Our Last Best Shot

GUIDING OUR
CHILDREN
THROUGH EARLY
ADOLESCENCE

Laura Sessions Stepp

RIVERHEAD BOOKS   NEW YORK

RIVERHEAD BOOKS
Published by The Berkley Publishing Group
A division of Penguin Putnam Inc.
375 Hudson Street
New York, New York 10014

Copyright © 2000 by Laura Sessions Stepp
Book design by Debbie Glasserman
Cover design © 2000 Tom McKeveny
Front cover photographs: Girl © Telegraph Colour Library/FPG;
Boy © Ron Chapple/FPG
Back cover photographs: Upper left © Telegraph Colour Library/FPG;
Right, both © Ron Chapple/FPG; Lower left © VCG/FPG

Published simultaneously in Canada.

First Riverhead hardcover edition: June 2000
First Riverhead trade paperback edition: August 2001
Riverhead trade paperback ISBN: 1-57322-875-3

Visit our website at
www.penguinputnam.com

The Library of Congress has catalogued the Riverhead hardcover edition
as follows:

Stepp, Laura Sessions.
    Our last best shot : guiding our children through early
adolescence / Laura Sessions Stepp.
        p.   cm.
    ISBN 1-57322-160-0
    1. Adolescence—United States. 2. Parent and teenager—United States.
3. Parenting—United States. 4. Teenagers—United States—Psychology.
5. Teenagers—United States—Family relationships. I. Title.
HQ796.S8268   2000   00-027974
305.235'5'0973—dc21

Printed in the United States of America

10   9   8   7   6

CONTENTS

Part Four: The Right Connections

To Carl, Jeff, Amber, and Ashli,
who teach me every day the miracle of family

Our Last Best Shot

This book began in a boat on a lake.

It was a school holiday for my son, then eleven, and I had taken the day off from work to relax with him at our favorite park in northern Virginia. I watched in amazement as he lugged a thirty-pound motor down to the shore of Lake Occoquan, attached it to a small skiff, and started us off. For three hours he steered us in and out of narrow inlets as we marveled at the fall foliage and the great blue herons who stood at the water's edge. We ate turkey sandwiches and sour cream–flavored potato chips; we talked about kickboxing and television commercials and the ups and downs of friendship.

After docking, we played eighteen holes of miniature golf. On the drive home, we bought a pumpkin for Halloween and a dozen apples. As we wove our way through I-95 traffic, we listened to Green Day on the radio. It had been a perfect afternoon, real quality and quantity time. "Thanks, Mom, I had fun," Jeff said as we pulled into our driveway.

He headed for the computer and a game of Red Alert. "Homework first!" I reminded him.

Kaboom. You would have thought I had asked him to hug me in public. "Why don't I ever get to decide things for myself? You're always telling me what to do!" As the argument escalated, he swept past, leaving me with this: "I hope you know how much I hate you right now."

Only a few hours earlier he had been piloting our boat with the assurance of someone twice his age. Now he had morphed into an angry toddler. One minute I was a hero, the next, a villain. I was confused. Was he becoming an adolescent? Please God, not yet. I wasn't ready for *that*.

Everything I had heard about adolescents up to that point made me want to skip town for the next eight years. Raging hormones. Mood swings. Weird hair, weird clothes, and friends who wore safety pins in their noses. Girlfriends and sex. Cars and beer. And worst of all: There was nothing I could do about it.

Fortunately, I was writing about kids and families for *The Washington Post* at the time and had been assigned to cover the release of a report called *Great Transitions*. Written by a panel of experts for the Carnegie Corporation of New York, *Great Transitions* reviewed and analyzed decades of research on early adolescence, defined as the years from age ten to age fifteen. I was fascinated, reassured, and challenged by the three big ideas of that report.

I was fascinated to be told that adolescence is a time of growth and change rivaling infancy in its speed and accomplishment. Bodies get taller and heavier, reproductive organs mature, and although kids flare up from time to time, most do not experience prolonged emotional turmoil. Over time and with help, they blossom rather than decay. The buds can first be seen in the early adolescent years: intellectual growth, expanding creativity, moral awareness—and other wonderfully human traits that are easily overlooked when we are barraged by television images of young teens gunning down their classmates at school.

I was reassured by the report's second big idea, that there are things that parents and other adults can do to nurture these seedlings. Biology is not destiny; for most kids, hormones are not navigating this boat. The intellectual and emotional changes we see in our growing children are largely the result of new experiences they encounter, their reactions to those experiences, and to the increased demands of friends and parents, teachers, and other adults.

The third big idea of *Great Transitions*, and its biggest challenge, was straightforward: In order to help our children navigate adolescence successfully we must board early. Early adolescence is our last best shot at preparing them for a successful life.

It is not our last opportunity, of course; our children's intellectual and emotional growth continues for years afterward at a slower pace. But it is our last *best* opportunity because they are beginning to adopt patterns of thought and behavior that will accompany them for years to come.

During early adolescence our kids first begin to ask, in a serious way, who they are, what they believe, and what they have to offer the world. Many encounter worldly temptations for the first time. If we don't show them how to find some answers and to make wise choices, they may drift in circles for years or even eventually beach the boat. But if we do provide the right kind of guidance, they stand a much better chance at sailing by the markers most of us would use to define success. They will become adults who are reasonably well educated, meaning they have had training beyond high school, preferably college. They will possess enough knowledge or skill to earn a living with pride. They will enjoy and be committed to a family and to friends. They will be ready to assume the responsibilities of citizenship and community involvement. They will be adaptable to change. And, as hard as it may be to believe, they will be able to live a good and meaningful life independently of us. In a nutshell: They will become the kind of guests we would like to invite over for dinner.

What kind of guidance, I wondered, do kids this age need from us in order to eventually achieve these goals? Are the problems they encounter today really that different from the problems of past generations, and, if they are, what can we do about that? Most important— since adolescence is often considered a time of rebellion and turmoil—how do we distinguish between signs of normal growth and trouble? What are the signals that let us know when to intervene and when to let them solo? Are those signals different depending on their skin color, income, family structure, or community?

In order to find children and families who could lead me to some answers, I had to decide first where to look. After talking to social scientists and other sources I knew from my years at the *Post*, and doing extensive reading, I settled on three communities: urban Los Angeles on the West Coast; the medium-sized city of Durham, North Carolina, in the East; and Ulysses, Kansas, a farm town slightly southwest of this country's center.

Each community provides a different context for raising kids. Los Angeles is home to more teenagers within its metropolitan boundaries than any other city in the country, and its combination of nationalities, incomes, and lifestyles is virtually unique. It is also the hub of a media industry that profoundly affects how our youths spend their time and how they feel about themselves.

In Durham, young people and their families are caught up in a major shift from a farm-based economy to an economy dependent on health-care services and technology. The area has grown rapidly, as has the cost of living, forcing a high proportion of parents to work and to work more hours per week than they once did. The city also has an interesting racial mix. Almost one-half of its two hundred thousand citizens are black, and an unusually high proportion of those black residents have a college degree. As I found out, racial issues are front and center in the daily lives of many Durham students, just as they are to young people in many cities today.

Ulysses, a town of six thousand tucked in the southwest corner of Kansas, also has experienced upheaval as hundreds of Mexican-American families have settled there. At one time removed from serious social ills, its families are living with early signs of gang activity, a teenage pregnancy rate that is among the highest in the state, and a general sense of uneasiness that often accompanies the ethnic assimilation that many communities are experiencing.

Once I had decided on these sites, I sought out their teachers, youth workers, and community organizers to identify potential kids. I interviewed dozens of young people and eventually chose eighteen to consider seriously, six in each of the three communities. Later, I picked twelve to report and write about in detail.

I was looking for typical kids living in typical families and quickly learned that there is no such thing. The Ozzie and Harriet family really is a myth and has been for years: Parents move in and out of jobs and in and out of kids' lives; so do sisters and brothers, aunts, uncles, and family friends. Chronic illness claims more adolescents than we realize, and the number of those affected is increasing; crime, violence, and/or drugs touch many families in ways we on the outside often don't see. As all biographers know, scratch beneath the surface of any family and you will find unusual stones.

I chose the original eighteen adolescents using measurable tools: family income, race, ethnicity, family composition, and school performance. I aimed for variety but avoided extremes.

I looked for kids in families who earned moderate- to upper-middle incomes. I selected white kids, African-American kids, and Hispanic kids in equal number because the proportion of minority youth in this country, already one-third of the population, is projected to reach one-half by the middle of this century. A slight majority of the kids I chose lived at home with their biological parents, but there were assorted other arrangements, including divorced parents, stepparents, grandparents, and a single mother who had never married. Most of the young people were B or C students, although a couple of girls made all A's.

I narrowed the original group down to twelve by asking one simple question: Could that child and his or her family teach me and, by extension my readers, something important about raising young adolescents? I had no doubt they all would have interesting stories to tell; most kids and families do. But would their stories help us understand our children and our children's friends?

Most of the kids with whom I talked, beginning in September 1996, were eager to participate once they understood that I wanted to observe them for hours at a time, to view the world from their eyes as much as a middle-aged white woman can. Few people had ever expressed that much interest in what they thought about things.

I won their trust by spending the equivalent of weeks of time with them. I visited their homes, sometimes staying overnight. I bowled with them, took them to dances, shopped with them, and ate more greasy pizza and burgers than I care to remember. I attended school with them, took them for rides in rented cars, sat next to them in church. I giggled and laughed with them. I observed them as they argued with parents, teachers, and siblings, and on more than one occasion I hugged a kid whose feelings spilled over into tears. When apart from them, I kept in touch by telephone and e-mail. I am profoundly grateful for the confidences these young people shared and the courage they showed in being willing to let me paint as whole a picture as possible, no matter how painful some of the details might be.

I also talked to the adults these kids identified as important: parents and other relatives, teachers, neighbors, youth workers, church leaders, store clerks. Parents, initially, were understandably protective. But when I assured them I would not use their names or the names of their children, in order to give their sons and daughters a measure of privacy, they opened up like a dam released. They couldn't stop talking about the changes they had seen in their pubescent children. While they knew adolescence has always been risky, they believed today's adolescents face different risks and they weren't sure how to prepare them for the future. They were fearful, as I had been, that they had a difficult few years ahead of them.

Most of them said they were spending less time with their kids now than they had in the past; all of them felt they were losing touch and losing control. Some of them had sought support from schools or churches, with mixed results. Like their children, they were hungry for information and conversation. This was especially true of the mothers, who wrestled openly with child-rearing questions that their husbands didn't want to philosophize about. These moms lamented the fact that the support systems many of them had had in place when their kids were younger had disappeared.

I learned an important lesson from these early discussions. One family's circumstances may differ from another family's, or one family's challenges may seem greater than another's. But the intellectual and emotional needs of the young adolescents in those families are the same and often show up in the same way initially. Also, the interventions that parents succeed with, as well as the mistakes they make, are strikingly similar to each other. Good parenting looks the same in all neighborhoods and all families. So does bad parenting.

During the year that I observed these children and into the next year, I scoured hundreds of books, scientific journals, magazines, and newspapers for findings that would help me understand my observations. I attended conferences of social scientists, physicians, and guidance counselors, and interviewed dozens of experts. You will find references to this research at the end of the book as well as a bibliography to point you to additional readings. You also will find a brief epilogue that will relate what has happened to the kids since my direct observation ended in August 1997.

I noticed that these kids spent most of their time and energy figuring out four things: what kind of person they were; how (and whether) they fit in with their friends; what they were learning; and how they could both create distance from and remain connected to adults. Each of these four pursuits forms its own section of the book, and each section is illustrated by the stories of three young people.

I also observed that while some adults deftly guide kids through these four areas of growth, others impede the process, either consciously or unconsciously. At the end of each chapter I summarize the ways in which we can act as guides.

I have written this book mainly for parents who are raising young adolescents or preparing to. (I use the word "parents" throughout the book to refer to a child's primary caretakers, whatever their actual relation to the child.) These are difficult times in which to do our job. We must contend not only with negative teenage stereotypes but also with a barrage of contradictory news and statistics. One day we read that crimes by kids are up, the next day, they're down. We ask ourselves, in an age of guns and AIDS and drugs and so many other dangers, can we make a difference? These families show us that we can, much of the time.

Of course, there are exceptions. We probably all know a couple of scoundrels whose parents did everything they could to raise them right. We can also probably name several sensitive, accomplished adults who were either ignored or abused growing up. It's impossible to know how any child will turn out. But it's also unthinkable to leave it to chance.

For teachers and others who work with kids, I hope my book will either confirm the approaches they already are taking or suggest new ways to reach kids this age. I have not made specific policy suggestions. That is not my expertise. But I have pointed out instances of certain programs and policies, in education and juvenile justice particularly, that I believe either damaged or helped specific kids.

This book differs from others about teenagers in several significant ways:

- It focuses on children ages ten to fifteen because young adolescents behave differently and have different needs than older kids. Grouping all adolescents together, as many popular books do, makes as much sense as combining babies and kindergartners.

  It also looks ahead to the kinds of skills, reasoning, and values kids will need as they get older. And it looks behind, to offer parents of younger children ideas on preparing for adolescence.

- It chronicles the lives of real young people, not composites, using real names for everyone except the kids and the kids' friends and relatives. Events and dialogues are taken either from direct observation or from firsthand accounts, interviews, school records, and newspaper articles.
- Most of the kids I followed are not in therapy. Books about young people suffering from eating disorders, clinical depression, and other severe disturbances perform a valuable service. But they also can frighten us unnecessarily. This book describes girls and boys struggling with universal concerns that, if not resolved, can lead to more severe problems but do not have to.
- The book's academic research is not limited to one particular expert but relies on studies and observations from an extensive list of sources. The main research, however, was simple, exhaustive observation. That is what I, as a journalist, have been trained to do, and have done for twenty-five years. I watched, I listened, and I considered all the data I knew to try to make sense out of what I had observed.
- Boys as well as girls are included. Adolescent girls received a great deal of attention at the end of the last century. With a couple of notable exceptions, writers ignored boys. Adolescent boys face a number of the same hurdles as girls as well as some that are unique. Others have said this but it bears repeating: One of the best things we can do for girls is change the way we raise boys.

Great Transitions challenged U.S. institutions to do better by our young people. My challenge differs slightly. Institutions are made up of individuals, and it is people, not programs, who are calling out directions to our kids. My wish is that readers, whatever their family circumstance, will come away from this book realizing how significant and fulfilling that job can be. And that they will feel equipped to begin, or to begin again.

PART ONE

Knowing Who They Are

It is 8:15 on a September morning in Ulysses, Kansas, and Sally Gollhoffer wastes no time starting her sixth-grade keyboarding class. "Sit back in your chairs, feet on the floor," Gollhoffer tells her class of twenty-two. "Keep your wrists down. We're going to practice jhjhjhjh. . . . Follow along on your orange sheets."

Alana Perales, wearing baggy jeans and a large blue-and-pink hooded shirt that hides her roundness, is staring blankly at a new Macintosh LC580 computer monitor. Her attention for the moment is on her hair. Wiry and brown like her dad's, it is driving her crazy and she fidgets with it, wishing like anything she could scrunch it down.

"Okay, which icon is the hard drive?" Gollhoffer will not let up. "We're going to the hard drive now. Type in your name."

At the prompt on her screen, Alana mistypes Aiana, then Ajana, then finally, Alana. "Are we going to play jigsaw puzzle?" she asks no one in particular. She presses several keys and zooms into a puzzle room on her computer. With a few quick strokes she is assembling a frog out of dozens of green pieces.

At age eleven, Alana sometimes feels like a jigsaw puzzle whose fragments are scattered. Last year in elementary school she was casually sure of herself. She knew she liked art, threw a pretty fast softball, and was good friends with Lisa and Ellen. This year, in a middle school three times the size of her old school, she feels she doesn't know anything. On days like this, she can't even type her name right.

A pretty, freckle-faced girl of Mexican-American descent living in rural America at the dawn of the twenty-first century, Alana has embarked on a journey as old as the human species—a trip into adolescence. Puzzle parts formed at birth, which fit comfortably together when she was a child, have broken asunder, and in the next few years she will discover that her body and mind are changing faster than she thought possible. She will look to adults to help her define, understand, and integrate those changes even as she distances herself from those adults. She will lose some friends and make others, hoping to become a valued member of each group to which she belongs. She will explore new ways of thinking, talking, and acting. She will change the way she eats, exercises, and sleeps. All of these activities will contribute to her major effort of defining who she is and where she fits in a world that also is changing rapidly.

Her quest for a distinct identity will be lifelong, of course; the puzzle pieces will take years to interlock and reveal a new, mature woman. But during her early adolescence she, like the other youths in this book, will fit the frame of the puzzle together, preparing to fill it in later. Many people, from well-meaning relatives to greedy advertisers, will want to choose the pieces for her. But ultimately she will have to make those choices herself if the completed puzzle is to be strong.

Social scientists have identified hundreds of elements that contribute to an adolescent's healthy self-image. Their research is replete with concepts such as "individuation," "diffusion," and "locus of control," which can overwhelm the ordinary adult seeking to understand the behavior of one very specific child. Many of these studies boil down, however, to three graspable ideas. Peter Scales, a research psychologist and expert on early adolescence, phrases these concepts as questions asked regularly by the ten- to fifteen-year-old: Am I competent? Am I loved and loving? Am I normal? In high school, the adolescent will add questions such as, What kind of work should I do? What kind of person should I marry? But during the gateway years, she is focused almost entirely on herself, looking outward in occasional bursts of altruism.[1] A parent's job is to try to make sure that his or her child can answer yes to all three questions.

All the children in this book, of course, are on a search for self, but I have chosen three through which to explore questions of identity in depth. Eric Stanton, in chapter 1, demonstrates one child's drive toward competence and how parents can facilitate that drive even if, like Eric's parents, they are divorced. Chapter 2 tells the story of Chandler Brennan, whose loving family began to disintegrate as she entered puberty, prompting her to look for love elsewhere. Chapter 3's Shannon Steele, over the course of a year, was learning to accept herself as normal even though, like many young teens, she could give you several reasons why she thought she was not.

Sometimes the adolescents in this book pondered their identity aloud, like the sixth-grader named Rodney (in chapter 7), who, when he couldn't figure out what part to play in a classroom drama, whispered, "Who can I be? I'll be nobody. That's good." More often, however, they barreled through each day, looking for answers with every choice they made, fitting together, tearing apart, and refitting the frame of their life's puzzle with no picture on the box top to follow.

CHAPTER ONE

Am I Competent?

(Eric's Story)

The morning sun shines through the bars of Eric Stanton's bedroom window in South-Central Los Angeles, waking him. Through a sleepy fog, he remembers he is supposed to do something new today—something that made him nervous to think about yesterday.

Oh, yeah, he thinks, he has to change his father's bandages. Eric the nurse. What a way to spend his Christmas vacation.

There's no one else to help Dad, says a voice inside his head. You know how modest Dad is. He doesn't want anyone else to see him this way.

"Eric? Are you up?" This time it is his father's voice, a booming baritone not easily ignored. Eric rises reluctantly.

Months earlier, an infection took hold of Eldon Stanton's sweat glands and the week before, a surgeon removed the sick glands from under his right arm. Then the doctor scraped a large piece of skin from Eldon's thigh and grafted it over the incision.

Eric hadn't been scared until he visited Robert F. Kennedy Hospital after the surgery. His dad, a normally robust man, lay limp in bed with plastic tubes attached to his arms and nose for feeding, breathing, and draining fluid. The doctor was worried about Eldon's blood pressure and his liver, damaged by years of drinking. He had ordered a biopsy on the glandular tissue.

As he left the hospital each night, Eric would ask himself, "What will I do if something happens to Dad?" His dad took him to ball games, stayed on him about school, and talked to him about mistakes he had made in his life that he hoped Eric could avoid. Dear, God, Eric would pray, let him come home well. No cancer, please. I need him.

The doctor told Eldon that someone would have to change his bandages at home. Could his wife do it? No, Eldon said, he was divorced. His girl-friend? No, Eldon said, he'd rather she didn't see him that way. But his thirteen-year-old son might be able to help. "Do you think you can handle it?" Eldon asked Eric one day at the hospital.

"I'll take care of you, Dad, don't worry," Eric said.

Eric's parents had split up when Eric was seven, and depended on him increasingly as he got older, a frequent consequence of divorce. Each had been raised with a strong work ethic and expected the same of their son. Eldon, who had sold remodeled cabinets for a couple of years, took Eric along to fill out order forms. Eric's mother, Denice, a medical secretary, spent weekends selling art, incense, and body oil; she also expected Eric to assist her. From 1994, when Eric was eleven, through the summer of 1996, they hawked her wares on the boardwalk of Venice Beach, that strip of sand and open-air markets known for its Rollerbladers, hucksters, and odd-balls.

Denice and Eric would idle in their folding chairs commenting on the crazies and school and discussing what Eric might want to do with his life. By the second summer, Denice decided that Eric, then twelve, was ready to sell by himself on weekdays while she was at work. She needed the money and Eric could use the experience. Unlike a lot of mothers, who hold their children back, Denice was nudging Eric out of the nest, telling him he could fly.

At noon Eric would hop on a bus and meet her at the clinic where the van was waiting, loaded with merchandise. She would drive a half hour to the beach, deposit Eric and her wares, and zoom back to work, leaving Eric to set up and sell until she returned about 6 P.M. He would make as much as $300 a day, turning most of it over to his mom.

He always sat in the same spot, next to a tiny, deeply tanned woman named Eva, who sold jewelry and kept an eye on him. Denice never wor-ried about Eric because of Eva, and because of the number of uniformed police officers around.

Eric eventually grew tired of the bums and weirdos. "I don't want to work here anymore," he told his mom toward the end of their third summer. Denice promised that she would search for another community in which to do business, but until then he would have to tough it out.

Tough it out, he tells himself this December morning as he goes to work on his dad's wound. As slowly and gently as his bearlike hands can manage, he unwinds the Scotchbrite surgical tape holding down the bandages and dismantles the layers of cotton protecting Eldon's wound.

He repeats the procedure regularly for the next several weeks. One night the skin graft becomes dislodged and starts bleeding heavily. Eldon yells to Eric, who wraps a towel tightly around the wound and calls for an ambulance. Eldon is taken to the hospital emergency room, where he is treated and released. Several weeks later, Eldon has similar surgery under his left arm. The night he comes home from the second operation, the new incision starts bleeding and won't stop. This time Eric summons his father's girlfriend to drive them to the emergency room.

A few weeks later, Eric drops by his youth club and encounters the club's president, Lou Dantzler. "I hear you've been a big help to your dad," Dantzler says.

Eric grins sheepishly. "Dad kinda needs me," he replies.

According to statistics, Eric Stanton should have been cruising the streets that morning with the brothers instead of taking care of his dad. He is a black teenage male, living with a single parent. His mother, married to his dad in a quick Las Vegas ceremony, left their home when he was seven. His father, formerly a heavy drinker, has been married three times and has held a variety of jobs. A half-brother, Sammy, his father's oldest son, used to run with a gang. Eric, "Sammy's little brother," would tag along until Sammy landed in prison for stealing a car.

Eric and his dad live on a street of tidy bungalows ringed by pansies and trimmed hedges in a neighborhood made famous in the gang movie *Boyz N the Hood.* One block north, in a faded white house that resembles a sharecropper's cottage, several members of the notorious Bloods gang hang out. One block south is the more prosperous, adobe home of a rival Crips associate. Eric grew up with friends who had nicknames like Fro, Little Chico, and Big Turtle.

Riding with those guys as he headed into his teenaged years would have given Eric a new family and a facade of being in control—powerful antidotes to the insecurities and self-consciousness that infect many kids as they enter adolescence. But he didn't head out to the streets. He knew his dad would get on him if he did, and he really didn't feel the need to. He was valued at home for his contributions there and at school for his achievements in mathematics, computers, and playing the drums. He didn't need gangbangers to make him feel worthwhile.

Doing Something Well

Social science suggests, and my own observations confirm, that the key task in a young person's search for identity is discovering what he is good at. True self-awareness and self-esteem come not from chanting "I am somebody" or receiving lots of verbal strokes, but from performing challenging tasks well in activities that are valued by the people one cares about.

With increasingly stronger bodies, keener cognitive skills, and budding creativity, young teenagers practically cry out for pursuits that go beyond filling out ditto sheets or washing the dishes. Yet parents and other adults sometimes don't take the time to observe what children are capable of, or they buy into the popular misconception that adolescents are lazy and irresponsible. Sometimes they're so worried about what a child lacks, be it an easy temperament, keen intelligence, or self-confidence, that they overlook what he offers.

Competence is not easily fostered in a society that values the shortcut, the quick fix, and just getting by. There are many distractions today, perhaps more than at any time in history, pulling adolescents away from the sustained effort that is required to do anything well, whether it be building a bookcase or playing Debussy's "Clair de Lune." But as Eric's experience illustrates, a child can discover and develop his talents with the help of parents who support and focus his efforts at home and position him within a community where he will encounter similar encouragement from other adults. This is true regardless of what kind of neighborhood he lives in.[1]

One way to detect and boost kids' natural abilities is by offering them meaningful work within the family, as Eldon and Denice did with Eric. Several of the boys I observed got that chance. Mario, an eighth-grader in Durham, helped his father, a construction worker, during a six-month suspension from school. Jack, also in Ulysses, took complete charge of a chestnut quarter horse named Whiskey: cleaning, feeding, mucking out the barn.

Few girls in my study were asked to do major jobs equal to what was expected of the boys. A couple of them were not even asked to do household chores on a regular basis. "You can't make them," was one mother's lament; another said, "As busy as she is at school and sports, I don't have the heart to ask her to do much at home." In one family, an eleven-year-old son assisted his father in the family furniture business while the twelve-year-old daughter roamed the malls with her friends. In this family and others, sex-role stereotyping seemed to be alive and well.

Teaching kids the basics of running a household—how to cook, clean, wash clothes, even help with the family budget as they get older—allows kids to exercise autonomy, a critical component of competence, and to assume increasingly larger roles when they're no longer children and not yet adults, a time that seems to them to stretch out forever. Work can also bring them the respect from adults that they long for at this age. And it can be enjoyable; for three decades adolescents surveyed by psychiatrist Daniel Offer have rated "a job well done" at or near the top of a list of things that give them pleasure. When kids complain about doing chores, as they inevitably do, parents would do well to consider what kind of work they are asking their young teens to do.

In the first half of the last century, adolescents proved themselves as a matter of course as they worked on farms or, during World War II, in factories. They provided essential income to their families. Long-term studies of Depression-era adolescents who labored in the Midwest show that they did better in later life than adolescents who had not worked.[2] But late in the twentieth century, largely for protective reasons, we relieved kids, particularly those between the ages of ten and fifteen, of the need to work, and in the process stripped them of opportunities for contribution, praise, and pride.

Affirmed for the Little Things

A healthy identity also comes from being appreciated for the seemingly ordinary things one accomplishes—a well-thought-out response to a question, for example. Eldon and Denice took notice of the fact that Eric was listening more carefully to them, following directions more precisely, and occasionally suggesting workable solutions to a particular disagreement. His head was growing, and obviously so was his brain's capacity for abstract, multidimensional, and reflective thought.[3]

Until recently, the prevailing wisdom among educators was that a pubescent child's intellectual circuits shut down temporarily as the emotional circuits ignite. Scientists now know that both kinds of circuitry are operating at the same time, each reinforcing the other.[4] Eric's parents began tapping into his maturing thinking skills.

They shared their opinions with him, and solicited his. At dinner with his father one night, several months after the second surgery, Eric said, "You always have to work for things but if you believe in God, things will come your way." God, he said, "sets our lives ahead of time."

"You mean predestination," Eldon responded. "That could be. But what about little children who are murdered? Do you think God meant for them to die?"

Eric paused. "Well everybody has a plan," he said, "but sometimes it gets thrown off by evil. I wonder if it's Satan at work."

Eldon and Denice had discovered one of the hidden gems of raising an adolescent: The same testing of ideas that pushes kids into exasperating arguments also makes them delightful conversationalists. They can talk about much more than how they did on their history quiz or how their day went ("Fine"). They enjoy sharing their ideas about current events and being consulted on important decisions at home, such as what kind of car to buy and where the family should vacation.

With "what about" questions such as Eldon and Denice asked, parents can stretch their children's developing capacity for abstract thought and encourage the moral reasoning needed to make wise decisions. Too often, we parents tell kids what we want them to think rather than demand that they wrestle with ideas themselves. Or we ask a question and don't give them time to think and respond.

We should talk to them as we would to our best friends—taking them seriously, being responsive. I once asked Eric how he was able to chat so freely with his mother. "I respect her," he said. "She has respect for me, too, you know."

High on the list of what teens want from their parents is to be listened to. When they say to us, "You don't understand," what they sometimes mean is "You aren't listening," or "You never talk about anything other than my grades," or "You don't allow me to talk before jumping in."

An example occurred one night with Jack, the twelve-year-old horse lover from Ulysses. He arrived home after basketball practice with exciting news to tell his dad: He had been chosen to lead the floor exercises. As he started to relate how he had been granted this honor, his father cut him short. "Get to the good stuff," he said. "Which team did the coach put you on?"

When teenagers turn mute, it helps if at least one parent is adept at conversation and not afraid to open up. Teenagers appreciate honesty from others since it is so often demanded of them. Eric was lucky; both his parents had the gift of gab. In one of my first conversations with his father, Eldon described himself as the kind of man who "if I sit next to you, we're going to talk." Eric had another model as well: a half-brother, Roger, handsome, in his mid-thirties, and successful at talking people into buying mortgage insurance.

Roger, Denice's son by another man, took Eric under his wing as Eric was starting fifth grade. The employees in Roger's office, United International Mortgage, came to know Eric well; Roger would put him to work at the office and invite him to office parties at his boss's house. One afternoon Eric walked me through the mauve-carpeted offices of United International. "Hey, Eric, how's it going?" Kim the receptionist asked. Two other coworkers came over to say hello.

A high-school graduate, Roger is one of the top-ranking salespeople in one of the largest black-owned businesses in the Los Angeles area. Looking natty that day in a tailored suit and pin-striped shirt with French cuffs, he described in his characteristically fast clip how he was encouraging Eric to set up a neighborhood car-washing business. He obviously relished playing big brother, a role he had assumed when Eric wasn't so little anymore. His timing couldn't have been better.

Timing Is Everything

It was the last year of elementary school, and Eric, going into puberty, was watching helplessly as his previously thin body was blowing up and out like a helium balloon. Adults should never underestimate the psychological impact on a child of such changes, which occur just as the young person is beginning to grasp how people look at him.

Eric's enlarging penis and testes and the growth of pubic hair didn't embarrass him much because he could keep these signs hidden under layers of clothes. What were not hidden were the secondary changes: longer arms and legs, broader shoulders, an expanded head and bigger feet, a reshaped face, deeper voice, and the additional weight. With his limbs growing faster than his torso and his bones faster than his muscles, Eric would bump into furniture and drop dishes.

He was especially bothered by the shape of his body. His father took him to a physician who, like many doctors, knew little about adolescent development. This doctor said Eric's weight gain was probably prompted by the steroid prednisone that he was taking for the asthma he had had since birth. Watch what you eat so you don't get fat, the doctor told him. What the doctor didn't explain to Eric is that puberty frequently causes weight to shift, and that there is a wide range for normal pubertal development. Boys' changes can come anytime between about nine and fifteen; Eric was simply at the younger end of the spectrum.

Compared to his shorter and lighter classmates, Eric felt like a giant. He began to withdraw, and his mother suggested that he see a counselor. His father, however, said Eric's behavior did not seem extreme. Let's give him some time, he said, and show him how he can use his size to his advantage—by working at Venice Beach, for example.

Eric's parents' friends openly admired his growth spurt, tossing off lines he remembered months afterward, such as "Just wait until you get a contract with the National Football League. Then you'll be glad you're big." In this way, he was lucky to be a boy. Research on puberty suggests that early maturation boosts boys' self-confidence even as it diminishes girls'. Psychologists believe that this is explained partly by the reactions of other people: Bigger boys win respect; bigger girls draw suspicion, as we will see in the next chapter. Such reactions may even influence the adolescent's behavior and feelings as much as the underlying hormonal changes.[5]

On his first day of ninth grade at William Howard Taft High School, Eric feels like the Pillsbury Doughboy, who might collapse if poked.

He is leery of walking fast to classes for fear of bringing on an asthma *attack but also afraid of making a bad impression on his teachers if he shows up late. He hustles from building to building on this sprawling suburban campus of 3,100 students, his shoulders hunched slightly forward as if to propel himself faster. By 2 P.M. he is exhausted from wandering around ten buildings, striking up conversations in the hopes of finding a friend, and listening to teachers tell him how hard he is going to have to work. He doesn't much like school anyway, except for math. Elbowing his way through crowds on his way to sixth period, he wonders whether he should have tried to talk his dad into letting him go to a smaller school closer to home with his best friend J.R. . . .*

He pulls open double doors leading to the band room, and his eyes take in rows of chairs, music stands, and sheet music ready to be embraced by first-time musicians like himself. To his left are saxes, piccolos, and flutes, next to them cellos, a double bass, and a bass guitar. In the center of the room is a piano, and on his right, the drums. He recognizes the Ludwig five-piece right away.

He takes a seat as the teacher, a tall man in his late thirties with blond hair sweeping his shoulders, introduces himself. Michael O'Conner tells his new students that he wants them to hear each instrument before they pick one, then proceeds to play every instrument in the room.

Eric opts for the drums. Having watched his brother Roger play, he has yearned to do the same. Sometimes he has found himself tapping out rhythms in midair with his forefingers, not even needing a radio to hear the beat in his head.

In the music room he wraps his fingers around two drumsticks worn smooth by preceding classes of would-be Buddy Riches. He thinks he has never felt anything so fine and smooth. Here is an opportunity to learn whether or not he has any talent.

This is my place, he thinks. This is me.

Adults sometimes forget the pure joy that comes from discovering something you love to do, something that may be a little over your head but is within your reach. Such a discovery takes hold of your creative side and lifts your mood, even making other tasks seem less dreary. Some kids will uncover these talents on their own. Others must be made aware of what they can do. Both kinds of kids then need opportunities and encouragement to explore their passions.

Young adolescents are ripe to experience what Mihaly Csikszentmihalyi, a psychologist at the University of Chicago, calls "flow."[6] Flow, he
believes, is a subjective experience that people report when they are
completely involved in something to the point of losing track of time and
being unaware of anything else. The experience of flow encourages kids
to work their hardest, to master a challenge, occasionally even to begin
considering a career. It can be spotted in younger children—the
preschooler playing make-believe, for example—but takes off in adolescents because of their rapidly expanding cognitive skills and their greater
ability to sit still.

Some kids this age can be turned on by academic challenges; they
find that they love to compose poetry or work mathematical formulas.
But the kids I studied who had found a passion—and sadly, fewer than
half of them had—were excited by sports, art, or music. These interests
shared the three characteristics that Csikszentmihalyi says young people
respond to most: They encompassed clear goals (perfecting a serve, creating more muted shades in a watercolor, playing a faster staccato), provided instant feedback, and offered increasingly complex challenges.
(Computer and video games share these traits also, which may help
explain why kids can play them for hours.)

The School as Fertile Soil

The school, Csikszentmihalyi argues, is the primary place for foster-
ing talents in children. Although parents, youth organizations, and
churches can do this as well, two-thirds of talent-related activity takes
place in school.[7] Such nurturing has never been more critical. Public
secondary schools like Eric's now approach or exceed a thousand students. For young adolescents already coping with enormous biological
and social changes, a favorite class or activity can be an anchor in a large
and churning sea.

As Eric could see from the first day in band, Michael O'Conner loved
music and hoped his students would learn to love it, too. O'Conner told
them that if they brought in any musical score, he would teach it to
them. He remained in the band room during lunch to help any student
who asked. By midyear, Eric and eight other students were spending
most of their lunch periods there playing jazz, R&B, and funk. As Eric

practiced more hours at home, some of his neighborhood buddies called him "stupid" for preferring practice to hanging out. But so what? With O'Conner's encouragement he had found a new group of friends who shared and respected his hobby.

The band room was also a haven from the high-fives, put-downs, and fights of the courtyards. Besides a place to cultivate their talents, young teenagers need a reprieve from the scrutiny of their peers. O'Conner provided Eric with both.

He also offered Eric a way to contribute to school. During Eric's second semester, O'Conner asked if he would like to play in the school's select marching band the following year. Doing something he loved and was good at? And that made other people happy? It doesn't get any better than that.

The Role of Parents

For much of his freshman year, Eric had no drums at home. Eldon wanted to see how serious his son was about music before spending a couple of thousand dollars that he wasn't sure he could afford. He also thought he shouldn't buy a drum set until Eric brought up his grades.

During the first semester at Taft, the typing teacher would call Eldon to report that Eric was looking out the window rather than doing his assignments. The physical education teacher would call to complain that he wasn't running track with the other kids. Eric would come up with reasons for his behavior—typing was boring, he didn't like running track because his asthma prevented him from keeping up with the other runners—but he was never able to explain fully to his parents or to me his occasional bouts of apathy.

Eldon decided to make the drums a reward. Show me improved performance in school over a couple of months, he said, and we'll talk about buying a set of drums. By March, Eric met that goal. For Eric's fourteenth birthday, Eldon allowed Roger to buy his brother a used CB Maxx Pro drum set. Eric spent three to four hours a day in his room on some weekends, tapping on his twelve-tom snare and working his foot pedals to keep bass and cymbals going. Roger occasionally dropped by to listen and critique. Eldon also became a big promoter. He hired a drum teacher to visit the house on Saturdays. He rarely complained about the loud booms that would bounce off the walls of their small house as Eric practiced. When Eric started talking about getting a gig somewhere, Eldon offered to drive Eric and his drums in his van. Together, Eldon and Roger were stoking the fire of a passion Eric had picked up in school.

Offering rewards to a recalcitrant student doesn't always work. But it can work if the child wants something badly enough and knows, as Eric did, that his parent can be trusted to follow through. Eric knew that his dad would find a way to acquire a set of drums *and* that he wouldn't hesitate to remove them if Eric's grades slipped.

Shortly after he received his drums, Eric also expressed an interest in learning the bass guitar. "I want to be the man who does everything," he told his dad, a typical statement for kids this age, who tend to adopt one pursuit wholeheartedly, then drop it and pick up another. But his father dissuaded him, saying, "You're good at the drums, keep those up."

How many pursuits should a child be allowed, Eldon wondered, if finances afforded them? He didn't want to stifle a possible interest, and how would Eric know what he was good at unless he tried several things? On the other hand, Eldon had seen kids overwhelmed by choices; such kids often dropped everything after a while and some never returned to any of them. Eventually Eldon told Eric that their resources and his time were limited. "You must learn to use them wisely."

The discipline and dedication Eric's music required, and the confidence it bred, were worth the investment. Increased competence in one area often leads to improved skills in others, and during the second semester Eric earned A's and B's in all of his classes.

I asked Eric midyear what "competence" meant. "It's staying on top of what you do and what you want to do," he replied. No expert could have said it better.

In the middle of an inner-city youth club, three college football players have silenced a gymnasium full of kids. These are boys and girls who know what it's like to grow up poor and defeated, and they watch, enthralled, as three men the same color as they are do push-ups and shadowbox and talk about being successful. Everyone is hooked, except Eric.

Eric, a member of the club for five years, is on his hands and knees picking up scraps of paper in the nearby arts-and-crafts room. This is his after-

noon to catch up with Barbara Brown, the art teacher, who threw a lifeline to him and his dad several years ago. They've been hanging on to it ever since.

He and Brown exchange the kind of "whatever happened to" tales that old friends swap when they haven't seen each other for a while. As he heads out of the room, he bumps into Laura Peterson, the club's communications director, who tries to talk him into returning to Saturday hockey games.

"I can't get into my uniform anymore," Eric says.

"That's okay." Peterson laughs. "I can't, either."

In a basement office he finds Kenny Rodgers, who runs a Leaders in Training program for ten- to seventeen-year-olds. Rodgers inquires about college plans, and Eric confides that he is thinking about the University of Southern California, if he can get a scholarship.

"We have connections, we might be able to help you," Rodgers says.

Connections. What a sweet sound to a boy whose world was disconnected for much of his life. With a father who drank too much and a mother who alternately yelled at her husband and withdrew to a separate bedroom, his early years were not idyllic. One afternoon shortly after Thanksgiving 1990, Denice announced to Eldon that she was leaving the family. She had had enough of his drinking, she told him. She was sick of his passive-aggressive way of dealing with her complaints. She had been working full-time since she was fifteen and had put herself through high school and two years of community college. She had raised two children prior to Eric and had almost always lived with a man. It was time to find out what she could do on her own.

"I won't stand in your way," Eldon said.

She took Eric into the bedroom and told him that she and Eldon were not getting along and she was moving out of the house. "I'm not moving very far away, and I'll see or talk to you every day," she told him. "Everything will be all right."

Eric remembers clearly the moment when his mother, a statuesque beauty with dark, kind eyes, the only person he could absolutely trust, walked out the door. He cried and pleaded with her not to go. The rest of that day is full of shadows, buried someplace he would rather not visit. "Some stuff you try not to remember," he told me.

After his mother left, Eric joined the millions of kids being raised in a single-parent home—about one out of every four, a growing proportion of whom live with their fathers. Eldon, who worked at an insurance company *about fifty miles from home, started searching for a place for Eric after school. Eric had been walking to his maternal grandmother's house every day, but that was now a sticky situation. Looking ahead, Eldon worried that if he let his growing son return to an empty house, Eric would be tempted to hang out with kids who had nothing to do. Eldon had lost one son to the streets; he didn't want to lose another.*

He and Denice worked out an arrangement they hoped would last only a few weeks. Denice would take a late lunch hour at work so she could pick up Eric at school and drop him off at his house with instructions to stay inside with the doors locked. Weeks turned into months as Eldon, like many parents with modest financial resources, found his choices of after-school care limited by cost and lack of transportation. But he continued to ask for ideas from anyone who would listen. One Sunday afternoon at a sports clinic, he struck up a conversation with a stranger and learned that the man was an ex–crack addict whose wife was dying of cancer. "I've kicked my habit," the man said. "But now I've got five kids to raise." Eldon volunteered that his wife had split and that he was worrying about how to care for his son after school.

"I know a place that might be able to help," the man said, and told him about a club that cost only $25 a year.

Only twenty-five dollars? Eldon thought to himself. That guy must still be on crack.

In 1992, when four white police officers were acquitted of beating Rodney King, a black man, the residents of South-Central burned and looted all the buildings in the vicinity of Vermont and 42nd Street save one: the Challengers Boys & Girls Club. This former supermarket, surrounded by tiny storefronts, taco vendors, and discount marts, was the only safe place they had for their children, and they dared not touch it. Challengers is where the addict sent Eldon, altering the lives of father and son forever.

It also is where I met Eric. A club employee had suggested Eric as a possible subject for my book and arranged this first meeting with Eric and Eldon. I interviewed them in an office upstairs and then we toured the building.

In the gymnasium, Los Angeles mayor Richard Riordan was hosting a boisterous meeting of community residents upset by recent drive-by shootings. An elderly woman in a black-and-white polka-dot dress, white stockings, and white shoes was shaking a long, bony finger at the mayor. "How can I let my granddaughter walk to school? Is there any place left that is safe?"

As Eric led me downstairs to a hobby area, sounds of the angry crowd upstairs faded. In a small basement room equipped with a couple of game tables and a desk, he showed me a Polaroid color snapshot of a miniature, motorized robot.

"This is Red Rover," he said proudly. "I built it here, out of LEGOs. It took me ten times to get it right."

Seeing the Possibilities

For a child to learn what he loves to do, he first has to find out what is possible. He must be exposed to new places, people, and ideas, and encouraged to try activities he has never tried and to hone newfound skills. As Eldon Stanton understood, parents often are limited in their ability to encourage such expansiveness. This is when they need to turn to outside organizations such as youth clubs, sports teams, and church youth groups.

The summer after Eric turned eight, he started going to Challengers every day, all day. That fall he went after school, catching a club bus that picked him up in front of his school. Club leaders made him do his homework first, then gave him a choice of computers, art, or shooting hoops. On weekends, he and his dad would take club-sponsored trips to Dodgers and Rams games, Michael Jackson's ranch, the San Diego Zoo, and leadership camps. After each event, they stored the ticket stubs in a shoebox.

Well-run clubs, organizations, and teams do more than open up the world to kids. They nurture a personal confidence that helps kids reject risky behavior. Young people involved in organized, group activities after school—about two out of three adolescents take part in at least one such activity, two out of five in two or more—are less likely to drop out of school, use drugs, or become teenage parents.[8]

The best organizations also offer kids opportunities for helping others, one of the most proven ways that kids can acquire a sense of personal worth and competence. At Challengers, Eric regularly was asked to help take care of the younger members—during Christmas parties, at Halloween's haunted house, and during the summer. He also helped cook and serve pancakes for more than a thousand community residents at the club's pancake breakfasts twice a year.

Challengers also puts its parents to work, surely one reason why in one generation it has grown from a dozen teenage boys in the back of founder Lou Dantzler's pickup to a million-dollar-plus operation serving twenty-two hundred boys and girls. Dantzler understands one principle of raising kids, especially young teenagers: They are more likely to take something seriously if they see that their parents do, too. At an orientation I witnessed, he made these dual responsibilities very clear.

"I'm going to start by telling you what we don't allow," he said in his commanding South Carolina accent. "We don't allow pierced earrings on boys, sagging pants, or earrings in the noses of girls or boys. No mushroom haircuts or braids on the boys. No green hair. No red or blue shoestrings, no sandals. Everybody must bring their membership card every day." Then he started in on the parents. "You must volunteer four hours a month at the club, at least. If you don't, your child cannot attend. We will turn your child away. You also must attend a monthly mandatory Saturday session. We're open Monday through Friday until seven-thirty in the evening; if you're late picking up your kid you will be charged two dollars per minute. This is not just some place you come to, to drop off your kids. Anyone want to leave now?" No one moved.

Competent Parents, Competent Kids

In all that has been written about youth organizations, the positive impact they can have on parents—which kids benefit from—is often overlooked. Depending on where they are in life, moms and dads of adolescents can feel as incompetent as their kids. Sometimes, they infect their children with these insecurities.

When Denice left, Eldon was in a bad way. As a new independent insurance agent he was having trouble persuading major policy writers to let him represent them. And overnight, he had become a single dad. He was angry and scared. At night he'd have one drink, then another. Sometimes he'd have friends over and they would drink. Denice recalls that more than once, her telephone would ring and it would be Eric.

"Mom, Dad's buddies are over here again," he would say. "Can you come get me?"

Eldon's life began to change when he started working with Challengers. He joined the board of directors and took charge of a late-afternoon tutoring program. It wasn't very long before he realized that Challengers was teaching him how to turn his anger into energy for others, how to make new friends, and, at the top of the list, how to be a good father. Gradually, he stopped drinking. Like Denice, who had struck out to shape a life of her own, Eldon was learning to be competent. And as the two of them became more satisfied with their own lives, so did their son.

Networking for Education

As much as Eldon enjoyed his and Eric's field trips with Challengers, he considered educating Eric his primary goal. This was fortunate for Eric, since doing well in school is one of the best guarantees for success later in life.[9] It turned out that Challengers could help Eldon and Eric with this, too.

Like many parents, Eldon wanted Eric to attend public school just as he had. In Wharton, the small town south of Houston where he grew up, the school was the center of the community. Kids and adults traipsed in and out of the well-kept building day and night, considering the school their property and an education their birthright.

Years later, Eldon looked at the locked-up, fenced-in, deteriorating compounds called schools in his section of LA and realized his son would never have that proprietary feeling. How could he keep his son focused on his studies in schools that lacked books, pencils, even toilet paper? The people at Challengers suggested a private school for Eric. They told him about a scholarship that put Eric in a Catholic middle school. Two years later, they told him that he could send Eric to Taft, a suburban high school, at the city's expense. From Lou Dantzler's secretary, he also heard about a Saturday morning enrichment program in math at California State University, Dominguez Hills. The summer before Eric started ninth grade, Eldon drove Eric to Cal-State every Saturday morning. The more he exposed Eric to college life, Eldon thought, the more natural going to college would seem.

In Wharton, everyone had assumed that bright young black men would attend college. Eldon did, graduating from Texas Southern University in 1966. He'd tell Eric, "You can have everything, lose everything, and get it back if you have brains and a college degree." He had had his share of financial problems and was convinced that his college degree and later a master's degree in finance that he earned through a special program at Stanford University were what kept him marketable. Denice, who had taken psychology courses at Cal-State, also urged Eric toward college.

When parents told Eldon that they didn't have the money to send their kids to college, his answer was always the same: Navigate the resources. Eldon had watched the way Challengers sought financial and technical help from the community, forming partnerships with dozens of businesses, universities, and government agencies. Eldon himself, in turn, became a master at networking for his son, a skill that he was passing on to Eric.

The network followed a curious route. At Cal-State, Eric picked up enough math so that in the fall, ninth-grade algebra came pretty easily. In Cheryl Snyder's algebra class, he often finished his class work early and would run errands for her. Toward the end of the year, Eric confided in Snyder that he was anxious about who his math teacher would be the following year. Snyder promised that she would see to it that he got a friend of hers and that she would be his teacher again in his junior year. The day, six years earlier, that Eric and his dad first opened the front door at Challengers, they set in motion a series of events that led to Eric's almost assured success in math.

A Supporting Cast

At Challengers and similar youth organizations, kids start dropping out in large numbers at age eleven or twelve, enticed away by television, computers, part-time jobs, and friends on the street. If parents stay involved, kids usually do, too, but sustained involvement can be difficult for parents who work. Eldon was lucky. Hesitantly, he asked his employer, Sedgwick James, Inc., for regular time off to help at the club. To his surprise, the executive vice president said yes. The company rewarded him several times for his community service, even sending him to a national competition.

Eric's mother, Denice, did not volunteer at the club, but she encouraged Eldon's and Eric's participation. She had to swallow her pride to do so because her ex-husband was often trotted out at club activities as a model father and she felt that such praise failed to recognize the role she had played in bringing up their son.

During the seven years she lived with Eric, Denice had been the primary caretaker. When she and Eldon divorced, she left Eric with his dad because she thought that in the long run, it would be better for her son. Her mother yelled at her for her decision; her girlfriends asked, "What kind of mother are you?" She told them that Eldon had never hurt Eric, and that as close as she and Eric were at the moment, she believed he would need his father more as he got older. Instinctively she knew what research shows, that boys who grow up without fathers at home tend to get into trouble more and do less well in school.[10]

Maybe if she left, Eldon would become a good role model, she thought. She knew one thing for sure: If she took Eric with her, Eldon would fall apart completely.

It was a gamble, and she did what she could to make it less of one. For months after her departure, she cooked Eric's dinner and took it over to her old house. She called him later to make sure he had eaten it and had had his bath.

When I met her she was working two jobs—at the psychiatric clinic by day and three nights a week at a car dealership—to keep up payments on what she called "my little piece of a house." She had stopped taking meals to Eric, but they still talked on the phone every night, and he spent the night at her house once or twice a week. She took him to restaurants and on a short cruise to Mexico.

When invited to banquets at the Challengers club, she attended even though it hurt her that everyone talked to and about Eldon. It would have been easier not to go, or to disparage Challengers in order to belittle her ex. But she would have been criticizing a group of people her son loved, people who were making him stronger and wiser. When Eric regaled her with stories of his latest adventures at Challengers, she put her jealousies aside.

From the time he set foot in his suburban high school, Eric has been afraid that someone would pick a fight with him because he is an outsider. On this nippy day in spring, his fears are about to be realized.

He and the other students are supposed to be reading silently in their seats. But on this particular morning, three tenth-grade football players have something else on their minds. Terence, tall like Eric but about a hundred pounds heavier, has spied Eric wearing an oversized, forest-green Nike jacket and decided that he wants it.

Terence and two accomplices have followed Eric into a reading room and locked the hall door from the inside. Should teacher Ed Hein wish to come in, he will have to walk outside the building to the room's other door.

"Hey, homey, I hear you want to fight me," Terence says to Eric. Eric, sitting near the front of the room, looks around nervously. "No, I don't. I don't even know you," he says.

"Then give me your jacket." Terence sidles up closer.

How ironic, Eric thinks. Here he sits twenty miles from the gangs of his neighborhood, in a middle-class school that employs more than thirty security guards and undercover cops. And he is about to be jumped for the first time.

As Terence hovers menacingly, Eric considers fleetingly whether to hand over the jacket. A present from his mom, it is not only a status symbol but also his security blanket, large and puffy and warm. He keeps it on during most of his classes. Give it away? Never. He begins calculating who in the room will come to his aid if he needs reinforcements. On the streets where he lives, reading people is critical. He is pretty good at it.

He glances quickly at Mark, a Korean student, and decides he would help. So would Paul, who's Indian, and Cambis, an Iranian. Why, he could have a multinational squadron at his command. He takes a deep breath and glares back at Terence. "You're going to have to beat me out of it," he says.

Suddenly Ed Hein enters through an outside door. Terence and his friends vanish. But Eric is shaking because he knows now that he is marked. When the brief reading period is over, he seeks out Scott McGorian, a gym teacher with whom he chats regularly, and tells him what happened. McGorian promptly escorts him to the dean's office.

Dean Howard Reisboard reaches Denice by phone and assures her that he will handle the situation. He calls Terence's little group into his office after Eric has left and warns them that if they threaten Eric again or harm him in any way, they will be kicked off the football team immediately and probably out of school.

That evening, Eric tells his father what happened. He paces the floor of the living room, visibly upset. He has broken the unspoken rule of the *streets and ratted on someone. Maybe Terence will persuade a friend to seek revenge. Maybe he should stay out of school for a few days.*

"You can't not go to school," Eldon tells his son. "Every time something like this happens, you've got to deal with it head-on."

Eldon offers to accompany Eric to school the next day and speak to the dean. Eric declines the offer, however. "Let's see if I can handle it," he says. "If you come out, it might make bigger problems."

Eldon doesn't want to fuel Eric's fear by appearing overly concerned and he does want Eric to learn to take care of himself. He appreciates the fact that Reisboard acted promptly. He decides against going to Taft but keeps a close watch on Eric for signs of trouble during the last three months of school.

Eric doesn't hear from Terence for the rest of the year.

Generations of young adolescents have left elementary school for secondary school fearful of what bigger kids will do to them. Today's kids are no different.

What is new, however, is the anxiety level of their parents. Barraged by news reports about crime and by talk shows parading forth despicable characters, many parents rein in their kids exactly when the kids need to begin to make their way into the world. Rather than teach their sons and daughters how to navigate the world as it is, they keep them home. This was particularly true for the girls I observed. In Ulysses, where a couple of spray-painted slogans are considered serious crime, eleven-year-old Alana was not allowed to walk six blocks to a friend's house after school. Fourteen-year-old Chandler had similar restrictions in her picturesque, wooded Durham suburb.

Such restrictions, while understandable and well intended, are also lamentable. Kids are programmed to want to explore the wider world at age thirteen as much as at age three. Those whose hunger is continually curbed will become dejected and apathetic. "It is a surefire way to turn a high-spirited youth into a demoralized one," says William Damon, professor of psychology and director of the Center for Adolescence at Stanford University.[11] Among the youth I followed, it was easy to pick out those who had been overly sheltered: They were either shyer and less self-confident than the savvier kids, or aggressive, even hostile.

Learning to Venture Forth——Carefully

It would have given Eldon greater peace of mind to forbid Eric to walk to his grandmother's house after school or, as Eric got older, to tell him not to go outside after dark. But he didn't do either. Instead, from the time Eric started school, Eldon taught him how to chart a course in dangerous terrain.

When you're out walking, stay on primary streets, Eldon would say. In our neighborhood, don't venture onto 73rd or 75th. Keep an eye on the people around you, and pick out a couple of busy stores or tidy homes with well-tended lawns that look like they'd provide sanctuary if needed. Stay away from neighborhood kids who are trouble and befriend neighborhood adults; they'll be more likely to help you in an emergency if they know you. Eric memorized blocks, streets, alleys, store clerks, and neighbors—not a bad technique for kids in any community.

When he did something foolhardy, Eldon jumped on him, hard. If he walked or rode his bike into forbidden territory and Eldon found out about it, he would be grounded. Once when he stayed out an hour past his 11 P.M. weekend curfew, Eldon came looking for him, took him home, and whipped him with a belt. That was the last time Eric remembers being spanked—or staying out too late.

Eldon also wanted to introduce Eric gradually to new situations. When Eric turned eleven, his father started dropping Eric and a friend off at the Great Western Forum, a professional sports arena in Inglewood. He would return when the event was over to pick them up. He also encouraged Eric to learn the city bus system; since he worked so far away from home, Eric couldn't always rely on him for wheels. Eric learned to navigate LA's five hundred-plus square miles of urban sprawl with an easy familiarity not often found among kids who do not yet drive.

Eldon had mastered two strategies that recent studies say characterize successful parenting of adolescents. He limited Eric's exposure to truly dangerous situations as best he could. At the same time, he encouraged Eric to gradually seek out new circumstances and taught Eric skills that would enable him to take care of himself wherever he was.[12]

As the jacket incident indicated, Eric had taken to heart his father's advice about making associations with people who could help him in uncomfortable situations. The school's decisive action on his behalf was also hugely important; it not only reassured him about the school's safety but also solidified his judgment that he had handled the situation well.

It would have done him little good to believe he was a talented drummer or a budding mathematician, or even a good person, if he didn't also believe he could take care of himself in tough situations. Terence's threat touched his core, and Eric found it solid.

His sense of personal competence drove everything else. In a year's time it moved him from being a guy who was as big, bashful, and awkward as a Saint Bernard puppy to a confident and considerate companion who frequently offered to pay for our meals.

He attributed his resourcefulness to his parents. Having made mistakes with their earlier children, Eldon and Denice had succeeded in not repeating history, first by putting aside their disagreements. Then, like other strong parents I was to meet, they had decided to both support Eric and demand a lot from him. They devoted most of what little free time they had and much of their energy to meeting his needs—not only for food, clothing, and a safe home but for music, entertainment, school, friends, and church. They included him in almost everything they did, almost every place they went. They enjoyed his company—but they did not spoil him. They expected him to set high standards of conduct and accomplishment for himself and to work as hard as they did toward achieving goals. They monitored his progress closely.

Realizing the limitations of their influence, they also built a community of other adults around him to keep him focused: his uncle Robert, his maternal grandmother, the staff at Challengers, teachers, neighbors, the pastor of their church, their coworkers. Eric lived in the inner city, but he was one privileged young man.

CHAPTER TWO

Am I Loved? Am I Loving?
(Chandler's Story)

As Hurricane Fran descends on the wooded suburbs north of Durham, North Carolina, one September evening, a pretty, blond fourteen-year-old named Chandler Brennan is staging her own personal fury. She stands outside her family's custom-built ranch house, ignoring the pelting rain and the wild wind that is snapping the branches of the skinny pine trees around her. "I hate you!" she screams at her mother, Tracy. "I wish you were dead!"

All she did was ask her mother to drive her to her boyfriend's house. So what if he is four years older than she? He is tall and good-looking, with a shaved head and baggy clothes that say, "I'm bad, don't mess with me." He could have any number of girls—has had them, in fact. But right now he has chosen her, Chandler, and that is enough. Why can't Mama under-stand that?

Why is Mama still trying to choose her friends? Why is she always on her case about her clothes, her music, her occasional smoking? Chandler remembers a summer-school tutor who said she had grown up "the hard way." Why can't Mama let her learn life the hard way? Something snaps inside Chandler that night, something that compels her to assert herself powerfully after a summer of small-time rages.

"I'm going to kill you!" she yells. "Or kill myself!"

It's true, Tracy doesn't like Jimmy. He's under house arrest for breaking into a neighbor's house, and she has heard that he runs with a local gang. His parents threw him out of the house and he's living with his grandparents. What mother in her right mind would let her daughter go out with someone like that?

She and Chandler have been fighting all summer. First it was over Todd, another punk. Then over Jimmy and parties and breaking curfew. During an argument on July Fourth, Chandler threw chairs around the kitchen, putting two holes in the wall. She slammed her bedroom door so hard that the door frame cracked. She threatened her younger sister, Ashley. A month later, she pummeled her mother in the face and legs after Tracy slapped her for cursing and talking back. Tracy drove to the magistrate's office with her husband, Daniel, the morning after that fight, and the two of them signed a warrant for Chandler's arrest. Chandler was hauled into court and lectured, then sent home. The judge, a family acquaintance, placed her on probation, telling her she had one year to shape up.

But her behavior hasn't improved. It seems to Tracy that nothing works, not grounding, not removing privileges, not going to court. The hurricane is tearing up her yard, and her firstborn is tearing up her family. "I'm going to call 911 to come take you to the hospital," Tracy says.

Chandler sniffs. "They won't do anything."

Tracy dials the phone. "Come get my daughter," she says.

The dispatcher tells Tracy they cannot take a fourteen-year-old child out of the house.

Three days later, on Sunday, Tracy has lugged the family's laundry to a Laundromat because, like most Durham families, even though the hurricane has gone, they still have no electricity. "Don't go anywhere," she tells Chandler. "Make sure the generator and the refrigerator are working." Several hours later, while the clothes are in the dryer, she telephones home and no one answers. She drives to the home of one of Chandler's friends and finds her daughter there. Mother and daughter fight all the way home; at one point Chandler grabs the steering wheel and tries to steer the car off the road. When they get to the house, Chandler starts threatening her mom, then her younger sister. Tracy dials the sheriff's department again and this time persuades a deputy to come pick up her daughter.

Four hours later, Tracy and Daniel are sitting in the emergency waiting room at Duke University Medical Center, where Chandler has been taken for observation. A physician appears to say that Chandler wants to apologize and go home. Tracy and Daniel look at each other and shake their heads. They're not ready to take her back. "We've got to find out what this is with her," Tracy says.

The physician checks to see whether he can admit Chandler into the adolescent psychiatric ward at Duke or Durham Regional Hospital. Both wards are full. He checks the local youth home run by the county's social services department. Also full.

By the next morning, Chandler is in the only place that will take her: John Umstead Hospital, the state psychiatric institution. Committed there by her parents, she has never felt more alone or more unloved.

Although Chandler experienced more problems as a young teenager than most children do, according to her parents, her early childhood gave few clues of what was to come. Her mother was twenty-four when she was born, her father twenty-six. She was their first child. "We were both crazy about her. She was like a miracle," Tracy recalls. When Chandler started preschool, she wanted to wear nothing but dresses so Tracy spent hours washing pink cotton and ironing lacy collars. On Saturday mornings, Daniel would take her out for pancakes, a tradition Chandler still remembers vividly. When she turned five and her younger sister, Ashley, was born, the pancake breakfasts stopped. But "I wasn't jealous," Chandler says. "Ashley adored me."

Early in elementary school, hints of a slight learning disability appeared, but after a year of special tutoring, school officials pronounced her abilities within a normal range. She learned to dance to jazz and tap at a well-known studio and attended a Baptist church with her family every Wednesday night. In seventh grade she took up cheerleading and soccer and joined a church youth group. On weekends and during the summer the family traveled to Kerr Lake, about an hour's drive away. There at a vacation house, they would hang out with other relatives, who attended to sweet, pretty Chandler.

As her hair got darker, Chandler wanted it lightened, and her mother took her to the hairdresser. Tracy showed her how to pluck her eyebrows into a perfect, thin arch, and how to apply makeup without looking like a hooker. Tracy also accompanied Chandler to have a "glamour photo" shot taken and placed it on the mantel.

Toward the end of middle school, Chandler asked to redo her girlish bedroom with its canopy bed and mauve color scheme. She wanted something more sophisticated and she got it: a walnut double bed, a black-and-white-striped comforter, black-and-white curtains, a black lamp, an art deco mirror, and an entertainment center with a random five-CD changer. Except for a stuffed black gorilla that she kept on her bed, her childhood disappeared virtually overnight.

In its place came adolescence and rebellion. She dropped soccer, cheerleading, church, and eventually dance between eighth and ninth grades. "I was doing so much, I just got tired of it all," she would later recall. She stopped being interested in school, abandoned friends her own age, and took up with older kids her parents didn't know as well. And she started being mean to her little sister.

Chandler was right—Ashley did adore her. If the two of them were in a crowd and Chandler was looking for someone, Ashley would hunt down that person. When they went swimming and Chandler showed off one of her high dives, Ashley would hold her breath until she saw her sister surface. Chandler watched over Ashley like a mama cat when they went out together. But at home, she began to include her sister in sweeps of violence.

Tracy and Daniel were stunned by these changes. They also were hurt, after all they had given her.

"I don't want to be a parent anymore," Tracy would say to Chandler. Her daughter would reply, "Well, don't then. Let me leave home."

By the time Chandler went to Umstead, she couldn't even say "I love you" to her mother. Tracy could get out the words, but only barely.

Testing the Limits of Love

By the time our kids reach adolescence, we assume they know we love them. After all, haven't we put their stick-figure drawings on the refrigerator, clapped until our hands were red at their plays, chauffeured them to ball games miles away? Must we continue to find ways to show our love?

The answer is yes. Demonstrating love—consistently and unconditionally—is the single most important thing we can do to sustain a young teenager's self-confidence and sense of self-worth. A close second is giving her opportunities to demonstrate her own capacity for love. A loving, supportive relationship between parents and teenager can usually sustain almost all conflicts that may occur. In fact, research shows that conflict within a healthy family environment can sometimes be a positive thing, promoting thinking skills, perspective-taking, and the ability to negotiate.[1]

But as the Brennans' experience illustrates, showing our love is far easier said than done. The pouty, loud, or smart-alecky fourteen-year-old is not nearly as lovable as the cuddly, pink-cheeked four-month-old. She may defy us at a younger age than we anticipate, and perhaps more forcefully. She may take risks that seem stupid and dangerous. Her behavior, at times, will annoy, provoke, and confuse us. It is tempting to yell back or, worse, to pull away.

But if we're confused, we need to remember that our children are even more so. Battered by physiological changes and by a world that is frequently hostile to teens, they will act in two seemingly contradictory ways. Sometimes they will be angry at us for the rules we put in place, and at other times they will reach out for the supporting structure of people who love them no matter what. Parents of adolescents are both punching bags and anchors, but they must never let their feelings about being the former get in the way of being the latter. For if their children don't find an anchor among adults close to them, they will turn to anyone else who throws out a lifeline, especially kids their own age.

Tracy and Daniel were caught off guard by Chandler's puberty and didn't know how to go about spending time with a rapidly maturing daughter who no longer wanted to do the things she once loved doing. Anxious about a community they believed was disintegrating before their eyes, they struggled over how much freedom she should be allowed. When they sought guidance from administrators and teachers at school, they usually came away disappointed and demoralized.

But the factor that best explained their daughter's erratic behavior, according to counselors who worked closely with the family after Chandler was admitted to Umstead, was their faltering marriage. It had begun to unravel just as Chandler entered adolescence, and their fights intensified over what to do when she acted out. Their ideas about how to raise a teenager differed dramatically, and each insisted on raising Chandler in the style in which they had been raised, failing to appreciate the need to speak with one voice.

Many parents of young teenagers wrestle with some of the same kinds of experiences and feelings that the Brennans did. But families can survive most crises if the parents work hard at providing a consistently loving home. Tracy and Daniel were unable to do this, and as a result, according to one counselor, Chandler "went through puberty pretty much without help."

Striding Toward Independence

Like most conflicts between young adolescents and their parents, Chandler's began over mundane issues: why she had discarded the preppy look in favor of grunge, why she wanted to listen to Ease Z rap. Chandler felt that her mom in particular constantly criticized her choices.

As the choices became more consequential, the mother-daughter battles escalated. Tracy would suggest a weekend curfew of 10:30. Chandler would argue for 11, Tracy would agree, and Chandler would come home at midnight. Tracy would find fault with Chandler's friends, and Chandler would sneak out with them anyway.

When she was punished for her defiance—Tracy would slap her or ground her or deny her the telephone—Chandler would react by screaming, crying, or withdrawing. These were typical coping responses for a young adolescent who hasn't learned yet to talk out a problem, make compromises, or seek outside help.[2] She went to extremes in flouting her parents' authority, but she was following normal impulses. Like the four-year-old who tosses her favorite possessions into a pillowcase and threatens to run away from home, she was seeking ways to define herself independently of her parents. New cognitive skills—what scientists call the beginning of formal operational thought—were pushing her to do so.

Allowing our child some early measure of freedom is one way we demonstrate our love. Going along with what seems to us a crazy dress style or tolerating music we privately can't stand are small concessions on our part but can be a big deal to our kids. But we don't want to be like the nincompoop parents portrayed on TV and in the movies who allow their kids virtually to raise themselves. Our maturing children need to know that we will pull them in if they fly too far away or too fast. Uncertain how independent they can be and remain safe, they want limits set on their behavior and consequences for when they misbehave. Tracy's instincts about the big issues—Chandler's violent behavior, breaking curfew, the kids with whom she hung out—were on target. Her problem was that she received little backup from her husband.

Daniel often agreed with Tracy's rules initially, but if Chandler broke one while he was home, he would frequently give in. "She's got to learn the consequences of her own behavior," he would say to Tracy, thinking back to his early teenage years when he got caught sneaking away in a Corvette or speeding on his motorcycle.

To Tracy, his reasoning sounded like "Let her dig her own grave." They would argue, and the arguments usually ended with Tracy giving in. ("It's the Southern culture, I guess," she told me.) Chandler, buffeted back and forth between them, saw that her dad didn't respect her mom, so why should she? When Daniel was away, which was often, since he worked two jobs, seven days a week, she'd resume her old habits. "I'm going to tell your dad," Tracy would say. Chandler's retort was always the same: "He doesn't care, he's not here."

Fighting over Chandler's demands wore both Tracy and Daniel down. They found themselves resorting more often to emotion than to reason, which provoked more emotional outbursts from Chandler. Daniel was right—Chandler did need to learn how to set limits on her own. But Tracy was also right: When Chandler broke the rules she had helped to set, she needed to be held accountable by both parents. Chandler was getting the extremes of the panicked parent: too much control from her mom, which only increased her appetite for the things she wasn't supposed to do, and no control from her dad, which made her feel unloved. Neither approach accomplished the Brennans' ultimate goal of teaching her to internalize and claim as her own some reasonable standards of conduct.

Parents do not have to agree on every rule or use the same enforcement techniques when a kid is pushing the boundaries as hard as Chandler did. But they should agree on most of the big rules and present a united front. Psychologist Wade Horn suggests a "first in, wins" rule: The first parent to discover that a rule has been broken may mete out discipline and the other parent should back him or her up. Discussion between the parents, and among parents and child, can come later.[3]

The most well-adjusted kids I spent time with benefited from such collaboration no matter what the family structure. Eric's divorced parents were an example, conferring regularly about what he could or could not do. Once a decision was made, they did not undermine each other. Feeling supported by each other, they could gradually allow Eric more freedom, taking their cues from his behavior.

Hurdles to Autonomy

Chandler's parents differed in another significant way from Eric's: They wanted to protect their daughter as long as possible from a community they viewed as increasingly dangerous. It is difficult for a parent to loosen restrictions and convey trust when that parent is terrified of what lies outside the door. Anxiety always accompanies parenting teens, but uncontrolled anxiety can inhibit rational, loving responses to our kids' lunges toward independence.

Like many baby boomers, Daniel and Tracy had worked several jobs and long hours to achieve and maintain a lifestyle that would give them some measure of security. But in their county of two hundred thousand residents, they did not feel secure. "They ought to erase Durham and start over," Daniel told me.

His attitude was formed in high school when several homes in the neighborhood in which he lived, a country-club area known as Willow Haven, were burglarized. Years later, just as his career was taking off, the local newspaper carried stories of teenagers being arrested in Durham in record numbers. When Chandler was two, Daniel decided to move the family out of the city into Durham County. The large, beautifully landscaped properties offered what he believed to be a safe haven as Chandler made her way through elementary school. But he no longer had that confidence as she got older and started riding around with her friends or bringing home boys he didn't know.

Tracy was equally fearful. She was amazed at what other parents allowed their children to do and by the excuses they made for their kids. "They just don't care for their young'uns the way I care for mine," she said. Chandler went astray because she got caught up in other kids' messes, Tracy said, echoing a complaint I heard frequently from parents.

Sitting one autumn night in her living room, a sunken, carpeted room with overstuffed furniture, dozens of candles, and a stag head above the fireplace, Tracy told a story to show what she meant. She had been driving by a nearby mall when she spotted a white car with her daughter in it. Chandler was supposed to be at her grandfather's house. Tracy beeped her horn and motioned for the car to pull over. The driver was a thirteen-year-old girl, driving without even a learner's permit. Tracy insisted that Chandler get out and ride home with her and later called the girl's mother. The mom "cussed me out and told me her daughter had never been to the mall." Tracy grounded Chandler for two weeks; the other girl was spotted cruising with her friends the next day.

It's not just other parents who are untrustworthy, Tracy continued. Chandler had told her that the arcade manager at this same mall left his car keys hanging on the wall in case any young customers wanted to take a spin. Another shopkeeper sold cigarettes to underage teens. The mall was the only place in their part of Durham County that young adolescents like Chandler could hang out, other than home, Tracy lamented, "and look what they run into there." As she talked, a wide-screen television was turned on behind her, its volume muted. The TV was like another member of this family, coloring their view of the world with its frequent reports of local crime.

Tracy and Daniel had some reason to be concerned for Chandler's safety. In 1996, 260 kids in Durham, or more than one-quarter of those referred to juvenile court, were charged with being truant or "out of control of their parents," the very thing about which Tracy complained. The number of ten- to fifteen-year-olds arrested for violent crimes such as murder, rape, and robbery rose from fifty-three in 1994 to seventy-six two years later. The victims were usually other teenagers, both black and white, in a county that was almost equally divided between the two.[4]

Yet as alarming as such figures were, they described only a fraction of the youth population. The kids arrested for violent crimes made up about one-half of one percent of the juvenile population in Durham. Chandler was far more likely to be killed in an automobile accident than murdered. It is difficult for parents to hold on to a realistic perspective, however, when the news media bombard us with frightening stories. And yet we must do so, lest we pass on to our children our own feelings of helplessness and incompetence.[5]

Distrusting One's Judgment

Tracy's self-confidence withered as Chandler continued to defy her. Early adolescence takes a particular toll on the mental health of mothers, according to researchers; in one study of about two hundred families, nearly half of the women showed a decline in well-being during their child's adolescence.[6]

Mothers of first daughters are particularly vulnerable, as Tracy's case illustrated. On the evening of our first interview, dressed in a waffle-weave jersey shirt and stonewashed denim overalls, with her shoulder-length auburn hair swept off her face, she looked almost as young as her daughter. But she had dropped thirty pounds over the last year, and, though she was still very attractive, her eyes drooped and her voice sounded resigned. "These kids have been my life," she said, sounding like someone on the verge of losing her best friend.

The family was to meet later that night with a counselor as required by Chandler's commitment to John Umstead. The sessions were not going well because Daniel didn't want to probe the role he had played in Chandler's problems. An electrical contractor, he had asked the therapist to forget past mistakes and lay out a blueprint for his family showing what they needed to do differently. The therapist had told him that this wasn't a matter of replacing a couple of fuses; the power line itself needed to be examined.

Earlier intervention might have been more useful, Tracy acknowledged. But she and Chandler had visited a psychologist together in Chandler's seventh-grade year and after seven meetings and no visible improvement, Tracy had dropped her. The counseling was not covered by their health insurance. Tracy decided it was too expensive.

"Was that wrong? Was I a bad mother?" she asked. As the parent who spent the most time with Chandler, she second-guessed herself a lot.

When Chandler was so busy in sixth and seventh grades, Tracy stopped pressing her to do chores around the house. She now thought that was a mistake. She also wished she had found Chandler some volunteer work, with younger children, perhaps, since Chandler liked little kids. Tracy's instincts told her, if not in these exact words, that requiring Chandler to donate time to others and to answer to adults other than her parents might have taken her mind off herself. She might have found other adults who cared about her at a time when she questioned whether her parents did.

Tracy's instincts were sound. So why didn't she follow them? As she would later come to see, Chandler's rebelliousness, coupled with what Tracy perceived as a lack of support from her husband, gradually chipped away at her confidence as a parent. Since parenting was the one job she thought she did pretty well, not doing it well threw her into depression. She kept trying to control Chandler, and each time she failed she felt more intensely that nothing she did would make any difference. As anyone who has ever lived through depression knows, it saps you of both energy and good sense.

Tracy's reaction to her daughter's adolescence was not atypical. Laurence Steinberg, a psychologist who studies the impact of adolescents on families, has found that many parents must cope with deep feelings of powerlessness as their kids assert themselves. The parent who exercises authority in a job outside the home may be extremely irritated that she can't control her kid as she does her employees, Steinberg says. But the parent who, like Tracy, doesn't even enjoy control in the workplace may, if constantly challenged by her child, come to feel "that there is no place, no situation, in which [she is] at all in control."[7]

Adolescence does not have to throw parents into depression, however. Steinberg found that a significant number of parents, including mothers, reported a growing sense of personal satisfaction over the course of their adolescents' maturation. Why? They did not take their kids' challenges personally; instead they saw them as inevitable, if sometimes flawed, steps toward independence that needed to be monitored. Also, they stayed emotionally close to their children and pursued other interests: work, hobbies, and activities with spouses and friends.

Their attachments to other adults were especially important, since others could help them realize that they were not the losers their children sometimes called them, that small rebellions do not inevitably lead to self-destruction, that there are not as many demons in the world as they imagined. One of Tracy's big problems was that when Chandler dropped all of her extracurricular activities, Tracy lost the support and advice of the adults who ran those programs. Except for conversations with her sisters and mother, she was flying solo.

Chandler's counselor at Umstead told Tracy that Chandler talked about her a lot, and that much of what she said cast Tracy in a positive light. Months later, as Chandler and I drove around Durham, Chandler would spontaneously point out places she associated with her mother: "Mama used to work there," she'd say, or "Mama takes her van there to get fixed." Late one afternoon at a swimming pool, she sang ever so softly, "My mama's off work! My mama's off work! She might want to lay out when she gets here." Such attachment confused Tracy in light of Chandler's behavior, but it was just as normal as her daughter's emotional outbursts. The research is consistent: Young adolescents vacillate between wanting to separate and wanting to connect. While they look to friends for guidance in dress, music, hairstyles, and entertainment, they rely on their families for affection and basic values. No matter how ugly they act.

Chandler is sitting in her room at John Umstead Hospital, staring at her poster of gangsta rapper Tupac Shakur. If only Mama and Daddy would get here. Because she has been making decent grades the last few weeks and obeying house rules, she has been allowed to leave the grounds for four hours. She can't wait. She still can't believe she's in a mental hospital. Why, there's a girl down the hall who screams all night and has to be strapped to her bed! Another girl is here because she stabbed her sister with a fork.

Two months have dragged by like two years. Mostly she keeps to her room. It's a depressing place with bare linoleum floors and boxy wooden furniture. Only Tupac, a red bedspread from home, and photographs of her family and friends keep her from going as crazy as everyone else seems to be.

The child and adolescent division of John Umstead, a series of two-story brick buildings in the woods of Butner, North Carolina, is a sleepy place today. Empty swings on the playground outside glide back and forth, pushed by a late fall breeze; tennis courts sit unused, a dozen girls' bikes, pink and purple and in all sizes, stand idle in an open storage shed. During World War II, these buildings housed prisoners of war for the army; today they hold about sixty prisoners of another sort: children and teenagers who parents, teachers, social workers, and judges aren't sure what to do with.

Next door, new construction is under way: a hundred-bed, four-story youth detention center enclosed by a tall steel fence with rolled barbed wire at the top. This will be part of the U.S. Justice Department's correctional facilities at Butner, and it reminds Chandler of the threat parents in her hometown would casually throw out to their kids: "If you're not good, I'll send you to Butner." Well, she's at Butner, but she desperately wants her friends back home to understand it's not that Butner. "I'm going to Bowling Green School," she writes them, a shortened form of the Bowling Green School of the Adolescent Unit of the Children's Psychiatric Institute of John Umstead Hospital.

Once Tracy, Daniel, and Ashley arrive in the family van, they head for Durham's South Square Mall. In the food court, Chandler asks to use the phone to call a friend. Daniel says no. Take me home, she says. We can't do that, it's against hospital rules, Tracy says. Ashley suggests that they go bowling. Chandler's rosy bow mouth turns down into a pout she has perfected over the years. "Oh fine," she says with unmistakable sarcasm. "I'm a teenager and I've got to go bowling with my family."

As she sits in the bowling alley, she realizes she can't remember the last time they all did something together, including eating dinner. She says to Mama, "Don't you think it's a little late to be doing this?"

For most girls, signs of puberty start appearing in sixth or seventh grade. Puberty for these girls is a continuous process stretching over four years, a time of weight gain, breast development, pubic hair, and eventually menstruation. It can be an annoying but not devastating transition. The changes embarrass but do not overwhelm.

Chandler was not like most girls. She started filling out and having periods in fourth grade. By sixth grade she had gone through a complicated series of physical changes at twice the speed of other girls. Only a few years earlier, she had been learning how to dress herself; now she was biologically ready to have a baby.

Like many early maturers, her cognitive and emotional development lagged behind her physical growth, leaving her especially sensitive to comments about her appearance. She felt on public display when all she wanted was to fit in. "I felt big," she remembers about her size. (The bodies of early maturers tend to expand and stay larger than those of average to late maturers.) She exchanged her dresses for a casual, baggy look, but still she was teased. Gradually she found herself attracted to troubled kids who also looked different and who behaved differently.

Chandler doesn't remember talking much to any adults, including her parents, about the changes and feelings she was experiencing. Tracy says she explained menstruation to Chandler and let it go at that. Then when Chandler was in fifth grade, her teacher pulled Tracy aside one day. "I've had other girls who develop early," this teacher told Tracy, "and they always get into trouble down the road. You better watch her."

Distrusting One's Child

Among kids who suffer during adolescence, early-maturing girls may suffer the most, exhibiting lower self-esteem, taking more risks and doing less well in school, particularly if they have older friends.[8] Researchers say that this has lots to do with how other kids and adults treat them. As boys mature, friends dare them in tests of courage and skill, but as girls mature, friends challenge their sexuality. "Tell how you lost your virginity on the playground in fourth grade," one of Chandler's friends yelled out to her one day when I accompanied her to school. It wasn't true, but Chandler winced. She had heard those kinds of comments for years.

Parents, teachers, and other adults sometimes compound the problem by being overprotective or suspicious. This was the case with Tracy and Daniel. They had heard nothing but bad things about girls who develop early and were unaware that problems associated with early maturity tend to solve themselves by the junior or senior year in high school.[9] They began to anticipate years of crises and to view everything Chandler did through that lens, unaware that negative expectations can influence a child to act out even more.

The Absent Father

By showing his affection in appropriate ways, a father can help his daughter accept her body's changes gracefully, even proudly. But what is appropriate? Daniel, like many fathers, wasn't sure.

Only a few years earlier, he could take Chandler on his lap; now he felt he shouldn't. He liked to ride his Harley-Davidson motorcycle with Chandler behind him; now she didn't want to do that. He liked to hunt and shoot skeet; those activities didn't appeal to her, either. "Chandler knows I can have fun, but she doesn't want to hang out with me," he told me sadly.

They still joked and laughed as he drove her to school in the mornings. She occasionally talked to him about boys on these trips and about her troubles with Tracy. "Me and my dad are real close," she told me at one point. But at home, conversations between them were confined increasingly to arguments. When her father wouldn't discuss extending a curfew or another privilege she cared about, she'd shut down and he'd leave the room. "Your walking away tells me you don't care," Chandler would holler after him.

"I won't lie to you, there were several times when I gave up on Chandler," Daniel told me. He turned his attention to Ashley, who still liked zooming around on Harleys.

His withdrawal from Chandler over several years may have been, in part, a reaction to events other than her maturation. As Steinberg and others have shown, parents of young adolescents, who usually range in age from thirty-five to forty-five, are often struggling with their own midlife crises at the time their children are in puberty. Personal or professional problems take up their time and energy just when their kids need them most. Daniel's mother died in 1984, and in 1990, when Chandler was nine, his father died. This left Daniel, the youngest of four, involved in a nasty inheritance battle that ensued just as Chandler was starting to challenge him and Tracy. Eventually he lost much of what he thought he was owed.

In 1992, when Chandler was eleven, he quit a $60,000-a-year job as a building supervisor and went into business for himself. Two years later, he added a grading company to his contracting firm. He didn't hire any employees—"I wouldn't trust them," he says—so he had to do every job he accepted. He drove his big white van all over the South. Tracy accused him of using his work as an escape from his family; he responded that two jobs were necessary to maintain the family's lifestyle. He and his sisters had been spoiled with cars and clothes; now it was his turn to spoil his children. "That's why I work, to buy them things," he would say.

His absence was not atypical. Only one in five teenagers reports spending time with their fathers daily.[10] Fathers and adolescent daughters do less together than fathers and sons, mothers and daughters, and mothers and sons.[11] More than half of the girls I studied showed visible signs of missing their fathers because their fathers either didn't live with them or, like Daniel, used home as just a place to sleep.

Fathers can do many activities with their growing girls—kayaking, cycling, cooking, listening to music. The possibilities are endless; they just need to take the time to find out what their daughters' interests are. The payoff is considerable, for on average, girls who enjoy solid, loving relationships with their fathers not only have more confidence in themselves but are higher achievers in school. They also are more likely to go to college and to establish successful careers than girls who don't.[12]

One week after he and Tracy sent Chandler to John Umstead, Daniel purchased several items he thought his daughter might want, including stationery, books, and a calculator. He headed to the hospital intending to give them to her. But as he rounded the corner of the road leading to the entrance, his eyes took in the outdoor playground with its old-fashioned swings and jungle gym. Overcome with grief for a little girl gone, he pulled his van into a parking lot and, through his tears, wrote his daughter a short letter.

"Signing you into the hospital was the hardest thing I have ever had to do," he wrote. "We will get through this together and things will be better."

He pushed the buzzer at the door and handed the letter and supplies to a receptionist instead of asking to see Chandler.

More than a year later, Chandler would tell me, "I still have that note."

On a sparkling and clear late March afternoon, Chandler lies dozing on the couch in her living room. On the television, Ricki Lake is chattering away about women whose husbands sleep with their wives' sisters. A visitor knocks. Chandler springs to the door in her short jean cutoffs and yellow knit crop top. Maybe it's Kenny.

But it's not. Her face falls.

Since she was released from John Umstead in January, Chandler has been dating Kenny, a high-school sophomore. "He's a pretty boy" is how she describes him as she shows off an 8-by-11-inch framed school picture of a young man with short blond hair, smiling blue eyes, and high cheek-bones. She met him three years earlier when he was her next-door neigh-

bor's best friend. They talked on and off while she was in middle school, and during her four-month stay at the hospital he would call her mom to find out how she was doing. Even her mother likes him, saying he's well-mannered, keeps Chandler at home, and doesn't get into trouble. What Tracy doesn't know is that Kenny and her daughter are sexual partners.

He is not Chandler's first lover. That was Todd, an older boy who smoked marijuana and carried a gun "to be bad." She was thirteen when she slept with him. The second was Jimmy, and now there's Kenny. Sometimes he uses a condom, sometimes he doesn't. Chandler's parents have not advised her to carry a condom and won't take her to a physician for birth control, even though a counselor at John Umstead suggested that they do both. The counselor explained that parents can preach abstinence and protection, and that doing so reduces the onset (or frequency) of intercourse and increases the odds that protection will be used. But the Brennans weren't buying it—yet. Tracy wants to raise the subject but says that Daniel doesn't because he believes that would be giving permission for something they don't believe in.

After working with Chandler for four months at John Umstead, the hospital staff decided she was ready to go home. In the structured, consistent environment of the hospital she was making A's and B's in her classes, keeping her language clean, doing her laundry, and had even opened up enough with the other girls to teach them some soccer skills. At the end of every phone call, Tracy was pleased to hear her say, "I love you, Mama." So one crisp January morning Daniel arrived, signed out his little girl, and took her right back into her old environment: same house, same parents, same school, same friends.

Behavioral scientists have known for a long time that environmental cues stimulate memories, which in turn prompt certain types of behavior. Put a recovering drug addict back into the setting in which he first started taking drugs, for example, and he is more likely to resume his habit than if he moves to a new setting.[13] For this reason, parents of truly troubled teens are sometimes advised to enroll their children in a new, and in some cases a private, school.

The Brennans considered moving Chandler but gave in to her wishes to stay at Northern High School, where she had started ninth grade five months earlier. For a couple of months, she minded them and her teachers. She reported to a psychologist once a week for individual therapy. Tracy and Daniel followed the doctors' orders to be firm and consistent with her and to back each other up. But by March, they had resumed their fighting, and signs of the old Chandler gradually started to appear.

She sneaked cigarettes at school. She wandered late into early-afternoon classes, having lingered outside at lunchtime with old friends with whom she once shared dope and now shared a probation officer.

Taking Risks: The Promise and Perils

From the time children come into this world, they take risks and watch for our approval. How we applaud them when they achieve those first milestones: rolling over, putting one foot in front of the other, riding a bike. Yet when they enter adolescence, all of a sudden we're terrified. "Risk" becomes a bad word, something to protect them from.

Lynn Ponton, an adolescent psychiatrist in San Francisco, says one of her biggest tasks is to convince parents that risk-taking is one way, perhaps the major way, young teenagers learn to separate from their parents. Taking risks forces them to think harder, try out new skills, tame their fears, and experience new impulses and learn to control them.[14] Psychologist Peter Scales agrees. "Borrowing other people's values without testing them is like borrowing someone else's ill-fitting suit," he says.[15]

As kids observe their parents' reactions to their adventures, they're also assessing parental love and trust. A parent's goal should be to help his or her child find ways to take risks that will contribute to, not damage, the child's health and well-being. Parents need to look for pursuits that are novel and that involve increasing levels of skill. They should not shy away from a challenge involving a moderate amount of danger if they think their child can handle it. In the coming chapters we will read about parents who came up with such adventures for their kids: in one case, roping on horseback, in another, flying overseas unaccompanied by parents.

Challenge should not be confused with thrill, however. When Daniel bought Chandler a Jet Ski, he was providing her with an exciting toy. It amused her and gave her a bit of a charge the first few times she rode, but it didn't call on any of her talents or require sustained practice.

The High-Flyer

And it wasn't even much of a thrill as far as Chandler was concerned. From the time they are born, kids have certain biological thresholds for risk. Some are cautious; others throw caution to the wind. Chandler was one of the latter. She needed to do more than skim across Kerr Lake in a Jet Ski to prove herself to herself and to others.

Many young adolescents will experiment with behaviors that scandalize their parents or that may be illegal. They may cut class, sneak booze out of the liquor cabinet, try a joint of marijuana at a party. For most of them, such instances will be few because they learn from the consequences to modify their behavior. But about one in five will adopt dangerous patterns of behavior—about the same proportion as adults. One experiment leads to another for this minority, each more dangerous than the previous one. For reasons that some scientists speculate may have to do with brain development, it takes these kids longer to develop an internal mechanism for self-control.[16]

Chandler's progression, which her parents say they didn't see at the time, was typical. When she was in middle school, she tried marijuana in a backyard clubhouse that her grandfather had built. By the end of eighth grade, she was smoking weed virtually every afternoon on her back deck. At parties with older youth, she was bumming cigarettes and throwing back wine coolers.

She was also running around with a couple of members of a well-known Durham gang. One afternoon she and these boys were riding around and spied a boy in another car who had mouthed off at one of Chandler's buddies earlier in the summer. The two boys nudged their car over to the side of the road, hopped out, and pulled a gun out of the trunk. They climbed back in the car and sped off after their would-be victim. "We're gonna punk him down," one of them told Chandler.

The two cars sped down a busy highway and ended up in a parking lot. Chandler's friends stepped out with the gun, then apparently had second thoughts about using it and passed it to Chandler. Hold it for us, they said, and if we yell for it, hand it out. "I thought to myself, what the hell am I doing?" Chandler would say months later. If her friends used their weapon, she could be charged as an accomplice.

Within a few minutes, the other boy had backed down, saying he never intended any disrespect. When her friends returned to the car, Chandler stuck the gun under the seat.

Cognitive growth occurs haphazardly in adolescence. Usually it isn't until late adolescence that kids can anticipate fully the possible consequences of their behavior. Chandler's thinking had matured enough to challenge the fairness of her mother's rule that she not see Jimmy, but not enough to anticipate how she was putting her future in jeopardy by running around with kids like him.

Risks and Bonding

Chandler realized that some of the choices she made were not what her parents and other relatives expected of her. But were they so bad compared to adults she knew? One close relative had had a baby while in high school. Several others had sold or used illegal drugs; one had been kicked out of college for dealing. She was growing up in a town whose name was synonymous with tobacco use; her mother, an aunt, and her maternal grandparents had worked for years for American Tobacco Company. The uncle of one of her boyfriends supplied her with free cigarettes. She took this as a sign of affection, not as a push toward a shorter life. "He just loves me to death," she once said, unaware of the double entendre.

As she rattled off the people to whom she felt close, who were risk-takers themselves, it occurred to me that her smoking and other high-wire acts were more than attempts at self-definition. They also acted as an adhesive to the people whose affection she craved. Parents need to understand that taking risks is one way adolescents seek close relationships with their collaborators or with those who attempt to rescue them.

Chandler knew that cigarettes could give her lung cancer, and that sleeping with guys could make her pregnant or infect her with disease. I never heard her—or other girls—say, "It can't happen to me," the explanation adults so frequently give for why teens as a group take risks. Nowadays kids live in an in-your-face world; I suspect they feel as susceptible to risk as the rest of us do. In fact one survey showed that adolescents feel more vulnerable to risk than adults.[17]

Chandler took risks at least partly because her need to feel connected was greater than her fear of negative outcomes. On the subject of pregnancy, for example, she confided one afternoon that she wouldn't mind having a baby to love. "I guess if I get pregnant, it was meant to be," she said.

Losing People You Love

Perhaps one reason Chandler sought out people she believed cared about her was that their number was getting scarcer.

In seventh grade, two of her girlfriends died in separate car accidents. And then she lost Carter. He was five years older than her, the brother she never had. His family lived in her neighborhood and also owned a house at Kerr Lake. In elementary school, she and Carter rode dirt bikes and talked about nothing and everything. Toward the end of his senior year, he was making plans to enter the navy. One morning, as Chandler was drying her hair in the bathroom, her mother walked in with tears in her eyes. Tracy could barely get the words out: Carter had committed suicide.

Two years later, Chandler thought she knew why. A couple of days before he killed himself, Carter had robbed a theater where he worked. He worried that if his girlfriend found out, she wouldn't want to have anything more to do with him. That may or may not have been the reason Carter killed himself. But Chandler interpreted the suicide as a love story.

Bad things continued to befall her. In the fall after she was admitted to Umstead, a high-school boy she knew hanged himself in jail. A few weeks later, her cousin's fiancé, nineteen, was shot and killed in his yard in front of her cousin and their baby.

As Chandler was exposed to more and more of these tragedies, she began to take them personally, almost as if she were responsible for them. "I guess these things are always going to happen to me," she said.

Young adolescents are naturally idealistic and tend to anticipate the best possible outcomes in all aspects of their lives. When things go awry, though, their idealism can turn to despair very quickly. Stressful experiences at this age have a multiplicative effect, meaning that several such events together cause a harsher emotional reaction than each event would separately.[18]

Those who experience or witness violence directly can become extremely angry, anxious, and depressed. Scientists now believe that violence and other severe stress actually alter the genetic makeup of these witnesses, making them prone to mental-health problems even after the stressful situation has passed. Some studies on puberty suggest that adolescent girls are particularly sensitive to negative events.[19]

The research is less clear on how kids are affected by traumas they learn about rather than witness—still the experience of most kids. But Chandler's reactions suggest one result may be that they, too, reject their natural optimism for a darker view of the world, particularly if they do not feel attached to adults who keep before them a sense of purpose and a positive view of the future. Earlier parenting is crucial here: If kids were held to rules and guidelines when they were younger, and possess the sense of control that flows from that, they will be better equipped to deal with life's misfortunes. If, as in Chandler's case, they have not been disciplined consistently, they may feel overwhelmed and helpless.[20]

Chandler's friend Brendan drags into math class five minutes late, his Boss jeans sagging, his eyes red and squinty, and his movements slow. The signs are unmistakable: He is totally stoned. "What's wrong?" Chandler whispers.

To her right, Mario from Mexico is slouched in his seat staring blankly into space. His sisters brought him to the States against his will, he doesn't speak English, and he doesn't want to be here. Next to Mario, nineteen-year-old Jared leans against the wall asleep. In front of Chandler, Michael shows her the superglue, now a hard mess, that he poured on the floor yesterday. Chandler's teacher Pamela Adams surveys her 8 A.M. introductory math class on this late spring morning and turns to me. What's wrong, she says, is that Chandler doesn't belong here.

The students have been asked to graph equations. Chandler finishes the assignment rapidly, then begins to chat with the guy behind her. Adams, who is completing the assignment along with her students, has pulled her chair over to the side of the classroom where I'm sitting. "This is the lowest math class there is," she says as she draws lines and angles and shades in squares. "Many of these kids have missed lots of days of school. If I can keep them in their seats a whole period, I've accomplished something. Chandler could be doing algebra, if you could just get her away from these kids."

Almost all of her school life, Chandler has been told she is dumb. A late-September baby, she started preschool a year early, at age two. As she approached five, her teacher assured Tracy that Chandler was ready for kindergarten. The kindergarten teacher, however, had another reaction. "Oh no," she said to Tracy at the first parent-teacher meeting. "Not another September baby." At that time, September 30 was the cutoff birthdate for starting kindergarten, and in this teacher's experience, students as young as Chandler weren't ready to sit still and learn along with their older classmates.

Chandler made it through kindergarten, but then had to repeat first grade. Her teachers told Tracy that she had trouble paying attention in class and showed little interest in reading. As Chandler entered third grade, Tracy asked that her daughter be tested for learning disabilities. She scored in a range that placed her in special education.

But the next year, when Tracy asked that she be tested again, she scored too high to qualify. Rather than feeling elated that Chandler had made progress, Tracy worried because now she wouldn't receive the smaller classes and special attention that a label provided. Each year after that, Tracy asked that Chandler be retested, and each year the decision came back that she was scoring within the normal range on her tests and didn't belong in special ed.

Where did she belong? She had a head for numbers, but by the time she entered sixth grade at Carrington Middle School, she had been grouped with the underachievers. "I stopped working in sixth grade," she told me. By the end of eighth grade, she had essentially quit trying in school and was in danger of having to repeat a year again. Daniel said she should be allowed to fail, but Tracy disagreed. Tracy hired a tutor to work with her during the summer and by fall, authorities said she could proceed to Northern. Tracy wasn't sure a school as big as Northern, with seventeen hundred students, was the appropriate setting for Chandler or that her Carrington friends, also bound for Northern, were good influences. "Please, Mama, give me a chance," Chandler begged. And her mother did. Two weeks after school started, both Hurricane Fran and Chandler exploded.

In 1984, Theodore Sizer wrote a book about a mythical high-school teacher named Horace who struck a "compromise" with his students:

Don't cause me too much trouble and I will allow you to pass with only a minimal amount of effort. This, in effect, was how Chandler was experiencing school. Rather than being encouraged to do more than the minimum, knowing that support was there if she failed, she was picking up a message that no one at school cared whether or not she stretched.

Next to home, school is the most likely place to make a young adolescent feel loved or unloved, loving or unloving. Caring teachers are the key. In the lower grades, students equate caring with teachers who are warm and nurturing. But by the time they reach middle school or junior high, a caring teacher is one who respects their increasingly sophisticated abilities and challenges them by giving them harder assignments and demanding quality work.[21] When pressed to name their favorite teachers, the youth I interviewed almost always chose the men and women from whom they were learning the most.

Chandler's teachers at Northern wanted to be good teachers. But they were frustrated by a tracking system that grouped students like Chandler, whose problems appeared to be more emotional than intellectual, with students who were not as bright. "This year's been the worst," said Pat Carroll, Chandler's science teacher. "Chandler is staying on task, but she'd do more than that if she were in a group where she saw higher-achieving kids doing better work." Carroll and Pam Adams, the math teacher, had reason to be concerned, for studies show that for lower-achieving students, tracking weakens their belief that schools care about them.[22]

Convincing a schoolchild this age that she is cared for is not just a feel-good proposition. A landmark national survey released in 1997 showed that a caring relationship with teachers was the single biggest predictor of young people's success in school, more important even than the amount of teacher training or class size (though of course it is easier for teachers to nurture supportive relationships when they have fewer students).[23] Another study by psychologist Carol Gilligan suggests that adolescent girls in particular thrive on caring relationships with their teachers because they depend more than boys do on the assessment of others.

Chandler felt that Pam Adams was the only teacher who really cared about her. One inspirational teacher is often enough, but for someone with as many emotional needs as Chandler, it may not be.

The Parent-School Divide

Chandler's low opinion of most of the staff at Northern was shared by, and perhaps fed by, her parents. Shortly after their daughter returned to Northern in January, Tracy and Daniel asked to meet with her new teachers and principal, Isaac Thomas. Twice a conference was scheduled, and both times the school canceled. On the third try, in March, Tracy and Daniel finally sat down with school personnel.

As soon as the lunch bell rang, Chandler hurried to a pay phone at school to call her mother and ask how the conference had gone. Walking out of school that afternoon, she was bouncing. "They gave me a good report," she told a friend. Much to Tracy's and Daniel's surprise, the teachers had said that Chandler was paying attention in class and getting B's and C's in most subjects. Tracy, showing the lack of faith in her child that she had harbored for several years, asked whether she should be placed in a class with learning-disabled kids. Chandler's guidance counselor said no.

Tracy was pleased, but one thought kept nagging her. If Chandler was doing so well, why wasn't she bringing any homework home? Chandler said she did it all in class. Tracy didn't think that was the whole story.

It wasn't. At that point Chandler was failing civics and art. In math, she owed the teacher six homework assignments. She refused to wear her gym uniform to physical education. She had been tardy four times to science. She knew that she was slipping, but she also knew that she was sliding by. Apparently the school, having given her a good report, expected little else.

Tracy and Daniel were in a bind. They suspected they weren't getting the whole story from either their daughter or the school. But, like so many parents of high-school kids, they had gotten the clear message from school authorities that they shouldn't intervene. Most of the time, high-school students should shoulder the responsibility for their learning, but there are exceptions. Tracy and Daniel could have done a little homework on the classes and teachers available to Chandler and then insisted on some changes. But by the time I met them, they seemed beaten down and resigned to never seeing improvement in Chandler's performance.

The Failing Marriage

As the school year came to a close, Tracy and Daniel's marriage was fraying fast. Not only did they find it hard to show that they loved her, they found it nearly impossible to demonstrate love toward each other. For models of what it was like to be loved and loving, Chandler would have to look elsewhere.

"It was really bad this weekend," she said to me over the phone one Monday night. What did she and Ashley do, I asked, when Tracy and Daniel got into a screaming match? "Usually we just laugh it off," Chandler said. "Or sometimes we go in our rooms and shut the door." Will her parents ever be in love again? "Maybe when I'm gone," she answered.

Marriages in trouble hit adolescents particularly hard because they are old enough to tell when the hostility has something to do with them, as it often does. This doesn't mean that parents should never air their differences, for in an otherwise healthy marriage, debate can stimulate an adolescent's thinking. But frequent arguments in an already shaky marriage raise a child's anxiety level, possibly leading to depression, aggression, and a sense of failure. This is true even if the parents take care to support the child.[24]

Thus, as difficult as it sounds, spouses have to work just as hard at their marriage as they do at the relationship with their child. In fact, the techniques are similar: learning to listen to the other person, giving more than you receive, using humor to defuse anger, saying more positive than negative things about a person, spending time alone together, doing something you both enjoy.[25]

A softball game one evening in late June could have been such an occasion for the Brennans. Although Chandler had dropped sports, her younger sister hadn't. Ashley was playing catcher on a team of ten- and eleven-year-olds, and Chandler, Tracy, and Tracy's father were there to cheer her on.

It was an exciting game, with Ashley's team coming from behind in the last inning. Chandler was dividing her attention between the field, a girlfriend, her mom, and her grandfather, who was sitting in front of her.

She lay her head on her granddad's back and tapped his balding head.

"Does that hurt?" she asked jokingly. He squeezed her arm and she cried out in mock dismay, "Hey, I bruise easily!"

All of a sudden she turned to Tracy. "Where's Daddy?" she asked. "He said he was coming."

Tracy shrugged.

Daniel never appeared, and as I climbed into my car that night after the game, I recalled the words of one of Chandler's counselors: "This child's problems are not going to change until the family changes."

CHAPTER THREE

Am I Normal?
(Shannon's Story)

On this early September afternoon, the Kepley Middle School gym is filled with sixty girls jogging, jumping, and hitting volleyballs. They are short and tall, these Kansas girls. They are fair and dark, blond and brunette and redheaded. Some are as thin as stalks of wheat, others round like a harvest moon. All are seventh- and eighth-graders who want to play volleyball for Kepley. None will be turned away; that would be unthinkable in sports-crazed Ulysses. So Alex Tuliosega, head coach, will divide the girls into four teams grouped by ability, A,B,C, and D. He will coach A and B, the top two teams, and his assistant, Julie Mirel, will coach C and D.

Tuliosega, or "Sega" as the girls call him, scans his eyes across several players and lands on Shannon Steele. Now there's a puzzle. Tall and lanky like a wolfhound, with angular features and coarse, reddish-blond, shoulder-length hair, Shannon is one of his most serious athletes. She always does what he tells her to do and has a hound's tenacity when it comes to staying with the ball. She sets up a volleyball better than anyone. But—and in volleyball it's a big but—she has trouble with her serve. Should she play on B or C? Sega can't decide.

Out of the corner of her eye, Shannon sees Sega watching her, but she barely thinks about it. As usual, her head is in the game that she loves, the game that frees her to forget for an hour how peculiar she otherwise feels.

Her face is blotchy with pimples. She can barely get out two words when she meets people. Her parents give her grief about her grades, and her classmates sometimes look at her strangely when she pulls out a syringe in the middle of the day to treat what has become the biggest problem of her young life. But on the court she plays like most of the other kids and better than some. Within that thirty-by-sixty-foot rectangle of well-worn floorboard, she is normal.

Sega spends a few more minutes watching and then calls the girls together to divide them up. Shannon is placed with the C's. Some of the other C's look disappointed at their placement, but Shannon doesn't. That's okay, she thinks to herself. As long as I get to play.

The girls in the gymnasium that afternoon illustrated one of the fundamentals about adolescents: When it comes to how they look, think, and relate to others, there is virtually no such thing as normal development. While boys mature between the ages of twelve and eighteen, and girls between eight and eighteen, every child's biological clock is different, and maturation is a process of fits and starts. How often have you heard someone say, She's only ten but looks like she's sixteen? Or, He's twelve and acts like an eight-year-old? Both statements can be true, and both kids are, more than likely, acting normally. Within one class at any middle school or junior high, there can be as many as six to eight years of difference in physical and emotional maturity.

But try explaining this to the young teen who's upset over her big feet or her chest size or even upset over being upset. The scientist extracts "normal" characteristics from more than half of a whole population, the adolescent from her world only. It may be "normal" for a ten-year-old girl to have budding breasts, but it doesn't feel that way if no one else she knows does.

At the same time that adolescents are comparing themselves to others, they're comparing how they are to how they could be. Younger children are concrete thinkers who focus on the present. They will tell you with assurance that they are smart or dumb, kind or mean. Certain behaviors are right, others are wrong. They don't talk a lot about feelings.

Adolescents, on the other hand, are increasingly able to think in the abstract. They compare how they acted yesterday toward Mom to how they acted today with their best friend and can detect inconsistencies in their behavior. They see exceptions to rules, consider extenuating circumstances. Their ability to imagine possible lifestyles and possible values expands dramatically. As psychologist Peter Scales points out, "In one five-year period, young people can go from being sure of everything to being sure of nothing and all points in between."[1]

Different kids react differently to this confusion. Some become exhibitionists, calling attention to the new person they are becoming. Lisa, a friend of Alana's in chapter twelve, relished cruising Main Street in Ulysses in a convertible in the hopes that everyone would see her "or else, what's the point?" Others, like Shannon, want nothing more than to blend into the crowd.

What Is Normal, Anyway?

Benchmarks defining normal physical development, such as breast growth for girls or a deepening voice for boys, are relatively easy to describe. But normal behavior, shaped by history and culture, is more difficult to discern for both kids and parents.

For kids, "normal" means feeling comfortable with themselves in relationship to others. In some ways, they have an easier time of it than past generations. Living with divorced, separated, or single parents no longer makes a child an outcast. Nor does being diagnosed with a psychiatric label and taking your "meds." Girls can now excel in math and not be considered misfits; boys can decide to play the piano rather than football.

By expanding the parameters of "normal," society has encouraged young people to become more authentic and more humane. But a more open society also presents an array of lifestyle choices that can bewilder a kid who is beginning to try on adult roles. Is it normal to curse like Howard Stern? To slug an opponent like a professional hockey player? To drink like your dad, pop pills like your mom, or diet like Ally McBeal?

This is where parents and other adults need to step in. But, as Shannon's story will show, we can feel almost as confused as our kids. We're not sure what normal means anymore. From what we hear from friends or see on television, normal adolescent behavior consists of screaming matches, the silent treatment, or other, even more dangerously erratic behaviors. Why should we want our sons or daughters to feel comfortable in relation to others if the others are troubled teens? What kinds of problems in our own children should we worry about?

We can thank early twentieth-century psychiatry for some of our confusion. Psychiatrist G. Stanley Hall proposed that rebelliousness and acting out were normal for teenagers. Psychoanalysts such as Anna Freud later speculated that turmoil was not only normal but also necessary for teens to form an identity separate from their parents. These observations were flawed in that they were based on very narrow samples, primarily white boys with diagnosed psychiatric problems. But the myth of teenage Storm and Stress has persisted.

About twenty-five years ago, a scientific view began emerging that is now considered more representative and helpful. Psychiatrist Daniel Offer sampled large numbers of girls and boys, including many who were not in treatment. He reported that the vast majority of these adolescents, about four out of five, experienced some day-to-day anxiety and conflict but generally were well adjusted. They enjoyed good relationships with their families and friends and accepted most of the values of their society.[2] Other social scientists such as Betty Hamburg and David Elkind have confirmed Offer's findings.[3] The current consensus can be phrased as follows: Normal means doing what is healthy and right, which is the way most kids are inclined to behave.

This is what parents need to remember as they watch their adolescents interact with the outside world. If they take time to discover what is considered normal in their child's world they can, without being overly judgmental, help the child exercise her judgment about whether her behavior really is normal. Then they can help her see that doing what is healthy and right sometimes means going along with the crowd and sometimes means standing apart.

Of course parents may find themselves wondering—particularly with a first child, like Shannon—whether the feelings and questions that their child expresses are normal for their age. "Isn't Shannon a little *young* to be using certain words about intercourse?" her parents, Brenda and Gary, asked themselves when Shannon was in fifth grade and they found an explicit letter that another girl had passed to her. Two years later, Brenda discovered an e-mail message that Shannon had sent to a girlfriend about a nineteen-year-old boy with whom she was corresponding.

Shannon had told her friend that she wanted this young man to kiss her and rub her shoulders. Brenda asked, "Is it *normal* in seventh grade to say that you 'need your man'?"

Yes, it is normal to be curious about sex when you're ten or eleven, to feel desperate about a first love when you're twelve or thirteen, *and* to express your feelings in the vernacular you hear. Young people need to be able to identify and think of their emotions and expressions as normal, not made to feel ashamed or weird for having them. The research by Offer and others suggests, of course, that it is not normal to obsess over a guy to the exclusion of everything else; adolescents taking any behavior to an extreme may need professional help. But most adolescents simply need reassurance that their feelings are acceptable and guidance in learning appropriate ways to express them.

As I discovered with Shannon and her family, this is far easier said than done. Several factors can conspire to make a young person feel weird and make her parents worry. Some of these things, such as Shannon's timid temperament and chronic health problems, will be obvious. Factors in the child's environment may not be, however: too many rules in school, for example, or an insensitive coach. A parent's job is to stay alert to these influences and their possible effects on the child, and to know when to intervene. And when not to. For too much parental fretting, as I also saw with Shannon, can make an adolescent feel both loved and helpless.

"My Shy Child"

From the day Shannon was born, Brenda was dogged by the possibility that her daughter was not normal. Shannon took thirty-five hours to be delivered, Brenda told me. She didn't walk until she was fifteen months old. Her face broke out in third grade. She had trouble with schoolwork in elementary school. And she was tongue-tied everywhere but at home.

I first met Shannon and her family on a Sunday morning in front of the First United Methodist Church. The autumn sky was as blue as Wedgwood china, the air breezy with a slight odor of manure. From the cattle yards or hog farms? Two craggy-faced farmers, dressed in dark Sunday suits, were debating this question when the Steeles' white Tahoe pulled up. Brenda and Gary, fair-haired and both over six feet tall, unfolded their lean frames and emerged from the car, followed by two fair-haired girls. I introduced myself, and Brenda turned to the girls. "This is Andrea," she said, pointing to the shorter ten-year-old, who, I would later learn, was a top student in the fifth grade and an accomplished swimmer. "And this is Shannon, my shy, quiet child." Shannon, thirteen and in seventh grade, flashed a wide smile, looked at her toes, and said nothing.

I saw what Brenda meant after church when we gathered at Pizza Hut, the family's regular stop after worship. During our conversation, Shannon would listen to my questions and then turn to her mother to answer.

Even normally gregarious youngsters can turn timid as they enter adolescence. Newly self-conscious, moving from elementary school to a larger, more impersonal middle school or junior high, they naturally seek to avoid exposure part of the time. In one U.S. study of eleven-year-olds, almost 40 percent described themselves as shy.[4]

But Shannon's reticence preceded adolescence. When she was about to finish preschool at age four, school officials tested her and told Brenda and Gary that she would benefit from another year because of her shyness. She stayed back. After she entered elementary school, teachers told Brenda that Shannon never volunteered answers and hung out by herself on the playground. As she grew older, friends would visit her at home, but Brenda noticed that their conversations included long, awkward pauses. Brenda encouraged Shannon to do things with other kids her age, but frequently failed.

Shannon and her family visited her aunt Gerry in Topeka two months after I met her. Her mom urged her to talk to her aunt on this visit, saying things like, "Shannon, tell Aunt Gerry about your applied economics class." Shannon complied, but Gerry, dusting or washing dishes, frequently changed the subject. Adolescents can tell in a heartbeat when adults aren't paying attention to them. Such slights sting even the self-confident and can devastate the timid. "When I talk to Aunt Gerry, she already has something in mind to say next," Shannon told her mom after their visit. "She's not listening to me. Why should I try to talk to her?"

Brenda saw Shannon's point. But still she worried, particularly after Gerry said to her, "I don't think she's going to be able to handle the real world."

It is easy for parents to obsess over their children's temperamental quirks, particularly when other adults call attention to them. But we must remember that a child's temperament is not set in stone. Personality is partly a result of genes *and* partly a result of how a child is treated. Shy adolescents, for example, are not shy all the time or with everyone. They may never become ebullient extroverts, though some in fact can turn out to be quite social. But with the proper encouragement most lead normal social lives.[5]

Such encouragement means normalizing the child's experience of shyness, not making too much of it ("my shy, quiet child"). It means pointing the child confidently in the direction you want her to go, saying things such as "You may feel timid now, but you'll get over it. I did. Let's practice."

It also means tuning in to how much the particular trait bothers her. Shannon's shyness didn't seem to disturb her; when I asked her about it on several occasions, she shrugged, grinned, and said, "That's me." Her classmates also seemed to accept it. If a child is comfortable with her quirkiness, a parent doesn't need to fret quite as much.

Worried About Sex

It's hard not to worry, though, because as parents we can see long-term implications of personality traits that our children cannot yet see. When Shannon once told Brenda that she was thinking about becoming a lawyer, Brenda replied, "Well, you might need to learn to talk." More immediately, she and Gary wondered whether Shannon would be able to stand up to the influences of coercive friends.

They were particularly concerned that boys would try to take advantage of her sexually and that she might be inclined to let them. Their fears were not unfounded. The average age at which young people begin to experiment with different forms of sexual behavior has declined significantly over the last two decades. It is not unusual for sixth- and seventh-graders to know kids their age who are engaging in oral sex and by eighth grade to be at least acquainted with those who have "gone all the way." This is true for kids in the cities, suburbs, and country alike. A majority of Grant County high-school students, surveyed the year I was there, said they didn't believe that having sex in their teens violated their personal values, an astonishing statement given the pervasive influence of more than two dozen churches in town, most of them conservative in theology.[6]

The possibility of sexual experimentation is one of the first things parents start to worry about when their children enter puberty. Embarrassed to discuss sex with their kids, many parents make the mistake of leaving such talk to the schools. Gary and Brenda did not.

They warned Shannon about sexually transmitted diseases. They told her that kissing and hugging were appropriate before marriage but that petting should be left until after the wedding. "I've told Shannon that sex is beautiful if it's between a man and woman who are married," Brenda said.

Shannon rarely responded during these conversations except for an occasional nod. The long pauses that are often part of any conversation with an adolescent can seem like hours when talking about sex. But Brenda persisted, to her credit. Regular conversations about sexuality, no matter how one-sided and uncomfortable, promote complex thinking patterns, build a young person's confidence, and help her assess the differences between healthy and unhealthy risks. If the parent clearly states her views about certain risky behaviors, the child is more likely to postpone those activities than if the parent equivocates or says nothing.[7]

As potentially helpful as Brenda's guidance was, it was only half the job. Shannon was hearing from her parents that sex was normal *after* marriage. But what about before marriage? If she went to college and landed a good job, as her parents hoped she would, she might not marry for ten years or more. The odds were slim that she would remain chaste that long; most young women don't.

More significant to her at the moment was the question of what to do with her impulses now. If instruction in abstinence is to succeed with young adolescents—and it can—it needs to be explained in a way that normalizes their curiosity and impulses and gives them some room for exploration.

Almost all kids learn in school the mechanics of sexual intercourse, the dangers of promiscuity, and the precautions they should take if they are going to engage in sexual activities. What they do not get—and need parents or other close adults to provide—is help in becoming comfortable with their sexuality without actually exercising their full biological capabilities. In the age of AIDS, scared parents often forget this.

This means helping them figure out what is normal and what isn't. Falling in love at this age, for example, is normal; it's a way of learning about themselves by observing how others see them. Erotic thoughts are normal and can be discussed with friends or adults they feel comfortable with (frequently not parents). Anticipating certain sexual situations is normal, and talking through how they would act is to be encouraged. Showing affection to someone they love without "doing the deed" is normal, and a parent can encourage a young person to think of pleasurable yet age-appropriate ways to do that (even if the parent has to hear "Oh, Mom [or Dad]. Puleeze"). Parents need not fear that talking about sex will encourage their kids to go farther than they normally would; studies have shown that this simply isn't true.

Parents and other adults must also convey the truth that all sexual behaviors, no matter how small, have the power to cause people pain as well as pleasure. The lusty, destructive relationships kids see on TV and in the movies aren't normal, and they need to be reminded of that. Carrying a condom around in your wallet when you're in the seventh grade (as one girl I interviewed did) isn't normal, and if a young person is encouraged to think about *all* the kids she knows, she will realize that. Engaging in oral sex, anal sex, or sexual intercourse at their age isn't normal. (Although the number of kids doing these things is increasing, most kids still don't.)

Brenda never knew how much of her talk about sexuality was getting through to her daughter. But she took heart from small clues such as one Shannon dropped on the way to school one morning: "Did you hear that Annie Potter got pregnant? Why did she go and do that?"

Gaining Confidence

Kids who hang back, like Shannon, need to find some activity that will force them out of their shell and help them feel accepted in their community. An activity that demands time and energy can also keep them away from risky behavior—sexual and other kinds.

Athletics was an obvious choice for any child growing up in Ulysses. In 1920, the last cattle drive passed through town, and the high school played its first football game. Old-timers spoke about these two events as if they were related, which in a way they were, for the town's attention gradually turned from tractors and cattle prices to balls and scoreboards. Ulysses boasts ten ball fields, a golf course, tennis courts, a state-of-the-art rubberized outdoor track, an indoor/outdoor swimming pool complex, and 227 acres of parkland. More than two-thirds of the kids in middle school and high school played or helped with a sports team the year I was there. Hoping that sports would give Shannon a group identity, and perhaps a personal one, Brenda and Gary enrolled her in T-ball at age five.

As she moved through the grades, Shannon continued with softball and took up volleyball, basketball, and track. She didn't excel in sports like her younger sister, Andrea. But she felt good when she did even reasonably well in something appreciated by everyone she knew.

When Sega placed her on volleyball's C team in the fall of seventh grade, she initially accepted the decision with aplomb. But one afternoon she overheard some girls criticizing her playing and she came home in tears. When she told her mom, Brenda hit the roof. A former volleyball coach, Brenda believed that Shannon possessed as much skill as several players on the A and B teams.

That weekend Brenda encountered Coach Sega at a local restaurant—one benefit of a small town—and mentioned how hard Shannon was practicing. Sega offered to open the gym on weekends and help Shannon improve her skills. "We need team players like Shannon," he said.

That was all that was needed to boost Shannon's spirit. She asked Sega if he would let her practice with the A and B teams in the mornings as well as with the C team in the afternoons. He said yes.

Doubling up carried a high price: Shannon had to rise at 5 A.M. on school days, an hour earlier than usual. She practiced from 6 A.M. to 7:30 A.M. and again from 4 P.M. to 6 P.M. On game days she would arrive home at eight or nine. The schedule forced her to do her homework, often a couple of hours' worth, late at night. She felt tired a lot of the time but was determined to make the B team before the season ended in late November. And she did, demonstrating how with only a modicum of outside assistance some adolescents move toward accomplishment.

Athletics, Carefully Considered

Athletics can empower an adolescent of any temperament. Regular, vigorous exercise builds strength in the arms, legs, and heart and steps up the brain's production of the chemical serotonin, which elevates mood. Sports can teach a child that, although she won't win all the time, she can increase her chances by practicing. A survey of Fortune 500 executives showed that most of them played high-school sports, and recent studies have demonstrated that girls who stay involved in athletics through middle and high school earn higher grades and go to college more frequently than girls who don't.[8]

But there are drawbacks, particularly in competitive sports, that kids and parents must consider. In a "win at all costs" atmosphere, the less skilled athlete may feel put down and not get enough playing time to improve. Shannon managed to avoid these pitfalls most of the time, largely because of her mother's vigilance, but not all youngsters are so fortunate.

Competitive athletics can also demand too much time, and if an athlete attaches too much significance to sports, she passes up other avenues toward building a strong identity. Shannon, for example, resisted her parents' suggestions to join her church's youth program, clubs at school, or community service projects.

When I asked her why sports were so important, she answered, "Because there's nothing else I'm good at." That was not exactly true at the time of our conversation; she was aceing English, general math, and business. But the fact that she *believed* it to be true was significant. Just as a deep bench is better than a few ballplayers, self-esteem is more solid if it encompasses several areas of development.

There was another downside to sports that Shannon, like many female athletes, experienced. Although the Ulysses community valued girls' sports, they valued boys' sports more. When basketball season began in early winter, Shannon and her teammates were given used jerseys while the boys donned new ones. They had to play most of their games in the afternoons because the boys played at night. This meant that many of the girls' parents couldn't make the games.

Parents also complained that the referees for the girls' games did not officiate as carefully as boys' refs. Brenda observed, "They never call

fouls on the girls' teams. It's like they just want to get the game over."
Jesse Archuleta, who was coaching the Ulysses girls, later agreed. "They
don't really care about girls' basketball," he said.

Shannon and some of her teammates wondered about Archuleta's
commitment. Prior to a game in nearby Liberal, for example, they put
on their uniforms as soon as they arrived, but then had to sit on the
bleachers for a half hour while waiting for his instructions. "He should
have us running around the gym right now, doing more drills," one girl
complained. Finally one girl mustered up the nerve to ask him what she
could do to prepare. "Just stand there and look pretty," he said, patting
her shoulder.

The saving grace for Shannon during basketball season was Archuleta's assistant, a young woman named Shan Britton. Shan would run
alongside her players as they practiced and, unlike Archuleta, would
move the girls in and out so all of them could play. She encouraged
them to play confidently, yelling, "Take that shot!" when they hung
back. Companionship and challenge, not condescension and coddling,
teach young adolescents to feel comfortable with themselves.

Shannon slouches in her chair in the back of science class, listening to
afternoon announcements over the intercom.

"Pssss! Hey, Shannon!" It's her talkative friend Tammy, whispering
something Shannon can't understand. Shannon glances over with a questioning look.

"Tammy? Shannon? Do you have something you want to share with the
rest of the class?" Gina Lyon's voice is easily heard over the announcements.
The girls shake their heads. Uh-oh, Shannon thinks. I'm in trouble again.
Some teachers spend all of their time figuring out how they can punish us.

When Shannon started sixth grade at Kepley she was shocked at the
number of things she was no longer supposed to do. She was slapped with
one detention for writing an assignment in pencil rather than pen, another
for leaving class without permission to go to the bathroom. (Going to the
bathroom during class time was an automatic detention for all but
straight-A students.) Shannon could understand enforcing prohibitions
against fighting, weapons, and smoking. But not going to the bathroom
when you really needed to? That was just stupid.

A couple of months earlier, in this same class, Tammy had tried to ask

Shannon something about volleyball and Lyon had given both girls after-school detention. Shannon had almost missed volleyball practice.

It had been a close call that Shannon didn't want to repeat this afternoon. She shakes her head no to Lyon's question and turns her attention to the science book in front of her. This time Lyon lets the disruption slide, and Shannon ignores Tammy for the rest of the period.

A generation ago, students new to junior high school encountered lots of new rules—more rules, in fact, than they had had in elementary school. Principals said this was because young adolescents were time bombs whose hormones could explode at any minute. The job of junior-high personnel was to keep the lid on.

What administrators didn't know then, but science knows now, is that the cognitive parts of teenagers' brains are as active as the emotions and exert a moderating influence. Young adolescents are more responsible than they were in elementary school and more capable of defining and enforcing their own rules in areas such as seating arrangement and classroom behavior.

Some schools in this country have reorganized their programs to give young teenage students a voice in setting norms for behavior and the consequences for breaking them. The authorities don't hesitate to enforce rules, but they tolerate a certain amount of messiness and loudness because they know that kids need to experiment in their search for normal behavior.

Most of the schools I visited, however, were still being run according to the time-bomb theory, still telling students to act like young adults while treating them like young children. Several, including Kepley, enforced more rules than even I remember in my junior high in the early 1960s. Many kids shrugged off the rules, but the more cautious, like Shannon, withdrew into their shells. The rules at Kepley didn't make her feel safer, she told me; she felt threatened by "nearly everybody."

Keeping Things Safe

On the first day I visited Kepley, a single-story beige brick building that used to be the high school, I was struck by the prohibitions posted every-where: in classrooms and hallways, on either side of the American flag in the gym. Some were age-old, such as "No chewing gum or candy." Others, however, were new, designed to discourage gangster wannabes. Boys and girls were not allowed to wear pants that "bagged or sagged," meaning that if trousers hit the floor they had to be hitched up and secured with a belt. Outfits in blue, red, black, or beige — supposed gang colors — were frowned upon, as were clothes carrying designers' initials. Overalls with big pockets were forbidden; so were hooded jackets, for, as Shannon said with a hint of sarcasm, "You could stash a gun in the hood." Students were not allowed to cluster, and if they got too noisy during lunch they were separated by class. If that didn't calm them down, they weren't allowed to talk at all, on penalty of spending four weeks in in-school suspension.

The main reason for the rules in Ulysses, as in the other communities I visited, seemed to be fear of two things: violence and change. "A lot of things kids do today are normal behaviors," Kepley's principal, Juan Perez, told me one day. "But these are not normal times."

Media coverage of homicides, kidnappings, and other gruesome acts blankets even the smallest towns these days, spreading a fear among adults that is taking its toll on children. Ulysses had never witnessed a drive-by shooting. Murders were unheard of. But residents and school-board members watched shootings in nearby Garden City on the local six o'clock news, gang wars in Los Angeles at 6:30, and worried that such outbursts could happen on their streets. Three hundred citizens crowded into the Kepley auditorium one night to hear a police officer from Colorado talk about gangs.

Not all teachers considered Kepley's environment a good thing. "There's no leeway given. It's, 'We're the adults and we know what's best for you,'" one longtime aide in the school said. "The kids take that as saying, 'We don't like you.'" But more seemed inclined to agree with Tim Hodges, a math teacher in his early thirties: "I'm not opposed to stepping on personal liberties to keep things safe for kids." He paused, adding, "I can't believe I'm saying that."

Longing for the Good Ol' Days

Residents also appeared unsettled by the pace of social and economic change in their previously stable community. Only twenty blocks square,

the town lived with one foot pointed in the direction of the next millen-
nium and the other clearly stuck in the 1950s.

This contrast occurred to me as I waited in Kepley's front office that
first morning. On my left hung a Norman Rockwell print of a proper-
looking schoolmarm in front of her class, a coat draped over her arm.
The children in the picture, all white, were sitting in straight rows, hands
folded on their laps. On the blackboard behind the teacher, they had
scrawled "Happy Birthday" and "Surprise!" dozens of times. Teacher,
who obviously had just arrived, looked pleased.

A few feet to my right, a Mexican-American boy was talking into the
office phone, obviously upset. "You have got to come get me now," he
said. "I got in a fight because they were throwing gang signals at me . . .
The cops are on their way."

Tucked into the southwest corner of Kansas four hours west of
Wichita, Ulysses was once a prosperous prairie community of white
settlers—mostly wheat farmers, cattlemen, and grain elevator operators.
Beginning in the 1920s, gas and oil companies moved in, bringing families with them and providing revenue that helped finance new schools,
parks, and recreational facilities.

In the early 1990s, reports surfaced that the gas fields were running
low and might be out of operation within ten years. Large commercial
hog operators, owned by out-of-state companies, moved into the area.
Residents watched in dismay as retired yellow school buses hauled hundreds of pigs away to Texas for slaughter and returned with hundreds of
unskilled laborers from some of the poorest regions of Mexico.

Ulysses natives like to think of themselves as friendly and helpful, but
the rapid influx of poor newcomers challenged that image. Teachers and
parents complained about rudeness and fights in school, particularly
among the young Hispanics at Kepley. Families bought police scanners
and phoned principal Perez, an American of Mexican descent, if they
detected the slightest rumble.

The school's rules were a response to community sentiment, Perez
said one afternoon in his small, square office. Residents believed that
their long-held standards of behavior, a consensus that strengthened and
protected their kids, were under assault, and they were fighting back as
vigorously as their pioneer ancestors had resisted the Pawnee Indians.

Perez achieved at least one thing with his discipline: The kids knew what was expected of them. Two-thirds surveyed in the spring said the school's regulations were clear. But if the goal was to encourage kids to think before they acted and to reduce the number who got in trouble, it wasn't working. Detentions and suspensions crept upward all year, and in the spring survey, Kepley students rated themselves less adept at decision making and more impulsive than they had two years earlier on a similar questionnaire.

Not all teachers at Kepley enforced the rules strictly, but Shannon's science teacher, Gina Lyon, did. Shannon was afraid to speak up in class when she didn't understand a particular concept, and by late January, she was flunking all her science tests.

Controlled at Home as Well

Shannon lived with lots of rules at home as well. Though her dad and mom agreed on most of them (a significant difference from Chandler's parents), Brenda was the enforcer. Gary was rarely home, and when he was there, he was easily frustrated by Shannon because he didn't understand her.

Gary was a joiner, Shannon's temperamental opposite. He was owner of Grant County Farm Implement, Inc., the town's John Deere franchise, as well as former president of the Chamber of Commerce, former director of the Emergency Medical Services team, board member of the recreation association, the United Methodist Church, and the swim team organization. He spent his days at the store and most nights in meetings.

Sensitive to his absence, Brenda doubled her efforts to be attentive. She wasn't confident that Shannon could manage without her, and in the first part of the year she didn't impart confidence to Shannon. She checked Shannon's homework every night. She went over every test, read virtually every essay.

When they were out in public and Shannon wouldn't answer someone's question, Brenda would answer. When Shannon left her snack at home, Brenda would take it to her at school. She would pick Shannon up for lunch and, later, transport her to sports practice four blocks away.

Shannon told me that she wished her mother wouldn't smother her with attention, and she was right. Secure attachments to parents or other caregivers are vital in early childhood, but so is the encouragement later to detach gradually, always with the assurance that the child can return to home base. Outgoing adolescents often demand responsibility earlier than we're ready to delegate it, but introverts like Shannon need to be persuaded, occasionally even forced, to accept it. The more choices that are made for adolescents, for girls particularly, the more likely they are in the future to allow others to make choices for them.

Shannon told me privately that she feared that as a B/C student, she could never do anything right, that her parents "expect me to be someone I'm not." When her sister, Andrea, brought home all A's on her report card, as she sometimes did, Shannon got a sick feeling in her stomach. She took pride in her sister's accomplishments but at the same time felt incredibly jealous. She would glare at Andrea or, when her parents weren't around, call Andrea names.

Her mom, an all-A student in high school and college, admitted that she had difficulty accepting anything less from Shannon. And she was bothered by the fact that she could no longer control Shannon's performance. "When I was in school, C's were F's to me," Brenda explained. "I now have to look and say C's are average, not low. It's hard to do that and not see it as a reflection on me."

Brenda's was a common feeling among parents of adolescents. She was beginning to discern what kind of a person Shannon was becoming. Some traits and skills pleased her. Others didn't. Was it time for her to start accepting her daughter's sum total and stop trying to change her? Or should she continue to push the parts she felt needed improvement?

Encourage but don't push, Shannon and other youths in my study would say to parents with such concerns. Challenge us to do better but loosen the ties. Let us start making some mistakes. Praise us when we exceed expectations; don't make us feel there is something seriously wrong with our half-finished form.

Too much parental intervention, like too many rules at school, can result in what psychologists call "learned helplessness," a belief that what one does or achieves is beyond one's control. This feeling can result in depression, lack of motivation, or hostility—and young adolescents are more susceptible to it than younger kids, according to a study by psychologists at Texas A&M University.[9] As parents we must, as an anonymous writer once wrote, learn the difference between holding a hand and chaining a soul.

One Intervention That Worked

When Shannon's performance in Lyon's class started to spiral downward, Brenda suggested to Shannon that she ask to transfer to another science instructor, Vana Campbell. Shannon asked, and the principal approved a transfer.

In her new teacher, Shannon found someone who understood adolescents, even shy ones. Rather than call on Shannon in class, or make her do work on the blackboard, Campbell passed by Shannon's desk several times each class period and checked quietly to make sure Shannon was following along. Shannon sought out Campbell after class and found her easy to talk to. Campbell was rarely sarcastic or cutting to students even when they acted up; to those kids she would say, "I am embarrassed by your behavior" rather than the more personal, "You are really getting on my nerves." Students who needed to go to the bathroom could do so, if they told her it was an emergency.

She posted a few rules in her classroom but they were short and funny, playing to adolescent humor:

"Say polite stuff, think positive stuff, respect other people and their stuff, have all your stuff ready in class on time, don't throw stuff, keep stuff out of your mouth."

In her firm and affirming classroom, a shy child like Shannon could do well. She began making C's instead of F's on her tests and breathed easier. After all, C was average. Normal.

It is after midnight in February, and Shannon has curled her five-foot six-inch frame into the fetal position on her bed, her head resting at the foot. She feels cold and incredibly weak, and although she grasps at the bedclothes, they keep slipping off. When Brenda comes in to check on her before going to bed herself, Shannon has trouble focusing on her mother's face. "Mom, I can't see," she whispers.

Brenda recognizes the symptoms of hypoglycemia, or low blood sugar, right away. "What's your sugar?" she asks in the shorthand that mother and daughter have learned since Shannon was diagnosed with diabetes ten months earlier. "Twenty-eight," Shannon replies. "I'll bring some crackers and 7Up right down," Brenda says.

Shannon is sliding into a coma. Normally people have 60 to 120 milligrams of glucose per deciliter of blood (slightly less than one-half cup). Twenty-eight milligrams means Shannon's body is producing too much insulin and digesting sugar and other carbohydrates too fast. If the symptoms go untreated, her brain could swell, seizures or paralysis could follow, and she could die within hours.

On her way to the kitchen, Brenda makes a stop in the bedroom and shakes Gary, who is asleep. "Shannon is really low," she says. He turns away and goes back to sleep. After Shannon has eaten her snack, she asks her mother to hold her. Brenda lies down with her, and Shannon wraps her long body around her mom. Brenda prays silently, "Dear God, don't let me lose this kid." Mother and daughter wait together without talking, wrapped in an old blanket, then measure Shannon's sugar level again. It has climbed to 95.

Before she falls asleep, Shannon offers up her own prayer. She doesn't expect God to take away her diabetes, but she wishes she would feel better. "Please, God, make me where I don't get low and shaky," she prays.

Right before dinner one night at the end of Shannon's sixth-grade year, Grandma Ruby, Gary's mother, noticed her granddaughter drinking glass after glass of water. Because of a family history of diabetes, she mentioned this to Brenda.

Brenda had Shannon tested, and the hospital in Ulysses confirmed Ruby's suspicions: Shannon suffered from Type I diabetes, also called insulin-dependent diabetes, meaning that her pancreas wasn't producing enough insulin to allow her to metabolize food. She was slowly starving to death.

The local physician admitted her for observation the night of the diagnosis. Shannon cried as she was hooked up to an intravenous pole and while Brenda tried to settle her down in bed. She had just heard that her life was going to have to change drastically but that if she took care of herself she could expect to live a fairly normal life.

What about Aunt Kate? she wanted to scream. Aunt Kate didn't lead a normal life!

Kate, her father's thirty-nine-year-old sister, had been diagnosed with diabetes at age eight. She had had three kidney transplants and most of her joints replaced. The previous winter, she had been hospitalized with an infection that her body, its immune system depleted, ultimately couldn't fight. On Valentine's Day, four months before Shannon was diagnosed with diabetes, Shannon and her family had visited Kate in the hospital.

"She died after we left," Shannon would tell me months later. "No one was with her." As she lay in the Ulysses hospital that night, Shannon couldn't shake the image of Aunt Kate, her face puffy, her arms and legs scarred from numerous surgeries and needles, passing away. Alone.

Shannon didn't know any kids who had diabetes. (There were only two in town, she would learn later, one in elementary school, one in high school.) If shyness sometimes pushed Shannon to the periphery of her crowd, diabetes threatened to place her in an entirely separate room.

Chronic Disease in Adolescents

Certain events can explode a child's sense of normalcy: the death of a parent, for example, a divorce, or the diagnosis of a serious medical condition.

Researchers estimate that at least one-fourth of all U.S. adolescents now live with long-term medical conditions such as asthma, cystic fibrosis, leukemia, spina bifida, and diabetes.[10] Some of these conditions, such as asthma, diabetes, and mental illnesses, including manic depression, are claiming an increasing number of young people. Scientists suggest various reasons: modern stress, environmental pollutants, medical technology that keeps more children alive who otherwise would die, improved diagnostic procedures.

Children born with disease know no other way of living, but children diagnosed in adolescence do. They may have a particularly hard time accepting their condition and the requirements for taking care of themselves. If their illness requires frequent hospitalization or doctors' visits, as Shannon's did, their friends may withdraw, making them feel more sensitive, isolated, and lonely.[11]

Chronic illness can bring families closer together. But it also inevitably tilts even the most loving of homes at such an angle that family members must constantly scramble to maintain equilibrium. The stress can be particularly acute on an adolescent because parents have to begin monitoring her habits just when she wants no part of parental scrutiny. As a friend of Brenda's, whose daughter also has diabetes, wrote to Brenda: "We walk an incredibly fine line between acting as if our kids are no different than any other kids, while knowing the potential dire consequences of allowing them to behave that way. Where does one negotiate and where must you be unflinching?"

So complicated are the dynamics in families with a newly diagnosed teenager that most physicians recommend family counseling during the first few months. The Steeles did not seek such assistance, although later Brenda wished that they had.

A Tall Order for Teens

After one night at the Ulysses hospital, the Steeles moved Shannon to St. Joseph's Hospital, a Wichita institution specializing in diabetes. They spent a week there learning about the disease.

Brenda and Gary heard that week that the outlook for Shannon's life was far from normal. Diabetics are more likely than most people to have heart attacks, go blind, lose limbs, or suffer from psychiatric problems. They generally live ten to twenty fewer years than non-diabetics.

Shannon was not told these things then. What she and her parents were told was that she would have to eat three balanced meals daily, counting how many grams of sugar, protein, and carbohydrates she consumed, and limiting herself to 2,100 calories a day. Sweets were forbidden except when her sugar level dipped low. So were potato chips. Snacking was encouraged but only on healthy foods such as apple slices. She had to prick her finger several times a day to test her blood sugar, and insert a three-inch needle into her upper thigh once a day to inject insulin. Exercising at least a half hour every day and sleeping ten hours each night were essential. Except for the exercise, which she did as a matter of course, it was a tall order that demanded that she show more self-control than most kids her age are capable of.

Like adults, many kids figure they will worry about long-term health later. Teens with chronic diseases don't have that luxury. Shannon discovered this over the Thanksgiving weekend after her diagnosis. Her blood sugar level started rising on Thursday night and by Saturday had hit 307 milligrams, more than 120 milligrams over normal. Brenda increased Shannon's insulin.

After her sugar level declined two days later, Shannon admitted that she had cheated on her diet by eating some high-calorie snack crackers. It wasn't the first time she had ignored orders—earlier in the month she had lied about measuring her sugar levels—but it had had the most serious consequences.

Blaming the Child First

Over time the fluctuations in Shannon's blood sugar levels could permanently damage her organs. Doctors at St. Joseph's had told Brenda that swings were not uncommon for teenagers because physiology and metabolism were always in flux. But Brenda's tendency, as Shannon's levels continued to fluctuate, was to blame Shannon. "Your first reaction with a teenager is: 'What did you do wrong? What did you eat?' " she admitted one day. Such words stung Shannon every time. Although she sometimes downplayed the severity of her condition (typical behavior for a chronically ill adolescent), more often than not she took it seriously. The fluctuations, she insisted to her parents, had nothing to do with her habits.

It occurred to Brenda that stress might be propelling Shannon's blood-sugar roller coaster. Stress affects hormonal secretions in all adolescents, and such secretions can upset the body's glucose. Like other young teenagers I interviewed, Shannon didn't appear intense on the outside, but privately she confessed to worrying. Her greatest concern, she said, was "that I will get to college and there will be no cure for diabetes and no Mom." Brenda suffered from allergies, headaches, cervical disc strain, and bouts of flu, all of which intensified after Shannon's diagnosis and worried Shannon.

Yearning for a Normal Family Life

Young people wonder not only whether they are normal but whether their families are. Mom may sing off-key or, worse, have a drinking problem. Dad may laugh too loud or, worse, turn abusive when he's angry.

The adolescent is not only embarrassed by such behavior, she is worried by it. She has no way of knowing how to distinguish between the serious and not-so-serious problems, and as she watches her parents she wonders, Is that what I will become?

Shannon's concerns revolved around her family's hectic schedule. Her parents worked long hours to provide all the outward signs of a comfortable life: a five-bedroom house, two computers, two sport utility wagons, satellite TV. I got a hint that their lifestyle came at a cost, however, when I arranged my first interview and Brenda suggested 10:30 P.M., the earliest time when they would all be home.

Gary was out of the house most often. His projects seemed to increase after Shannon's diagnosis—a not uncommon response to problems at home—but his work habits had been in place from a young age. As a sophomore in high school, he had stocked the shelves of his dad's John Deere business every day after school. After attending Fort Hays State University, he returned to Ulysses and he and his dad expanded the business into the nearby town of Hugeton and later into Wichita. He added recreational vehicles and prefabricated roof panels to his Ulysses inventory of tractors and combines, more than doubling the size of the store.

Like many modern dads, Gary compared his fathering role to his own dad's and believed he came out favorably. The family took a couple of trips out of town each year to places like Disney World and Six Flags Over Texas, he said one spring morning in his kitchen. Also, he went on, "I take off for lunch with them or to go to their ball games in the middle of the day. And a lot of the community projects I'm involved in, the kids will benefit from."

Gary spent a fair amount of time with Shannon's younger sister, Andrea, partly because Andrea liked to work with her hands, as he did, on renovation projects. Also, once Shannon reached adolescence, he found Andrea easier to get along with. "Shannon tunes me out," he said, echoing almost verbatim Daniel Brennan's rationale for turning his attention away from his oldest daughter, Chandler, to his youngest.

Brenda had fought privately with Gary about his workaholic habits for several years, saying he wasn't doing enough at home, and Shannon's diabetes intensified their arguments. Chronic disease can act like a telescope, putting sharply into focus once-blurry accusations and dodges.

Brenda felt she needed more help from Gary because she was on the

run all the time. She was the company's financial manager, often working the ledgers for more than five hundred accounts at night after the
girls had gone to bed. She was also the family's chief operating officer,
cleaning the house, doing the laundry, and cooking the meals. She shut-
tled Shannon to her games and Andrea to her swim meets, making trips
of four to eight hours. She sang with and composed music for a Christian
music group and attended swimming board meetings. And this was all
before the diagnosis of Shannon's round-the-clock disease.

When dads underfunction in a family, moms frequently go into over-
drive, particularly if there is reason for perpetual oversight. "I'm sure
Gary feels like we share Shannon's care equally," she wrote to me in
early December, "but in reality I have the majority of it. . . . If I'm gone
for some reason, I usually have to call back to make sure shots are taken
on time and meals gotten ready because he doesn't watch the clock or
the kids."

In the months following Shannon's diagnosis, Gary promised he
would contribute more to the family, but little changed. Brenda found
herself resenting Gary's church work in particular and even resenting
her kids. One night after a game that Gary had been too busy to attend,
Shannon asked Brenda whether she could go shopping for clothes the
following weekend.

"I just bought you clothes a couple of weeks ago," Brenda said, a note
of exasperation in her voice. "Sometimes," she said, addressing me, "I
think I should never have had children."

Shannon's brown eyes widened. "You mean because I asked you for
new clothes?"

Shannon and her friends commiserated with each other about their
parents' stressed-out working lives. Such conversations made me realize
that no matter what their own families look like, many kids still carry
around mental pictures of "normal" families that resemble Ozzie and
Harriet.

"Dad spends way too much time working at the church," Shannon
said one afternoon while eating a hamburger pizza with her friend
Melanie.

"Yeah," Melanie agreed. "He's never home. He's always helping other
people."

Melanie empathized: "My dad hasn't been home for a full week in three months. He's a manager of a gas company and right now they're laying off people. He's afraid he might get laid off, so he has to work a lot."

Shannon sighed. "In a normal home, you would have time for family."

Sympathetic Ears

At an early age, Shannon learned to seek out the company of a family next door that seemed to her to keep a normal schedule. In the late afternoon, tired of being home alone or with her sister, she'd walk next door to visit Maxie and Richard Coffey. The Coffeys got home from work about 5 P.M. With their children grown and gone, they welcomed the diversion.

"I'd be doin' something and look up and there would be Shannon, usually with her little dog right beside her," recalled Maxie, a petite older woman with friendly blue eyes. "I'd have to ask the questions, of course, but I'd get her talking." Coffey would nod sympathetically as Shannon talked, and she didn't tiptoe around important issues. Shannon, like most adolescents, took forthrightness as a sign of interest and opened up to her neighbor more than she did to most people—discussing her acne treatment, for example, or a party to which she hadn't been invited.

Shannon also found sympathy over the Internet. Brenda and Gary had purchased computers for their daughters' schoolwork, but Shannon quickly discovered a community of diabetic friends on line. With Brenda periodically monitoring her e-mails, Shannon talked with Jeannie, a diabetic in Virginia, about their disease, guys, and parents who bug you. With Jeremy, a Montana diabetic, she discussed music.

The Internet supported Brenda as well. Late at night, when everyone else was in bed, she would sit at her Gateway 2000 and research the latest findings about diabetes or discuss with her on-line friends her frustration with her husband and her children. To friends in Ulysses, she couldn't disclose her most intimate problems and feelings for fear that rumors would fly. On the Internet, she felt safe. Her on-line friends became increasingly significant over the year, reassuring her and encouraging her to relax and allow Shannon to plot more of her own course.

. . .

On a warm *May afternoon at school, Shannon yawns and wonders how long the awards assembly will last. Hopefully until the last bell rings; she doesn't feel like doing any more schoolwork today.*

She is preparing herself mentally for watching her friends file up on stage, one by one, to receive their orange and black letters signifying extraordinary achievement in sports. She'll have to content herself with a certificate for participation, just like last year, and that's okay. She just hopes her mom and dad, sitting in the back of the room, are satisfied with that.

Coach Sega has walked to the front of the stage carrying the letters for girls' volleyball. He reads the names out slowly so that each star has time to leave her seat and walk up to the stage.

"Melanie Patterson . . . Lydia Rehm . . . Shannon Steele."

Shannon sits up with a jolt. Slowly she rises from her seat and squeezes past her classmates, a goofy smile on her face. As she makes her way forward, Brenda and Gary look at each other, then applaud loudly. They do that again a few minutes later when Shannon is handed a letter for track. After the assembly, Shannon and her family fairly float home. The school year is finishing well. Shannon has brought up all her grades, including science. She has been elected treasurer of the student council for next year, after giving a speech that was videotaped and shown to sixth- and seventh-graders. In that speech she described running The Cub Stop, an in-school store whose profits go to community charities. Brenda and Gary have agreed to let Shannon go away to overnight camp this summer—a big step given the precariousness of her health. Shannon is proud of the responsibility they are beginning to place on her.

The day after the sports awards, her friend Melanie sniffs, "I don't see why they gave you a letter in volleyball. You didn't play that much on the B team and you never played for A."

"But I came to practice early in the morning and after school, too," Shannon protests.

"That shouldn't matter," Melanie says. Shannon walks away mad.

I deserved that letter, she thinks to herself. I worked hard for it. I've always had to work harder for everything.

If contradictions in personality and behavior are to be expected at this age—and experts say they are—Shannon was the perfect representative.

She lacked conversational skills, harbored resentment toward her sister and her parents, struggled to find meaning in school, and sometimes disregarded her medical treatment plan, knowing how risky it was to do so. However, by the end of the year she also showed competence in sports and several courses, had assumed a leadership role in school activities (of her choosing, not her mother's), and continued to display a deep affection for her parents.

Sheer maturation had something to do with her progress and so did the relentless attention of her mother. For as overbearing as she sometimes was, Brenda never let Shannon forget how much she was loved, both by her family and by the God in which their family believed.

Just as She Was

From the time Shannon was very young, she and her mother had said bedtime prayers together. Even when her mother wasn't there, Shannon said she prayed. Questions about her faith occasionally crossed her mind—why God allowed her to suffer from diabetes was a big one—but she didn't spend a lot of time thinking about them. More significant for her was the idea of a superior being who loved her just as she was, faults and all, who would take care of her no matter what.

Brenda also began to find solace in her faith in early spring after much soul-searching and praying over her relationships to her daughter and husband. "I've done everything I can do," she wrote about both Shannon and Gary. "I'll just have to turn the rest over to God." This faith bestowed an occasional peace of mind, which in turn allowed her to give Shannon more responsibility for her own care.

In March, she started making Shannon take her own lunch and snacks to school. "If she forgets and faints from not eating, then she'll have to suffer those consequences," Brenda wrote to me. "Of course, you'll have to chain me to the chair if that happens!"

Faith did not eliminate all her anxieties but allowed her to ask the right questions. "Shannon depends on me way too much and yet at the same time is testing her wings," she said. "I want my kids to be independent but raised with the values and sense of responsibility that will carry them through the hard times. . . . How can I let Shannon know how very much I love her and yet step back further than she's ever let me before and let her take more charge of her own life?"

Knowing when to intervene and when not to is one of the toughest assignments we parents have. How well we do it goes back, in large part, to our assumptions about adolescence. If we believe the teen years to be a stormy and risky time, and if our child shows even a hint of being different from other children, we may hover too much and criticize too frequently. Our child may feel loved but not accepted, and we may end up seeding the storms we fear.

If, on the other hand, we understand that there's a wide range of normal behaviors during this period, we can relax while remaining vigilant. We will more easily see the positive traits we want to promote and want others to encourage as well. And we will learn to provide assistance based on the clues our kid herself gives, not on some false stereotype.

Becoming Comfortable with Herself

We need to watch and listen for those clues, for our assumptions can be way off-base. I learned this from Shannon near the end of the year I observed her.

One afternoon as Shannon's basketball team prepared for an away game, she had a choice of riding to the game with her mother or on a rickety yellow school bus with the team. She chose the bus. But after taking a seat on the right side next to a window, she laid her long, left leg across the seat so no one would sit next to her. As the bus bounced over rural roads and the other girls gossiped and snacked on cookie dough, Shannon kept her head in a book or stared out the window.

Later that afternoon, watching the match prior to her game, she sat in the gym with her mother rather than with her teammates. Perched one bleacher below Brenda, she occasionally leaned back against Brenda's legs and allowed Brenda to rub her shoulders. It was a sweet scene and an unusually public gesture of affection for a teenager.

Three girls stopped by briefly to chat, then left. Poor Shannon, I thought to myself at the time. She doesn't know how to mingle with kids her age. She's probably dying for the other kids to ask her to join them.

As my year with Shannon came to a close, however, I suspected that I had been wrong. She was shy, but from what I had seen no lonelier than any girl her age. She seemed to have accepted her shyness, as well as her diabetes, as parts of who she was. I decided to ask her why she chose to sit by herself that day on the bus.

"So I could do my homework," she said.

Why did she choose her mother's company over that of her friends? Was she afraid of crowds? Had someone in that group hurt her feelings? She shook her head.

"I'm more into the game, and Mom is, too," she said matter-of-factly. "All these other girls do is talk about boys and they don't even watch. It's like they don't even want to be there."

In both cases, Shannon did what she wanted to do no matter how it appeared. It occurred to me that she was learning to value her own judgment about the right thing to do over the norms of the group, a major step toward building a strong identity that usually first appears in middle adolescence. Her friends noticed her independence and admired it. Melanie, when asked in the spring what she liked about Shannon, replied, "She's funny, nice, cool, and doesn't try to impress people."

When Shannon compared who she was to who she wanted to be, she still felt deficient in specific areas. On a self-esteem questionnaire I asked her to fill out late in the year, she replied that she was only "sometimes" satisfied with herself. But when she compared herself to others, she felt better; on that same survey, she said that she felt she had "a number of good qualities" and that she was "a person of worth, at least the equal of others."[12] Despite the labels that other people wanted to give her, she felt normal at least some of the time.

AS PARENTS WE CAN

• Encourage our child, as she grows, to take on tasks that involve increasing levels of skill and responsibility, showing appreciation for effort as well as accomplishment.

• Expose him early to a variety of possible interests and talents, enlisting support for his enthusiasms from others.

• Ask her opinions about consequential matters and show respect for her answers.

• Prepare him for the world outside and then propel him toward it.

• Find ways to show how much we love her even when she is being her most unlovable; fathers of daughters, especially.

• Ask him to help set his own rules and the consequences of failing to abide by them; enforce consistently.

• Quietly observe her world and the people in it. State clearly what is acceptable behavior, while allowing her as much room as possible to act normal according to her definitions.

• Hold to family routines; find one activity to do together regularly.

• Work to keep our marriage healthy, spending more time in conversation and play than in criticism.

PART TWO

The Company They Keep

Alana Perales has walked halfway to her friends in the school cafeteria, food tray in hand and right ankle throbbing after a fall, when she remembers. She has to sit with her team during lunch, a group of about a hundred sixth-graders who share teachers. Sitting with friends on other teams is forbidden. That's the new rule at Kepley Middle School since her sixth-grade class became too noisy for the lunchroom monitors. She crosses the room, easing herself into her team's assigned table. She leaves an empty spot on either side and makes sure there are boys on her right and left. Another regulation: Kids must sit at every other place, boy-girl, boy-girl.

She bites into her hot dog and looks wistfully across the room at Meredith and Lisa. They're on the same team, so they can talk at lunch. Wonder what—or whom—they're talking about? Both girls belong to the popular crowd at school. Meredith, the quieter of the two, is friendly and fair-minded but somewhat cautious. Lisa, outgoing and spontaneous, has had several boyfriends already and boasts about having dyed her hair nine times with homemade solutions ranging from peroxide to Kool-Aid. Alana has been trying to work her way into their group ever since she started at Kepley a little over four months ago.

It has not been easy; sometimes she thinks middle school is organized precisely so that she cannot make and keep friends. She doesn't share any classes or activities with Meredith and Lisa, she's not allowed to eat lunch with them, has no time to talk to them in the four minutes between classes and no time after school because she must catch the school bus. She plays volleyball and basketball like they do, but the sixth-graders have been divided into teams based on ability. Meredith and Lisa, thin and quick, are on a more advanced team than she is.

Some of her classmates find ways to sneak past their friends' tables at lunch when they're putting away their trays. But she has always been afraid to risk that. Just as she's about ready to get up to leave, she spies Meredith rising from the table. Please swing by my table, Alana prays.

To most adults the idea of friendship is so ordinary as to seem inconsequential. In a grown-up world where alliances pass for friendship and dinner talk for intimate conversation, soul mates can be an afterthought.

Not so for young adolescents. Ask any twelve- or thirteen-year-old what the best thing about her life is and she will probably say, "My friends." U.S. teens spend more time with friends, and report more satisfaction doing so, than teens in other countries.[1]

As friends like Meredith and Lisa talk to and about Alana, they will be supplying their answers to those questions she is asking: Am I competent? Loved and loving? Normal? Because Alana's thinking has matured, she will be able to put herself in their shoes and for the first time divine their answers. These friends and others will join her family members in adding their own pieces to her life's jigsaw puzzle.

Some of Alana's friends will inevitably band together as a group. Group behavior frightens parents. But as you will see in chapter four, it does not have to. Friends' opinions, while increasingly significant, are not omnipotent. Libby Sigel and her parents had a great deal to say about the friends she chose and the effect those friends had. In chapter five, you will see through the story of Chip Thomson what can happen to a child who does not fit into a crowd. Chapter six looks at the benefits of best friendships through the eyes of Angela Perales, Alana's older sister.

All three chapters demonstrate a key point for parents to remember: Friends are not just nice for kids to have; they're critical for healthy development. Indeed, some scientists now believe that the best predictor of how well children will adapt to life as an adult is not their IQs or grades in school but how well they get along with other kids.

While certain friends may sway Alana in unhealthy ways, other friends will provide positive influences, complementing what her family is trying to teach her. Some of them may hurt her feelings, but others will provide shoulders to cry on. (Occasionally, the same friend may do both.) Some friends may encourage her to take dangerous risks, but others will rein her in. Some friends may draw her away from her studies while others will encourage her to learn and achieve.

Some friends may pull her spirits down, but others will infect her with joy and inspire her to worthwhile adventures and projects she might not attempt on her own, teaching her the value of collective work. All of her friends will give her the opportunity to learn more about other human beings and contribute to someone else's life. Being befriended, and being a friend, will encourage her to be adventurous, generous, compassionate, patient, and humble—values that will mark her as a person of character.

CHAPTER FOUR

Hangin' with the Crowd
(Libby's Story)

Libby Sigel, the black-haired, seventh-grade child of Israeli immigrants, is sitting at a weathered gray picnic table in a suburban Los Angeles park. The sun is setting and the late September air is remarkably clear for LA, throwing the sand-colored mountains to the west into large relief behind her as she tells me about her life.

She has mountains of her own to scale, and first impressions suggest she won't have trouble making the climb. She is self-confident: "I make all A's." She is thoughtful: "Will society get to the place where we have too much technology?" And she is bold: "I would like to walk naked down the street."

But first impressions, I would learn with Libby, do not paint a full portrait. She has an experimental side that will get her into trouble as the year passes. Like many kids her age, she can be remarkably mature one day and a bat brain the next. I get a hint of this the first day when she starts talking about her friends. "Kids know more about a lot of things these days," she says. "Sex, drugs . . . I bet ninety-nine percent of my friends do drugs."

Does she? "Not yet. But I'll try drugs. Also smoking. I want to have the experience of getting high." She pauses, catches herself as the more mature Libby takes over. "But now I'm too young. I'm gonna tell my parents before I do anything stupid." This declaration, I would later see, was not as far-

fetched as it sounded; in her house, family members talked about every-thing. And yet . . .

Fast-forward to New Year's Eve, three months later.

Libby and her crowd have been invited to a party at a Beverly Hills mansion. One of the girls has smuggled in some beer, courtesy of her mother's boyfriend. It is quickly consumed in a bedroom. Someone else brings out a stash of marijuana, and the group wanders out to the back fence to smoke a little grass.

"Say, what are you guys doing?" bellows Carl Adams, father of one of the girls. He is taking care of this multimillion-dollar estate while the own-ers are away, and has allowed his daughter to throw a party. Before the kids can hide the evidence, he's there. "So you've been drinking?" he asks. They shake their heads no. "Then what's this?" He holds up an empty beer bottle he found under a bed.

The party's over, Adams says. He sends the boys home but allows the girls to spend the night as planned. Early the next morning, he calls the girls' parents to tell them what happened.

"I was just trying stuff. I'd never get in the habit of smoking or drink-ing," Libby insists when her mother, Rebekah, picks her up in the family van. Rebekah, however, is furious. "It's not so much that you tried these things," she says. "It's that you did it somewhere besides home. What does it mean to do it with friends?" She reminds Libby that two girls at the party had been picked up by police for shoplifting only a few days before. "What if your friends are not as strong and smart as you? Their actions affect you and yours affect them, too."

It is the struggle of Libby's seventh-grade year—how to weigh what her instincts tell her is right against her desire to fit in with new friends and a new crowd. At the moment, she only shrugs off her mother's questions. When she arrives home she grabs the portable phone, slips inside her bed-room, and shuts the door.

Groups, cliques, and crowds: Nothing prompts more conversation and anxiety on the part of the adults who are raising adolescents. We can accept the need for close friends, but crowds scare us, particularly in a society that increasingly equates group behavior with gangs and trouble. Shannon's mother worried that Shannon didn't fit in with a crowd, but Libby's mother worried because Libby did.

Like many moms, these women were used to playing the role of social director when their children were younger. They had orchestrated play-dates, sleepovers, and birthday parties according to their tastes as well as their kids' preferences. Now they heard their kids talking in reverent tones about girls and boys they had never met, whose families they had never heard of. Most of these acquaintances came from school, sports, or clubs. But sometimes they were friends met over the Internet, intimate strangers whom the kids themselves had never seen. Staying on top of these friends and what they were doing seemed an impossible task. As Rebekah told Libby, "I can't stay in your pocket all day."

There was some justification for their concern. Groups frequently act differently than members do on their own. They wield influence on people of all ages, but particularly on young adolescents, and surprisingly, they are more influential than best friends.[1] Sometimes, that influence is harmful; as we saw with Chandler Brennan, if a kid runs primarily with a group of delinquents she is more likely to get into trouble than if she hangs out with the nerds.[2] But groups can also be a powerful force for good, offering kids opportunities to feel appreciated and to learn valuable skills in relationship-building and leadership.

As Libby's father, Aaron, in particular would come to realize with Libby, when a kid does something wrong it is easier to find fault with the other kids involved than to assign responsibility to our own. But blaming friends misses the point and drives a wedge between child and adult. Instead, parents can begin to build a bridge to their children by taking the time to consider the positive, as well as the negative, lessons their child may be learning. They need to embrace the regular opportunities that group behavior provides for discussion about the values their family holds dear. And they need to help their son or daughter balance his or her social life with the demands of being a student and a member of the family and the larger community.

"Everybody's Doing It"

Rebekah, a nurse-turned-homemaker, and Aaron, a carpenter, came to the United States from Israel to introduce Libby, their first baby, to a couple they had known in Israel. Originally intending only to visit, they were seduced into staying by visions of living in a country where, as

Aaron put it, "money grows on trees." They settled on Calhoun Street in Van Nuys, a San Fernando Valley suburb of flat, wide streets, modest stucco ranch houses, and young families. Here they sought out new friends to substitute for the family they had left behind in Tel Aviv.

As we talked on the afternoon of our first meeting, friends moved in and out of the small but airy living room of their three-bedroom home, grabbing a cold drink from the refrigerator, an orange or strawberry from the table, joining in the conversation. They were comforting and unremarkable to Rebekah and Aaron, who could not say the same about some of Libby's acquaintances. "My daughter tells me there are drugs in her school and cigarettes," Rebekah said that afternoon. "She tells me how you get high from drugs, and how does she know? From her friends." Rebekah remembered trying marijuana herself several times with groups of friends when she was nineteen or twenty. "But we never had this idea at her age, you know. It's pretty scary. It's the same with sex. 'I feel like doing it,' she says. Why not? Everybody is."

Searching for Community

Several months earlier, in June 1996, Libby had said goodbye to the fifty kids who made up the sixth grade at Corinne A. Seeds, a small, private K–6 school on the campus of UCLA that she had attended since kindergarten. She and the other graduates scattered to seventh grades across the metropolitan area. Libby entered her neighborhood middle school, Roger A. Millikan, in Sherman Oaks, a sprawling public campus with sixteen hundred students in grades six through eight, including more than five hundred seventh-graders.

Moving to a new school is hard on a child of any age, but particularly on young adolescents, who are undergoing so many changes already. Libby knew no one that first day of school. She suspected that most kids in her class had already formed their groups in sixth grade the year before. To make matters worse, the composition of each class changed every fifty minutes.

A lot of kids would have kept to themselves that day. But Libby, a child with natural social skills, dove right in, preferring to select her friends rather than wait to be selected. Over the next few days she put together her own informal class, choosing friends, as most kids do, whose interests and attitudes resembled hers. Jamie in art, who was blond, beautiful, and impulsive, was one. "Hi," Libby said. "I'm a new girl. Who are you?" Callie in science, a short and smart girl, was another she approached. Then Megan, then Angela. Within a couple of weeks she had assembled a pack of about a dozen girlfriends.

Young adolescents run in packs because packs are safer at first than single friends. If one member of the group betrays you, a replacement can be found quickly. If one member can't think of anything to do, another can. Today's public secondary schools are large, impersonal, and contain disruptive students who wouldn't have been there twenty-five or thirty years ago. Kids catch on quickly to the fact—demonstrated so tragically in the 1999 high-school shootings in Littleton, Colorado—that loners do not do well at school.

Libby had lived almost her whole life on Calhoun Street. But like other youth I interviewed, she felt no attachment to her neighborhood. The San Fernando Valley—the "valley" of Valley Girls and Valley Speak—is 275 square miles of flat brown dirt, irrigated to support 1.2 million people in thousands of apartment complexes and tract homes like Libby's. Nearly everyone there seems to have come from somewhere else and to be headed for someplace better. In the late afternoon, the doors to most houses on Calhoun would be shut, the shades drawn, and the sidewalks empty. "I'll put it this way," Libby said. "I wouldn't borrow a cup of sugar from our neighbors."

It wasn't hard to see that absent any feeling of closeness to her neighborhood or her school, Jamie, Callie, and the other kids whom Libby befriended became her community. They assumed such significance that, like Chandler Brennan, she dropped outside activities to make time for them. She stopped taking lessons in dance and piano, abandoned horseback riding, and hung out at her house, her friends' homes, or at the mall.

A Little from This Group, a Little from That

Some Millikan students loved rap music; others couldn't stand rap but loved ska. Some were studious; others were slouchers. Some of them wouldn't be caught dead in anything other than frayed jeans and worn T-shirts, while others carefully coordinated short skirts and spaghetti-strap camisoles. For the first half of the school year, Libby jumped from one of these groups to another, trying out different parts of her emerging personality and personal taste, or what some psychologists would call her "possible selves." This was natural and healthy.

Parents often make the mistake of assuming that if their child gets in with a particular group, she will assume all the characteristics of that group. Most kids, however, are smarter than that. Libby said she took from each group what she wanted and ignored the rest.

The challenge for parents like the Sigels is to figure out the mostly good crowds from the mostly dangerous. That means finding out the names of these new friends and then asking the son or daughter about them. If consulting the child proves unproductive, as it frequently does, the parent can seek out teachers and guidance counselors. What kinds of grades do these kids make? What kinds of after-school activities are they in? What kind of family life do they have?

This doesn't mean a parent should become alarmed if a couple of bad apples turn up within a given group. Having one or two troubled friends usually will not harm a child if her other friends are pretty good kids.[3] But if a whole group of friends seems risk-prone, the experts say, the parent will want to discuss his or her reservations. The child needs some time to make her own judgment after that. But if the friendships persist and serious harm may result, she also needs help in pulling away and finding a new crowd.

During the year I observed Libby, her parents were in the stage of talking to her about her friends but doing little else. They had chosen her school environment carefully—the private school at UCLA and then honors classes at Millikan—and were leaving the rest up to her.

By the time of the Beverly Hills party, she had sorted her friends into concentric circles, with four or five girls in the center clique. "Basically I'm the same person with everyone," she said, "but with my closest friends, I'm more open." These closest friends were attractive girls who preferred shopping and parties to schoolwork, something that was beginning to have serious implications.

The Odd Girl Out

The clique had pulled together after a painful skirmish in the fall. Young adolescents sometimes pick on someone outside of, or on the periphery of, their group in order to divert attention from themselves.

Libby fell victim to such an assault shortly after Halloween when a girl she was trying to get to know, a lanky black-haired beauty named Megan, started circulating rumors about her. Boys liked Libby only because she had large breasts, Megan whispered. Taking their cue from Megan, the other girls started inventing secrets to tell about Libby. Rebekah caught snippets of conversation between Libby and her so-called friends but decided to stay out of the fray, at first.

Then one evening Libby called home from a friend's house asking Rebekah to pick her up. In tears, she told Rebekah, "I'm not going to take it. I'm not going to sell my soul to be in the group. If it means I won't have friends, I won't have friends."

Unlike younger children, adolescents tend to keep peer problems to themselves, fearing that their concerns will be dismissed by adults worried more about mortgage payments than meanness. Libby, however, was lucky. She felt comfortable talking to Rebekah about the whisper campaign. Rebekah, once she recognized how seriously Libby took these smears, didn't brush off her feelings by saying something like, "Don't let it bother you. They're just kids." She also didn't encourage Libby's initial impulse to drop her friends, to run away from the pain. Instead, she and Libby analyzed the problem and shared ideas for resolving it. They even devised possible retorts to caustic barbs.

"Meanieheads," as Libby called them, usually go after girls they think are most likely to crumble, Rebekah told her daughter. Libby needed to project an image of strength.

"You go to school and smile, walk with your head up in the air like a queen, come back at them with humor," Rebekah advised. "Whenever you feel down, sing or hum. I will be with you in spirit every day."

The next day, Libby walked into one of her classes and a classmate moved away from her. "Ooh, I have an allergy," the girl said.

"I have a doctor," Libby replied. "Want his number?"

Another girl called Libby "a cow." Libby shot back: "I wish I could give you some milk. Let me think how."

After one of the girls threw a soda can at Libby, Rebekah went to Millikan and spoke to the assistant dean. The dean promised to look into the matter and get back to Rebekah but never did. As we will see in the next chapter, school officials frequently fail at resolving social problems. Parents have to push them, and Rebekah wasn't a pusher. She considered calling the parents of the offending girls but feared, probably correctly, that that might cause more trouble for Libby.

She suggested to Libby that Libby wait out the girls and look for other friends with whom she could be herself. Libby turned to girls and boys she knew in other groups—an advantage of being associated with a larger crowd. Slowly the clique members began calling her, asking for forgiveness and advice because Megan had turned on them, too. Libby became a mediator, helping clique members understand one another. She was beginning to comprehend what her mother preached—that friendship was not just about what it did for her, but also what she could do for her friends. Eventually even Megan called Libby wanting to make amends.

"Why don't I have any friends?" she asked Libby.

"Friends do not hurt or manipulate other friends," Libby told her.

"You sound like God," Megan complained. But she listened and began renewing her friendship with Libby.

Although girls at this age battle more openly than boys, they also tend to discuss and settle their conflicts more quickly. As the next chapter shows, boys tend to let disagreements slide and may nurse hard feelings for months or years after an incident. By weathering Megan's abuse with her pride intact, and helping other girls do the same, Libby learned to manage conflict. She also became what young adolescents aspire to and need to be: a valued member of her group. Rebekah talked to her about the power she now had over her friends. "How will you use that power?" she asked.

Competing Voices

In the Sigel household, such questions were not unusual. Debates among Rebekah, Aaron, Libby, and her three younger siblings filled the home at teatime after school and at the Sabbath meal every Friday evening. Anyone dropping by, young or old, was likely to be drawn into a discussion about religion, education, or any one of dozens of other topics.

Such questions and conversations were beneficial to Libby because they encouraged her to reason in a group setting, to arrive at her opinions independently of others and be able to defend them. But unfortunately for Libby, Rebekah and Aaron argued opposite positions on almost everything, including how and whether to discipline their children. Like Chandler Brennan, Libby sometimes sought out friends to give her shelter from their storms.

Aaron, sounding a lot like Daniel Brennan, believed that his children needed to learn things for themselves. On the afternoon I met them, for example, he volunteered that he was thirteen when he first had sex. I asked him what he would say if Tobias, Libby's eleven-year-old brother, came to him in two years and said he wanted to sleep with a girl. "I think I would talk to him and find out what his feelings are," he said. "If they need a place, I would try to arrange it for them." He looked over at Rebekah. "What's wrong?"

"It's unbelievable," she sputtered. "Is that how you teach them? I tell you, last weekend Libby came and told me she wants to experience drugs to get high. And I started talking how I don't believe in life you have to experience everything in order to know this is not the right thing for you. . . . Being like everybody else is not what we want to do in life, I told her. We want to elevate ourselves, not degrade ourselves by using drugs."

Aaron posed a classic dilemma: "But unless we're real open with them, they're not going to feel comfortable coming to us."

He continued, "They're going to do this stuff anyway. Who am I to tell them what I want them to do?"

"You are their father." Rebekah sighed, having had this conversation dozens of times before. "You tell them to choose something right. You don't tell them what to do at the age of twenty, but you do tell them what to do at the age of eight or eleven or twelve."

Rebekah knew that Libby needed to hear a chorus of voices in her head, including Aaron's, telling her not to be stupid when she considered making a potentially harmful choice. Rebekah's voice by itself was easy to ignore among the clamor of friends.

Libby later informed me that she had learned to play her parents so that her father's hands-off attitude usually prevailed. Rebekah and Aaron did not look over or inquire about her homework. They did not insist that she take part in her synagogue or retain at least one of the activities she had dropped. They did not give her appointed times to be home when she went out, and they certainly did not try to influence her choice of friends. What they were doing was giving her a blank page to fill in—or for her friends to fill in. Only her mom continued to provide some margins through conversation and occasional punishment.

Peer Pressure: The Real Scoop

After the New Year's Eve crisis, Rebekah forbade Libby from visiting her friends for several weeks. The two of them discussed the idea of atonement, perhaps through volunteer work. Libby didn't resist the idea, even though she thought her mom was blowing the incident out of proportion.

Rebekah wasn't. The younger kids are when they try smoking and drinking, the more frequently they end up doing both regularly. Young abusers are also more likely to move on to harder substances than older kids who experiment. Rebekah acted properly in coming down on Libby harder than she usually did.

Privately, Rebekah asked herself, "Why would Libby want to do such things?" Sometimes she was fooled into believing that Libby would stay away from drugs and other risky substances because Libby argued so intelligently about complex social ideas. It's an assumption that many parents make, and it is wrong. Neuroscientists now know that different parts of the brain develop according to different timetables, and that one of the last regions to mature is the part that determines sound judgment.[4]

The only answer Rebekah could come up with was this: "Libby wants to fit in with the crowd, which is a bad influence. It makes her feel she needs to be like everyone else."

Rebekah did not say that Libby's *friends* were a bad influence. She understood that peer pressure is misnamed, that teens who drink or smoke usually do not stand over their more reluctant friends coaxing them to join in. What they do is convey a sense of fun and relaxation, and the young person who wants the others to like her, who knows of no other way to unwind, or who simply wants to try something new and forbidden, may be inclined to experiment. If something goes awry, she figures someone in the group will be there to help. Peer pressure, then, is really "me pressure," stress the child imposes on herself.

Also, a kid is likely to choose a crowd who is already like her in important ways. Her values—independent of the group's—play a role in whom she chooses to run with.[5] And not everyone is equally susceptible to the influence of a crowd. Younger adolescents are more vulnerable than older teens, eighth-graders especially so. Boys succumb to deviant behavior more often than girls. And boys or girls who are socially awkward are more likely to go with the flow than the socially adept.[6]

Just because a kid tries something risky with a friend doesn't necessarily mean she will adopt that behavior. Controlled studies have shown that when kids start to drink or smoke regularly, it's for reasons related to friends or acquaintances less than half the time.[7] The child may be responding to a physiological addiction or, as we saw with Chandler, to an emotional need for support from people she cares about. Also, she may be imitating not only her companions but adults who either unconsciously or consciously encourage her. Libby's choice of a free-wheeling, experimental group to hang around with resembled her father's choices decades earlier. She and her siblings knew about his early sexual activity and that he had tried various drugs after joining the Israeli army. He still smoked cigarettes that he rolled himself, a habit his children criticized.

Too Much Time with Friends

Libby spent few waking hours without a friend in tow or off the phone, a reflection in part of her parents' own socializing and open house. Having Libby's friends around a lot meant that Rebekah and Aaron got to know several of them. But it also meant that Libby spent little time alone with her family.

In this she was not unusual. Starting in puberty, kids pick up messages from other teens and from television that it's not cool to hang out with their moms and dads. Parents often go along with this near-alienation, assuming that it is inevitable and maybe even good for the kids.

Gradual separation is healthy, but isolation from the family is not. Even as friends command more attention from teenagers, parents must seek equal time. Studies show that the more time young teens spend with their families, the less likely they are to engage in risky behavior.[8] Experts suspect this is partly because time together acquaints parents with the new person their child is becoming—and familiarity can breed respect as well as contempt. Time with a parent also allows a kid the opportunity to test out new ideas and feelings on someone other than kids her age.

Parents sometimes complain that their kids never want to do things with the family. But my observations suggest that if kids enjoyed being with their family prior to puberty, they can usually be persuaded to continue, assuming they have a voice in deciding what to do. If, during their elementary-school years, the amount of family time has diminished noticeably, which is what happened to Chandler, Shannon, and Libby, it can be difficult to restore.

Friends were cutting into Libby's attention to schoolwork as well. A straight-A student at her old school, she was making B's and C's by November at Millikan. Rebekah told her she needed to spend more time on her studies but didn't take any steps to assure that Libby complied. Instead, Rebekah rationalized privately, "Learning is not only going to school, and life is not only the next math problem. I remind myself, she needs to do other things."

Certainly kids Libby's age need to do things other than schoolwork. But parents sometimes forget that success in school *leads to* success in those other things, including social competence.[9] The most popular kids in any given school are usually at least moderately high achievers as well. Parents would do well to teach their kids during the elementary-school years how to manage their free time smartly before adolescence's highly social stage kicks in. Course work in middle school and high school will demand more hours in their day, but if they have already learned how to prioritize, they will be able to balance their assignments and their friendships.

The Classroom as Social Playground

Libby's attention in class was also waning, partly because some of her teachers seemed clueless about how to engage their chatty, convivial students. The most vivid example occurred one morning in art class. The regular art teacher was attending a staff meeting and a substitute had been called in. The sub, an unemployed actress in black leggings and a multicolored sweater, sat at the teacher's desk the entire period reading a paperback novel.

The class had been asked to cut out three photographs from magazines. The sub instructed them to remain in their assigned seats while they worked, but Libby, Jamie, and a friend named Melanie left their desks anyway to sit together. As they turned the pages of their magazines, they gossiped and giggled. Other girls joined them, and the hum of voices grew louder.

"I've told them twice to get in their seats," the teacher complained to me. "I'm not going to do it any more. They don't pay me enough. I try to avoid subbing for this age. They don't do anything you tell them to do."

Later that day in an honors social studies class, chaos threatened again, but this teacher knew how to handle it. The class was being drilled on the trade patterns of ancient African civilizations, and twice, as he turned his back to write on the blackboard, gummy worm candies sailed back and forth. The teacher caught on and chastised the class briefly about their antics. Then he asked them what they would like to discuss. One student suggested the current and controversial subject of ebonics, or whether "black English" should be taught in schools. The teacher promised they could turn to that discussion as soon as they finished the chapter in front of them. The worms disappeared and the kids became students, hands in the air and ideas at the ready.

By early January, Libby's grade in math was plummeting. Her teacher had disciplined her several times for talking in class, making her stay in his classroom during free period and write hundreds of times: "I must contemplate my actions and their sources and use self-control to display my inherent respectfulness for all living things." Her friends told her this teacher had singled her out. In a' move of quiet rebellion, she stopped doing her math homework. Rebekah and Aaron did not realize she had done so. They were not contacted by the school nor did they get in touch with school administrators until late in the year.

Aaron held Libby's close friends responsible for her sliding grades, saying they were pushing her toward mediocrity. Rebekah, on the other hand, argued that doing well or poorly in school was Libby's choice: "She is moved to the middle because her priorities are socializing first and talking on the phone."

Instead of intervening at the first serious signs of trouble, they preferred waiting for the day when she would resume her earlier, more studious habits. Privately, Libby interpreted their inactivity in a way they did not intend. "My parents don't really care about grades," she told me.

. . .

Tuesday afternoons are half-days at school, so by one o'clock Libby, Jamie, and Lynda are hitting the tarmac of the Millikan parking lot.

Jamie resembles a bad-girl version of Clueless star Alicia Silverstone, dressed in a black Replay T-shirt, black stretch pants, and stacked heels. Lynda, also blond, looks more like a baby doll, her petite frame swallowed up in a Jolly Green Sprout sweatshirt and sporting a star on her cheek. Libby, with her dark coloring, frayed jeans, and a blue, short-sleeved mechanic's shirt, completes the picture of three totally distinct styles. No adolescent clones here except for one detail: the pastel candy necklaces each wears on her throat.

The three girls pile into a waiting car, ready to take on the Northridge Fashion Center. Near the intersection of the Ventura and San Diego freeways, the mall offers three levels and two hundred stores, including the names that make teenage girls glow: Hot Topic, Contempo Casuals, Spencer Gifts. But their first stop has to be the food court. Over Sweet and Pungent Chicken at Plum Tree Express, they share confidences:

Jamie: I really hate the fact that whenever a guy and a girl do something, like, you know, the guy always gets "Yeah, you go, boy." But for the girl it's always, "Oh, you're such a slut."

Lynda: Why can't the girls be like guys?

Libby: It's a double standard.

Jamie: I know a lot of girls who are doing the deed.

Libby: I think you can do everything but sex. That's okay.

Jamie: Is giving a blow job considered losing your virginity?

Libby: No.

Jamie: Are you sure?

Libby: Because it's oral sex.

Jamie: Somebody said it was. Because the man or boy can ejaculate.

Lynda: What?

Jamie: Ejaculate.

Lynda: Is that why they call it jacking off?

Jamie: Uh-huh.

Lynda: I never knew that.

Jamie: What do you feel about Joey?

Libby: I barely know him. He calls me up. He's like, "Hi." I'm like, "Oh, who's this?" "It's Joey."

Jamie: He does that to everybody.

Lynda: Who is Joey?

Jamie: I've been on the phone with him three times when he said, "I have a knife in my hand. I think I'm going to kill myself." And then he goes, "Bye. I love you." And the next day he calls me back and he goes, "What's up?" He doesn't take life seriously.

Libby: His brother was killed in a drive-by shooting.

Lynda: I didn't know that.

To adults, such meandering conversation in a food court may seem pointless. But these three girls were doing nothing less than translating for each other the language and dynamics of human relationships. Where else would they be able to talk so freely about embarrassing things that matter so much? At school? Hardly. At the dinner table? Unlikely.

Adults forget how important such translation is to kids just learning the language. Friends are their support group for the "little" problems that beset them in the present, as opposed to the "big" future concerns, such as education, which may obsess their parents.

Adolescents act as the eyes of friends whose vision is temporarily clouded. Of course the friends' vision may not be 20-20, either, and for that reason adults must help them sort fact from fiction, particularly on topics such as sexuality and drug use. But kids must also be able to talk and mingle without an agenda designed and managed by adults, to relax and be silly without embarrassing themselves in front of adults, whose approval they still privately seek. Anyone who insists that teenagers are consistently sullen should hear a bunch of them "chillin'" in a place where they're comfortable. The laughter and teasing can make even the biggest grump smile.

The Soda Shop of the Late 1990s

Kids who are lucky can find such a place to hang out at home or at a friend's house. I remember Michelle, the sixth-grade girl in chapter ten, telling me that on a particularly stressful day at school, "I started running around on break outside yelling, 'Are you a wild child? Are you a wild child?' My friends and I decided to form a Wild Child

Club. That night we met at a friend's house. We sat on the patio, lit candles, said a chant, and had a little feast of bread and tomatoes. We meditated and told fortunes and drank pop out of chalices. I felt much better after that."

Many kids don't enjoy such freedom at home, especially in the afternoons. Their parents work and refuse, with good reason, to allow friends over when they aren't present. On street corners and in parks, kids are likely to be dispersed by police for loitering. Certainly recreation centers, youth clubs, and, increasingly, schools stay open weekdays until the early evening, and several of the kids I followed took advantage of such after-school activities. Friendships can thrive in such places, built around specific skills.

But such organizations usually insist on scheduled events, including homework. They don't provide much time for the unbooked, unsupervised "hangin' " that kids this age need in addition to lessons and games. Enter the shopping mall. For all the concern that malls inspire in parents, they are one of the few places kids can cluster informally on their terms, in relative safety.

Rebekah was home in the afternoons, but she understood Libby's desire to be somewhere besides Calhoun Street. She remembered what it was like to have wanderlust. "When I was her age, I had the outside where I was boss," she recalled. "I did things I was not allowed to do, climbing on roofs, stealing fruit from the neighbors, all these naughty things that a child does and learns that it's wrong."

Rebekah wished the family could move back to Israel, where living was simpler and freer. "I think this is the biggest loss that I cry about for my kids. They have no neighborhood, no experience of being outside and doing really what they want to do. They come home, watch TV, and it's always the same. They're living their lives in boxes."

At Northridge Mall, Libby, Jamie, and Lynda could climb out of their boxes. They could play at being children—doing jumping jacks to Muzak's version of "YMCA." Then they could pretend to be adults, trying on Jamie's frosted blue lipstick and checking out the erotica at Spencer Gifts.

A slightly spicy novelty store three decades ago, Spencer Gifts has turned into a sex- and dirty-language emporium—at least this one in the Valley was, located in the heart of the country's adult entertainment industry. As the girls walked in, a display of shopping bags greeted them with a picture of a homeless man giving the finger and saying, "Times are hard / Life's a shit; / So here's your friggin' birthday gift." The seventh-graders glanced at the display, then headed for the back of the store where a sign read YOU MUST BE 18 TO BE IN THIS SECTION. No clerk pursued them.

They passed around a package of Body Likker and a Dick Massager for "those muscles that don't get enough exercise." They thumbed through a joke book entitled *More Dead Dicks*. Libby wanted to buy a Love Coupon book containing coupons for a "head massage." Jamie asked if I would buy her an Exotic Condom. "I won't use it; it's just cool to carry in your wallet," she said. (The request was denied.)

Later on, they hit Hot Spots, a boutique specializing in T-shirts, funky clothes, and punk jewelry. Libby slid into a tight, black, floor-length satin skirt. While Lynda was trying on a smaller size of the same skirt, Libby stood in front of the three-way mirror moving her hips back and forth, watching the black satin swirl at her feet.

The mall was Libby's soda shop. She associated the warmth of friendship and the power of free expression—both healthy, desirable experiences—with buying things. The real problem with shopping malls is not, as many parents suppose, that other young people will be there whom the parent may not know, or that kids together get in trouble. What parents should worry about more are the acquisitive, sometimes vulgar values that some stores parade in front of kids who are just beginning to think about what kind of people they want to become. Parents and communities must provide attractive places other than malls for young adolescents to "hang."

The two seventh-grade *girls are in the junior section of Macy's department store, trying on tank tops and leggings and other casual clothes. One of them has an idea. "Let's push these clothes down in our shopping bags and walk out with them. Chances are we won't get caught. And if we do, they'll just ask us to put them back."*

The other girl agrees. They saunter out of the dressing room and a suspicious clerk stops them. "May I see what's in your bag?" she asks.

That night Libby gets a phone call. "Ohmigod, you'll never guess what *happened," says the voice on the other end. "We were in Macy's today and . . ." The girl says that she and the other girl were arrested, finger-printed, and charged with shoplifting more than $100 worth of merchandise. They are going to court. She is freaked, and the person she thought to call was Libby.*

Libby appears distressed after the conversation. Her seventh-grade year began with two friends being arrested for shoplifting, and it has ended the same way. "If I had been with them, they wouldn't have done it," she says with certainty. "I would have told them it's stupid."

In any group of kids, one or two will emerge as leaders. Over the year I followed her, Libby began to play this central role not only in her little group but among others at school. She possessed several traits that young people identify with popular teens: she was self-assured, a good listener, tolerant, had a sense of humor, and generally was in a good mood. Her family had had something to do with that, raising her in an open, spontaneous environment that encouraged her to speak her mind.[10]

Increasingly like her mother, she was able to perceive the needs of her friends, predict their reactions, and care for them in times of trouble. In nine months she had moved from knowing no one to being one of the most popular kids at school. At lunchtime she would dart like a dragon-fly from group to group, crossing with abandon the little territories on campus that each group had carved out for itself.

"I have a million friends," she said toward the end of the year. "Let's see, there's Ziva, Valerie, Megan, Jamie, Greg, Ashley, Chloe . . . two Robbies, five Daniels . . . oh Jema, how could I forget Jema . . . and there's Harold and Dustin . . ."

Within thirty seconds she had named thirty-five friends. Most adolescents go through consolidation and expansion in their friendships; Libby was clearly in an expansionist period. Making and keeping friends had become her badge of competence, and she was as proud of it as Shannon was of her volleyball skills and Eric was of his music.

Her primary allegiance was still with the small group of girls she had hung out with for most of the year. From the outside, they appeared to be a good-time crowd, prone to taking risks. But slowly and painfully some of the members, including Libby, were learning about good judgment and how to encourage their friends to use it. The Swiss psychologist Jean Piaget believed that moral principles governing relationships between people, such as empathy and resolving conflict, begin as norms applied between young friends.

Kids are more perceptive about their friends' strengths and weaknesses than we realize, and they try to help their friends more than we know. Libby's friend Jamie, for example, was boy crazy, and Libby worried about her. A boy named Hugo had cheated on Jamie by going out with other girls four times, Libby said, and Libby had tried to warn her away from him. Libby also came down hard on Megan and Valerie for shoplifting, which is more than the legal system did. A judge ordered the two girls to perform community service but they never complied, and the court never forced them to.

Taking Her Own Advice

But was Libby learning to be a good influence on herself as well as on her friends? Sometimes she would say things that made Rebekah think so. On a shopping trip for sandals after school, for example, Libby turned to Rebekah in the shoe store and said, "I know sometimes I am a hypocrite. And it may look as if I don't listen to you. But you have a great impact on me."

Other events left Rebekah wondering. For a school assignment on the 1960s, Libby videotaped her brother Tobias lying on a mattress, his shirt off, snorting sugar made to look like cocaine. She stayed out with a friend one afternoon after school for five hours without telling her mother where she was, prompting Rebekah to call the police. She invited friends over to her house for a party, and Aaron had walked in on a couple "vigorously rubbing" on the couch, as Libby's younger sister put it.

Had they relinquished too much control in light of the crowd Libby ran around with? they wondered. They were right to be concerned: Young adolescents rarely keep friends for a long time whose values they do not share.

Together, they decided to step up their involvement, subtly. Aaron began asking Libby and her friends to go horseback riding with him on weekends. He listened carefully to their conversations, and what he heard upset him.

"Valerie has no father figure at all," he said on a quiet summer evening at home. "Megan's mother is so bitter about Megan's father that she told Megan that her father didn't love her and that's why he left." He shook his head and took a drag on his cigarette. "How can you guide kids if you don't clean up yourself? I could take these girls and change them in three months if they didn't see their parents."

Parents should pay attention to the relationship their kids' friends have with their own parents. In a recent analysis of dozens of studies on peer influence, the authors were surprised to learn that, all other factors being equal, kids whose friends enjoyed a good rapport with their parents did better than kids whose friends did not have such rapport. "Friends who get along with their parents are protective," the authors wrote. "Friends who do not have good relationships with their parents may enhance risk for others."[11]

Rebekah's questions to Libby became more numerous and more pointed. "Why would you want to be friends with someone who steals?" she asked one day after Megan and Valerie were caught shoplifting.

"They're my friends," Libby told her mom. "I may not approve of what they do but they're still my friends." Loyalty is a trait learned painfully and valued highly by kids this age.

"Well, what do you want to do in life? Do you want to be somebody?" Libby had always cut off any discussion about her future with a quick, "I don't have to think about that now." But it was time for her to start thinking about it, Rebekah decided. "All I know is I don't want to work in an office," Libby responded. "That's why you need to read more, get the good grades, maybe choose different friends," Rebekah said.

By this point, other parents might have forbidden some of Libby's associations, possibly enlisting the support of the school. They might have limited Libby's time with her friends until she brought up her grades. They might have organized more family activities to replace some of Libby's group get-togethers.

Rebekah and Aaron chose not to do these things. They thought they saw signs of increasing maturity: how Libby helped her younger siblings now instead of fighting with them, how she chastised her dad for not supporting Rebekah more often, recognizing the need she had for more consistent parenting. They were encouraged that on her own she expressed an interest in taking piano again, maybe singing in a band. Ultimately, Libby would choose to live by the right values regardless of who her friends were, they believed.

CHAPTER FIVE

The Loner
(Chip's Story)

"Have you heard the latest cut by Sublime? It's really awesome." Chip Thomson, barely fourteen, pops a new compact disc into his boom box and looks over at his new friend Mike sitting at the end of Chip's twin bed.

"Nah," Mike grunts, staring out the window of the bedroom into the dark, late-summer North Carolina sky. A skinny kid with a shaved head, he recently began living with his mother, and she is already on his case. He reaches into his jeans pocket and pulls out a joint.

Chip checks to make sure his bedroom door is closed, then walks over to a window and raises it as high as it will go. Good, he thinks, there's a wind tonight. He hands Mike a lighter, switches on the black light that makes his posters glow in the dark, including his favorite, a giant caterpillar grinning from the top of a mushroom. Soon, both boys are sharing marijuana, deep into their own thoughts.

Chip thinks back over his eighth-grade year at Githens Middle School. He started out wanting, as always, to be one of the best-looking, most popular boys at school. To be lounging in a hallway after lunch, talking to some other good-looking, popular boy, and not to be ignored when other members of the in-crowd appeared.

The jocks were admired. But Chip had never been much of an athlete; although almost six feet tall, he was stocky and not well coordinated.

Another way to be cool was to dress the part. But the porous soccer shorts and shirts that were all the rage didn't look right on him. He had adopted skater dress instead—baggy khakis and brand-name surfer shirts, chain wallets and the flat-toed sneakers that fit easily on a skateboard. He had let his blond hair grow to his shoulders so it would cover some of his fair-skinned, round baby face. He had pierced his left ear.

Still, the kids he wanted to call didn't. He had his friends Ward and Jeremy, of course, neighborhood buddies since elementary school. But they weren't as popular as he wanted them to be. The most well-liked boy he knew smoked marijuana and occasionally tripped on LSD. Maybe drugs were an entrée into the desired crowd.

It hadn't been difficult to acquire the goods. Githens, under a voluntary desegregation plan, had opened its doors that year to seventh- and eighth-graders from Rogers-Herr Middle School in a low-income Durham neighborhood. Chip wasn't afraid of the new kids like some of his friends were, and he found he could get drugs on short notice. He became someone to know if you wanted to get high. Students began sidling up to him in the halls. Cute girls flirted with him. He assumed an identity that would prove later to be difficult to deconstruct, that of a drug user and seller.

A small band of white, well-to-do seventh-grade boys seemed especially to like him. One weekday afternoon during spring break, several whom he knew only slightly telephoned him from a nearby convenience store and said they were meeting at their old elementary school to do some skateboarding. Would he like to come?

He was alone, having just finished volunteer work at his church. His parents were still at church. Sure, he told the guys. He'd be right over.

Condemned a year earlier as a fire hazard and planned for demolition, the abandoned seventy-year-old brick school was a skateboarder's paradise, ringed with pine trees and pavement. Chip didn't like skateboarding much, and after a few minutes, he came up with another idea. Wouldn't it be fun to slip into their old school and look around? His friends agreed. Chip broke a window in a side door and the boys walked in. The dusty old rooms were so dark that they decided to make a torch to light their way.

One of the boys picked up a broomstick and handed it to Chip, who wrapped an old sweater around the handle. He and another boy then poured some cleaning fluid they found onto the sweater. Chip pulled a lighter out of his pocket and got the torch going. They tramped through the halls until they reached the auditorium. On stage, one boy wondered aloud whether they could explode the can of cleaning fluid. They grabbed some rags that were lying around and stuffed them into the can. Chip put a lighter to the can and within thirty seconds it was ablaze. "We better put this out," Chip told his friends, but it was too late. A stage curtain was in flames and a fire alarm had sounded. The boys split for home. That night on the television news they learned that a blaze "of unknown origin" had demolished most of the school.

Two weeks later, one of the boys who had been involved told his parents, who contacted the police. All five turned themselves in, were tried on charges of breaking and entering and arson, and found "delinquent." They were ordered to perform one hundred hours of community service, some of it at a local hospital burn center. They were also suspended for the rest of the school year.

Chip's mom, Marianne, his dad, Brian, and his aunt Joanne took turns staying home with him. His parents told him that he could not talk on the telephone, use the computer, watch television, or see friends. Occasionally he was allowed to go over to his grandparents' house, where he was expected to do lawn work and other jobs. "This is one way to repay us," Marianne said.

As mid-summer approached, Marianne and Brian began to allow Chip to contact some of his old friends. He started with Ward, someone they trusted. Ward then introduced him to Mike. Chip's parents did not know Mike but assumed he was okay because he was Ward's friend.

They assumed too much. Mike introduced Chip to cocaine and acid. Marianne and Brian didn't have a clue.

On this particular summer evening, Mike spends the night. The next morning, Chip gets permission to walk Mike home. As the boys wander down the road toward Mike's house, Chip spies his Sublime disc sticking out of Mike's pocket.

"What are you doin' with that?" Chip asks.

"Oh, sorry," Mike says, handing over the CD.

"Whatever." Chip is saddened by his friend's betrayal but doesn't say much about it then or later. It's not the first time someone has stolen something from him. He turns around in the middle of the road and heads back home, alone.

. . .

A few months into Chip's kindergarten year, the negative school reports started coming home. Chip was acting up in class. He was bullying the other children. "Nobody likes me," he told his parents. He was exaggerating but not by much. Unlike Libby in the previous chapter, Chip started school as a loner.

We don't think of boys needing friends as much as girls, maybe because they don't talk about it as much. But they crave the validation, support, and affection that can come with friendship just as much as girls do, and, like girls, their need increases during adolescence.

We also don't think of boys having trouble keeping friends. Girls are known for their cliquish, even catty ways. But boys, too, can be cutting and devious, and in fact are more likely than girls to report feeling lonely and dissatisfied with friends.[1]

A child's skills with playmates are evident early. On any toddler playground, some boys can be seen chasing one another around the jungle gym while others hang back. Some chatter confidently and confidentially to youngsters they barely know, while others are quiet. Some jump into any fight they see, while others run at the first sign of conflict.

Once they reach elementary school, most boys and girls, no matter what their temperament, will be perceived as friends by their classmates. But a few will not. These are the teased kids, the ignored kids, the kids chosen last for kickball. They tend to be the most insecure, and the more they are excluded, the more insecure, even hostile, they become. The signs of their discomfort—numerous fights, perhaps, or their own complaints about other kids and teachers—are almost always evident.

Unless these cries for help are recognized for what they are and are acted upon early, these kids' behavior will probably worsen as they enter adolescence. They may withdraw completely into their own world. They may, as we have seen in the last two years, decide to take out their frustration Rambo-style on a school campus. Or they may do what Chip did and seek to gain friends by doing risky things. Cigarettes, drugs, even acts of vandalism become social calling cards, attracting friends who also feel lonely.

About 5 to 10 percent of any class can be counted among the rejected, a figure that has been consistent over many years of surveys. What's different today is the young age at which lonely kids can acquire the cards.

Parents of "outsiders" must start earlier and work harder at all the things good parents of adolescents do, focusing on their child's self-esteem and relationship skills in particular. Parents can be a mighty force against the pulls of the crowd and illegal behavior, but only if they tune in early to their child's social needs. As the Thomsons would find out, in adolescence, timing can be everything.

A Promising Start

When we meet socially awkward youngsters, we immediately think the problem must have started with Mom or Dad. Sometimes we're right. Remote or unloving parents can destroy a baby's natural empathy within a few years, and as we will see in the next chapter, the adolescent child of such parents may move from friend to friend trying to recover a feeling of connectedness.

But in other cases, parents can hardly be held responsible for social skills that are twisted in early and middle childhood in reaction to cruel playmates, unobservant teachers, and other uncaring adults. Genes, physical appearance, the arrival of a sibling, and the ready opportunity for mischief can also contribute to social awkwardness. The combination of these factors over time produces the lonely child.

Chip's earliest memories of home are warm. He was adopted at five weeks by Marianne, a nurse in her early thirties, and Brian, an easy-going city employee about the same age. The Thomsons' application for adoption had languished with the Durham County social services department for five years, and they were delighted to receive a phone call telling them a healthy boy born to rural, teenage parents was theirs.

The day they brought their son home, Marianne's sister Joanne, as well as Marianne's brother and parents, came over to help them celebrate. That evening marked the first of many extended family gatherings—at the beach, at ski resorts, in each other's backyards. The Thomsons celebrated Chip's birthday each year as well as the anniversary of the day he arrived at their home. As Joanne would later say, "We all feel as if we've raised Chip together."

On one of our first visits together, Chip and I sat on the front-porch swing of his house, a contemporary two-story home on a heavily wooded street. Surrounded by bikes, Rollerblades, and other boyhood paraphernalia, Chip recounted fondly some of his earliest memories with his parents.

"I remember when I first learned to take my overalls off and put them back on," he said. "I must have been about two. Mom was in the kitchen cooking dinner. I showed her what I could do. She was so proud.

"Me and Dad played all the time. Like every day, I had a bike and he'd push me down the street. We'd go to the pool a lot, or the park, swing and everything. I would always wear this red jacket with a zip-up hood. Every night, we'd watch TV upstairs and cuddle, the three of us. We were real close back then."

Three years after Chip's arrival, Marianne got pregnant, and by the time Chip was four he had a brother named Justin. "My dad stopped playing with me a lot," Chip said. "We started doing things like all together."

Sometimes siblings bring out a child's insecurities, making that child less sociable, particularly if a sibling is the same sex. Being an adopted child when your sibling is not can add to the insecurities. Chip's aunt Joanne says she saw Chip begin to build a shell around himself in the months after Justin was born. As Justin got older, it became clear that he and Chip were, in Marianne's words, "as different as night and day." Justin was short, skinny, cheerful, and outgoing, with lots of friends. He was quick in school and had ten times the amount of energy that Chip did. Early in Justin's elementary-school years Marianne and Brian found out why: Justin suffered from attention deficit hyperactivity disorder (ADHD). Try as they might to divide their attention equally between the two boys, and as sensitive as they were to Chip's feelings as an adopted child, Marianne and Brian found themselves spending much of their time managing Justin.

"He demanded a lot of attention," Chip told me. "I was jealous of him. He made jokes about my being adopted. That bothered me."

As Chip got older he learned to ignore his little brother's remarks but they left a scar. "We're not close," Chip said.

On the Playground

Most of Chip's darker memories were of the world outside, beginning in kindergarten. He was one of the youngest in his class and also the biggest. He stood, literally, head and shoulders above them. Rather than take pride in his size, he felt humiliated by it, partly because classmates started calling him names. The taunts continued even after he reported them to his teacher. He and his parents now think that this was because of his size. He was so big, and got angry so frequently, that teachers couldn't believe he was not the bully.

Harassment early in a child's life should never be taken lightly; it can seriously damage a child's self esteem and his attachment to school.[2] The Thomsons decided to play down the playground banter, however, as many parents probably would have. "It's just kids being kids," they told Chip. "Ignore them. They'll stop eventually."

As he moved through elementary school, Chip sought out individual friends, thinking they would be less hurtful than the little groups who still, from time to time, picked on him. In first grade, he made friends with a boy named Carter, with whom he shared a love of Nintendo games. Carter moved away in third grade and was replaced by a boy named Paul. At a sleepover, Paul stole $20 from Chip's backpack, and Chip then made friends with Ward. After Ward came a boy next door named Alex. That friendship lasted for a year until one afternoon, for reasons he doesn't fully understand to this day, Chip stole a bottle of Alex's cologne off Alex's bedroom dresser. Alex and Alex's parents found out, Chip replaced the cologne and apologized, but the friendship was never the same.

The Lure of the Crowd

By middle school, Chip was determined to find a group that would accept him. Being male, he would have to prove himself in some way first. Some boys do this in sports; others, in academic competitions. Chip found his talent in securing drugs. Unlike Libby in the previous chapter, who counted a number of "straight" friends in her crowd, virtually everyone Chip hung out with at the end of middle school did drugs.

Chip was particularly influenced at Githens not by kids he was close to, such as Ward, but by the students with whom he *wanted* to be close. Psychologists call this the "reference group." Parents know it as "everybody"—as in "everybody is doing it." If a child is already respected as a core member of a certain group, "everybody's" influence will probably be minimal. But if a kid, like Chip, is constantly on the fringes, trying to move into the core, "everybody" can shape behavior more than individual friends.[3] This suggests that parents need to figure out not only the values of their children's friends but also the values of wished-for friends. Parents can pay attention to a son's or a daughter's casual remarks about the kids they don't know, and to the tone in which such comments are made, or they can solicit information about the different crowds at school from teachers, counselors, and other parents.

Safe Time vs. Free Time

When Chip came along, Marianne and Brian both had full-time careers that became more demanding as Chip, and later Justin, entered school. Marianne would rise at 5 A.M. and leave by six, well before the boys were up. Brian would give them breakfast and get them off to school before he left for work. Once Chip's last class in elementary school was over, he would join the after-school program. He hated it, particularly in fourth and fifth grades. College students organized games and crafts in which he had no interest and made little effort to draw him in, he recalls. "They spent a lot of time doing their college homework," he said.

Chip says he begged his parents during those years to let him come home each day when school was over. But they did not want him home alone after school and, through sixth grade at Githens, required him to stay at school until one of them picked him up. From their point of view, it was a workable plan: When they arrived, he seemed to be enjoying himself, and he was safe. In Chip's eyes, however, they did not trust him and were trying to control him.

Theirs was a dilemma known by many working parents: what to do with school-age children between 3 P.M. and 6 P.M. These are the much-publicized hours when young teens, left alone, are most likely to get into trouble, and the solution, many experts say, is to enroll them in organized activities. But by early adolescence, kids don't tolerate what they consider make-do work, and unless a program offers a pursuit in which the child is already interested or skilled, an after-school program can feel like prison.

Also, young people want downtime. As much as they enjoy being around friends, they also need a comfortable place to relax away from

the stress of constant social interaction. Insecure kids such as Chip especially need time alone.

As I watched Chip negotiate times to see his friends, it occurred to me
that those of us who work full-time outside the home have taken away
from our children the casual, relaxed pace under which friendships bud
and flourish. When they are very young, we schedule playdates. When
they get a bit older, we send them to after-school care with kids they
don't know or care about or fill up their afternoons with lessons and
sports. When we finally let them stay home alone, it is with the admonition that no friends may join them. Their social life is planned from the
time they are small. When they become old enough to be spontaneous,
many don't know how to be.

Organized Friendships

Beginning in middle school, Marianne and Brian steered Chip into one
activity after another: basketball, baseball, Boy Scouts, serving meals to
the homeless. The Thomsons hoped Chip would discover some element
in one of these groups that would give him a sense of purpose, that he
could succeed at, that would draw admiration from his peers. As Eric
Stanton and Shannon Steele showed, young adolescents will go to great
measures to feel competent, and the Thomsons' strategy probably would
have worked with most kids. It didn't with Chip, though. What he
wanted was to fit in, and within any program his focus was on that goal
rather than on building his skills, which might have been a means to his
goal. He would stick with an activity for a while, then drop it.

The Thomsons had assumed that these groups would give Chip lots
of practice negotiating alliances with boys and girls they considered
"good kids." They discovered that this was not necessarily true. In the
recreational ball leagues, for example, adults decided who would play on
the teams, when and where the teams would play, and how disputes
between boys would be settled. Gone was the old-fashioned negotiation
among kids that Brian remembered from his sandlot days, when kids
learned to compromise and use a little tact.

It appeared that before Chip ever donned a basketball jersey, he could
have used help breaking down the challenges of socialization into small
steps. In *Playground Politics*,[4] psychologist Stanley Greenspan offers par-

ents several suggestions on how to do this in the elementary-school years, before the child becomes a thin-skinned adolescent. Encourage the child to do something regularly with someone new, Greenspan advises. When another kid hurts his feelings, help him put the moment in perspective by asking questions such as, "Could it have been any worse?" Encourage him to identify the feelings of the other child and to talk about his own feelings. If such intentional measures fail to work, Greenspan says, don't hesitate to seek the counsel of an older, experienced teacher, friend, or professional.

The Role of Biology

As Chip got older and, it seemed to them, increasingly antisocial, the Thomsons found themselves wondering how much of his behavior was genetically based. This is a question all parents ask but is particularly perplexing for parents of the approximately 1 million adopted children in this country.[5]

Scientists now know that the child of a parent who suffers from major depression is predisposed to depression. If a child is consistently impulsive, the odds are better than 50-50 that impulsivity is a family trait.[6] Since the Thomsons had received no medical information about Chip's birth parents, they knew nothing about the mental health of his biological parents and were severely handicapped in knowing how to help him. Situations such as theirs are one reason why adoption experts argue for open adoption records or at least for making the health records of birth parents available. Such information is critical to have by the time the child enters adolescence, when serious disorders may surface.

Chip's temperament had been consistent from the time he was young. One-on-one, he was delightful to be with. He would listen carefully to his companion, respond appropriately, speak honestly. He could also be very thoughtful. Before Christmas of his eighth-grade year, his father took him and his brother to The Dollar Store to buy gifts for all the relatives. Justin raced up and down the aisles picking up the first things he saw, but Chip spent time trying to find items suited to each person.

In larger groups, however, Chip retreated into himself. He could also be willful and impulsive. Even as a preteen, when he wanted something, he took it, using the reasoning of an early elementary school–age child. On why, at age eleven, he stole Alex's cologne, for example, he said, "I didn't have any cologne. I thought it would be nice to have." At the moment that he grabbed the bottle from Alex's dresser, he didn't see how taking it would hurt Alex; Alex's family had money and Alex could always get more cologne, he thought. He did not understand that the theft would hurt Alex's feelings or that it would destroy the trust he enjoyed with Alex. Like most young adolescents, he swung back and forth between lower and higher levels of moral thinking, but his overall progress was slow.

Chip was also noticeably pessimistic. Occasionally a smile would trip across his face, but I never saw him laugh. "I'm never satisfied with what I'm doing. I always wanna do something bigger or better," he once told me. His dark moods inhibited his ability to make and keep friends because kids, like adults, prefer their acquaintances to be outgoing and cheerful. Brian and Marianne, who enjoyed teasing and joking, regularly tried to loosen him up. "Not only does he see the glass half-empty, he doesn't like what's in the glass," his father sighed.

Attention Deficit Disorder

When Chip was in fourth grade, the Thomsons took him to a psychiatrist who gave them a partial explanation for his troubling behavior: attention deficit disorder, or ADD. One of the most commonly diagnosed psychiatric diseases among children, claiming some 2.5 million kids, ADD and its sister, attention deficit hyperactivity disorder, are believed to be partly the result of an imbalance of three chemicals in the brain. Typically, ADD kids are described as having difficulty focusing, paying attention, and regulating their behavior. This described Chip to a T. Like many ADD children, he was prescribed the medication Ritalin. His grades improved almost immediately, from D's to B's and C's. "Rit," as he later would call it, became his first drug.

As he entered puberty, doctors were less certain how to treat his disorder. Behavioral illnesses in adolescents, clouded by the normal hormonal activity and stresses of puberty, are difficult to recognize and treat. A family doctor started him on drug number two, the antidepressant Prozac, and he began visiting a psychologist once a week.

Brian and Marianne were told that ADD would make it hard for Chip to pay attention in class and be motivated to learn. What was not made clear to them was that ADD could also make it more difficult for Chip to move easily within a group of friends, pick up visual as well as verbal clues, and understand why other kids behaved in certain ways. Chip regularly attributed other kids' negative responses to the fact that they didn't like him, for instance, rather than considering whether they might be shy or preoccupied.

Neuroscientists now know that the part of the brain that modulates emotion and rash decisions, the prefrontal cortex, matures slowly in most adolescents, and that ADD may delay the process. One way to speed up development, scientists speculate, is to exercise the cortex by pursuing activities such as sports or music *and* healthy interaction with friends. If, like Chip, one doesn't like doing those things or isn't good at them, maturation takes longer.

Youths like Chip, with underdeveloped cortexes, seem to learn only by doing things they're not supposed to.[7] "If there's a crack anywhere, Chip will jump right into it," Brian told me. During Chip's eighth-grade year, after Githens merged with Rogers-Herr, he had plenty of cracks to choose from. Tension escalated between the different groups at school, and it showed in the discipline reports. The number of in-school suspensions rose from 0 to 520 that year, according to school records. Out-of-school suspensions more than doubled to 434, and violent incidents more than tripled, to 44.[8] Chip was, in a way, the victim of bad timing. Had he finished Githens before the merger with Rogers-Herr, he never would have encountered the number of tough street kids who became his suppliers. Had he arrived a couple of years after the merger, when things had settled down somewhat, teachers might have paid more attention to his increasingly errant behavior. But during that first transitional year, he had lots of company in the "bad boy" category, and school authorities had bigger problems to handle than him. Or so they thought.

Progressive Delinquency

Following the footsteps of generations of boys before him, Chip lit his first cigarette in the seventh-grade bathroom. Smoking quickly became more than just a temporary act of rebellion, however; it turned into a conversational tool. "You meet people by going up and asking them if they have a cigarette," he explained one afternoon at a McDonald's restaurant. He had just crawled over a seat to get a light from a leggy brunette puffing away by the window, then returned. "You sit there talking, relaxed, smoking. It's like smoking cigars at a party, or playing golf, or sipping a glass of wine."

He started smoking marijuana for the same reason in the same grade, joining the 9 percent of boys in grades five through eight who report having taken illegal drugs in the past month, a proportion that is increasing.[9] Marijuana makes some people withdraw, but it relaxed Chip and made him feel more outgoing. It was a comfortable antidote to Ritalin, which juiced him up, and he gradually increased the frequency with which he smoked it.

Chip says that during those middle-school years he heard few voices at school telling him not to use marijuana. He hadn't talked about drugs with his parents, who at this point were unaware of his use or of how easily available drugs were. (They were not alone; according to a recent national poll, most parents discount the presence of drugs in their kids' lives.[10])

Moreover, he knew students who used cocaine with no visible ill effects, and, like many adults, he was persuaded more by personal example than abstract facts. What could be wrong with a little marijuana? This is one dangerous side effect of the increase in this country of harder drugs such as crack and heroin among a very small proportion of teens; it makes marijuana seem not so bad to kids looking for just a little high. For Chip, however, there was a lot wrong with smoking marijuana regularly: It exacerbated the symptons of his ADD, including his short attention span, failing short-term memory, and loss of motivation.[11]

By the spring of his eighth-grade year, Marianne and Brian had caught on to some signs of Chip's increasingly serious misdeeds. Brian began noticing that bottles of wine cooler were disappearing from the refrigerator. He discovered a 1-900 phone pornography number charged to his monthly telephone bill. Marianne found a cigarette lighter in Chip's room. Then the elementary school went up in flames, pushing Chip into the category of a serious delinquent.

The Thrill of Leadership

The prosecutor in the arson case, as well as Chip and his family, say Chip and his buddies did not visit their old school intending to burn it down. They went there first to skateboard and, later, to poke around.

Breaking a window to get into a building that was scheduled to be razed didn't seem like a big deal. Constructing a torch to light their way seemed harmless enough. With each small step, Chip exercised more leadership over the four younger boys. He enjoyed the rare feeling of being in charge. Had he not been with a group, he now says, he probably would not have set off on the adventure. The thrill for him was not in destroying property but in leading.

Typically for this kind of crime, Chip did not know his accomplices that well. Neither did his parents, but they let Chip run around with them because the boys came from respectable families. As Brian would wryly say later, "They were the kind of kids we had always hoped he would hang around with."

The four younger boys were tried together first, separately from Chip. Their attorney made the only statement. Then came Chip's trial. At his parents' urging, he spoke directly to the judge. He provided the lighter, he said, but another boy set the can on fire. When the fire started to blaze, they all tried to put it out. It was his idea to break into the school, he said, and he had made a dreadful mistake.

Durham County District Judge Carolyn Anderson gave all five boys the same sentence. Then she turned over their names to Githens school administrators, who suspended the boys for the rest of the year. Chip was called at home and told not to return to the building to pick up his possessions or to say goodbye to his friends.

A Wake-up Call

Eight months later, on Christmas Eve of the year I was observing him, Marianne made a significant discovery.

She had slipped into Chip's bathroom to prepare it for guests who would be visiting on Christmas morning. On the sink, she spied an item that resembled a piece of a marijuana bong. She and Brian confronted Chip. He said he had smoked marijuana in the bathroom earlier that day but swore it was the first time. They were furious and once again grounded him.

They also put their whole family into counseling, which continued on and off for more than a year. In counseling they learned for sure something they had suspected: that covert behavior such as Chip's is the hardest of all problems to identify and treat. A delinquent child detaches himself more and more from the parent, making it hard for the parent to find out what is going on. To further confuse parents, a kid may act out with his friends but be well behaved at home.[12]

Chip had demonstrated small signs of disturbance all along the way: increasing hostility that lasted for days, indifference and lethargy, dropping old friends for children they didn't know. Their alarms hadn't gone off soon enough, however, because most of the traits had always been part of his character. "I was acting weird and they just thought that was normal," Chip would tell me later. Marianne and Brian also thought teenagers were supposed to act erratically and rudely. The myth of adolescence as a naturally turbulent state had blinded them to the fact that something really was wrong with their oldest son.

The tan Plymouth Voyager winds its way up a wooded slope and stops in front of a stately redbrick, plantation-style building. Marianne, casually dressed in khakis and a short-sleeved shirt, hops out and opens up the back doors of the van. "Here are the essentials," she jokes, handing over to Chip a can of air freshener, Roach Bait, a couple of two-liter bottles of diet Coke, and a stack of clean laundry.

It is a balmy Sunday morning in early March, and Chip is back at a military academy after spending the night off-campus with his parents. Marianne and Brian enrolled him at the school in the fall after the fire. "It's like going back to prison," he says to me as we enter the residential hall. We climb four flights of stairs and as we walk down the dark hallway to his room, past rows of narrow doors, all closed, the click of our shoes echoes off a gray cement floor and concrete block walls.

Chip opens the door to the room that he shares with another cadet. It is a narrow, rectangular room with bunk beds on the left, two desks on the right, and a window at the end. The only signs of life hang on the wall over Chip's desk: a cross and posters of singer Bob Marley and Bud Light beer. A photograph of Chip's family taken the previous Thanksgiving at his grandmother's house is pinned to his bulletin board next to a map of Scotland marking the original village of the Thomson clan.

Usually the room is spit-polish neat. But today, something is terribly wrong. "My footlocker's been busted!" Chip cries as we enter. "They've torn pictures off my bulletin board, taken down my mirror . . . Look, one of the black wires running from my CD player to this speaker has been torn. . . ."

"Do me a favor," Marianne interjects. "Let Wes give his side of the story." Chip shakes his head. Wes, his roommate, is not present.

"It's probably not him, it's probably his friends. He lets them in. They've done this before." Chip's voice and shoulders drop as he moves around the room, checking the few personal belongings he is allowed to have.

"Don't get discouraged. Stand up for yourself. You've got to tell someone," Brian says.

"They won't do anything, they never do," Chip shoots back. "I had a black light, and someone colored it in. I've had my shoes stolen. One night, someone wrote all over my desk with a Hi-Liter. No one cares about anyone up here.

"They want us to learn to work together but it's hard when some guys are real jerks."

When they enrolled Chip in military school, Marianne and Brian joined thousands of other families who send their kids to private schools each year. As public schools have grown in size and enrollment, parents have sought out other institutions that offer smaller class sizes and more personal attention from teachers. The Thomsons were looking for something else as well: a more structured environment in which Chip could make new and better-behaved friends. They would soon learn that private schools have their own problems.

Only two private schools in Durham would have considered accepting someone with Chip's history, and officials at both said they had no openings. So the Thomsons decided on the academy, a school of about four hundred students. On paper it had everything they were looking for: a schedule of supervised classes and activities from 6 A.M. to 10 P.M., required military drills, religious devotions, and a student-teacher ratio of 12 to 1. Hazing of freshmen was prohibited, they read in the school's brochures. Talking with the staff convinced them that their annual $15,000 payment would be money well spent.

Progress in the Classroom

Chip told his parents on the phone during the first week of classes that he hated school. He threatened to do something "so terrible that the school will throw me out." But when they visited him on parents' weekend, he asked to go to the gift shop to purchase a school sweatshirt. Adolescents are masters at giving mixed signals. The Thomsons focused on the positive ones.

Academically, Chip did relatively well. For the first time he could remember, he enjoyed math. Pre-algebra, he said, was his favorite subject "because I can do it." The math teacher, he added, was "the best teacher there." All his teachers provided extra help when he needed it, he said, and moved him quickly ahead in his texts when he was ready. "They show they care," he said. How? "They make you do your work. They don't sit down, they walk around the room working with the students."

After dealing for years with schoolteachers who were impossible to track down, Brian and Marianne were amazed to find teachers who returned their phone calls promptly. They appreciated the school's rules. For example, if Chip were caught smoking he would have to march outside carrying a thirteen-pound rifle. Spiritually, Chip seemed to be making progress as well. He read his Bible every night. He joined the Fellowship of Christian Athletes, which met once a week. He volunteered to seat people at chapel services three times a week.

Their relationship with Chip began to improve. "I'd give it a six on a scale of one to ten. It used to be about a two," Marianne said in March, three months after she had found the bong in the bathroom. On home break, he would ask her to take him to the shopping mall, to walk around with him. Sometimes she would put her hand through his arm and he wouldn't resist. Troubled parent-child connections often settle to a slow simmer as the youth enters midadolescence. Marianne and Brian hoped it would last.

From Rejection to Harassment

What wasn't going so well at school was Chip's social life. He didn't have trouble making friends with his roommates, he just had trouble keeping them. Wes was his fifth.

As a freshman in a company of fifty upperclassmen, Chip was, once again, one of the youngest. "They could tell I was not cool," he would recall later. Hazing might not be allowed officially, but cadets on his hall had their own set of rules, as he found out.

His first roommate, a soccer player, stole his homework. His second roommate bossed him around and made him clean up the room. Boys started ganging up on him in the shower. Once they poured shampoo and shaving cream into his sleeping bag; another time, one cadet held him on the floor while several others pummeled him. After that assault, he told his parents, who drove to the school midyear to meet with the assistant commandant. Brian and Marianne were assured that the room-mate would be dispatched and that an unidentified senior on the hall would be assigned to watch over Chip.

Two more roommates followed in short order, then Wes arrived. Chip got along fine with Wes until Wes started bringing in friends who loved to torture Chip.

When Chip telephoned his parents with some of these stories, they didn't know whether to believe him. Adults who run to a crying young child with a concerned "What's wrong?" can find all kinds of reasons to dismiss the negative feelings of the adolescent. Marianne and Brian knew Chip could be belligerent. They knew he didn't trust other people and sometimes didn't listen to legitimate explanations. They suspected he exaggerated others' reactions to him as a way of justifying his own sense of isolation.

Like many parents who leave public schools for private ones, they wanted to believe the school officials, who said everything was under control. By their March visit, however, they had begun to question Chip's safety.

Buying a Protector

When Chip returned to the school after spring break, he had a new roommate, a cadet captain named Seth. Seth had heard about Chip's run-ins with Wes's friends and didn't like what he'd heard. He enlisted the help of a friend named Rhett. Rhett and Chip made an informal deal. Chip would give Rhett some of his Ritalin from time to time. (Ritalin is popular with "normal" kids as a stimulant, particularly before exams.) In return, Rhett, a tall, muscular guy known, as Chip put it, for "kicking kids' butts," would protect Chip. No one messed with Seth and Rhett and, now, no one would mess with Chip, either. "We got very close. I started to enjoy life," Chip would say later.

Marianne and Brian didn't know about this arrangement and if they had known would not have approved. But parents sometimes need to remind themselves that what young people do—even if it's risky or not right—may make sense in the context in which the kids live. School authorities had not been able to stop other cadets from harassing Chip, so Chip did the only thing he knew how to do. He bought himself protection.

Since his Ritalin was rationed through the infirmary, giving some to Rhett meant he didn't always take his prescribed dosages. It is a sign of how important these friendships were that he started doing better in school anyway, probably because he was less afraid and less distracted under the umbrella of his new friends. Shortly before he left school, he was awarded the rank of corporal.

On a balmy summer *night following his year at military school, Chip comes bounding downstairs about nine o'clock. "I'm going for a walk up the street," he says. Marianne and Brian lock eyes.*

"Fifteen minutes," Marianne says.

He's out the door, a clean-cut-looking young man. Polo shirts have replaced surfer shirts, and his long hair is gone. In its place is the military-style buzz he chose to keep. Once again, Marianne and Brian think they're seeing progress and hope it lasts, but they keep him on a pretty tight leash. After he leaves, they settle into the family room to watch television.

Chip's long legs take him to the corner of his street in under a minute. He scans the intersection. In this woodsy neighborhood, a dark sedan is difficult to spot. The driver actually sees him first and pulls over. Chip joins a couple of other guys in the back of the car. The driver hands him a small plastic bag filled with tiny brown buds.

"How much?" Chip asks.

"Twenty-five," the driver replies.

Chip pulls out his wallet. For a couple of years he has been stealing small amounts of money from his parents to support his habit. Now he's making his own money legitimately, bagging groceries at a local super-

market. Still, $25 for such a small amount seems like a lot. He hands over several bills reluctantly.

The driver steers the car onto the road leading out of the neighborhood. Some nights they drive to the parking lot of a nearby gas station that is closed, roll their marijuana into a cigar-shaped "blunt," and smoke. But tonight the driver, Ethan, suggests that they cruise over to his house.

"I can't stay long," Chip says.

Mike, Chip's friend from the previous summer, had introduced Chip to Ethan before Mike headed for California. Chip already knew about Ethan from his days at Githens. A short kid who wore wide-legged jeans, Ethan was always cracking jokes at school and making kids laugh.

Once they are in Ethan's bedroom, the boys put on some Wu-Tang Clan and it booms out through Ethan's giant speakers. They get two bongs going and soon the room is filled with smoke. A couple of them plop down on Ethan's futon; Chip takes the swivel chair under the High Times magazine poster. Like military officers mapping a campaign, the boys trade stories about the relative potency and cost of marijuana strains such as Kind Bud, Chronic, and Commercial. They plan how to buy more drugs and how to expand their sales territory. Chip keeps looking at his watch. A half hour passes, then forty-five minutes. He knows his mother will be getting worried. He starts thinking how to ask Ethan to drive him home.

Marianne is worried. She slips into her car and drives the streets of the neighborhood slowly. She has overheard some conversations on the phone between her son and someone he calls Ethan. Something tells her Chip is with him. So she winds up one street and down another, peering over the headlights into the darkness, looking for someone she knows very well and someone she doesn't know at all.

She gives up after a while and returns home. Just as she is getting out of the car, Chip saunters up the driveway as if nothing has happened.

"Where have you been?" she asks.

"A long walk," Chip answers. "I just needed to clear my head."

Since she has not seen anyone else, Marianne chooses to believe him. But he has broken his curfew. "Tomorrow you're grounded," she says.

Chip decides to sit out on the front porch for a while. As he rocks back and forth in the swing, he thinks ahead to the fall. His parents have agreed to let him go to Jordan High School, his assigned public school, under sev-

eral conditions. He will have to keep a C average, take part in at least one extracurricular activity, and not get into trouble.

He is looking forward to September. Jordan will be easier academically than the military school, and he will fit right in—with the drug crowd.

"No one will be making fun of me anymore," he says to himself.

The darkness that engulfed Marianne and her car on that summer evening could have been a metaphor for how little she knew about Chip and his friends even after all that had happened over the previous year. She didn't have a clue what Ethan looked like. She had seen Mike only once or twice. But . . . the biggest surprise was Ward. Just because parents know the habits of their kids' friends when the friends are young doesn't mean they will know them as those kids get older. They wondered whether they should tell his parents about the kids Ward was hanging out with.

A Hundred Questions

Substance abusers tend to come from lower-income, less well-educated, single-parent families. Brian and Marianne did not fit that mold. They were college-educated professionals pursuing successful careers, who knew enough to have a hundred questions but not enough to answer any with certainty. To their credit, they didn't write off Chip's problems as the result of genes and adoption only.

They had made sure that Chip was supervised after school through sixth grade, but had that been enough? Should one of them have stayed home? Or arranged his or her schedule in order to be at home during critical times such as after school?

Like most of us with a first child, Marianne said she had not foreseen how much time and attention kids, including adolescents, could take. She had not realized how much easier it is—not necessarily easy, but easier—to stay on top of the evolving connection if one is at home much of the time that the adolescent is. Some kids need more monitoring than others; Chip fell into that category.

Another question Marianne asked herself was whether she and Brian should have spent more time with their own friends. As Chip and Justin grew older and more demanding, Marianne and Brian focused on family-related activites: scout meetings, church work, family reunions, and even family therapy. As important as those things were, they crowded out Marianne and Brian's social life. It is a sad fact of contemporary professional life that many of us don't spend the time previous generations did chatting with and helping out friends; we rely on therapists, e-mail, and answering machines instead. If we don't work at having meaningful friendships, how can we expect our children to do so?

When they did things with her family, Marianne wondered in retrospect, should they have encouraged Chip, starting at a young age, to bring friends along on family outings? They might have gotten to know the friends better. They could have observed Chip with friends and been able to advise him later on how to act. One or two of his friends might have struck up a relationship with them as well; it does happen. This could have helped Chip appreciate them more.

Had they not spent enough time volunteering in activities at Githens? When Chip was in elementary school, they had sold books at the book fair and hot dogs at fund-raisers. But when Chip moved to Githens they backed off. "I always got the feeling that Chip did not want me in middle school," Marianne said, a common observation among parents of young adolescents. She now thinks that involvement would have made her privy to the warning system that gossip provides.

She and Brian didn't feel the school counselors and teachers had helped them much, focused as they were on his academic deficiencies. They also wondered how smoking and illegal drugs could be so pervasive at both schools Chip had attended and not attract the attention of school authorities.

A Matter of Containment

Finding the bong in the bathroom on Christmas Eve had jolted Marianne and Brian into their son's world. Their eyes now open, they were able to piece together over the following months what Chip's reality was and shape their behavior accordingly. They stepped up family counseling sessions. They told Chip there were some friends he wasn't allowed to see at all. They began setting rules and consequences and sticking to them. They thought they had been doing that all along but realized that they had allowed Chip to talk them out of enforcement more frequently than they should have.

Sometimes they felt as if all they were doing was containing their oldest's worst impulses as they waited for him to grow up. Chip's adolescence had brought them face-to-face with the fact that sometimes there are no simple answers why kids act the way they do. Because human beings are so complex, no single remedy would turn Chip into a happy, healthy, and responsible kid overnight. The best they could do was to do their best, now that the blinders were off, and take heart from people who said that he was better off with them than without them.

They marveled at the fact that even in his period of heaviest drug use, Chip never stopped believing that he, not the drugs, was winning. Or that he had a future. "After I go to college . . ." he would say regularly and then fill in the blank with something different each time: a policeman, a music producer, even (and he would smile) a psychologist. Marianne would listen to such statements and shake her head. "He gets over things much more quickly than we do," she would say.

Some experts would say he was in denial. But others might suggest that he was a dreamer. Most young adolescents are; it is one of their endearing qualities. As they mature, they begin to shape their dreams according to what is possible, to understand what they have to do or not do to achieve their goals. Some are able to do this by high school, some by college, and some not until their early twenties. Marianne believed Chip would be one of the late bloomers—if she and Brian could get him safely into the next decade.

"Right now, I'm just trying to get him through high school," she said. "Then maybe the military, or a technical school . . .

"If you're waiting for an ending to this story, it isn't going to happen anytime soon."

CHAPTER SIX

Best Friends
(Angela's Story)

It is October 5, and Angela Perales feels she has finally arrived as she cruises through town with her volleyball team in the Ulysses High School homecoming parade. Dressed in Tiger colors of orange and black, and with a black paw painted on her face, she waves from the back of a white pickup to dozens of little kids, who wave back enthusiastically as the truck passes Sullivan Elementary School. A few minutes later, the parade turns onto Wheat Street and glides past Kepley Middle School, where the students do more watching than waving. Angela understands their restraint. In seventh and eighth grades it isn't cool to suggest that you'd give anything to be in a parade.

It has been a great weekend so far. Yesterday she was in the football stand, cheering the undefeated Tigers as they ripped apart the Hays Monarchs 56–14. Tonight, a dance will cap everything off. Only one cloud threatens to rain on her personal parade: Until yesterday she had a date to the dance and now she doesn't.

She isn't allowed to date officially, of course. Martha and Louis Perales, her grandparents who are raising her, consider fourteen too young for dating. But she has a boyfriend, a junior named Lucian, whom she has been "seeing" at school. She learned on Friday that he is ineligible to go to the

*dance because he is flunking three of his courses. She might have been dev-
astated but for one thing. Her best friend, Kimberly, doesn't have a date,
either, and the two of them can go together.*

*Angela got to know Kimberly in seventh-grade basketball. The two girls
passed notes in class and quickly became attached despite obvious differences in background, personality, taste, and looks. Angela comes from a
family of Mexican-American farmworkers; Kimberly's parents are Scotch-
Irish professionals. Angela is a Roman Catholic; Kimberly is a Baptist.
Angela is boisterous; Kimberly is quiet. Angela likes girl-rock; Kimberly listens to oldies or country and western. Angela plays volleyball and basketball aggressively; Kimberly prefers to be team manager. Schoolwork comes
easily to Angela; Kimberly has to work hard to keep A's and B's.*

*They carry their physical contrasts into the gym that night: Angela, tall
and muscular with dark, curly hair, and Kimberly, petite with dark,
straight hair. Almost immediately, they start dancing with Vincent, Abi-
gail, and other friends, coupling and decoupling as kids this age often do.
They confiscate several balloons and engage in a balloon fight. Someone
steals Angela's sandals and hides them in the trash can; she dances bare-
foot for a while.*

*"We had such a good time," she tells Lucian on Monday. "I wish you
could have been there."*

As young adolescents mature, they become increasingly dissatisfied
with cliques and crowds and begin to seek out close friends. Groups can
criticize and ostracize, but best friends value them as they are, even
make them believe they're better than they think. Groups allow them to
try on different lifestyles, including some they know are risky, but best
friends usually encourage them to listen to their better angels.

Intense attachments form much more quickly at this age than at any
other. Overnight, a daughter or son may start talking in reverential tones
about a bosom buddy she or he just met. But these friendships can also disintegrate quickly and therein lies a problem. Other, less desirable acquaintances may be hovering on the fringes, waiting for an opportunity to claim
the adolescent's time. Adults must understand that by themselves, best
friends often cannot silence the competing voices of these others. And, in
cases like Angela's, they also cannot completely fill in the holes of a
painful early childhood. Best friends are valuable but not omnipotent.

A Tough Beginning

Angela's first best friend in adolescence was blond, blue-eyed Stacy Kramer. Besides her fair, good looks, Stacy seemed to have everything Angela didn't, including two loving parents. While Angela called a small, rented bungalow home, Stacy lived in a brick split-level with a backyard deck, patio, and circular drive. Stacy, her parents, and her three siblings were so middle-class wholesome that friends had dubbed them the Brady Bunch, and Angela loved hanging out at their house just to watch them laugh and joke with one another.

One Friday night around Christmas in her sixth-grade year, Stacy and a couple of other girls stopped by Angela's house. The other girls made some unflattering comments about the house, and after that visit Stacy stopped talking to Angela. Angela was devastated. Because Stacy meant everything to her, she assumed she meant everything to Stacy. The two girls didn't talk for the rest of the year.

Angela had trouble replacing Stacy. Other Mexican-American girls thought she was stuck-up, a white wannabe who sought out Anglos to boost her status. And the white girls had already formed their own little cliques. "All these other girls would go to eat lunch with their friends and no one ever invited me. So I, like, hated everyone," she recalled the first night I met her.

She had just come in from pitching a softball game and was talking to me at the linoleum table in her grandparents' kitchen with her grandmother and her younger sister, Alana. Tears rolled down her cheeks. "When someone would ask me over to their house, they'd say, 'Ask your mom,' and I'd say, 'I live with my grandparents,' and they'd say, 'How come?' "

The answer was more complicated and painful than she wanted to tell to a stranger that night. But the shaky attachments of her earliest years helped explain why friendship—what Ralph Waldo Emerson called "the solidest thing we know"—was so important to this fourteen-year-old girl whose bulletin board was covered with more than fifty photographs of friends.

Her father, Harold, started dating her mother, Jessica, when he was in his early twenties and Jessica was in her late teens. An oil rig worker who put in sixty hours of work or more a week, Harold had wanted a child "to settle me down," he said during our first meeting. He and Jessica, living together but not married, had Angela first and, two years later, Alana. They moved into a tiny garden apartment in Garden City, about an hour's drive north of Ulysses.

The two daughters did not slow him down a bit. He would depart from the house at daybreak and return late at night. Jessica, a pretty, slender woman with freckles and blue eyes, wasn't ready to settle down, either. She started drinking, and when Angela was three, left Harold and the kids. She returned six months later, pregnant with another man's child.

Angela learned at a very young age to take care of herself and Alana. She heated up bottles of formula and fed her baby sister while her mother entertained friends on the patio. She went out in search of her mother if Jessica left, going from apartment to apartment with her little sister in tow, asking if anyone had seen her mother. She would cook hot dogs for herself and later for her dad when he got home from work. She taught herself to ride a bike without training wheels and started learning to read. She was four years old at the time.

One night shortly before Angela started kindergarten, Jessica announced to Harold, in front of her daughters, that she was leaving. Harold asked his parents, who had kept Angela and Alana from time to time, if they would take care of the girls temporarily. Louis and Martha were tenant farmers on a large corn and wheat spread west of Ulysses; they were starting to build a little nest egg and thinking about retirement within five to ten years. But they agreed, and their other two grown children offered to help: Louis Jr., a paraprofessional in the school system who lived at home, and their oldest child, Pam, a computer analyst.

"Temporary" turned full-time, and Angela and Alana became two of the rapidly growing number of children—currently about 3.9 million— being raised in grandparent-headed homes.[1] The family of five—Louis Sr., Martha, Louis Jr., and the two girls—lived on the farm until midway through Angela's elementary-school years, when they moved into the small rental house in Ulysses. Louis Sr., nearing seventy by then, took a job as a maintenance man at a motor shop, and Martha went to work cooking at the senior citizen center.

Harold, by then a foreman earning about $50,000 a year—twice what his parents did—settled into a large mobile home about four blocks away. He furnished his new living room with overstuffed couches and the latest in video and sound equipment, including a sixty-inch screen TV. The comfortable, wood-paneled room, so much bigger than any room in her grandmother's house, appealed to Angela as a great place to hang out with friends. But when she would phone on a Friday night to suggest a sleepover, her father would tell her that he was on call or that he was going to St. Louis the next day. As a result she had never spent the night there. "It might have been better if he hadn't been there at all," Angela said during one of our last interviews. "Look up the definition of a dad. I don't have a dad."

Harold was an easy target for Angela's anger because he lived in town. Her mom, who lived out of state, didn't provoke the same amount of rage. Angela cut a stamp-sized picture of Jessica holding her as a baby out of a larger family photograph, placed it in a tiny frame, and tucked it next to the knickknacks in her bedroom bookcase. She wrote Jessica asking if she had been a mistake. No, her mother wrote back.

Jessica called her daughters twice, maybe three times a year. She kept promising that she would visit soon. Harold regularly told Angela that he would take her shopping or swing by her ball game but more often than not he would call and say that something had come up. In Stacy for a while, and later with Kimberly, Angela found girls who would show up on her doorstep when they said they would.

The Value of a Best Friend

She also found someone to whom she could bare her soul, someone who would keep her secrets and help her solve problems. Children share toys with their friends; adolescents share thoughts and feelings. Some psychologists say this intimacy marks the beginning of adolescence.

When she and her dad got into a screaming match because he was reneging on a promised trip to Colorado, she could call Kimberly in tears. When she started hearing rumors that Lucian wanted to break up with her, she could ask Kimberly what Kimberly had heard, knowing she would get an honest answer. When she got a D on a computer science test, Kimberly would assure her that lots of other honor students had done just as poorly. Kimberly often knew what she was thinking before she said anything. "She's living my life," Angela said.

Angela didn't enjoy that kind of intimacy with her family. Like Libby in Los Angeles, she was a forthright, lay-all-the-cards-on-the-table kind of person. But, unlike Libby, she didn't have at home an adult of similar temperament who knew how to listen to and challenge her ideas without sounding judgmental. Effervescent kids like Angela need a listener who can reflect back to them what they've just said. Her relatives tended to listen, keep a check on their emotions, and tell her what she should and should not do. If she spoke privately to one of them, she felt she risked being told she was making a mountain out of a molehill and, later, being lectured by all.

It is important for parents or other caretakers to identify their child's style of communication and, if it differs from their own, to adapt to the child's. Studies of both at-risk kids and high achievers show that a significant predictor of how well they do in school and life is their ability to talk openly with at least one adult with whom they are close—usually a parent.[2] Angela's reticence to talk things over with her family would prove to be a severe handicap later as she faced several crucial life choices.

Her grandparents, uncle, and aunt had woven a protective web around Angela and Alana. Pam would go to bat for the girls at school if she thought they had been wronged; Louis Jr. would watch their faces for signs of unhappiness and stress. Family conferences were called in times of crisis. These strong threads did the job most of the time. The girls were turning into excellent students, competent athletes, and faithful churchgoers. To a maturing Angela, however, the threads of the web felt like rope. Even her uncle Louis, in whom she had once confided, seemed increasingly critical of her. "He doesn't realize the things I feel," she said.

By their own admission, young adolescents are often relaxed and open around friends but critical and withdrawn around parents or others who are raising them. Their "attitude" is not necessarily a sign of trouble, however; frequently it is merely a sign that they know who's in charge at home and are beginning to be uncomfortable with that. This makes egalitarian relationships with friends even more desirable.

Martha, a plump, white-haired woman with a generous nature, understood this. She encouraged Angela's friendship with Kimberly, whom she called "my other granddaughter." She realized Angela needed to let off steam, and that their small home would be more peaceful if Angela was able to do that. She respected Kimberly's mother, Katherine Lasch, comfortable that the Lasches shared her values, and she allowed Angela to go anywhere with her friend. Her trust was well founded because the two girls acted as tethers to each other, talking each other out of doing reckless things.

Once, Angela wanted to sneak out, and Kimberly argued her out of it. Another time, Angela dissuaded Kimberly from throwing a party when her parents were out of town. Friends can persuade an adolescent to try something he or she shouldn't, as Chip discovered, but close friends are a good influence at least as often.[3] Their influence is especially powerful during the period when the friendship is stable and exclusive, as Angela and Kimberly's was for a while.[4]

The Value of a Best Friend's Parent

Angela adopted the Lasches as she had the Kramers, and spent the night frequently in their country-style home. She and Kimberly held private conversations in Kimberly's bedroom, which, unlike Angela, Kimberly didn't have to share with a sister. Sometimes Kimberly's mother, whom Angela called "Mom," would wander in and listen. Angela was constantly comparing herself to her classmates and felt competitive "with everybody over everything," from grades to boyfriends, she said. She took offense easily. With the Lasches, she would spill her guts, then listen as daughter or mother offered advice. "When Angela was in pain, we all were in pain," Katherine Lasch told me.

Because Angela seemed more headstrong and volatile than Kimberly, Lasch had some concerns about Angela's influence on her daughter. Frequently she would find some excuse to check up on Kimberly when Kimberly was with Angela. If the girls headed over to the Pizza Hut for a late-night snack, for example, she might walk in unexpectedly and ask her daughter, "Did I give you enough money?" She told herself that in doing so, she was protecting both her child and her child's friend.

She was the kind of adult confidante from whom all adolescents could benefit—responsive, available, and most important, not related. To adolescents from split families in particular, such adults can mean the difference between normal crises and deep depression. Angela was lucky; the proportion of such adults in lives such as hers is paltry.[5]

Trust can be hard to sustain, even in close friendships, particularly if one's attachments in the early years of life are as fragile as Angela's. Angela had to work harder than she made it appear to maintain her relationships, and even a day or two away from Kimberly and Kimberly's mom could feel like a chasm. The Lasches couldn't provide all the reassurance she needed all of the time, and increasingly she turned to boys to fill the empty spots.

*"**Hey, girl. Me** and Austin are going to Sonic for lunch. Wanna come?" Lucian, Angela's boyfriend, appears at her locker out of nowhere. He is always doing that, showing up unexpectedly, phoning her at odd hours, surprising her with his impersonations. She likes his spontaneity and sense of humor.*

"Sure." She doesn't have to think twice. When the lunchtime bell rings, Angela, Lucian, Kimberly, and Kimberly's boyfriend, Austin, head to the parking lot and pile into Austin's sporty red '96 Ford.

The Sonic drive-in, a favorite hangout for Ulysses teens, is a throwback to the 1950s. Cars pull into their own stalls next to a menu and a speaker phone; customers place their orders and wait for a waiter or waitress to carry their food out. Sonic is famous for its cheese fries and vanilla Dr Peppers. But teens like it because they can be "seen" and talk privately at the same time.

On this particular fall day, Lucian decides to sing to Angela in the backseat. He is a big guy with a black bowl haircut and a goatee that makes him look dangerous. But when he scrunches up his face and croons the words, "You are so beautiful . . . to me," even Joe Cocker couldn't sound any better, Angela thinks.

On her way to class after lunch, Angela runs into John, who is one of the smartest kids in the freshman class. He punches her in the upper arm. "Hey, what's happening?" She punches him back. "Not much. I just ate lunch with Lucian at Sonic."

John looks hard at her and walks on. Lucian is a gangster. What is she doing hanging around with him?

Young adolescents discover that one close friend cannot satisfy all their needs. Thus begins a search for other individual soul mates that can resemble a pinball bouncing from one side of the machine to the other.

Usually the adolescent arrives at a number ranging from three to six, a couple of whom may be friends of the opposite sex.

The Friend Who Happens to Be a Boy

At this age, the separation of the sexes has collapsed in almost all activities, including gym class. Jogging around a track and pitching baseballs together encourage boys and girls to consider each other as more than objects of lust. Teenage boys and girls today enjoy a level of comfort with each other that was unheard of in their parents' generation. This is generally healthy, researchers are coming to believe, because platonic friendships can be protective. Recent research on adolescent friendships in fact recommends that girls be encouraged to hang out with boys who do well in school and don't get into trouble.[6]

During the winter, Angela chose to manage the boys' basketball team. She served the boys water, set up equipment, cleaned up after them, and joked around with them. She was hard-pressed to explain why she would want such a job except to say, "They're my friends."

John, tall, skinny, and blond, was one of them. Angela had met him at the beginning of the school year because his locker was next to hers, and she liked him for many of the same reasons she liked Kimberly. She could tell him anything, seek his advice, have fun with him. He teased her unmercifully, slipping her a liquor-filled chocolate on the school bus and laughing as she spit it out. He made her giggle by prancing around in one of her grandmother's frilly dresses at a family yard sale. One night he surprised her by suggesting they go to the Pizza Hut for dinner; they discussed girl and boy problems. He was smarter, cleaner-cut, and closer to her age than Lucian and other boys she had started running around with. He wished he could steer her away from some of those guys but wasn't sure how to do it.

Being friends with John felt easy to Angela. She enjoyed getting to know boys who weren't her boyfriends, particularly since she had no brothers. Boys enjoyed talking to her about topics they wouldn't discuss with other guys, and she got a charge out of attracting their attention.

The Boy Who Is More Than a Friend

The age when boys and girls start dating has fallen consistently since the 1980s. These days, some boys and girls begin what they call "going with" each other as early as fourth or fifth grade. "Going with" usually means that they talk at lunch or recess, pass notes at school, maybe walk home together. Interest in the other sex fluctuates each year, but by the time they reach ninth grade, at least half report that they're dating, according to one survey, which can mean anything from meeting at the movies to "hooking up" at a party. Like Angela, the majority of the ninth-graders surveyed said they date without their parents' knowledge,[7] a finding replicated in another survey as well.

What prompts such early activity? Experts such as Sarah Brown, executive director of the National Campaign to Prevent Teen Pregnancy, point to a media and fashion culture that trumpets sex and sexiness. Brown also suggests that adults unwittingly launch kids on the road toward dating by saying in jest, but at remarkably young ages, such things as, "Got a girlfriend [or boyfriend] yet?"[8]

Sexual curiosity is always a factor, of course, and today's girls aren't nearly as afraid to explore it as they once were. "We girls have hormones and impulses, too, you know," Angela said. Encouraged by society to be more assertive, many eleven- and twelve-year-old girls think nothing of calling boys on the telephone or asking them out. As they get older, they may be the ones to initiate sexual play.

According to the National Campaign, a research and advocacy organization, parents should discourage or forbid one-on-one dating until a child is sixteen. Dating before then can lead to early intercourse, campaign officials say, and all the risks that accompany intercourse, including pregnancy, disease, and broken hearts.

The research also shows that kids who date early tend to come from single-parent homes and divorced families. But the youths in my study suggested that separation from parents was less significant than the strength of the connections to their parents wherever the parents lived. In particular, girls who had weak or distant relationships with their fathers—sadly, the majority, including some from two-parent homes—sought out boys who paid them special attention.

Lucian did that to Angela. Large for his age, Hispanic in a predominantly Anglo community, son of parents who were separated, and a poor student, Lucian was somewhat of an outcast. Before moving to Ulysses, he had lived in Liberal, a larger community about ninety miles away, where he belonged to the Spanish Disciples gang. He told Angela that he'd had a gun pointed at him twice and that he sometimes carried a knife. There were no gangs in Ulysses, and Lucian insisted that he wasn't a recruiter, but occasionally he would pencil the Spanish Disciples' sign on his notebook or on the corner of a table.

With Lucian, Angela could act any way she wanted, the crazier the better. He took her to lunch, bought her little gifts. The big draw, she told me one evening, was that "he respects me. That's good." Unlike other upperclassmen she was getting to know, Lucian never pressured her to have sex. From the outside, he looked like he could be a bad influence—that's why she had not told her grandparents about his background. But she felt safer with him than with some of the more "acceptable" guys.

Angela "went with" Lucian for several weeks in the beginning of the year. (Dating relationships at this age are notoriously brief.) They broke up because he accused her of flirting with another boy, and she started "seeing" a senior who was a failing student. Within a couple of weeks, she heard rumors that this senior was snorting cocaine.

She left the senior and took up again with Lucian about the time teen heartthrobs Leonardo DiCaprio and Claire Danes were playing Romeo and Juliet on the screen. She saw that movie several times, intrigued that a playwright more than four hundred years earlier had known what it was like for a girl to love a gangster. She bought the CD sound track and listened to it over and over. One song in particular grabbed her, performed by the girl group The Cardigans. Riding around town in Kimberly's car, Angela and her best friend would sing at the top of their lungs, "I don't care if you really care, as long as you don't go." In December, Lucian returned to Liberal.

Sex in a Small Town

Kimberly could not understand Angela's attraction to boys such as Lucian. "Their IQs combined wouldn't match hers," Kimberly said, and she was relieved when the relationships fizzled midyear. The rest of the year, Angela played the field, basking in the attention of upperclassmen. She continued to circumvent her grandmother's dating prohibition by going to movies and parties and leaving early to ride with boys to favorite parking spots, including a railroad trestle known as "the Bridge." Occasionally, her uncle or grandmother would hear about one of her escapades and ground her, but that didn't stop her from sneaking out again.

Some studies of early daters suggest that such relationships are primarily exercises in risk-taking. Angela's flirtations seemed to have had that element, first in choosing two wild young men to go out with, later in where she chose to go. She said she was never seriously in love. She was, however, increasingly physical with some of these guys, enjoying the touching and holding that she didn't get a lot of at home.

Parents who easily demonstrated love when a child was young can be uncertain how to behave once puberty starts. They pull away rather than giving a hug in private, a kiss on the head, a squeeze of the arm. This is unfortunate, Angela and Kimberly agreed one afternoon as we sat in a booth at a popular hamburger joint, because adolescents crave physical contact.

The sixties' songs we were listening to, "My Boyfriend's Back" and "Soul Man," seemed quaint compared to the nineties' trends we were discussing: petting in middle school, oral sex by freshman year of high school, and intercourse by year's end for one-fourth of their fellow freshmen. By the time senior year rolled around, more than half of the seniors would have had intercourse, they predicted. A town survey several months after I talked to the two girls showed that their estimates were not far off, and only slightly higher than national averages. Not "going all the way" with guys who expected it, Angela and Kimberly said, was the single biggest stress they faced.

The two girls had made a pact early in the year that they would not have sex in high school. They were up against enormous odds, however, precisely because so many of the couples they knew were already so engaged. Parents often worry about the effect on their child of certain promiscuous kids in a class. If there are not many such kids, they probably needn't worry. But if the proportion is as high as half of the class, they should pay attention, because the risk of sexual debut for all kids goes up.[9]

Angela said there was another reason kids her age had sex: "What else is there to do?" Ulysses offered little entertainment for teenagers other than traditional school activities, such as sports and occasional plays. One cinema showed one movie, which changed once a week. There was a small bowling alley but no ice skating rink, shopping mall, dance club, or video arcade. The nearest large town, Garden City, was an hour's drive away along a dark country road, not the kind of route parents wanted their kids to take on a weekend night.

As we saw with Libby in LA, teenagers need safe, chaperoned places to get together. In Ulysses, the situation was going from bad to worse, from the teens' perspective. A teen center that held dances every weekend was closed the year I was there for being a fire hazard. A bond issue (promoted by Shannon's father, Gary) was put on the ballot to support the construction of a new community center that would have included a large, separate space for teens. But it was defeated as being too costly, even though the solidly middle-class town could have paid for it in less than three years. The directors of the senior citizen center, which sat vacant on weekends, refused to allow dances there, saying they were afraid teens would damage the building. The only spot teenagers claimed as their own on weekend nights, other than the Bridge, was a parking lot downtown, but the sheriff's department threatened to run them off.

Having a Baby

The first day I met the Perales family, Martha had just returned from a party for a fifteen-year-old friend of Angela's who was seven months pregnant with twins. During that school year, twenty-five high-school girls were either pregnant or had recently had a baby; at least two middle-school girls were pregnant as well. A candidate for homecoming king was a father (the year before, the homecoming king himself had been a father); a cheerleader was a mother, and in the spring, a star athlete on Angela's softball team became pregnant. Grant County's rate of teenage pregnancy jumped that year from the eighth highest in the state to second.

Mirroring a national trend, these young mothers were keeping their babies, partly because abortion in the highly religious community was discouraged and the closest hospital performing abortions was four hours away. Giving the babies up for adoption was also discouraged among Mexican-American families, and increasingly Anglo girls followed in the footsteps of their Hispanic friends, deciding to raise their babies with the help of their families. The stigma of single parenthood in Ulysses, as elsewhere, was virtually nonexistent, according to the director of a teen pregnancy program in the community.

Angela promised herself that if she ever slept with a boy she would make sure he was wearing a condom. (Acquiring birth control pills violated her Catholic upbringing.) She didn't rule out having sex sooner than her grandparents would have liked. She certainly was not going to wait until she got married. Why should she? Her parents didn't.

Her grandparents, approaching their fiftieth wedding anniversary, were one model of restraint, her uncle Louis another. But her mother was eighteen when she got pregnant with Angela and she never married Harold, a fact Angela learned only shortly before I met her. Jessica had then had a baby girl by another man, and after Harold split up with Jessica he fathered another woman's son. Angela talked to her half-sister and half-brother on the phone and each year taped their school pictures on her bedroom wall.

As she became increasingly involved with boys, Angela worried that she might become "just like my mother." Unless someone pointed out to her regularly the many ways in which she differed from her mom, this fear could become a rationalization for doing things she wouldn't be proud of.[10] But, except for Kimberly, no one came forward to discuss these worries with her and to offer support.

She also did not seek help. Like most of us, she found it difficult to talk about her physical desires and the conflicts she felt. Adults whom she might have sought out lectured too much, she said. At church, her confirmation class teacher told her that sex before marriage was sinful. At school, guest speakers preached about sexual diseases that would scar girls and boys for life. Her grandmother didn't invite conversation, preferring instead to give her articles to read or quick admonishments such as "Just remember, if you got pregnant you couldn't play sports."

Martha opened her home to the "good kids" with whom Angela was close, like Kimberly, Stacy, and John. She discouraged risky associations when she knew about them, and she never stopped reminding Angela of the severe consequences of certain actions. But what she didn't do—and what a wealth of research now shows that parents or caretakers need to do—was establish a running, age-appropriate dialogue with Angela about love and sex from the time she was very young. Talking about the physical and emotional implications of sex will not cause a child to run out and experiment, as many parents fear. Neither will explaining one's own feelings and values in very specific terms, such as "I want you to wait until you're married," or "Wait until you're in college." Kids hate "The Big Talk," but they are hungry for good advice on how to say "no" and how to manage emotional relationships.[11]

Martha was not alone in her reticence. Surveys show that the majority of parents do not discuss sexual relationships with their kids in a comprehensive way, which is why an increasing number of churches and other organizations now run sex education programs or offer courses for parents on talking to kids about sex.

Her fear of getting pregnant was Angela's main restraint from "going all the way." She didn't want to disappoint her grandmother, and she didn't want anything to interfere with her dream of becoming the first child in her family to graduate from a four-year university.

That dream was significant. One possible explanation for some teenage pregnancies is that the girls see limited choices for their future and exercise little power in their world until they have a baby.[12] Angela believed—on some days more than others—that she did have a choice. A mention of the University of Notre Dame, or East Texas State, which boasted one of the country's top women's volleyball teams, made her eyes light up. "Work at your dream every chance you get," her uncle Louis told her.

But expectations can dim as young adolescents get older and reality sets in. As Angela headed into winter, she worried more and more about how she would pay for college. Her family couldn't provide a quick answer to that question. Would a dream about a school she had never visited, paid for by funds she didn't have, be enough to keep her from having sex? Would her promise of abstinence to Kimberly hold up? By early January, she wasn't sure of the answer to either question.

. . .

On a hot, dusty June night, Angela arrives home from a softball game and collapses on the couch. "You better go on to your room," her grandmother suggests. Any other night Angela might have argued, but she is too tired to fuss. She rises, walks the few steps to her doorway, and freezes. Stacy is sitting on her bed waiting for her, has been there in fact for a couple of hours.

Angela can't believe it. After their contentious sixth- and seventh-grade years, she and Stacy had reconciled in Bible school during the summer after seventh grade. In eighth grade they spent most of their free time with Kimberly. The three girls formed a detective squad and solved imaginary cases. They talked about politics and debated which of them would someday be president. They took turns spending nights at each other's houses, and Angela was in heaven, having two best friends.

Near the end of eighth grade, however, Stacy phoned her one night and told her that Amoco Oil, Stacy's father's employer, was transferring the Brady Bunch to Tulsa.

Less frequent contact with a friend often weakens the bond, but Angela worked hard at staying in touch with Stacy the year after she left. The two wrote each other almost every week and telephoned every other month.

The week that Stacy returns for a visit, she and Angela are inseparable. One afternoon they pick up Kimberly and head for Duckwall's Variety Store on Main Street, where they buy plastic handcuffs, a toy gun, and masks. On their way back to Kimberly's, Stacy and Kimberly don the masks and pretend to hold up Angela. A few minutes later they cross the street to their old elementary school and play tag in the schoolyard. "It was just like old times," Angela recalls later.

The night before Stacy leaves for Tulsa, the three friends spend the night at Kimberly's and watch a movie: A Very Brady Sequel.

So many things seem out of the young adolescent's control: body changes, assigned subjects at school, parents' relationships to each other, how much money her family has. Friendship can be just as ephemeral. Friends can fight with you, break up with you, or move away. Some families had lived in Ulysses for several generations, but others came and departed according to the whims of the area's major employers, the oil and gas companies. Far more families were in transition than one might have assumed in this sleepy little Midwest community. And so were the friendships.

Learning About Yourself, Good and Bad

Angela had matured a lot the last year Stacy lived in Ulysses, in part, she said later, because of Stacy's family. The Kramer children were individualists, encouraged by their parents to speak their minds. Angela, outspoken by nature, felt confirmed by them. "Stacy taught me to be myself, not to follow the crowd," she said. This conviction had a very positive side: When other students gave her a hard time about making A's in school, or accused her of "kissing up" to the teachers, she was able to shrug off their comments and keep studying.

Stacy and her family applauded Angela's community involvement. They commented when Angela sang and led the hymns at mass or ran the video camera at the Christmas bazaar. Angela kept abreast of who was ill in the community, who had died, and who had given birth, to an extent unusual for someone so young, the Kramers noticed.

Throughout ninth grade, Angela showed remarkable empathy for others: On her volleyball team, she regularly encouraged her teammates; in a reading class, she lent a book to a girl who was about to receive detention for forgetting hers; in a health class, she deliberately held back a ditto sheet she had finished until other, slower students were ready to turn in theirs.

At the same time, her independent streak was evolving into an in-your-face attitude toward her family and the values her grandparents held dear. So what if she stayed out past her curfew? So what if she was acquiring a reputation around boys? Who cared, really?

Kimberly cared, but she and Angela had fought during the latter part of the year over Austin. Austin was Kimberly's boyfriend and also a close friend of Angela's. Kimberly kept hearing rumors that Angela and Austin were more than friends. Angela denied it, but Kimberly wasn't convinced. Conventional moral standards, sworn between friends early in adolescence, become harder to keep as friends get older. When even one standard is violated, the friendship feels severed.

Angela suspected that Stacy wouldn't approve of some of her actions, either. Friends help you discover who you are by allowing you to be who you are not—but only to a point, she thought. "Stacy wouldn't like me if she knew everything I do," Angela said. By the end of the year, she found herself being more guarded with Stacy on the phone, and that felt dishonest. "All we share now is the past," she said, sounding the plaintive note of many who have headed down a path in life that differs significantly from the life of a previously close friend.

Teenagers are notoriously fickle, moving in and out of friendships over the course of a year. Only about one-third of them report having friendships that last more than a year.[13] Earlier stages of friendship are easier. In sixth and seventh grades, kids seek out friends with whom they can share activities: playing ball and going to the movies. In eighth grade, an understanding ear and loyalty are most important. But by the time they reach ninth grade, young adolescents are beginning to look for girls and boys whose backgrounds, values, and character resemble theirs.

Like most kids her age, Angela was not yet sure which values to claim. She could be sweet-natured toward her friends one day and mean the next. She could swear to her grandmother that she would stop seeing a particular boy and then hook up with him at a party the following weekend. These inconsistencies bothered her now that she was able to reflect more deeply on her actions and better anticipate the negative consequences. As she put it, "In high school, you find out what you're capable of. You don't think you'll do things, then you do."

Conflict among friends frequently is higher in this third stage of friendship, but friends can learn to accept each other's contradictory qualities.[14] Angela didn't know that. From what she had observed as a child, when a relationship became uncomfortable, you walked away and sought another.

Each night, in a journal that by the end of the year filled 366 pages, Angela would analyze that day's events, victories, and discontents. "Ga, this town is boring," she wrote one night. "There are probably a lot of parties going on, but they are all drinking parties. Drinking is nasty."

Another evening she described in detail her confusion about a particular boy. Then she wrote: "I just realized you are the only true friend I have because I can tell you everything and you never ever get mad. Thanks truly!" Angela figured she would have to be her own best friend, at least until she found someone who would like the person she was becoming.

AS PARENTS WE CAN

• Encourage our child in her effort to find a good group of kids to run around with, and keep our home open to friends all the time.

• Stay on top of the kids in his circle by listening to the parents' grapevine at school, games, and concerts.

• Listen to her casual remarks about the boys and girls with whom she would like to spend time.

• Inquire about the relationships his friends have with their parents.

• Refrain from automatically blaming her friends if she starts acting out. Instead, ask questions: Is her life missing something? Is she under unusual stress? Is she following the example of adults she knows?

• Expand conversations about sexuality to include relationship issues such as hurt feelings and loyalty.

• Show physical affection regularly, in appropriate ways.

• Keep family time sacred and give him plenty of opportunity to choose what to do. Be a good companion.

• Make time for our own friends.

PART THREE

Learning In and Out of School

Alana takes one taste of the gelatinous mass she has made and smiles. It is sweet, cold, and creamy—just the way ice cream should be.

Ice cream in science class? Proof to some parents at Kepley Middle School that Alana's science teacher is daffy. But proof to many sixth-graders who have had Ruth Cones over the past twenty-five years that their teacher is cool. Making ice cream is a great way to watch liquids turn to solids and a pretty good reason to discuss chemical reactions.

Cones, a plump, curly-haired woman who tends to speak in exclamation points, believes that students Alana's age learn basic facts best by using objects that relate to those facts. With her own money as well as the school's, she has set up a series of experiments through which her students rotate, in pairs. During her one semester with Cones, Alana studies energy by twirling a yo-yo, electricity by taking apart a radio, and machines by working levers and pulleys.

"Students this age are like little sponges going suck, suck, suck, at every little detail you give them!" Cones proclaims during an interview. She knows what some adults don't: Young adolescents are easy to inspire. They are beginning to catch on to the power of their minds and think of themselves as learners. It's a big piece of their identity puzzle. In one national survey, two out of three teens polled just before their school year said they looked forward to "learning new things," a proportion almost as large as those who said they were eager to join "the social scene." The two responses are not exclusive. Kids' interest in each other can be used to encourage learning, as Cones knows when she pairs up her students.

The middle-school years will be a turning point in Alana's education. If her performance is going to slide, it likely will begin to do so then. If it is going to take off, these years will provide the launch.

To take the giant intellectual leap for which her brain is preparing, she needs adequate physical resources: clean, safe, and cheerful classrooms; modern science laboratories; textbooks she can take home; and a well-stocked library, including great books as well as computers. Such resources show her that learning is valued by the adults of her community and that *she* as a learner is valued. She also needs the emotional resources available in classes that are not too large, where teachers have time to get to know how she learns and can tailor standards of achievement that are high but not impossible to meet. And she needs parents or other caretakers who are familiar with the challenges she faces at school and who support her accordingly. In chapter seven, "Little Rodney" Kincaid demonstrates what can happen if a child does not enjoy such resources and expectations for learning.

In chapter eight, Jessica Johnston's experience will demonstrate how fiercely today's young adolescents wrestle in the classroom with ethical concepts. Middle schools have become the laboratories in which communities work out complicated moral issues of race, ethnicity, and income disparity; middle-school students are the laboratory rats. Jessica's year illustrates that some teachers run the experiments better than others.

Chapter nine's Jack Richardson will take you out of school almost entirely to look at the learning that can take place when a child assumes a hobby or a job. You will see how parents who feel limited in their influence over a kid's performance in school can, outside of school, fuel a love for learning that can accompany their child for years to come.

Such motivation is essential because the goal for kids like Rodney, Jessica, Jack, and Alana is to take charge of their own learning. If parents and teachers inspire them to become their own best teachers, they will clamor for better resources and seek out resources on their own. They will set their own standards and try to attain them. They will learn to tol-erate poor teachers and to engage good teachers. They will be on their way toward a rich and fulfilling life, instructing and amusing any adults who are willing to observe and listen.

CHAPTER SEVEN

Low Expectations
(Rodney's Story)

Amid the early-morning bedlam of the front office at Audubon Middle School, a dark-skinned, bulky eighth-grader named Roosevelt offers to lead me to room 203. As we wind our way down long concrete corridors and across a vast quadrangle, I am grateful for his help. No wonder they call this a campus. The seven buildings, separated from one of the poorest communities in Los Angeles by a high, wire fence, would comfortably accommodate a small college. Only the occasional sneaker-clad child slipping between buildings reminds me that this is a school serving eleven-, twelve-, and thirteen-year-olds.

Roosevelt brags that his school won a beautification award because of the raised bed of green grass and mature trees that break up the gray of the quad. Would I like a quick tour? No thank you, I reply, for I have spotted a dark, shaved head no bigger than a peanut peering out an upstairs window and I know that Little Rodney is waiting.

I had met Rodney Kincaid, called "Little Rodney" by his mom and dad, at home the previous morning when both his parents were off work. Right away I was struck by his small, slender stature. Dressed in a fuchsia T-shirt and matching shorts, he couldn't have been more than four-feet-six. His arms and legs were no bigger around than broomsticks. The hormones of

*puberty that spur bone, muscle, and head growth were working slowly in
this one, I thought.*

He smiled a lot, a big wide grin, and his eyes never left my face as I
talked at the dining room table with his parents, Veronica and "Big Rodney" Kincaid. He flitted like a mosquito on the periphery of our conversation, occasionally buzzing in with a few witty words of his own. As I
prepared to leave, I said I might meet him at school the next morning. His
parents, both college-educated, seemed like solid representatives of the
black middle class who enjoyed an easygoing relationship with Rodney
and his older sister. I probably could learn a lot from them. But several
questions nagged at me about Rodney. Was he mature enough? Would he
have enough to say? Several other kids seemed more likely choices.

I opened the door of my rental car, and as I turned toward the house one
last time I spied him alone on his gray-and-white front porch, waving. "See
you tomorrow!" he sang out in a sweet, high voice that pierced my doubts.
He had, in fact, chosen me.

As Roosevelt and I approach the classroom, Rodney is waiting, dressed
in the school uniform of gray flannel slacks and a white short-sleeved shirt.
An amiable-looking white man in his late thirties is expecting us; he
unlocks the classroom door and ushers me into a plain classroom sparsely
decorated with posters of Martin Luther King, Jr., Cesar Chavez, Gloria
Estefan, and a map of the United States. He introduces himself as Steve
Marcy, Rodney's English and social studies teacher. "It's kind of wild in
here right now," he apologizes.

He explains that the students, grouped in threes, are working on reports
about a newspaper article of their choice. One student in each group is
supposed to read the article and tell the others what it's about. Another student is a reporter who writes a story about the article. The third is a tester
who makes up questions about the article. The students are to decide
among themselves who will play which role.

Shredded remains of the Los Angeles Times and Los Angeles Daily
News litter the brown linoleum floor. Students are huddled, some working
together quietly, others arguing over which article to summarize and who
should assume each task. Rodney's group is having trouble deciding
among several sports stories. Finally they agree, and Martin, the biggest
talker, parcels out the roles.

"I'll be the teacher," he announces. "John, you be the reporter, and Dar-rell, you be the tester. Now let's get started." This group, unlike most of the others, has four members, and Martin has given out only three roles.

"Who will I be?" Rodney asks himself so softly that only I can hear him. "I'll be nobody. That's good."

Not that long ago, the middle grades, whether they were called junior highs or middle schools, were little more than holding tanks. Educators didn't expect much intellectually from their students because science was telling them that young brains went into hibernation at about age twelve and woke up at about age sixteen. What their students really cared about was socializing, so the theory went, and a school's job was to keep the hormones at bay until pupils moved on to high school.

These assumptions began to be questioned in the late 1980s. Organizations such as the National Middle School Association and the Carnegie Council on Adolescent Development argued that young adolescents were smarter than had previously been believed and vastly underchallenged. As neurobiological research progressed through the 1990s, scientists began reporting that, from about age eleven, the brain's frontal lobes grow, particularly in the spread of cells that enable the child to select and act on knowledge accumulated in earlier years. At rates that vary with the individual, ten- to fifteen-year-olds can think more quickly than before, reason more abstractly, solve problems more creatively, and work better in groups.[1]

"Young adolescents are capable of far more than adults often assume," the National Middle School Association wrote in 1995, urging teachers and administrators to "hold and act upon high expectations for all students."[2]

"High expectations" has become a cliché today, but their importance for young adolescents cannot be overemphasized. Why? Because by fifth or sixth grade, kids are more sensitive to what others think of them—and more likely to believe those assessments—than they will ever be again. When they move into high school, as we saw in the last chapter with Angela, they will begin to form their own judgments about what they are good at and not so good at. But the evaluations of others during those middle-school years will whisper to them ever so softly and persistently for years to come. As psychologist Jacquelynne Eccles says, "Kids will leave early adolescence either believing in their own potency or doubtful about it."

Over the last decade, many middle schools and junior highs have restructured themselves to better serve their students. They have grouped pupils into teams of eighty to a hundred and twenty kids who share the same teachers. They have instructed teachers to assess children's abilities individually and to teach lessons that will move children forward at their own best paces.

Audubon Middle School, in South-Central Los Angeles, adopted these strategies but did not have the resources to fully carry them out. As Rodney's sixth-grade year demonstrated, high expectations can diminish considerably when learning resources are inadequate, when teachers are poorly trained and given more students than they can handle, and when parents are distrustful of the school. Kids quickly pick up on what is expected of them as learners not only by the way they are grouped but also by the school buildings into which they are sent, the classwork and homework they are assigned, the men and women they are provided as teachers, and the attention and emotional resources they receive from parents.

Crowded Schools, Crowded Classrooms

Built for eighteen hundred students and holding twenty-one hundred, Audubon was too big for children just out of elementary school. Child psychologists and educational researchers have long agreed that middle-level schools should have no more than eight hundred students. Anything larger makes it easy for students to get lost, especially marginal students. Many of these students never establish that feeling of connectedness to one or two teachers and one group of kids that can inspire effort and learning.[3]

During his first two weeks of school, Rodney took English, social studies, math, and science with more than forty other students in each class, or fifteen more per class than is recommended for his age. The number was pared to thirty-five after additional teachers were hired, but very little work got done during those first two weeks. Rodney quickly figured out where he could sit in each classroom—usually in the front row in the corner—to be away from troublemakers and the teacher's eye. As his experience with the newspaper group assignments indicated, he was not one to seek out work or attention.

He could sit for three weeks next to someone who did not know his name. On that first day I observed Rodney's class, Steve Marcy passed out books for silent reading. Rodney read with his seatmate, Estevan Abolanos, who had chosen a big picture book about the animal kingdom.

In a few minutes, Rodney sidled up to tell Marcy something. Marcy walked to the front of the class and cleared his throat. "Rodney tells me that some of you are saying he is a foster child and that is why we have someone in the room observing him this morning. That is not the case." He explained why I was there.

Estevan raised his hand. "Who's Rodney?" he asked.

Navigating Solo

Rodney belonged to a team of about 120 sixth-graders, all of whom were taught English and social studies by Marcy, math and science by a woman named Golden Quinn, and electives by several other teachers. The team offered a certain degree of intimacy, but Rodney still felt overwhelmed by the sheer logistics of changing classes and teachers and keeping up with his assignments. He knew the school presented opportunities for learning new skills and having fun, but he didn't know how to go after them.

As he was playing a Super Munchers vocabulary game on the computer, for example, a voice erupted over the loudspeaker: "All students are expected to fill out their ballots for student government."

"Who's running?" Rodney wondered to himself as he moved from Munchers to Print Shop. "Do I know them?"

After reciting the pledge of allegiance, the disembodied voice continued. "Band tryouts will be in room 401."

"Where is 401?" Again, he was talking to himself.

As they move through adolescence, most kids will acquire what psychologists call a sense of self-efficacy: a belief that they can accomplish tasks they set for themselves and the knowledge that when they have questions, they know how to find the answers. In sixth grade they are just starting down that road and can benefit enormously from regular adult assistance. Some kids need more attention than others.

Rodney was one of those. He needed someone who would seek him out to ask what he was interested in knowing about the school, someone who not only could tell him where the band room was but would take him there and encourage him to try out a horn. As we saw with Eric, even small accomplishments can bond kids to school and make learning seem less burdensome. Rodney, like many kids in middle school, simply heard what programs were available. The rest was left up to him.

Rote Learning

Teachers in the holding-tank schools of the 1970s and 1980s strove for what was called "horizontal enrichment" of their students as opposed to individualized instruction. They presented the same lessons at the same time in the same manner to all their students. The lessons usually consisted of lectures at the blackboard followed by questions and reading from textbooks.

This teaching style, sometimes derided as "the sage on the stage," fell out of favor in middle schools for a while but gradually has wormed its way back into many classrooms, partly because of the increasing emphasis in school districts on standardized testing and memorization.

Rote instruction filled Rodney's day after the newspaper assignment, beginning with social studies.

A student handed out textbooks, and Steve Marcy wrote a question on the blackboard: "What does it mean to be a U.S. citizen?" Three hands shot up, led by Estevan, whose parents immigrated to the United States from Mexico.

Marcy was not actually seeking an answer or a discussion. He was looking for something more basic. "How would we begin to answer the question?" he asked the class.

"With a complete sentence," a girl answered. Marcy nodded, then continued. "What is the question one wants to know?" After several shrugs and wrong answers, he called on a student who understood. "The question one wants to know is what does it mean to be a U.S. citizen," she replied.

Marcy nodded. "Now who can find the answer in the book? Use your scanning finger . . ."

A boy read, "To be a U.S. citizen means to be a member of our nation."

By now, Estevan was staring out the window. Rodney, back in his seat, had written two words: "The question."

"If you answer all your questions like this, in complete sentences, you'll get A's and B's," Marcy said. "Teachers love complete sentences." He posed a final question. "The three ways a citizen can become involved in American government are . . . ?"

Finish the sentence, he told the class, and get the answer out of the book. "Teachers want the answers in the book."

Rodney's right index finger searched for the right paragraph. He copied directly from the book onto his paper "1. Voting, 2. Working for a political party, and 3. Taking direct action."

"I got it!" he muttered. "Hallelujah!"

Marcy had started out the year hoping to teach primarily in groups. He had read that students in small groups learn assigned material more quickly, develop a better attitude about learning, and think better of themselves. What he did not realize at first was that small-group instruction requires a healthy investment of teacher training and preparation time. He didn't have enough of either. He gave Rodney and his classmates too much control—allowing them to decide their roles, for example, a tactic that would have made even adults uncomfortable. The result was confusion, and after a couple of other attempts at grouping, he gave up. "They just can't handle groups," he told me, obviously disappointed.

I heard this complaint frequently from other teachers in other schools all year. There was some truth in it: Over the last decade, more and more students whose learning and behavior problems once would have kept them separated have become a part of regular classrooms. As classes have grown and students become more diverse and challenging, teachers have resorted to routine methods of teaching to maintain control.

This is unfortunate because children's brains develop in fits and starts, and each young adolescent is different, depending on physical maturity and past experiences. Some students in Rodney's class had no trouble reading a page and quickly summarizing the key concepts; some could hypothesize new scenarios from what they read; and some, like Rodney, were happy when they could simply repeat a couple of paragraphs. To expect all of these students to learn the same information the same way was not only wrongheaded but could actually stunt their cognitive growth. Stimulating them with material slightly beyond their capabilities—and using both group and individualized instruction to help them stretch—could encourage higher-order thinking skills and a more mature attitude toward learning.

Steve Marcy was correct that many of the students needed help in focusing their thoughts on "the question(s) we need to know." Organization is not a high priority for most kids this age. The workings of Rodney's mind resembled his home, a place of casual chaos with clothes strewn about and tables piled with knickknacks, papers, and hairbrushes. Writing down the question his teacher asked, then the answers as they appeared in his social studies book, swept away some of his brain's clutter, making room for learning.

Confining instruction to mechanics, however, ignored the way Rodney and his classmates learned. Basic skills are retained longer if they are included in a curriculum to which the children can relate personally. Judging by the hands that went up when Marcy asked what it meant to be a U.S. citizen, several students would have liked to discuss the question. Estevan, for one, could have told his classmates about his parents, who had recently been awarded citizenship. Other students might have enjoyed voicing their opinions on whether illegal immigrants should receive social services, a hotly debated issue in California at that time. The students could have been encouraged to see how issues surrounding immigration resembled their own struggles to be accepted by cliques at school. Such dialogue would have signaled to the students that they were intelligent and had ideas to contribute. A dumbed-down exercise suggested to them that they were, well, dumb.

Teacher Training

Marcy had had very little training in how to make groups work. He had become a teacher four years earlier, having spent fifteen years selling car stereo systems. A bachelor's degree from college (where he majored in drama), twelve credit hours of instruction in education, and a brief internship in an elementary school qualified him to exchange warfs and woofers for chalk and blackboard. His biggest hurdle, he said he realized very quickly, was that schools of education "don't train you to teach."

Like other systems around the country, the Los Angeles Unified

School District suffered from a chronic shortage of teachers, particularly for the middle years. As a result, district officials had loosened considerably the credentials needed to teach either full-time or as a substitute. Marcy was able to leap into the void.

Dressed the first day we met in khakis, a gray T-shirt, and Converse sneakers, he told me that he had been drawn to teaching because "you work nine months, and then there's June, July, and August!

"My wife's a teacher," he continued. "I thought it sounded like fun. I like the regular paycheck." He discovered he also liked kids. "At this age, especially," he said. "They still like their parents and their teachers."

Marcy was patient, upbeat, and had a biting sense of humor that kids like Rodney reveled in. But an expert in the unique needs and capabilities of young adolescents he was not. He taught by instinct, not principle, and had never been evaluated by his administrators.

Middle-school and junior-high teachers are probably the most ill prepared of their profession. Most have been trained in elementary-school education, as Marcy was briefly, a few in a high-school discipline such as science or English. Only about one in five has had any undergraduate training in teaching young adolescents.[4]

Few of the teachers I met had majored or minored in college in the subjects they were now expected to teach. If teacher expertise accounts for as much as 40 percent of variation in student achievement, as studies show, their students were at a big disadvantage.

The most capable, successful teachers I observed taught me this: To teach students just beginning to delve deeply into core subjects, it's not enough just to love or understand kids. You also have to know and love your subject and keep up with the knowledge base that supports it. Partly that's because the world is changing and so is what kids need to know. And partly it's because knowledge and love of knowledge are essential to inspiration. To reach kids these days, with all the distractions that pull on them, you have to inspire them. Teachers trained in specific disciplines tend to do that.

"Mr. Bald-Headed Man"

Students' need for sophisticated, well-trained teachers highlights a very real problem: the abundance of substitute teachers used in middle schools and junior highs. Not long into my year of observation, I started noticing that every child I was following had at least one sub at any given time. Two of them, including Rodney, were instructed by substitutes who taught them for more than a month. This was not a statistical aberration, I would later learn. Climbing enrollments, an aging teacher workforce, and increased demand by regular classroom teachers for out-of-school training have sent the number of substitute teachers in this country soaring. With demand exceeding supply, some states have lowered their qualification for "emergency subs" to a high-school diploma.

Rodney's class loved their regular math and science teacher, Golden Quinn, a patient, experienced teacher who always found something positive to say to a child no matter how he or she answered a question. Early in the school year, however, Quinn's mother became seriously ill and she went on leave. A substitute took her place. The first day I followed Rodney around was the sub's first day teaching Rodney's class.

The kids called him Mr. Bald-Headed Man. He was young, had thinning hair, and was smartly dressed, sporting a white shirt, dark navy blazer, gray slacks, and cordovan loafers. He told me he had been a math major in college and a counselor to youngsters at the local Boys & Girls Club. He was looking forward to explaining integers, decimals, and division.

But the instructions Quinn had left told him to emphasize order and following directions. As a regular substitute three to four days a week, he knew the key to getting called back was to do what the regular teacher told you to do.

Seconds after Rodney and his classmates were in their seats, two boys came straggling in. Immediately, the substitute sent them to stand in the back of the room. "I'm going to take attendance now," he said to the rest of the students. "Just raise your hands. Don't say, 'Here.'" Several students spoke up anyway and they, too, were dispatched to the back of the room.

Worksheets and textbooks entitled *Introduction to Mathematics* were passed out. Voices escalated.

"I'm going to turn off the light and when I turn it back on, I don't want to hear any talking." Banks of fluorescent lights blinked off, then on again. The din subsided but did not disappear. This time, two chatty girls were sent to the front corners of the room.

"Everyone look at your worksheet," he continued. "This is not difficult at all. Let's read the directions. You are to build a chain of mathematical words. Choose a word. The next word must begin with the last letter of the first word you chose. Each time you write a new word, draw an arrow from the last letter of the last word to the first letter of the new word."

One boy asked if they could work in groups. The substitute said no. "This is not an exercise in learning new words," he reminded the class. "This is an exercise in learning to follow directions."

Math is Rodney's favorite subject. He went right to work. "Divide," he wrote. Then, "equation." Then "negative integer." He picked the words out quickly from the glossary in the back of the book, not pausing to read the definitions. Meanwhile, his teacher had run out of corners into which he could send talkative students. He started taking down names instead, and informed those acting out that they would have to write two hundred times: "I will not talk in class." As the end of the class period approached, everyone's name was on the list except Rodney's and Estevan's.

Rodney raised his hand and pointed proudly to his completed worksheet. The substitute walked over to examine it. "The answers are right," he said. "But you've got the arrows all mixed up. You have to follow directions. Go get another worksheet and do it over again."

Mr. Bald-Headed Man subbed in this class for five weeks. Rodney never had to stand in the corner, but he later said, "I didn't learn nothin'."

"Two households, both alike in . . . What's that word?" Rodney, slowly reading aloud, is stumped before he finishes the first line of Romeo and Juliet.

"Dignity," Veronica replies.

"Ddddddd . . . ," Rodney stutters. Veronica, a slender woman with a model's angular features, lays her hand gently on his forearm.

"Take a deep breath," she counsels.

"Dd . . . dignity!"

His face lights up and he continues. "In fair Verona . . . Hey, that's like your name!" he exclaims.

Veronica sighs. "Yes, now go on."

"In fair Verona, (where we lay our scene) / From an-ci-ent grudge break to new mu-ti-ny . . . . Mama, what does that mean? Mama?"

He looks over at his mother, sitting next to him on the concrete front steps of their bungalow, and he can tell. She doesn't know what this old guy named Shakespeare was talking about, either. He'd bet his Nintendo game on that. So why are the two of them spending a clear, cool, autumn evening reading something neither of them understands? Couldn't they just have gone to see the current movie with the same name?

Veronica catches herself wondering the same thing. But she knows the answer. They're trying to read this excerpt from Romeo and Juliet because Steve Marcy suggested she buy the book What Your 6th Grader Needs to Know, an anthology of lessons in language arts, social studies, the fine arts, math, and science. An abridged version of the Capulet-Montague struggle is its first selection.

"Read this from front to back," Marcy told her at their first parent-teacher conference. "I'm going to be using it this year. If Rodney reads ahead of me a little, he will be better prepared."

Veronica was so grateful for any advice that she sought out the book immediately. Her heart sank though when she saw how thick it was. Rodney will never read all that, she thought. But she shelled out $22 anyway for the last copy in the store, a steep price for someone who sells cosmetics at Macy's department store.

On this September day, her husband, a city bus driver, was working a double shift and wouldn't be home until eight or nine. It fell to her, as usual, to encourage her daughter, Simone, a senior in high school, to get off the telephone and into the kitchen to make dinner so she could sit down with Rodney and go over his homework. After standing on her feet all day, she was always tired when she sat down next to her son on the porch or on their living room couch.

Rodney made her even more tired. He read out loud slowly. Sometimes he stuttered. He had been taking special speech classes on and off for four years; she had seen some improvement but not as much as she'd like. His handwriting was virtually indecipherable, and she often had to ask that he write assignments over. In math, he occasionally still used his fingers to count. Some days she wondered whether he was making any progress at all. Would he end up like his sister, totally uninterested in learning, having to repeat a grade, clueless about what kind of career he wanted to pursue?

Reading with his mom was no picnic for Rodney, either. He could tell *that he disappointed her. When he did pronounce a big word correctly, or added a sum of numbers, she rarely praised him.*

After Rodney and Veronica finish a page of Shakespeare, with Veronica reading the last two paragraphs, it's time for Rodney to bathe and assemble his backpack for tomorrow. Rodney's dad gets home and warms up some macaroni and cheese. Then he and Veronica settle into the living room to find a movie to watch, which isn't difficult since with their new cable system they can choose from eighty-four channels. They settle on Eraser, *an Arnold Schwarzenegger action movie that Veronica has seen four times. By ten-thirty, they are both asleep, Veronica in the recliner, Big Rodney on the couch. Rodney has fallen asleep on their bed watching the ten o'clock news on another TV.*

What a precious moment when a child is born. How big the parents' dreams that follow that child through his first few years. If he's interested in writing, perhaps he will be the next James Baldwin. If she spends hours with her first microscope, perhaps she'll be another Madame Curie. But passions change with time, and the child's talents, as he gets older and into classes with kids just as skilled or more so, can appear more faded pastel than brilliant acrylic. Disappointment can set in, in both child and parent.

It is at this point that the child most needs his parents to hold on to dreams even if they must be adjusted. Parental expectations, more than anyone else's, including those of teachers, neighbors, and friends, will influence how much he accomplishes at school. High expectations will motivate him, low expectations will discourage, even alienate him.[5]

By observing the Kincaids and other families, I saw that parental expectations shape not only the goals we set for our kids but also the effort we put into helping them meet those goals. If we expect a lot, we usually give a lot; if we expect little, our efforts will be minimal as well. Our expectations also affect the amount of autonomy we allow our kids as well as the kind of discipline we apply and how consistently we apply it.

Veronica began receiving negative reports from teachers when Rodney entered fifth grade. Teachers complained that he had an attitude, wouldn't sit still in class, and was easily distracted. Part of the reason may have had to do with his size: Several of the boys in his class were starting to grow and he wasn't. He felt like the odd man out and used a quick tongue to compensate. Veronica attributed his behavioral problems to puberty. She consulted with her sister, who had raised several teenagers. "When they hit puberty, you might as well trade 'em in for stuffed animals," her sister said. Veronica began to anticipate the worst and wished she could keep Rodney a child forever.

Big Rodney's expectations were a little harder to define, but it was clear that he believed his job was to toughen Rodney up psychologically. The two spent a lot of time together and were quite a contrast to look at: Big Rodney, rotund and more than six feet tall, Little Rodney barely reaching his dad's elbows. They bowled together, played basketball and golf, and Big Rodney would tease his son about his inferior playing. Rodney learned to come right back at him. "I could beat you now. You just haven't seen me lately," he would say to a father he obviously adored.

Big Rodney's teasing was good-natured but unrelenting. "When you don't get picked to play on a team at the club, you cry, do you not?" he asked his son on the first morning I visited the family. The family was seated around the dining room table, enjoying glazed donuts and talking into my tape recorder.

"I used to. I don't anymore," Rodney said softly.

A few minutes later, as I was asking Rodney about possible girlfriends, Big Rodney jumped in. "Have you kissed a girl yet?"

"First kiss? Not yet," Rodney replied.

"Do you look at their bods?"

"Their what?"

"You know, their booties. Do you look at girls' booties?"

"This is nasty. I don't want to talk about this anymore," Rodney protested, leaving the room. Seconds later, he returned, tears in his eyes and a blue tissue in his hand.

"He's temperamental," his mother explained.

Rules, Inconsistently Applied

A high-school graduate with two years of community college, Big Rodney saw the result of too little education every day on his bus: testy young men who would harangue his passengers until he kicked them off. It was up to his children to decide whether they wanted to go that way, he thought. "They're either going to learn or not. And if they don't learn, they'll get it later on. I'm not one to hassle."

Big Rodney could have afforded to be somewhat laid back about his son's performance in school if Rodney had been naturally self-motivated, as some kids are, or involved with friends who were high achievers. But with most young adolescents, parental laxness is dangerous. Veronica believed this and, in light of her husband's attitude, fretted full force over Rodney's schoolwork.

She set rules for him at home, such as doing his homework before watching television. She told him she wanted him to ride the bus to the Boys & Girls Club every day after school. She threatened to take the TV out of his room. But she wasn't home to make sure he did his homework, she didn't get on him too badly when he slipped home instead of going to the club, and she rarely removed the television. Rules about schoolwork are the same as any other rules: If kids aren't asked to follow them regularly, they ask themselves privately, Am I expected to do this or not? Consistent expectations build up their sense of personal control; inconsistency leads to feelings of helplessness.[6]

Early in the year, she thought she saw signs of progress. "He's trying to be a little bit more responsible with school, like getting there on time, doing his homework," she said. But then she went on. "His handwriting is bad, and he doesn't like to read. He can't get the basics, that's what I have a problem with."

She motioned to Simone, who at seventeen was taking night classes in subjects she had flunked the year before. Veronica had used every psychological weapon she knew to push Simone in school, and she was about to give up. "I told her to hurry up and turn eighteen so she could move out," she said one afternoon. "Now they tell me at the Boys & Girls Club that Rodney's starting to get an attitude about school, like this one. I see signs of it, too." Rodney had to live not only with his past failures but also with those of his sister at the two places he spent most of his time—home and the club. He bristled at such comparisons: "I don't get in near as much trouble as she does."

Veronica believed that Rodney's intelligence and disposition were fixed. She didn't realize that each child's brain power is different and forever changing, depending on the stimulation a child receives from his surroundings.[7] She also didn't know—as many of us don't—how to accept Rodney's failures without letting her expectations diminish further. We frequently need to tell ourselves the same thing we tell our kids: Failing is okay as long as they're working as hard as they can. How hard they work, not how smart they are, will determine how well they do.

Veronica's low expectations for Rodney surfaced in small and large ways at home. She refused to let him slice his own birthday cake on his twelfth birthday. She confined his household chores to folding his laundry and occasional vacuuming. What she did not know was that children whose parents ask them to start making decisions at a young age, gradually increasing their responsibility, tend to do much better in school than those who are not asked. Depending on their age and maturity they can plan and make meals, shop for groceries, manage an allowance, and offer advice about the choice of a new family car, among many other possibilities.

In middle school, Rodney was expected to take more control of his learning. But with little responsibility for his personal life, there was no reason to think he would suddenly seize responsibility at school. As the fall progressed, Steve Marcy marveled at how often Rodney would say he "didn't understand" why he had received a bad grade.

Content with Their Lives

The Kincaids' expectations for Rodney were really just an extension of their expectations for themselves. They enjoyed steady jobs, had enough to eat, and owned their own home. Their kids were not in jail or strung out on drugs like other young people they knew. "I'd like a Lexus truck, but I'm pretty comfortable with what I have," Veronica said. Big Rodney said, "Society will let you keep what you've got but it don't want you to get more. So you have to make do with what you have."

Their attitudes, so different from upwardly mobile parents with higher incomes, have been echoed in various studies of working-class urban families. As one such study explained: "Most parents set the bar at a level not so high as to invite disappointment."[8] Making do in a city of the rich and famous, rather than doing better, helped these not-so-rich parents get up and go to work every day.

A near brush with unemployment sobered their sense of control and supported Big Rodney's notion that God was in charge of their lives, not them. One weekday afternoon, Big Rodney drove his bus over a mattress lying in the middle of the road. The mattress got stuck in the engine and caught on fire; before Big Rodney knew it the back of his bus was smoking.

He steered over to the shoulder, helped his passengers off the bus, and radioed his company. A couple of days later, he was charged with gross negligence and fired. "But that's not fair! It's not your fault!" Rodney told his dad. "No, it's not, son, but some things are out of our control," his dad answered.

Big Rodney sought out his union representative for help in getting his job back. Over the next five months—with Rodney taking everything in, as kids this age do—Big Rodney made a halfhearted attempt to find other jobs. Construction? Not good for his high blood pressure. A taxi-cab? No way. A job at the post office? It paid only $5 an hour.

At a church retreat one weekend, he decided to place his situation "in God's hands." He told the bishop he needed a job, and he prayed about his needs with a group of men attending the retreat. The day after the retreat, his union representative called to tell him he had been rein-stated. He is convinced that God gave him his job back, with an assist from the union rep.

The pastor of the church the Kincaids attended, the large West Ange-les Church of God in Christ, regularly preached to his congregation to accept what they had. "He says 'Don't move, improve,'" Big Rodney told me when I asked him once why the family hadn't moved to the LA sub-urbs with their presumably better schools. In addition, the house they were living in had been Veronica's home growing up, and she was reluc-tant to leave it.

Another strategy the Kincaids could have pursued in Los Angeles would have been to send Rodney to a suburban school, as Eldon Stanton did with Eric. Big Rodney said they had considered that. They thought that Rodney possessed a flair for drama and would have liked attending a magnet school for the arts. They rejected the idea, however, for several reasons. Transportation was one. Another he phrased this way: "Rodney would see things the other kids had that we couldn't provide."

To achieve in school, kids need to believe they can make things hap-pen, that if they work hard they can realize any goal. It is difficult for them to believe that if their parents don't.

Involvement, but What Kind?

Veronica was becoming increasingly disenchanted not only with Rodney's lackluster performance in school but also with her ability to help him improve. She checked the homework he said he had and talked to him at night about his classes the following day. She made sure he prepared his backpack the night before and fed him hot cereal for breakfast every morning. These were the methods she had used when he was in elementary school, and she had no reason to think they would not work in middle school. When they didn't produce results, her self-esteem as a parent declined, which led her to feel worse about Rodney, and then to feel even worse about herself. She was trapped in a vicious cycle.

Research by Laurence Steinberg, a professor of psychology at Temple University, suggests that once kids move into adolescence, parents should gradually relinquish control over schoolwork and increase their involvement at school. There are several reasons for this. Young people need to take responsibility for their assignments—some, like Rodney, gradually, others more quickly. At the same time, they need to see by their parents' example how important education is. Veronica might have been better off volunteering at his school on her lunch hour and getting to know the staff. This would have required more time and effort—she would have had to take time off from work, and that would have been difficult—but Rodney would have noticed.

Such visits also would have helped her become familiar with Rodney's teachers and the school counselor, and would have relieved her somewhat of the responsibility she felt for Rodney's academic problems. Perhaps together they could have discussed new ways of motivating him. The teachers could have filled her in on Rodney's admirable traits and skills—there were several—and that would have given her positive comments to make to her son in addition to her regular critique.

Steinberg has found that two out of every five parents of older students never attend school events, and only one out of five attends regularly. His and others' work demonstrate that parent participation drops off dramatically between elementary school and middle school, especially among African-American and Hispanic families. This may be partly because the low-wage jobs that many of them have do not allow for flexible hours.

But it also indicates the degree of discomfort that many minority parents feel inside a school building.

Veronica and Big Rodney admitted that they never felt comfortable in school when they were students, and they didn't enjoy visiting Audubon years later. With the exception of Golden Quinn, Rodney's teachers did not listen to their concerns, they said. After Steve Marcy gave Rodney his first F in language arts, Veronica forbade Rodney from watching television for a week. But neither she nor her husband contacted Marcy. (Marcy didn't try to reach them, either. "If I called the parents of everyone who got F's, I'd have no life," he said.) Parental involvement is a two-way street, but, as Anne Lewis, a national education policy writer, has observed, "Just when the lives and schoolwork of young teens are becoming more complicated, schools tend to do less to involve parents."[9]

So profound was their distrust of school that when the staff offered to provide Rodney with free tutoring twice a week after school, Veronica refused because she did not want to fill out the required financial form.

Books vs. Television

Reginald Clark,[10] an educator who studied at-risk students, found that those who spent at least twenty-five hours a week outside class on what he called "high-yield" learning activities, including homework, were more likely to succeed than those who didn't. One of the most important of these activities, he said, was leisure reading. Rodney did almost none of that, and neither did his mother or Big Rodney, who told me point-blank he didn't like to read.

Rodney's lack of interest in reading could also be explained by what he read at school. If national studies are any indication, as much as 90 percent or more of what Rodney read at Audubon was textbook material: boring, simplistic, and unrelated to his life. Absent other, more exciting models, he equated reading with sentences such as "To be a U.S. citizen means to be a member of our nation."

Like other middle schools, Audubon pulled out students who were having reading difficulties for special instruction. Educators there failed to realize how embarrassing special pull-out classes are to young adolescents. Rodney would find all kinds of excuses not to go so as not to be laughed at. He also found the reading exercises he was asked to do "dumb." His failure to read smoothly and his disinterest in reading helped explain his failing grades, his faltering self-esteem, and his inability to see any way out of his situation. It also boded poorly for his future, because competence in reading must precede the abstract thinking skills required in later grades.

Like so many American families, the Kincaids spent far more time watching television than reading. Their living room was dominated by a big TV, and each of their three bedrooms had one as well. One night that I slept in their home, we watched three movies on TV—eight hours' worth. All three were action adventure movies, the Kincaids' favorite genre.

Some parents worry about television violence. Others worry about the amount of television watched, with some justification because at ages ten to twelve, kids spend more hours in front of the TV than at any other age. But the real disadvantage to television shows for youngsters like Rodney, which not many people talk about, may be how few words and concepts they expose kids to. They rarely contain unfamiliar words or sentences longer than five or six words.

If a child is doing well in school and is engaged in outside activities, a parent may not need to restrict the quality or quantity of television a child watches. But if, like Rodney, he isn't faring as well as he could be, the parent should step in, perhaps allowing the child to help decide how much he should watch and then monitoring his use. When the Kincaids thought Rodney needed to do something besides watch TV, they unplugged the set in his room. Frequently, he would plug it back in after a short while. Sometimes they noticed, but more often they did not.

They encouraged his participation in the Boys & Girls Club in part because it kept him off the living room couch. But he figured out ways to be home after school, particularly when his favorite TV wrestlers, Gold Dust and The Undertaker, were fighting.

By 5 P.M. on one such day, Gold Dust had trounced The Undertaker, but Rodney didn't feel quite ready to start his math dittos. So he picked out one of his favorite Disney videos from a bookcase of more than fifty. Within thirty seconds he was flying with the world's most famous elephant, Dumbo. A few minutes into that, I suggested we read together. "What is your favorite book?" I asked. He suggested Where's Waldo?, a large picture book with virtually no words. Together we searched for a skinny, goofy Waldo among hundreds of other images on each page.

"The sermon this morning is about success." Bishop Charles Blake's voice booms out through his handheld microphone in the cavernous sanctuary of West Angeles Church of God in Christ. "God rarely comes to us in our comfort zone. No, He makes us leave our comfort zone. He asks us to show our faith in Him before He gives us something. . . ."

"Amen!" "You're right!" "Tell us, Bishop!" Fancily dressed parishioners shout out their enthusiasm as this tall, handsome pastor in his flowing beige robe delivers the Old Testament story of Abraham and Sarah.

About eight hundred souls have filled the church this rainy January Sunday. Rodney, dressed in a purple suit ("I got it last Easter"), white shirt, and tie is sitting in a folding chair in the center aisle, four rows from the front. A woman in a floppy pink hat leans over and whispers to me that he's there, in that same spot, almost every Sunday. He says he enjoys the music and the idea that he can yell out "Hallelujah" whenever he wants to.

Several minutes into the sermon he leans over and asks me the time.

"It's almost one o'clock," I whisper back to him. "What are you thinking about?"

"I'm thinking about what I'm going to do in school tomorrow. I wonder whether, with all the rain, we're going to have PE on wet ground."

"Is that all?"

"I'm hoping we don't have a lot of work in history and math." For someone who says he doesn't like school very much, Rodney spends a lot of time thinking about it.

Less than twenty-four hours later he is in Steve Marcy's class, history book in hand.

"Rodney, tell me one aspect of a civilization."

"A stable food supply." The correct answer slips out of Rodney's mouth. He looks surprised.

"My man!" Marcy gives him a high-five.

I have returned to Rodney's class, now almost halfway through the school year, hoping to see that he has made some progress. It is early in first period, and the class is running smoothly with only twenty students. Rodney answered the first question right away. So far, so good.

But latecomers start straggling in and the distractions begin. Marcy sends several students to the office to get a late slip. Others are dispatched to the auditorium for not wearing their uniforms. One boy returns and Marcy remembers that he wasn't in class the Friday before winter break. "Get your butt outta here and to the office, and the rest of you, too," he tells the boy. If it were up to Marcy, the kids would be allowed to come in and take their seats at any time. "We've got to get out of this military model," he mutters as he fills out an attendance report. "Especially at this age. We're losing 'em here."

Marcy assigns the class homework but allows time to do most of it in class. Rodney diligently writes down what he is supposed to do: copy a poem, write out what the poem is about, and answer question 3, page 190, in the social studies book.

He finishes copying the poem, "Merry," by Shel Silverstein, then writes: "My poem is a story about Christmas without happyness." Marcy passes by and glances at Rodney's desk. He doesn't comment on the content of Rodney's answer. He says, "That's chicken scratch. There will be no farm animals in this class. Do it over." Maybe things haven't changed after all.

Rodney says Marcy is his favorite teacher. But physical education, the last period of the day, is his favorite class. Because the ground is still sodden from rain, the PE staff has canceled any organized games outside. So three hundred sixth-graders and six teachers assemble in a small gymnasium. PE teacher Maggie Small, in charge of Rodney and forty-nine other boys, tells her group that they can march outside on the blacktop for what is called "free period." But she is not allowed to provide them with equipment during unstructured play. The boys, without a word of protest, race to get outside and scatter across the yard.

Most stand around in groups, shifting about aimlessly. They're not allowed to bring any sports items from home. But one boy, Gary, has sneaked in a basketball. Rodney and nine other boys start to fight over who will play. Small shakes her head. "We have equipment," she says, "balls, bats, basketballs. Why they won't let us give it out, I don't know. What are these kids supposed to do for the next half hour?"

School officials later said they couldn't allow Rodney and his classmates to play with balls or other gear during free time because the equipment might have gotten damaged and wouldn't be available for later activities. They didn't have money in their budget for replacements.

Low Expectations for Public Schools

Ever since California taxpayers capped local property taxes in 1978, halving the amount of local revenue available for schools and other public services, the state's public schools have deteriorated—a frightening development considering that one out of every eight children in this country attends school in California.

From 1990 to 1995, allocations dropped $10,000 per classroom and continued to decline until recently. Only three states in the country spend less per pupil.

The crisis meant that after Rodney inevitably lost the fight for the basketball, he spent most of PE horsing around, squandering his only opportunity for the regular physical exercise his growing body needed. It meant that he rushed to each class to make sure he could get a desk, since some classrooms didn't have enough. It meant that he made sure he sat next to a window in science so he would have enough light to read—one out of three banks of fluorescent lights was out in September and by January, two were down. It meant that he worked entirely out of a science textbook because there was no money for lab equipment and experiments that kids his age love. It meant that he could not take home any books, that "homework" had to be done in school or on ditto sheets.

It meant that the only computers to which he had access were two outdated Macintoshes in Marcy's room. He and his classmates were assigned a weekly time slot during which they could use the computers for schoolwork; his time was Wednesday at ten, whether or not he had work to do. Like several children I observed in Durham, heart of a high-tech corridor known as the Research Triangle, it made no difference to Rodney's life that he lived in a state known for advanced computer engineering.

The financial crisis meant that lunchroom offerings consisted of fast food from Pizza Hut and Taco Bell and that the kitchen often ran out of such items well before lunch was over. One day Rodney stopped to talk to Estevan for a couple of minutes and by the time he reached the window to buy his lunch, all that was left were chocolate chip cookies. He bought one and it disappeared in two bites.

It is impossible to say with precision what toll such systemic deprivations take on kids, although some researchers have found a correlation between daily stresses and physical complaints such as skin rashes and earaches—both of which Rodney complained of throughout the year. But surely the condition of his school and its resources compounded the helplessness Rodney felt about his life in general.

The children I got to know in Los Angeles shared a resignation about schools that was palpable. Libby Sigel, for example, who had transferred from a pleasantly modern, private school to Millikan in suburban Van Nuys, was asked about the soiled condition of her school after drinking from a water fountain grimy with black dirt. "What do you expect?" she asked. "This is a public school."

A Death Grip on Childhood

By midyear, Steve Marcy was increasingly frustrated at his inability to inspire any sort of personal responsibility in Rodney. Rodney would lose his assignments or not complete them. When any group of students got in trouble, he always seemed to be on the periphery. "Rodney is in total denial," Marcy told me. "He has a death grip on childhood, and reality doesn't faze him."

A couple of months after that conversation, Marcy decided he had to do something to attract the Kincaids' attention. During a spelling assignment, he caught Rodney talking to another student. "Rodney," he said, "I'm suspending you from class and you can't come back until your parents come in for a conference."

Rodney looked up in surprise. "I was helping Jared with his spelling."

Steve shook his head. "You heard me. I want you to go to the dean's office and tell him what happened."

The next morning, first period, Rodney slipped back into class. When Marcy asked him what he was doing there, Rodney said, "You only suspended me from period two. This is period one." Before Marcy could send him out again, Big Rodney arrived. He had heard from his son a few details about the day before and he happened to be off work.

Marcy excused himself from class and headed off to find the dean and

Golden Quinn. An impromptu conference was held in the hall outside room 203. As Rodney listened, Marcy told Big Rodney that his son didn't pay attention in class and that he had assumed the role of class clown. He wasn't turning in his assignments on time or at all.

"The work is too hard!" Rodney responded, his eyes misty. "I don't understand it. I lose my notes, and Mr. Marcy won't let me take my book home. No one helps me."

At home that night, Rodney was told he couldn't watch television for a week. That Saturday he wasn't allowed to play basketball with his friends on the street or go bowling. Instead, he rode with his dad on the bus all day. That turned out to be not a bad deal. "We'd ride and talk, ride and talk," he reported. "At the end of each trip, I would sit in his seat and play bus driver."

Veronica was surprised to hear that Rodney wasn't completing some of his assignments. She wished he had a planner like he had had in elementary school. "Last year, I would go over it and sign it when his work was done," she said. "Now all I can do is ask him what kind of homework he has and he tells me. If he don't tell me, I don't know."

Had she approached the teachers about writing down his assignments and asking that she sign each one, they might have agreed. But she didn't ask and they didn't volunteer.

"He's just like Simone," she said. "You have to slap him in the face to make him wake up."

Small Victories

Like a small ground creature, Rodney's initiative would poke its head out every once in a while before quickly retreating underground. He designed a science project to determine the most effective cleaner for tennis shoes, for example, and received an A minus. And in drama one day he enjoyed five minutes of fame.

Asked to perform something musical, he walked up to the front of the class, took a bow, and sat down at the piano. In front of his thirty-plus classmates he improvised a tune he called "My Year in Outer Space," a concerto-sounding piece that included several tempo changes and a long, soulful ending. As the class applauded loudly, he took a final bow and swept out of the classroom. That night, he told his mother about his performance. They had an old piano that he enjoyed fooling around on. Could he take lessons? he asked. Veronica said they couldn't afford lessons, believing his interest wouldn't last. Rodney let it drop and didn't even mention it to his dad.

Not all kids enter the land of learning through the same door. Rodney's aptitude may have been more creative than analytical, and music might have unlocked it. Parents and teachers must pay attention to a child's gifts as well as his inadequacies. Some middle schools have adopted programs that identify and enrich the natural strengths of their borderline students. They have found that when they do so, most of these kids start doing better in their regular courses.[11] Unfortunately for Rodney, Audubon was not one of those schools.

On to the Next Grade?

By June, the temperature in Los Angeles was stuck in the high nineties. Audubon's classrooms had no air-conditioning, no drinking water (fountains had been turned off for conservation), and students were told not to bring water bottles to school for fear of water fights. In an irony that did not go unnoticed, the sprinklers that watered several new flower beds got stuck and could not be shut off.

For a few weeks after his piano performance, Marcy saw a slight improvement in Rodney's attitude and work. Rodney turned in a take-home exam in English and history, touching on all twenty-five concepts he had learned about civilizations. It was organized and the best work he had done all year.

But as the year came to an end, so did Rodney's enthusiasm. Marcy designed an oral history final for him, figuring that his verbal ability might help him pass. Rodney bombed the exam. He acted up so often in class that Marcy began sending him to another room to stand in the corner. Marcy believed, as did Big Rodney and Veronica, that Rodney should repeat sixth grade in order to pick up the skills he hadn't acquired in what had been a difficult year. But school district policy prohibited that. "It would damage his self-esteem," Marcy said sarcastically.

Promoting a kid when you know that he will fall only further behind made about as much sense to Marcy as watering flowers instead of people. "Rodney has many talents," he wrote me, "but reading and writing are not his forte. Not because he can't. I believe it's because he doesn't see a need to. Rodney prefers to get all his information from TV or radio and he would rather talk to you than write anything. He has not progressed in his writing skills at all since September. His dubious reading skills are masked by his constant chatter. If only the educational system offered more for students with his type of intelligence. It wouldn't harm the situation if he developed a little more self-control, also."

Students like Rodney made Marcy question his own efficacy as well.

"Alas, I am a mere classroom teacher," he continued, "sent forth to keep the pupils quiet and in order while providing their parents an escape from their responsibilities and affording the administration the pretense of doing something. Along the way I try to include a little education for those who are interested and a little motivation to those who are not interested."

On the last day of school, Rodney received his report card: Two C's from Golden Quinn and two D's from Marcy. He was promoted to the seventh grade.

CHAPTER EIGHT

Learning Values and Being Valued
(Jessica's Story)

The five girls have been called to the assistant principal's office after several days of sniping at one another. Two of them are petite, blond, and white; the other three are taller, wirier, and black. All five are sixth-graders in their first year at Chewning Middle School in Durham.

"All right, girls, let's get everything out in the open. Why are you taunting each other?" The assistant principal, Edna Vann, wants answers, now.

Jessica Johnston, a white wisp of a child, glances over at the black girls. Speaking up has never been easy for her. How can she describe what she has been going through?

So far she likes the learning part of sixth grade. "You have more chances at doing things, a lot more teachers, and you learn mainly different things every day," she says two months into the school year. But the social part, well, that's another story. She doesn't know many kids because her friends from elementary school attend a different school. She thought she was going to their school because it was close to her house. But when fall came, she discovered that she lived in a neighborhood assigned to a school across town for purposes of desegregation.

She is one of only three or four white students in each of her classes. Many of her classmates come from the projects in Durham. Taller and more outspoken than she, some of them call her "Mickey Mouse" because of her protruding ears. Every morning she climbs the steps into the school bus with a big knot in her stomach.

When I first met Jessica one Sunday morning in the spacious sanctuary of Fellowship Baptist Church, she was sitting ramrod straight in a wooden pew, a blue leather Bible with her name embossed in gold on her lap. She wore a blue-and-white-checked cotton jumper that was soft and faded from many washings. Thin white socks covered ankles smaller than my fist. She showed hints of approaching teenage years: mascara dabbed on thin eyelashes, blond highlights in her long, naturally light brown hair, artificial fingernails painted white.

Her eyes were glued on the young, round-faced preacher, Rick Finley, as he explained the dismayed confusion of the twelve apostles after Jesus warned them of his impending death. "When Jesus leaves, who's going to be in charge? That's what they wanted to know," Finley bellowed. "When somebody's not in charge, there are a whole lot of people who think they ought to be."

Jessica smiled knowingly at his point, her hands busy picking at her fake nails. By the end of the service, she had peeled off each tiny piece of painted plastic, revealing her own nails that were chewed to the quick.

Church, I would later learn, was one of her favorite places, a haven in her increasingly fractured life. When she was seven, her mother, Teresa McNamara, a licensed practical nurse, had left her father, Ray Johnston, and moved herself and the two youngest of her six children, including Jessica, into a cheap apartment in a poor neighborhood. Two years later, after divorcing Ray, she married an electrician named Glenn McNamara. Glenn, also divorced, had brought two sons to the marriage, Justin, eleven, and Joel, eight. Shortly after they were married, Teresa and Glenn had had a baby boy they named Denver. The new blended family moved into a three-bedroom yellow frame house in a working-class neighborhood.

The house was less than a five-minute walk from Jessica's dad's house, but Teresa forbade Jessica to visit him, saying he refused to pay child support.

"Dad lives two blocks from here. I haven't seen him in two years," Jessica said one afternoon, sitting on her bed and wearing an olive Champions sweatshirt Ray had sent her. She looked away and swallowed hard. A tear rolled down her cheek. A minute or two elapsed.

She continued, "Mama don't let me go because she's afraid I'll go live with him. That would hurt her. But sometimes I sneak and talk to him on the telephone."

Home life was forcing her to question the values she heard about at church, such as trust, respect, and forgiveness. So was life in middle school. Already, one of the toughest sixth-graders, a girl named Jenelle, who lived on the infamous Canal Street, had threatened to fight her. When Jessica reported this to a guidance counselor, she was told to just ignore her. Ignore? She had tried that and Jenelle just seemed to taunt her more. Her next plan was to avoid Jenelle and Jenelle's friends.

When the bell rang signaling a change in classes, she would exit the class and flatten herself against a hallway wall, trying to avoid hundreds of kids who would swarm past her, shrieking and calling out to one another. In gym class, where some fifty kids came together daily, she would steer a wide berth around the black girls during warm-up jogs, keeping an eye out for Jenelle and her friends.

Wouldn't her PE teacher stop any foolishness that threatened her? I asked.

She shook her head no. "There are so many students in here moving around, he wouldn't notice anything right away."

One of the girls she stuck close to was Beth Blake. Beth, quick-witted and sharp-tongued, was Jessica's friend and protector. It is Beth who is in the assistant principal's office that morning with Jessica, and Beth's behavior that has prompted the black girls to complain to a teacher, who sent them to the office.

"Beth says bad stuff to us, like 'West Side' and 'What's up, dog?'" LaTisha, one of the black girls, tells Edna Vann, citing two popular gang expressions. "She and Jessica stare at us in class."

Vann turns to Jessica and Beth. "Why do you do that?" she wants to know.

"It's not true." Presumed guilty, Jessica feels forced to defend herself and her friend. "We mind our own business. They stare at us, they call us names, they throw things at us when no one's looking."

Vann sighs. She has heard it all before, dozens of times. Young adolescents are acutely self-conscious, sensitive to the smallest slight or hint of a put-down. Fights at this age are almost never over what adults regard as big things. It is her job to help the two sides here understand why innocu-

ous looks or words can be misunderstood and hurtful. The division this morning along racial lines adds another, delicate dimension. She's pretty adept at handling these disputes, but right now she has a meeting down the hall.

"I want you young ladies to mind your own business," she says. "Don't stare at each other. If someone says something you don't like, forget it. Before you leave this office I want you to promise you'll try to get along."

The girls mutter niceties to each other, file out, and head for math, Jessica and Beth walking on one side of the hallway, the other three girls on the opposite side.

With all the attention we pay to grades and test scores, it is easy to forget that schools are the primary places where kids learn to get along—or fight—with others and be tolerant or intolerant of individual differences. Home life provides the foundation for values, but schoolyards and classrooms are where those values are tested hour upon hour, day after day.

This is particularly true in the middle grades, when young adolescents are beginning to actively define the moral principles by which they will live. At this age they are able not only to grasp concepts of right and wrong but also, for the first time, to detect exceptions, inconsistencies, and conflicts among competing viewpoints.[1]

Getting along with others, or doing the right thing, can be tough in their world, which is considerably harsher, with more obvious temptations, than the world many of their parents knew. Sassy attitudes are in, as is at least a passing knowledge of where to acquire drugs or cigarettes. The language they hear from adults is rough, the images ugly: athletes talking trash, talk show guests throwing chairs at each other, parents cursing in the car at aggressive drivers.

And yet it is not difficult to persuade them to care for each other. Cactuses on the outside, inside they want more than anything to be liked by other kids. Earlier they were good because of what was in it for them; now they want others to respect them, and they want to respect themselves.[2] Educators and parents can seize this opportunity to inspire and teach humane values.

Currently, many teachers are trying to do this. Some of them are caught up in moral training known as character education, teaching a specific curriculum in core values. But as Jessica's year illustrated, character education is less about lessons taught than lessons observed. Character is learned when kids feel their viewpoints are sought and respected on matters that affect them. Character is learned when children feel safe telling the truth and confident that their observations will be acted upon or at least listened to. Character is fashioned when students are engaged in challenging assignments that involve other pupils and when they are taught not only how to answer questions but also how to reflect on their answers.

This is a tall order for teachers, who, as we will see, have been given numerous tasks to perform by a society that expects schools to cure virtually every ill. But as parents we have a right to expect our kids' teachers to be decent moral guides. Most Americans now place teaching values to kids at or near the top of their list of things they want schools to do. We are coming to understand that positive values improve our children's mental health, boost their performance in school, and increase the odds that they will contribute to their community.[3]

All instructors teach and model values, of course, even in the middle of a geography lesson or math drill. The question is, which values? As I learned watching Jessica, a teacher's instructional style, the ideas she is trying to get across, even the remarks she casually tosses out, convey a lot. Parents can pick up significant clues simply by observing their kids' teachers in the classroom. The parent who does this will be better able to understand what her child is facing each day, better able to help her think through any puzzling or unpleasant encounters. Teresa, Jessica's mom, never found the time to observe Jessica's teachers in middle school, a fact she regretted later.

Teaching Civility: The Official Line

As the middle-school teacher in Ulysses observed, young adolescents are like sponges. They absorb, then release, much of what their environment throws at them. That's why the social climate of a school is so crucial. Civility from teachers and students begets civility; hostility breeds hostility or, as in a situation like Jessica's, forces a child to retreat into her shell.

As America's schools become increasingly diverse, schools are learning what a challenge it can be to establish a civil atmosphere. Jessica's example could teach them a thing or two.

Four years earlier, Chewning served a mostly white population in a rural area of Durham County. But in 1993, city and county schools merged in an effort to save the city's mostly black schools. A combination of magnet programs and busing went into effect. Students from poor neighborhoods in East Durham, some of them white, like Jessica, but most of them black, were bused to Chewning. The school's population of about eight hundred students went from majority white to majority black overnight. The proportion of students qualifying for free or reduced-fee lunches doubled, to more than half.

Generally, the transformation was accomplished without major disturbances. David Dennis, a white principal well liked at his former, predominantly white elementary school, was assigned to Chewning, partly to ease the fears of white parents. He solidified the school's middle-school structure of small teams. He signed Chewning up for an after-school, homework-and-activities program known as Save Our Schools. He hired new teachers, black and white. He supported special activities during Black History Week. He encouraged his teachers to group kids heterogeneously rather than according to ability, believing that tracking young adolescents did not enhance achievement and was a surefire way to segregate kids within his school.

What he did not do was train his staff in teaching and supervising the diverse populations. This was not entirely his fault: The county provided no training before the merger and very little afterward, according to county school authorities. He also did not organize discussions among students on the advantages and problems of learning in a multiracial setting. Working side by side with classmates who vary in background, income, and lifestyle—one great benefit of a public education—occurs more smoothly if students are asked to do what psychologists call "perspective taking," that is, imagine what it is like to be the other person. Jessica and her schoolmates could have compared favorite rock groups and athletes, then been asked to talk through their prejudices and figure out how they should and would act. They could have shared their common feelings of anger, fear, and hurt.

Dennis did ask a teacher, Melissa Bartlett, to write a program in conflict resolution should it be needed. Bartlett wrote the program and Dennis directed his staff to use it. Fewer than a dozen of the fifty teachers complied, however, according to Bartlett, and Dennis didn't seem concerned.

"We haven't had any problems with race relations," he told me.

But from Jessica's Point of View . . .

Jessica saw things differently. Several years after the Durham school merger, signs of segregation and racist attitudes still prevailed, she said. In hallways, in the cafeteria, and in classrooms with no assigned seating, most students grouped themselves according to race, the girls particularly. Threats and taunts, such as Jessica and Jenelle exchanged, were not uncommon. Jessica could cite half a dozen examples of small provocations that, in her mind, added up to an unfriendly atmosphere:

"On the bus they'll throw paper and either hit me or someone else and in school they call me 'Monkey' or 'Mickey Mouse.' They talk about how the white girls get away with everything, and when white people say something about their fake hair they'll get really mad and end up fighting with you. Jenelle threw an eraser and hit one of my friends in the eye. Another girl took my friend's hair and yanked it real hard. There are all these little groups, black groups and white groups, and they're like too good for anybody else."

If there's one thing educators have learned from more than two decades of school desegregation, it's that simply mixing kids together doesn't assure increased tolerance. Small incidents, if not handled promptly and fairly, can merely reinforce stereotypes.[4] Jessica said she never heard racial issues formally discussed. Without guidance, she felt compelled to identify and classify people so that her world at school made sense. The most obvious label to apply to people was skin color.

She started describing behavior she didn't approve of as "black." Black boys let their underwear show; black girls wore short skirts, wiggled their behinds, and made obscene gestures. Black teachers were meaner than white teachers.

She also perceived unfair treatment of black and white students. One morning a white friend had to write five hundred times "I will not swear" after a teacher heard her call someone a "motherfucker." That afternoon, a black girl used the same word in class and a different teacher only admonished the girl to sit down.

Her sensitivity to racial issues was not without its humanity. One day one of her teachers teased a boy named Jared, calling him stupid. Jared was large for his age, not a stellar student, and black. Jessica had seen this teacher pick on Jared before, and it always bothered her. On this day, she decided to act. She took her friend Beth with her to the principal's office. David Dennis listened to the girls' complaints, then turned to Beth.

"So how's softball this year?"

Dennis later told me he changed the subject because it was inappropriate to talk about personnel matters with students. But instead of explaining his reasoning and commending their courage in speaking up for someone else, he left Jessica and Beth with no idea whether their visit had done any good.

The Color-blind Approach to Education

Jessica showed she was capable of considering complex moral concepts such as prejudice by being uneasy with her biases. Before saying something critical, she would preface her remark by saying, "I don't want to seem racist but . . ."

She *wanted* to talk out her confused feelings about race, and did so with her friends and brother, but never with adults at school who knew the context of her comments and could guide her reasoning. Without adults to gently challenge their thinking, eleven-year-olds see behavior as right or wrong, fair or unfair, with no mitigating circumstances allowed. She said to me in the spring, "I think they should have an assembly or something because it's getting worser and worser. I don't think you should be racist. You should get along because you're going to end up working with some when you get older, so it's like an opportunity to learn how to work with people when you go to school."

When I asked several of Jessica's teachers why racial issues weren't discussed more at school, they said they and their colleagues had enough to do to cover curricula quickly and thoroughly. Another mandated change—state-required, end-of-grade tests for all students—had forced them to set aside social goals, they said. Some of them were also uncomfortable discussing race, preferring what has been called a color-blind approach to education.[5] Race and ethnicity should be irrelevant and ignored, they said; problems were socioeconomic, not racial.

Certainly kids should not be reminded constantly of their differences. Color blindness has been shown to reduce the potential for overt racial conflict in the short term. Yet Jessica's experience suggests that it does little to prevent or extinguish underlying hostilities. It's not enough to assume that, as kids mature, they will outgrow their prejudices. Teachers, like parents, must actively challenge their thinking about race and other moral issues in order to help them move beyond thinking only about themselves.

Opportunities for such teaching arise naturally in later grades: in interscholastic sports and after-school plays, for example. But at Chewning, as in most middle schools, sixth-graders like Jessica had to wait until seventh grade in order to participate in the most coveted extracurricular programs. Midway through the year, for example, a counselor, impressed by the way Jessica had helped contain a conflict between black and white students, approached her about becoming a peer mediator to help settle disputes among students. Jessica proudly announced this to her mother one evening, only to learn the next day that the program wouldn't start until the following year.

The subject in *Wendy Martin's math class is ratios and proportions, the problem to find what "n" represents if* $6/24 = 50/n$. *One girl is combing her hair, another tapping a yellow pencil on her desk, still another muttering to herself nonstop. Jessica, sitting in the back of the room, stares straight ahead. An A student, she knows the answer. She learned much of what is in her general math textbook last year. But she doesn't volunteer.*

All desks, arranged in vertical rows, face the blackboard. Twenty-two boys and girls sit with their math books opened, ditto sheets in front of them. Cardboard boxes and manila folders are stacked in piles around the room, and a fan sits, unused, on top of a gray filing cabinet. Windows are closed; the linoleum floor is scuffed with the marks of hundreds of students of past years who have shuffled into class to be drilled on ratios and equations.

Martin, a serious-looking woman with very short, brown hair, has tried using beans in a bag to demonstrate the lesson, then moved to an overhead projector. Her kids are reviewing for a test they'll take tomorrow. She is worried that they don't yet grasp the key concepts. A tenured teacher at Chewning, she can recognize signs of confusion in a heartbeat. She calls on Jessica's friend Beth for the answer. Beth shrugs and smiles.

"Look, she's smiling. She must have a date this weekend." Martin is growing increasingly frustrated. This is one of her better classes, but the period is not going well.

She turns back to the overhead, and Beth mouths to Jessica, "Click your duck." Beth brought two toy clickers to school this morning, a frog and a duck. The clicking drives Martin crazy and Beth knows it. She and Jessica call the toys "teacher buggers." Jessica shakes her head no.

"Now you may never need this again, I know that," Martin continues. "My job is to expose you to stuff, a little bit about probability, a little bit about fractions." She looks at Beth. "I'm real tired of people making noises. If you don't want to learn this, just put your head down on your desk." This is one order Beth obeys.

Martin writes the answer, n = 200, and Beth looks up and raises her hand. "I don't know how you got that." Martin looks at her quizzically, and several students jump in to try to explain. Their explanations are ragged, not well thought out. Rather than let them struggle on their own for a while, Martin tries to explain the answer herself. With fewer than three months until end-of-grade tests and more than half the book left, she feels she doesn't have a minute to waste.

A boy raises his hand and asks a question. "I can't understand your English," she replies. "You've got thirty seconds to explain." He starts to repeat himself and the bell rings. Time for language arts, not explanations.

Several times a year news reports remind us how poorly U.S. secondary school students perform in mathematics compared to pupils in other countries. On standardized math tests in 1995, for example, American seventh- and eighth-graders ranked in the bottom half of students from forty-one countries even though they spent more class hours on math, covered more topics, were tested more often, and received more math homework than students in most of the other countries.[6] Research suggests that the reasons for such underachievement may have less to do with which particular concepts are covered in U.S. classrooms than with how American students are taught.

The Value of Collaboration

About ten years ago, the National Council of Teachers of Mathematics recommended teaching practices in line with the Japanese model. Japanese teachers place math students into small groups, give the groups one or two complex problems, and ask them to come up with solutions together and to be prepared to defend their answers in class. The teachers then highlight and review the proposed solutions and summarize the main point of the day.[7] The focus is less on the instructors and individual students and more on the students as teams.

The national council said that memorization and drills, essential for proficiency, should be included in elementary-school instruction. But by middle school or junior high, an instructor's goal should be to teach students how to solve problems by thinking and working effectively with others. Such collaboration, which is the way most great scientific research is done, works a child's cognitive and moral reasoning skills.

Some teachers have adopted this approach. But as we saw in the last chapter and again in Wendy Martin's room, other teachers have not. Lessons are taught from an overhead projector or the blackboard, and students work individually, sometimes racing each other. Students are not inspired to think deeply and independently, to connect disparate but related bits of knowledge, to be creative in their solutions when something goes wrong, and to reflect on and evaluate their own and each other's work. Indeed, what I observed in many classes was that traditional instruction values individualism, competitiveness, and speed over teamwork, reflection, and cooperation, not the ideal preparation for the working world, personal relationships, or civic engagement in a democratic society. Rote work also alienates adolescent students because it says they are, in the words of education writer Alfie Kohn, "so many passive receptacles to be filled, lumps of clay to be molded, pets to be trained, or computers to be programmed."[8]

For Wendy Martin, like Steve Marcy in the last chapter, the specter of end-of-grade testing and the enormous number of facts her students needed to know in order to pass pushed her toward lectures and drills. She was caught up in a movement that had started nationally several years earlier as an effort to raise student achievement. By the time Chewning started administering the tests — Jessica's sixth-grade year — all states reported some kind of requirement that secondary students take multiple-choice tests in their core subjects at the end of each school year.

The stakes were high: A majority of Chewning students would have to score a 3 or higher (on a 1–4 scale) on the final test. If they did not, the school would be rated a "low-performing" school, which could lead to the principal being replaced and teachers losing their teaching license. David Dennis and teachers like Wendy Martin were concerned: Many of their students read at only a second- or third-grade level. Their jobs were on the line, and this took their minds off almost everything except teaching for the tests.

According to Dennis, Martin was the kind of teacher who believed every child in her class should understand every principle she taught before she moved on to the next idea. When she didn't accomplish this, she was hard on students and hard on herself. Testing at the end of the year only increased the stress.

Martin had reached out to Jessica early in sixth grade, occasionally putting her arm around Jessica's shoulders and asking, "How are you doin', pumpkin?" But Jessica did not warm to her in part because of the way she treated Beth. Young adolescents judge adults by the way their friends are treated as well as the way they are. Beth was sassy from the beginning of school, and she and Martin didn't get along. Jessica also didn't like Martin's sarcasm.

One morning in homeroom, Martin walked over to see if Jessica had finished her math homework. Jessica had not. "Why don't you have your homework?" Martin asked. Jessica shrugged, and Martin turned to me.

"Write that down," she said. "When asked by her teacher why she didn't have her homework, Jessica didn't respond and didn't seem to care, either."

Jessica winced.

As the year moved on, Jessica began to dislike not only her teacher but math itself and to think of herself as not very smart in a subject she had done well in the year before.

"Trip, trap, trip, trap, trip, trap."

A soft female voice rings out, stilling the whispers and giggles of eighteen

*other voices in room 239, Melissa Bartlett's language arts class. A tiny figure
under a white sheet starts across a makeshift bridge on her hands and knees.*

"Who's that trip-trapping over my bridge?" *growls the young male voice
of a troll dressed in dark, baggy clothes and a werewolf mask.*

"It's only me, the littlest billy goat Gruff," *answers the white sheet.*

"Then I'm coming to gobble you up!" *the troll continues.*

"Oh, please don't gobble me up!" *protests the sheet.* "Wait until the second billy goat Gruff comes along. He's much fatter than I am!"

*Through slits in her sheet Jessica can see that she and her acting troupe
have a hold on her classmates and Ms. Bartlett, who is partly hidden
behind a video camera.*

*Jessica barely knew her three fellow actors when they were assigned to
come up with a folktale and present it to the class. Nearing the end of the
third quarter of school, she still was keeping pretty much to herself. Melissa
Bartlett, recognizing that the group might feel awkward working together,
had assigned them a game before they started the skit. Think of different
items you would like to bring to a dinner party, then agree on a menu, she
told them.*

*When they moved to the folktale, the group had to decide whether to
make up their own story or agree on one they all knew. They mulled over
that decision for almost a full class period. When it came time to assign
parts, they went by size, and Jessica became the littlest billy goat. They
wrote their script during the next couple of class periods and then—the
most difficult step—decided by what measures they should be graded.
What would distinguish an excellent performance from a mediocre one?
Was it the quality of the script or of the acting? Should they be judged as a
group or individually?*

*Jessica had to hand it to Ms. Bartlett. She was one cool teacher. You
could tell when you walked into her classroom. It was clean, for one thing,
empty of the boxes and papers that cluttered other classrooms. Batik wall
hangings from Kenya and Egypt brightened the cinderblock walls. An
apple tree made of green and blue felt and filled with brightly colored trop-
ical birds hung over a coffeepot that Ms. Bartlett, always in motion, gradually emptied over the course of a day. A quizzical felt eye adorned the
loudspeaker; above it a computer banner proclaimed:* EXCELLENCE WITH-
OUT EXCUSE—A SHARED RESPONSIBILITY.

Under that banner on the afternoon of their skit, the biggest billy goat

Gruff knocks the troll into the river and joins the other goats across the bridge. The cast then disrobes to take their bows. The next day, they watch themselves on videotape. A stellar performance, everyone, including the teacher, agrees. As the bell rings to go home, goats and troll trip-trap out of room 239 smiling.

Wheels turning, light bulbs going on, name any inspirational metaphor you like and you can see it in a classroom of young adolescents learning from a teacher they admire. They ask questions constantly, listen to each other, and if a head or two rests on a desk, it's up again in a matter of minutes. Melissa Bartlett's students behaved as if they wanted to be in her classroom. Taunts were rare; the students were more likely to be helping each other.

As her banner indicated, Bartlett understood the three R's of working with young adolescents: respect, responsibility, and relationship. She treated her students with respect, gave them responsibility for their learning, and worked at keeping a healthy relationship with them. "It was the better part of the day," said Jessica, who had Bartlett for her last period. "It wasn't boring. Ms. Bartlett was the only teacher who cared."

Modeling Respect

Bartlett, an English and linguistics major in college, spent a year student-teaching in a middle school in inner-city Norfolk, Virginia, in the 1970s. But she never thought she would end up as a middle-school teacher. She taught remedial reading to adults on Saint Thomas in the U.S. Virgin Islands, joined the Peace Corps and taught Kenyan high-school students, left Africa for Cairo, where she taught adult students again at the American University, and eventually moved to Durham to train teachers how to teach non-English-speaking children. When a job opened up at Chewning for the 1996–97 school year, she decided to try her hand once more at middle school. After teaching older students, she found sixth-graders refreshing.

She tried to explain her preference for younger children one after-noon in her room after tutoring a dozen students who had failed an important English test. Because of a recent burglary in which her pocketbook had been stolen, all the windows were locked except one, which she kept open for air. It was not an ideal teaching environment, but as she pushed back strands of auburn hair that kept slipping from a makeshift chignon, she could barely contain her enthusiasm for her task: "These kids have not learned to recoil in fear, or felt public ridicule for being curious. They see things I never see. I learn from them."

Bartlett's teaching style was rooted firmly in the principles of Swiss psychologist Jean Piaget, who observed that it is in children's nature to want to learn and that they do so primarily by interacting with things and people. The job of the teacher—like the job of a parent—is not so much to tell students what to do or how to think as it is to structure the students' environment so that they do the doing and thinking—and then help them reflect on what they have learned and what they still need to learn.

Bartlett understood that not all of her students learned the same way. Some, like Jessica, responded best to words. Others, like Dennis, the troll, reacted well to movement. She was skilled at figuring out each student's abilities and then grouping them so that they would complement one another. Jessica, for example, brought thoughtfulness to the billy goats' project whereas Dennis provided exuberance and creativity. Another member of the group, Lana, would say, "Let's get it done," and the fourth participant, Tawana, was able to moderate disputes.

Unlike Rodney's teacher Steve Marcy, Bartlett decided which roles each student would play within a group (who would be the leader, who would take notes) and thought up exercises the group could do together before they started their main assignment. Knowing how quarrelsome kids this age can be, she would weave her way around the room constantly, encouraging the hesitant and helping students resolve petty arguments. "You have to be hyperactive to stay on top of groups," she would admit. She almost always demanded that the groups present their final product to the class, since middle-schoolers are inspired not so much by acquiring knowledge as using what they've learned, not so much by consuming knowledge as producing it. She would ask some groups to write down what their individual contributions had been, any problems they had encountered with classmates and how they had solved those problems. This was the first time many of her students had been asked to reflect consciously on their behavior.

Moving Kids Forward

One way to nudge young adolescents' moral reasoning forward, according to Thomas Lickona, a developmental psychologist at the State University of New York, is to substitute specific expectations for rewards and punishment. Extrinsic incentives that elementary-school students respond to, such as candy or a trip to the principal's office, can actually decrease adolescent motivation to do well and be good.[9]

Wendy Martin was a reward-and-punishment type of teacher who would entice students to finish an assignment by, for example, promising that if they did, they could watch a video the next day in class. Bartlett, on the other hand, ran her classes according to plans that she and each student set out.

At the beginning of each year, she gave students a written overview of the reading and writing they would be doing each semester and an explanation of how their grades would be determined. Each semester, she handed them a week-by-week syllabus listing topics, readings, writing assignments, and tests. She told the students to share these handouts with their parents.

Within such a framework, she gave students as many choices as possible, knowing that choices increase a student's desire to learn.[10] She helped students design their own test following a model that told them in broad strokes the items a test should cover. She asked them to write at the top the grade they expected to get. Her goal was to instill in her students the belief that they were in control of succeeding or failing at school. They might not be able to control other parts of their lives, but they could determine how much—and how quickly—they learned.

Pushing Kids Deeper

When her students showed interest in a particular topic, Bartlett would let them run with it for a while before bringing them back to the next topic she needed to cover. She rarely spent more than a couple of minutes talking at one time. Talking was the kids' job.

"Who or what did Daisy think caused her car to wreck?" Bartlett asked a class reading an excerpt from *Driving Miss Daisy*.

"The car!" several students chimed in.

"We do that all the time, blame someone else or something else for our behavior. It's called projection." She wrote the word on the blackboard.

"Oh I know, like what I do to my cat . . ." One girl was off and running with a rambling account of how she blamed her cat for opening the back door of her house. Bartlett let her go for a short while, pleased that the girl had grasped the analogy of *Miss Daisy* to her life, and knowing that kids at this age don't talk so much as gush, dribble, and sputter. Given time to do that, they are capable of uncovering levels of meaning they didn't know they knew.

Entering Their World

Bartlett knew that if she wanted her students to try to see the world through other people's eyes, including hers, she would have to put on their glasses as well. "If you don't have a good relationship with kids this age, they hate you," she said.

She sat and chatted with students in the cafeteria during lunch, while most of the other teachers clustered at tables off to the side. She was good-natured even when having to play the bad guy. Spying a collection of boys playing a game of Uno, she rose and walked over to their table. "I think I need some cards," she said with a smile, removing the deck quickly to a few groans.

She stood in the halls between classes greeting some pupils and reprimanding others, as other teachers remained in their rooms. During her poetry unit, she encouraged students to analyze the lyrics of popular songs; anything was permissible as long as it contained no curses or explicit sexual references. She watched lots of movies so that when her students referred to particular films during class discussions, as many did, she could talk about mood and violence in *Daylight* or stereotypes in *White Men Can't Jump*. She didn't hesitate to let her students know how she felt about what they watched, but she didn't put down their opinions.

She also shared her world with them. She brought in songs she liked—"Imagine," by John Lennon, and "Redemption," by Bob Marley. She told stories about living overseas. Her sociable young adolescents devoured such personal details as if they were Jolly Rancher candies.

Ethicist Amitai Etzioni says morality (as well as English and math) is best learned when students bond with a teacher. If that is true, Bartlett's students were off to a good start.

Creeping Discouragement

However, one dedicated teacher can do only so much for a child like Jessica, who feels boxed in by a school environment she perceives as unresponsive. Jessica started the school year bursting with enthusiasm for "learning mainly different things every day." By spring she was questioning "whether anyone, students or teachers, care whether you learn or not. Except for Ms. Bartlett."

Her dismay at the lack of attention to hostile relations between students had expanded to dismay at teachers' tolerance for other negative behaviors. One day during a computer typing test, she and her classmates were asked to place covers over the keys and type without looking down. The teacher left the room for a long time, and many of the students peeked under the covers while he was gone. Jessica came home that day angry at her classmates for cheating and at the teacher for making it so easy.

She also got riled when she noticed that students in some of her courses who were not turning in their homework were still passing. But by the end of the year she was slacking off along with them. "You're punished all day with work, why should you have to do homework?" she asked.

Back at Home

School was not solely responsible for Jessica's discouraged attitude. Her stepfather, Glenn McNamara, was starting to terrorize the family. At first he only injected rules and structure into what had been a laid-back household: Kids had to be in bed by 9:30, keep the house clean, wash their own laundry, and make good grades in school. Failure to abide by these rules brought swift punishment, usually grounding.

An electrician who strung wire for a small company, he frequently worked seven days a week, and deep into Jessica's sixth-grade year the stress started to show. "My job's killing me," he said one night about

8 P.M. when he had just gotten home from work. "My mind's tired, my body's tired, I haven't had a vacation in three years."

When his son Justin started bringing home failing grades, he hit him. He hit his other son, Joel, on the head when Joel gave him a demerit slip to sign. It seemed to Jessica that he could flare up over anything. One time he accused her of being sneaky for opening the refrigerator to grab a piece of bologna. He never hit her, but she learned to stay in her room with the door closed until he fell asleep in front of the television in the living room. His outbursts caused friends like Beth to cut back on visits to her house.

Jessica didn't feel comfortable talking to anybody about her problems at home, not even Ms. Bartlett. What could one teacher do? she asked herself. One of her older brothers had called the county social services department to complain about his stepfather. Her mother had filed charges of abuse with the police department, and Glenn had pled guilty. But he had returned home and nothing had changed.

In the spring she brought home a C in science after turning in a project late. It was her first C ever, so her mother, Teresa, knew something was wrong. But Jessica shrugged off Teresa's questions, and Teresa let it go. "Maybe she's just in a slump," Teresa thought to herself. "She'll pull herself out of it." A few days later, Teresa told me that Jessica was "really working hard now in science."

"Not really," Jessica told me that same day. "I never really work very hard in that class."

At that moment, Teresa had other things besides Jessica's report card to worry about. She was searching for a new job, finally taking her ex-husband to court for child support, and trying not to antagonize her second husband. Each day she took Glenn to and from work and dropped off and picked up two-year-old Denver at day care. She also drove the other kids to three different schools and back. She wore a beeper so that her kids could reach her, and it seemed like it was always going off.

When Derek, Donald, and Linda, her three oldest, were young, she had baked cookies for their school parties, chaperoned their field trips, known all their teachers. She wasn't working outside the home then. Now, she was employed and had children and stepchildren in grades five through nine who counted more than twenty teachers among them. She couldn't remember the last time she had been to a parent-teacher conference at Chewning. "The kids usually bring home the flyers after the event," she said with a wan smile. Had Jessica ever mentioned Melissa Bartlett, her favorite teacher?

"I vaguely remember the name. It's hard to remember unless there were some problems," she admitted.

A Fresh Start, but to Where?

It is not unusual for girls' spirits to flag during sixth grade. The decline, not as evident in girls who attend K–8 schools, usually reverses itself by eighth grade with parental support, cooperation with school authorities, and maturation. But some parents don't want to take a chance over three years and they seek out private schools. This is what Teresa did. Rather than take her concerns about Jessica to Chewning administrators in the hope of improving Jessica's seventh-grade year, Teresa started preparing to send Jessica to the private school run by their church the following fall.

The Fellowship School was not accredited in North Carolina. If Jessica ever wanted to transfer back to public school, her credits might not be accepted. In addition, if she chose to graduate from Fellowship, she probably would not be accepted into any non-Christian colleges.

It is doubtful that she understood these risks. If she had any second thoughts, they were erased by her happy experiences with the church over the summer following her sixth-grade year. At a week-long church camp in the mountains, she swam, played volleyball, and studied the Bible. When she returned, she began riding a van into the housing projects of south Durham every Saturday morning as part of an evangelizing team. On Sunday, the team returned to the same neighborhoods to pick up the children for church. It was during this summer evangelization campaign that her thoughts about race began to change noticeably.

Race Revisited

On one such visit, she and three others on her team approached a duplex door riddled with bullet holes. A tall girl opened the door and ushered them into a living room that held nothing but a torn gray couch and a wooden chair. Food and clothes were scattered on the floor. Odors of stale grease and dirty diapers hung in the air. The girl, carrying her nine-week-old baby, was twelve, Jessica's age. Jessica handed her a religious brochure and told her a little bit about Fellowship Baptist.

As the van left the projects that morning, Jessica thought about how some people had it so much worse than she did. She imagined her old foe Jenelle leaving a neighborhood like the one she had just visited for the rural surroundings of Chewning. Maybe Jenelle was one of ten or twelve kids in a family and would do anything to attract attention. Maybe Jenelle threw erasers because her father threw punches. Maybe Jenelle had been as scared of her dad as Jessica was of her stepdad, and maybe Jenelle's way of dealing with insecurity was to act bossy. Jessica wished that she had gotten to know Jenelle better. Her pastor was right: She needed to work on her attitude.

"When I was at school, it made me feel racist," Jessica said. "But after getting out into those neighborhoods with my church and thinking about it, I realize kids like Jenelle probably had problems at home and are just getting them out at school."

Like the younger child who can't stop asking why, Jessica was beginning to challenge her earlier assumptions. She was entering what has been called "the second age of reason," in which she could spot and name what she and others had in common and be more forgiving in her moral judgments.

Significantly, it was her service in the projects that forced her to rethink her prejudices. Certainly, her day-to-day experiences with black students at Chewning had prepared the ground, if a little unevenly. The give-and-take discussions of Melissa Bartlett's class had helped spread the seed. But had she not knocked on the doors of south Durham and talked to girls her age about her faith, the sprouts of new moral growth might not have appeared that year. Water and sun came from outside, not inside, school.

CHAPTER NINE

Outside the Box
(Jack's Story)

Crouched on the hard brown Kansas sod behind his house, Jack Richard-son, twelve, surveys the pile of weathered gray scrap lumber he has gath-ered. He closes his eyes against the late summer sun and asks himself, What would a birdhouse look like? How tall should it be? How wide? How big should the door be? On the tablet of his mind a design slowly emerges. He holds the picture in his head for a minute, then picks up a saw and attacks a large plank, cutting it down to a width of a foot and a half.

Oblivious to the hum of the semis on the highway in front of his house, he grabs another board and saws, then another and another, five boards in all. He then drills four overlapping holes in the piece of wood he has des-ignated as the front to create a door about two inches wide and three inches tall. Sweat beads accumulate under his short, caplike blond hair, and he raises his arm to wipe them away. Halfway to his father's workshop, in search of hammer and nails, he remembers. Nails would split wood this dry. Better to use screws.

When he rose early this morning, he hadn't a clue how he was going to fill the long summer day. His parents were already at work, Gay in the loan department at the local bank, Phillip at a meat-packing plant. His brother, Zeb, a year younger than he, was still sleeping. Now that they lived in the country, he had no way to get to his friends' houses. He had poured himself a bowl of cereal and was idly watching the sparrows and swallows outside the kitchen window when he spied a glossy black bird with red-tipped wings. The bird gave him an idea. Maybe it needed a home. He went outside to look for some scrap lumber and his dad's tools.

By the time his mom's Honda Accord turns onto their dirt driveway around 6 P.M., Jack has finished building the birdhouse. He meets his mother as she steps out of the car.

"Come see what I did," he says.

"Can't I change into my jeans first?" Gay, tall and slender like her oldest son, with shoulder-length blond curls, can't wait to take off her suit and panty hose. A Nebraska native, she doesn't fit comfortably into what, even at thirty-nine, she still considers grown-up clothing. But the brief look of disappointment that passes over his face tells her to put her needs on hold for a minute. Mother and son walk around the house to a post-and-wire fence in the back. The birdhouse, about a foot tall, sits on the ground next to the wooden post on which Jack will attach it.

"I made it huge, for several birds," Jack explains. "I had no help, not even a little. I cut everything, drilled everything, screwed everything. It don't look too good but I built it all myself. Look here, I even wrote my name at the bottom with a one-inch bit."

Gay is impressed. "Let's put it up," she says. Jack lifts up the house, then realizes he will have to take the roof off in order to drill screws through the floor into the post. As he works at this, Gay changes clothes, then returns. "What kinds of birds do you think will come live in this house?" she asks.

"I'm hoping for a pretty bird like a cardinal, or a blue jay, maybe even a parrot. You never know."

Gay chuckles. A parrot in Kansas? She is pleased nonetheless that Jack has spent his day outside, using his imagination. This is one reason she and Phillip moved from Colorado four years earlier and used all their money to buy thirty-two acres just outside Ulysses: The outdoors would give their two boys more opportunities to explore, discover, and work.

From the time Jack was nine and Zeb eight, they had stayed home by themselves after school and during the summer. Gay and Phillip believed the family had little choice. The schools didn't offer after-school activities until seventh grade, and summer camps were too far away and too expensive. Their relatives lived hundreds of miles away. They didn't make enough money to hire an adult to stay in their house, and they had run through all *the high-school sitters they knew. So they told the boys to ride the school bus home after school and laid down rules against having friends over or watching television unless it rained.*

The more projects the boys have to do the better, Gay believes. She has been shaken by an attitude change she has seen in Jack, who worked hard through elementary school to make A's and B's. He seems, she says, "increasingly content to be mediocre," to do C work in school and say, "It's good enough." She isn't sure why this is. Is he rebelling against Phillip, who expects perfection? Copying his friends? Turned off by a boring curriculum? Whatever the reason, he needs a jump start. So a few days after the birdhouse is completed, when Jack asks Phillip if he and Zeb can turn the back quarter of Phillip's workshop into a clubhouse, Gay privately lobbies on the boys' behalf. She also starts squirreling away money to buy a couple of horses. The family owned two horses when the boys were much younger but couldn't afford to keep them up and eventually sold them.

The shop, a weathered white building no bigger than a one-car garage, sits a few hundred feet away from the house, adjacent to a slightly larger barn. It has a hard dirt floor and unfinished, rough-hewn rafters. Field mice scamper in and out; snakes coil in its dark corners. The way Jack carries on about it, however, you would think that Phillip has presented him with a luxury suite at the Best Western.

True education, the philosopher Socrates said, is the kindling of a flame, not the filling of a vessel. Twenty-four hundred years later, Gay Richardson, a bricklayer's daughter with a high-school diploma, is feeding the fire of her sons' learning in the ways she knows best, through adventures in the country. It's not that she doesn't think formal education is important. She and Phillip pay close attention to the boys' work at Kepley Middle School in town. But she believes—correctly—that her real goal as a parent is to instill in Jack and Zeb a love for learning that will last a lifetime. Let teachers teach the facts, she says. She will provide the inspiration.

If her methods succeed, she will have handed her sons one of the most precious gifts she could bestow. Scientists now know that pursuing knowledge throughout life helps people stay happier and live longer.[1] Given the speed of change in jobs as well as families, people must keep learning in order to lead even approximately successful lives.

Parents marvel at the toddler who starts to recognize colors, the six-year-old who adds and subtracts, the eight-year-old who rattles off twenty-five kinds of igneous rock. Dozens of books are available suggesting hundreds of ways in which parents can foster intelligence and creativity in their young children.[2]

Yet parental mindfulness often flags as kids enter adolescence, sometimes because parents think they have done all they can do. This is unfortunate, for it is during grades five through nine that learning either takes off or does a nosedive. One of the best things we can do for kids at this age is to continue to feed their natural hunger to learn new skills. It is also one of the best things we can do for ourselves. Young teens begin to articulate concepts in ways we never thought of. Their ideas enrich our lives as well as theirs.

Our kids' enthusiasm for learning is far more important in the long run than whether they make the honor roll. Parents, like teachers, sometimes make the mistake of focusing entirely on grades and test scores as measures of how intelligent their children are, ignoring the possibility that a child may have talents that have nothing to do with school, may even be stifled by school. An article on young teenage prodigies showed what can happen when parents of gifted children pay attention to their children's instincts and give them opportunities to hone those inclinations: These twelve-, thirteen-, and fourteen-year-olds excelled in areas such as painting, cooking, and public speaking, and almost all of their talents blossomed outside school.[3]

Extracurricular education, at its best, allows young people to choose what they will do and to dig deep into that in which they're interested. It forces them to gather and organize information, to evaluate their work, and to solve problems creatively even if they must work a long time on them. In effect, they are their own teacher. The fact that they decide what is worth knowing and mastering is the fuel that keeps them learning through high school, college, and their adult years.[4] As Jack's story indicates, such education can be pursued alone or alongside savvy adults, including but not limited to parents. And it need not cost a lot of money.

Coming Up Short, at School

The evening I met the Richardsons, I had just stepped into their small frame house when Jack's younger brother, Zeb, an impish-looking sixth-grader in wire-rimmed glasses, pushed open the side screen door. In three quick strides he was through the kitchen, passing the remains of a hot-dog-and-beans supper. He came to a full stop in the living room.

"I was chasing a bull snake. It was huge!" he exclaimed to his dad, a tall, broad-shouldered man lounging in his recliner in blue jeans and a long-sleeved white shirt. Phillip, exhausted from standing on his feet all day picking shards of bone out of ground beef, listened with one ear while he watched television, a nineteen-inch screen flanked by decorative steer horns and an old set of *Encyclopedia Americana*. Jack, meanwhile, was standing in the kitchen with Gay, telling her how much Pepto-Bismol to pour for him. Sick with the flu for most of the week, he had missed several football practices in which his team had learned about kickoffs, punts, and punt returns. He was not happy about it.

Jack was beginning to compare himself to other students and was deciding he came up short. He had been placed in the top math group, for example, a pre-algebra class in which he had to work hard. "I don't know why the teacher put me in that class," he said. He had gone out for football for the first time, on a team of two dozen seventh-graders, and he noticed that many of the other boys seemed more skilled than he and saw more action on the field. They were the town boys, the bigger and faster receivers and tackles who had played years of football in the Ulysses recreational league. He was a country boy so thin he would, as his favorite author, Louis L'Amour, wrote, "have to stand in the same place twice to cast a shadow."

He said very little on my first visit to his house. When I returned the following afternoon, however, he volunteered to show me around the homestead, the outside classroom where he did what he really enjoyed. Would I like to see the barn, where he and his brother once raised peacocks until the neighbors' dogs attacked them? Would I care to look in the shop, where they were building their clubhouse? How about the birdhouse, would I like to see that? No birds had come to roost there yet, but his parents told him it takes a while for birds to settle into a new home. It could be any day now.

As I got to know Jack, I came to realize that these outdoor projects— as well as certain solitary assignments in class—allowed him to create things without the threat of being compared to other kids. Achievement, by itself, he found, was fun.

Exercising Choice, Being in Control

American philosopher John Dewey argued that schools should give children lots of opportunities to make meaningful choices in order to prepare them to become competent citizens.[5] One could argue that this holds true particularly for the middle grades. More than the three-year-old who insists on wearing pajamas to preschool, young adolescents hunger for the opportunity to feel autonomous, to be able to say, "This is my life!" in ways other than fighting with their parents. Parents must help them find self-directed projects that they can stamp as their own, particularly if their teachers do not.

At Kepley, Jack had to be in Pat Mapel's English class every day at 8 A.M. Math teacher Georjean Perez told him when he had mastered algebraic definitions and could move on to formulas. At home, however, he was able to decide when to launch a project and how to accomplish it.

Working on a project one chooses and controls actually stimulates the growth of new neurons, according to research. During the task, the brain secretes endorphins, which produce a feeling of excitement and energy. Whether building a birdhouse or a skyscraper, the creator gets "high" and wants to keep creating. Outdoor projects are especially stimulating, according to education professor Susan Miller, because they involve "almost every competency one can imagine: observing, inventing, problem-solving, decision-making."[6] To construct his birdhouse, for example, Jack had to make a plan ("How big should it be?"), imagine different ways of carrying it out ("Should I use nails or screws to secure it?"), and consider the merits of each alternative ("Nails would be easier, but screws wouldn't split the wood").

The ability to control their environment is a better predictor of kids' satisfaction at school than report cards or levels of self-esteem, Jacquelynne Eccles, a psychologist at the University of Michigan, has found.[7] Jack was not the only student who did not feel in control in school: In a survey taken of all Kepley students by the Search Institute, a national research organization, fewer than half said they had a sense of personal power and purpose.

Classes in which Kepley students did exercise some initiative—and typically described as their favorite courses—were electives that resembled out-of-school activities, for example, ceramics. The first time I visited Jack in the ceramics studio, I arrived a few minutes late. Pat Kistler, the teacher, was not in the classroom yet, but Jack and his eleven classmates were working away without her, focused and quiet. One girl was making a mask of her friend's face. A boy was touching up a wall plaque of two faces: one smiling, the other in a deep frown. Jack was at the potter's wheel, smoothing a cone of grayish-brown clay with a wet sponge.

"What is it going to be?" I asked.

"Whatever I want," he replied without looking up.

Kistler arrived a few minutes later and told me it is difficult for some of the students to make what they want because they've never been able to choose a task in school before. She suggests ideas for the clueless, then watches them take off. "Go slow, use lots of water, and you will not fail," she tells them. She turns to me and says, "They can't control their friends or their parents but they can control the clay." Clay is also forgiving, she added. They can throw a lopsided planter back on the wheel, or shape a pot that has fallen on the floor into a plate.

Enjoying the Doing

Pat Kistler was a little too cheery for Jack's taste. But he loved what he *did* in her class that first semester and chose to take the class again the second half of the year. In the art room, as well as the backyard, he reminded me of the toddler who learns to pull himself up in his crib, then stands there bouncing and grinning even if no one else is in the room. As Jack worked his clay, or cobbled together his birdhouse, he was saying to himself, just as that toddler does, "Look what I can do!"

Therapist Michael Gurian says that boys' brains have been wired over millions of years of evolution to be object-oriented, to want to take things apart and put things together. In *A Fine Young Man*,[8] he urges parents to make sure their boys find such opportunities, if not in school then out of school. My observations support this. Mario Rawlings, a kid from a working-class family in Durham who appears in chapter eleven, showed me early in the year a small wooden race car that he had built in his shop course at school. In a competition with other cars, it proved to be the speediest and was his proudest accomplishment in an otherwise up-and-down year.

Jack's birdhouse, like Mario's car, provided him with something else he didn't always enjoy at school: tangible evidence of accomplishment. Too often, educators focus on external rewards far removed from any actual specific effort. Kepley, for example, had structured an elaborate reward system each quarter to encourage good grades. The student who earned all A's received a gold card, entitling him to free products at participating community businesses as well as certain school privileges, such as moving to the front of the lunch line. The student who earned mostly A's got a white card carrying somewhat fewer privileges, and the B student received an orange card. During his seventh-grade year Jack consistently won an orange card but almost never used it.

Why not? "Oh I don't know, I'd forget it, I guess, or lose it," he said.

Laying the Groundwork for Learning

Jack's parents encouraged him and his brother from an early age to play by themselves. "We couldn't afford the latest toys," Gay recalled. "But he and Zeb would play for hours with toads or the neighbor's chickens. They'd swing on rope from rafters in the barn, or use rope to build things. They could make a toy out of anything." By the time Jack was nine, Phillip had showed both boys how to safely use the tools in the back shed.

That was about the age that the boys started staying home alone after school. In addition to restricting access to TV and friends, Gay required her boys to call her at work regularly and to do chores during those afternoons, such as feed and exercise their animals.

Depending on which survey you read, one-half to two-thirds of young adolescents take care of themselves after school at least a couple of days a week. Some research suggests that this is risky, that kids in charge of themselves experience, on average, more social, emotional, and academic difficulties than those who stay at home under adult supervision or are engaged in organized activities.[9]

Several recent and more refined studies indicate, however, that self-care is not always harmful and that the degree of risk is moderated by several factors: whether the child is at home or someplace else (home is usually better), whether he is with friends or by himself or with siblings (by himself or with siblings is preferable), how much monitoring the parent does (regular is crucial), how long he is alone (no more than a couple of hours, depending on maturity), even the particular personality of the child and the neighborhood he lives in.[10]

To that list I would add one more, inspired by observing Jack and other kids: Those kids who do well at home learned how to play by themselves when they were younger, to create and make things that pleased them and for which they were praised. John Taylor Gatto, twice named New York City Teacher of the Year, argues that parents of young children do their youngsters a disservice by cramming their agendas with soccer, music lessons, ballet, golf, and foreign languages. Children need to be able to create meaning on their own, Gatto says, to conquer solitude by pondering and following out their thoughts.[11]

It was admittedly easier for the Richardsons to allow their boys to stay home in the country than it would have been had they lived in a city. But even parents living in distressed neighborhoods can create routines during the after-school hours that enable their children to be both safe and increasingly self-sufficient. A variety of activities can be knitted together both outside the home (visits to a neighbor or relative, the library or a club) and inside (homework and chores, then relaxation).[12] Eldon Stanton did this for Eric. Both he and Gay did something else equally important: They told their boys that, until proven otherwise, they were confident that the boys could take care of themselves.

Lapses in Judgment

Jack did get into trouble occasionally while home alone or with his brother. The worst of these incidents occurred in his beloved clubhouse.

It was late fall and Jack and Zeb were goofing around, drawing silly pictures. Jack decided to try a little experiment. He rolled up a tissue and put a lit match to it. The tissue went up in flames, and a piece of it fell on the old sofa. Jack blew out the flame, patted out the spot on the couch, and thought no more about it.

At eight o'clock that evening, a neighbor banged on the screen door. "Your building's on fire!" he yelled. Phillip, Jack's dad, phoned the fire department, then called his sons outside. Jack saw the clubhouse smoking and knew what had happened. The firefighters extinguished the fire and Jack confessed.

The consequences of his antic were severe. The clubhouse was charred beyond repair, and Phillip's custom-made saddle had been destroyed. Jack cried himself to sleep that night. He was placed "on restriction" for a month after the fire, which meant he could not leave the house except to go to school. He was assigned to clean out the shop and to polish the metal bits that had survived. The weather had turned bitter, and he caught a chest cold. He moped his way through each day, not wanting to talk to anyone.

Gay allowed him to feel remorseful but she saw no reason to overreact. Jack was normally a cautious kid. To pull him out of the doldrums, she increased her deposits into the horse fund, and one weekend she and Phillip bought two small quarter horses for $1,400.

"I felt strongly that if we didn't get 'em now, the boys wouldn't want 'em later," she told me.

One crisp Saturday morning in early spring, Jack and his horse are separating cattle for a Ulysses rancher when Jack spies a cow off to the side by herself. Something looks strange about this reddish Hereford crossbreed, and he rides over to take a closer look. His eyes come to rest on her vagina, out of which, to his amazement, a basketball-sized mass of red tissue is hanging, scabbed over. He rides over to Jess Hammer, his new boss and, increasingly, his teacher.

"Hey, Jess," he says, nodding to the unfortunate animal. "What's wrong with her?"

"That's a prolapsed cow," says Jess, who has been up all night birthing cows. "I've got to take her to the vet."

Hammer is a laid-back, friendly guy in his mid-fifties whose round face wears a perpetual tan from working outdoors. He owns thirty-six hundred acres of land three miles from Ulysses on which he raises livestock and grows wheat and milo, also called sorghum. Like other farmers and ranchers, he hires young men and an occasional young woman to help him, usually on weekends and all day during the summer. He pays them $3.50 an hour to start and $5 when they "know a thing or two." But as Jack attests that spring, the young workers acquire a lot more than a paycheck from him.

Gay had hooked her boys up with Hammer the previous year. As much as they enjoyed doing projects at home in their spare time, she figured they *also needed someone to teach them new skills and talk to them about what was in store for them as men. Their dad did these things, too, working with them in the shop out back. He attended their ball games, gave them tips about playing sports. But sometimes he was out of town working, other times out of work and depressed. Both he and Gay felt the boys needed a grandfather figure, and their own fathers lived too far away to play that role.*

Jack's first job was leading cows out of the barn and down a green metal chute to be vaccinated. This was not easy because the cows seemed to know what was in store for them and balked at the idea of getting their hides punched. Over the next year, Jack sorted cattle, hauled bales of hay in the pickup, put up fence posts, and strung wire. Usually Jess worked with him but sometimes he was left alone, forced to make his own decisions about how tight to stretch the sixteen-gauge wire or what to do with an ornery steer. He learned how to castrate young bulls and to take care of a prolapsed cow whose vagina had ripped during the birthing process.

"Wanna go with me to the vet's?" Hammer asks Jack and Zeb. The boys nod eagerly. Hammer backs up his pickup, attaches a trailer to it, and tells Jack and Zeb to move the cow into the trailer. They grab a couple of short sticks and prod the cow up the ramp, then set out for the veterinarian's office, where they watch the surgery.

From their earliest years, kids are fascinated by what grown-ups do and how they do it. One sees this particularly in middle school–aged kids, who enjoy working alongside adults, learning essential skills of teamwork and joint decision making.

We have taken away many such opportunities that once existed for kids under sixteen. Child labor laws, passed early in this century in the wake of abuses to child workers, eliminated formal apprenticeships and discouraged even informal jobs for kids twelve, thirteen, and fourteen. Social attitudes changed from what kids could do to what they could not do. Today, although many middle schools foster adult-student work arrangements through community service, school is still largely a solitary pursuit that gives kids few ideas about how they might make it in the world. The result, longtime middle-school educator Chris Stevenson suggests, is that children are "growing up more sophisticated but less mature than their counterparts of earlier generations."[13]

A Jack of All Trades

As kids move into middle to late adolescence many will begin to zoom in on one or two particular interests. But at younger ages they are curious about everything and will try anything. They ask why—and why not—almost as often as a preschooler.

They are thrilled not so much by learning facts, which is what they enjoyed when they were younger, or by analyzing facts, as they will do in high school, but by using facts to complete interesting projects. If they're lucky, school will give them opportunities for such firsthand applications, as when Jack learned in math class to graph how he spent his time each day. Jobs outside school frequently provide them with such chances as well.

At Hammer's ranch, Jack applied his math skills and learned the basics of carpentry by building a fence. He learned biology while attending the birth of calves. He was forced to think about economics and probability as he watched Hammer draw up a plan for the number of acres of grain he had to plant in order to support the livestock. And he saw how the things he was learning worked together: Corn had to be sown in straight rows in order to produce a healthy harvest, which was necessary to fatten up the cattle in order to bring a good price at auction. This sense of integration appealed to his newly developed appreciation for patterns. He rarely saw such connections at school except in an occasional interdisciplinary unit in English and social studies.

Jack couldn't help but compare how much he accomplished on the ranch to what he did in school—in, for example, his vocational agriculture class. "The class is supposed to be hands-on," he said. "We just planted corn and radishes in pop bottles. But everyone is fooling around so we don't do that much." Contrary to what people think, many kids Jack's age would rather work hard than goof off.

They also enjoy being practical. On one of my visits to Jack's house, he proudly showed off the products of his ceramics class: a mustard-yellow coffee mug (which he talked me into buying for $5) and a couple of planters for his mom. Why did he like ceramics? "Because I make a bunch of cool stuff that I need," he replied.

Young adolescents are rarely shown the utility of what they're taught in school. I observed an exception in Jack's life science class, listening to

Gina Lyon, his teacher, discuss roundworms. Lyon, a young, forceful teacher, had placed her twenty-two students into small groups and had passed around a jar of cylindrical worms resembling fat, brown pieces of pasta. She reminded them that roundworms could invade the human intestine, blood, and central nervous system, doing harm if left unchecked.

Lyon asked a girl in one of the groups the roundworm's range in size. "I don't know," the girl responded.

"Is that how we answer?" Lyon asked.

"Noooo . . ." The girl smiled slightly. "We'll figure it out and tell you tomorrow."

"That's more like it," Lyon answered approvingly.

Lyon was attempting to teach kids how to uncover facts that are changing rapidly as human knowledge expands. She was also showing them that they can produce better results working with someone else than working alone. But these gifts are not as obvious as a coffee mug. Jack could not see them or hold them in his hand. The uses one can derive from a good education are frequently long-term rather than immediate—a disadvantage to kids raised on Nintendo and computer games and who live fully in the present.

We adults tend to roll our eyes when students question the relevance of school, as they start doing at this age. But as Stevenson reminds us in *Teaching Ten to Fourteen Year Olds*, young adolescents who issue such challenges are "re-examining the context in which they live, critiquing the way things appear to be and . . . theorizing alternative possibilities."[14] In return, we must take more pains than we normally would to think about education's merits ourselves and spell them out to our kids. Collaborations with the outside world can provide occasions for such conversation.

The tangible results Jack achieved on the ranch were sweetened by the fact that they benefited someone he cared about. If he failed a test in school, he was the only one who suffered. If he aced the test, he boosted his chances for a good report card. But if he stretched Hammer's wire too tight when building a fence, it might snap later and a cow could slip out and wander away, getting lost or hit by an 18-wheeler. Hammer could be out as much as $700 or $800. If he followed Hammer's instructions to the letter, the cows would be contained and Hammer would be content.

Young adolescents want to feel that there is something at stake when they work. They are increasingly able to see how their actions can help or hurt others, and they like knowing that what they do will make a positive difference to someone besides themselves.

Teaching While Doing

Hammer was an excellent teacher, partly because he loved what he was doing and had been doing it for a long time. He bought his first heifer while in high school and his first acres of land after he graduated from high school. He added on to the ranch as he and his wife raised two sons and a daughter.

He learned from his kids that communicating is easier when you are doing things together. As he and Jack worked side by side, he would test Jack's book knowledge. Jack might be directing cattle into the chute and Hammer would say, "You know, I'm thinking of selling twenty-six of these cows. They'll bring $330 a head. What will I make?" Slow to answer at first without a calculator in his hand, Jack got faster after Hammer explained the tricks he used to make quick computations.

Sometimes, Hammer talked to Jack about college. Hammer hadn't attended college and wished that he had. "If you want to be a pen rider in a feedlot, you'll get by without it," he'd tell Jack. "But if you want to be a buyer, you need the paper. The boss is going to look and see that you've done something steady for four or five years of your life and now you're ready to go to work."

Jack told Hammer he wanted to go into the cattle business after college. Hammer thought that was a fine idea, but he wanted Jack to appreciate how rapidly the business was changing. Beef companies were talking about going the way of hog operators, Hammer told Jack, raising and fattening their own cows rather than buying someone else's. Jack would accompany Hammer to a sale barn with a hundred cattle, each weighing six to seven hundred pounds, and both would return shaking their heads at the low prices Hammer had received from the big feedlot operators. "The conglomerates are going to own it all," Hammer would tell Jack on his darker days. "Ten to fifteen years from now I'll be out of business." Then prices would start to creep up and Hammer would confide to Jack that he still had several goals: buying more registered cattle, better horses, a fancier tractor.

Hammer found it difficult to explain to Jack the vagaries of a volatile farm economy, trends that Hammer hadn't worried about much when he was starting out. Why did the price of wheat fluctuate so much when the cost of a loaf of bread stayed the same? Could Jack be a rancher and hope for a steady income?

Adults who see themselves only as advice givers sometimes back away from adolescents, fearing that they won't know the answers to such questions. But Hammer knew that having the answers wasn't nearly as important as helping Jack frame the right questions.

Together they could speculate on the economy, with Hammer asking that question so precious to someone Jack's age: "What do *you* think?" Occasionally Jack would be able to tie into these conversations something he had learned at school, as when his social studies class discussed genetic engineering. "The world will be different by the time I get into ranching," he told Hammer one evening. "I may be just cloning my good animals."

Learning a Code of Conduct

Hammer didn't let just anybody work on his place. One time a parent called him complaining that the parent's son had gotten drunk at a party and "needed to be taught a thing or two." Would Hammer take him? No, Hammer would not. Work was not a punishment, it was a privilege. Another time, a boy he had hired blew off a job Hammer had asked him to do. When Hammer asked why the job wasn't finished, the boy shrugged, replying, "Don't worry about it." He was shown the door. In Hammer's book, you had to keep earning the privilege.

Without stating it as such, Hammer was teaching Jack about character. He knew it sounded corny, but he believed in the maxims written in 1939 by cowboy singer Gene Autrey. The cowboy, Autrey wrote, "must never shoot first. He must never go back on his word. He must be a good worker. He must keep himself clean in thought, speech, action, and personal habits. He must be gentle with children, the elderly, and animals." It might be manlike to plow nonstop, but if Hammer saw a bird's nest in his path, he would stop his tractor in the middle of a furrow, step down, and remove it. Jack had seen him do that.

"Most people wouldn't go around that bird," Jack said one Saturday morning in Hammer's kitchen. "I probably wouldn't have. I don't know if I would even have seen the bird." Hammer, listening to our conversation, smiled and said nothing. He doesn't preach to Jack on these finer points of morality. He can tell that Jack is rolling them around in his mind, and that is enough for now. Young adolescents are beginning to wrestle with questions of right and wrong, but most are not able to articulate their beliefs until later in adolescence. That is why mentors are so important; they provide words until those under their care can find their own.

"Hammer helps make me a better person," Jack said privately to me later. "I don't know how, but I'm pretty sure he does."

This is the day, Jack thinks to himself one late afternoon in May as he slides into his Wrangler jeans and pulls on his boots. "I'm gonna get Spook into the box if it's the last thing I do."

He is headed for the roping arena with his mother and brother and their two horses. Several months ago Gay decided that she and the boys needed to learn to do something new together. Roping was an obvious choice. They loved to ride, and Phillip already knew how to rope from his days herding cattle. They could join the local roping club, travel to rodeos, and rope for fun and competitively, as a family. As members of the county roping club, they would be tutored by men she knew to be courteous and patient.

The boys hoped to rope steers, an activity increasingly popular with kids their age. Their two horses, Whiskey and Phantom, were not strong enough to pull five hundred pounds of beef and bone. So they were sold and the family bought two other, more muscular quarter horses: a chestnut for Zeb named Pete, and a gray horse for Jack named Spook.

Phillip first taught the boys how to capture a bale of hay, standing on the ground. Then he and the boys built a dummy steer out of gray metal pipes and wire. They roped it next, first on foot and later on horseback.

Pete was already a roping horse. Spook, picked up from a feedlot, was more cautious, or "box sour" in cowboy terms. The first few times Jack had tried to ride him into "the box" at the arena, a square frame stall out of which horse and rider bolt to chase the steer, Spook had turned away. Jack began to get discouraged. Then one evening he watched his dad try to ride Spook into the box, spurring the horse vigorously. Eventually, Phillip succeeded, and this inspired Jack. Maybe he could do the same thing but more gently. Spook just needed additional training. And so did he.

The timed event known as steer roping, cowboys say, is 80 percent horse and 20 percent rider. This is because the rider's attention must be focused on the rope and the steer. Everything else—the velocity of the chase, the angle of the ride, the turns and quick stop—are the horse's responsibility. Before the steer is released, the horse must stand quietly in the left corner of the box. When the rider nods for the steer's chute to be opened, just to the right of the box, the horse must remain calm as metal doors open with a bang. The steer charges out, setting off a light that signals the start of the time clock. If a skittish horse bolts out prematurely, the rider is fined ten seconds, catastrophic in a competition that sees the best riders complete their routine in four to five seconds. Once the chase begins, the rider sights the steer's horns and tosses out the loop, attempting to place it over the horns or neck.

After he made up his mind to train Spook, Jack spent time watching veteran riders at the arena, comparing what they did to what he was doing. The good handlers were calm and focused, traits he needed to practice.

Over the first few weeks on roping nights, Jack didn't enter Spook in competition but would walk him up to the box several times, talking quietly all the time, stroking his mane and neck. No matter how many times Spook turned away, Jack would turn him back around. Horses, like people, learn by repetition. "You're going to go in that box if we have to stay here all night," he would whisper to Spook. "If you go in there right away, you won't have to work so hard." It was difficult to tell on these nights who was learning more, horse or rider.

Meanwhile Jack was teaching himself to rope on Zeb's horse. His first night in the box, sitting on Pete and waiting for the steer to charge out of the chute, he was haunted by questions. What would the steer be like? Fast, powerful, and kicking, or slow and meandering? You never knew. In his right hand Jack held a loop he had built out of twenty-five-foot rope, scratchy and stiff as a cable. In his left he held reins and the rest of the rope, coiled three times between his thumb and forefinger. He quickly ran through all the things he was supposed to do. His armpits were sweating through his T-shirt.

He nodded to the man to open the chute and "Bang!" the doors swung open. Immediately he leaned forward, prompting Pete to run out at a clip of about thirty miles per hour. Pete was steady but Jack's right hand wasn't, *and as he swung the rope out in the direction of the steer it sailed off over the steer's head and fell in the dirt. Over the next four hours he took nine more turns in the arena—true to the saying that there is no quit in a good cowboy. He managed to land the rope neatly over a steer's horns twice.*

A number of accidents could have happened that night or in the nights to come. Even a well-trained horse will buck if annoyed by a stickler caught under its blanket. A steer can go crazy and gore horse or rider. A rider can get thrown and break a collarbone, or worse. Gay never watched the boys loping into the arena without feeling fear snake through her stomach. Her anxiety lessened, however, as she herself learned to rope.

Her first two times in the arena, she didn't bother holding a rope. She just tried to stay on the charging horse. She graduated to holding a rope, then throwing it, and eventually she landed it over a steer. The rush of adrenaline she felt that night was like nothing she had ever experienced. "Now I understand why you love this so much," she told the boys as she practically bounced off her horse.

She stands nearby on this evening in May as Jack mounts Spook and lopes him in a circle a couple of times before heading for the box. Amazingly, Spook walks right in and assumes his position in the left corner facing out. Seconds later, boy and horse charge into the arena after a steer. Gay leans on the fence watching, alert, a bit fearful, and very proud.

As kids move into adolescence, father and daughter can go whitewater rafting, mother and son can camp, the whole family can cook a gourmet dinner. Relationships are strengthened or repaired as rafts sail over choppy waters, tent stakes are pounded into the ground, or vegetables are chopped for stir-fry. Activities with kids this age are a lot more fun than playing Candy Land for the thousandth time.

Even better, particularly from the kid's point of view, is for parent and child to learn to do something new together. Gay Richardson had always learned from her boys. When Jack and Zeb were younger, they had taught her how to build a two-room cabin out of Lincoln Logs and how to throw a football. She had done these things with them partly because she enjoyed being with them and partly because she noticed that the more time she spent with them, the better behaved they were. As they got older and were no longer interested in "baby games," she realized she would have to find a new pursuit for them all, something physical and risky enough to hold their interest. She felt she had only a year or two to hook the boys before they started driving cars and getting wrapped up in high-school activities. She herself was ready to learn a new hobby as well. "Otherwise, life gets dull and mundane," she said. "I figured if I didn't learn to rope then, I never would."

Setting an Example

Unlike some of the other parents I observed, Gay, approaching the age of forty, infused her own life with learning. She attended classes in leadership training, paid for by the bank. She was promoted twice at the bank the year I observed her family, to the job of salaried loan supervisor. Phillip, who had trouble keeping a steady job, often traveled out of state looking for work, and she had to learn to do dozens of jobs that she never thought she would need to know—like buying and hauling pigs.

At daybreak one Saturday morning in May, before the temperature had had a chance to climb much past 40 degrees, Gay rose and woke up the boys. "Time to get the pigs," she told them.

Boys and girls all over Grant County were purchasing young hogs that weekend and having them weighed. They would fatten up their hogs until late August, when the animals would be auctioned off at the county fair. With Jack's assistance, Gay hitched a trailer onto the family's red pickup, drove her boys to a farm to buy their pigs, then stopped by the scales at the Grant County fairground. When the workers waved her over, she realized she was going to have to back the trailer plus its two animals down a long, narrow driveway with about forty people watching. She had never backed a trailer before. She took a deep breath, shifted gears into reverse, and steered so adroitly that when she stepped out of the cab, a man standing at the scales said, "You ought to get an award for that." She grinned.

By seizing the opportunity to learn even minor new skills, Gay risked looking dumb in front of her kids, a condition not too many parents willingly put themselves in. Like Eldon Stanton in chapter one, she did not mind acknowledging that her child could do some things better than she and turning to him for advice. In her view, every member of the family could be an expert at something and share his or her knowledge with the other family members.

She rarely got discouraged; even while roping she was happy to go, as she put it, "from point A to point B." Each day she showed her kids that perseverance and hard work, more than brains and luck, lead to success. Young adolescents tend to think just the opposite.

Months after he and his mother had started roping, Jack recalled for me something his dad said one night while watching Gay in the arena: "If you boys would put half as much effort into roping as your mother does, I'd be happy." Said Jack, "My mom's not very good, but she tries hard."

Learning by (Negative) Example

Jack also learned perseverance by watching his father's ongoing attempts to acquire and keep a job. He knew his dad's history: After high school, Phillip drove trucks, dealt cards in Nevada, worked on one ranch, then on others, in Nebraska and Colorado. When Gay met him at age twenty-five, Phillip, then twenty-four, was a bouncer in a bar in Denver. They got married soon after they met and moved around as Phillip continued to search for a job he liked. When he landed one at a Grant County feedlot he told Gay, "This is it," and they settled in Ulysses. He started college at age forty, when Jack was in elementary school, and finished with a master's degree in agribusiness the year Jack started at Kepley.

To Phillip's dismay, his degree didn't guarantee him a management job. It got him into the offices of some plants, but layoffs and his temper would sideline him. Eventually he found himself riding through feedlots again, looking for sick cows, first in Texas and, when that job ended, in Colorado. Toward the end of my year with the Richardsons, he applied to become a meat inspector for the U.S. Department of Agriculture.

"They didn't need him in Texas" is how Jack described his dad losing one job, then later, "They didn't need him in Colorado, either." Unassisted, Jack could have looked at his father's work patterns and asked, Why go to college? But Gay and Phillip didn't want him thinking he would end up like his dad; they wanted him to learn how not to. They talked to him candidly about the economy, timing, and temperamental flaws. As a result he learned other lessons. What were they? "To try again," he told me. And "to go to college before I'm forty."

By Year's End

Jack had earned a secure spot on Kepley's honor roll by the end of the school year. His adventures outside school had made him a better student inside the classroom. Building a birdhouse honed his imagination and creativity. Working on Hammer's ranch taught him to follow directions and finish a job. Roping taught him to figure out what he didn't know, to think quickly, analyze, and correct his mistakes and to keep doing something that was difficult until he mastered it. All of these skills were turning a shy, self-deprecating boy into a young man of poise and self-respect who, like his mother, continued to seek new challenges.

The summer after seventh grade, he tried his hand at photography and brought home a blue ribbon from the county fair. He enjoyed similar success at a pole-bending competition sponsored by the roping club.

Pole bending, a staple of horse shows, is a timed obstacle course on horseback. When the flag went down the day Jack competed, he ran Spook as hard as he could from one end of the arena to the other. Then he wove Spook back around six poles. Rider and horse wove up one more time, then headed back to the starting line as fast as they could. The entire event took only twenty-five seconds, winning applause from dozens of spectators. He received a silver belt buckle measuring two inches by three inches and engraved with the sweet words "First Place."

"We told Jack his horse is worth a whole lot more now than when he first got him," Gay said proudly. Spook was no longer willing to be mediocre, and neither was Jack.

AS PARENTS WE CAN

• Make sure our child is connected to an adult at school who can guide him through the maze of opportunities for learning and fun.

• Sit in on her classes for a day. Observe the balance of individual effort and group work, and whether students are engaged. Listen to the teacher's tone of voice and observe whether teachers mingle with students outside class.

• Pay attention to the teachers and subjects he talks about and why. Look for opportunities outside school to enrich both the subjects he likes and doesn't like.

• Discuss with teachers ways in which she can combine schoolwork with her outside interests.

• Gradually decrease oversight of homework but stay involved in school activities that put you into the school building regularly.

• Watch for major changes in school policies, curricula, or school population that might affect how he thinks about himself and others.

• Make home a haven from the trashy language and behavior she sees elsewhere.

• Encourage him from an early age to entertain himself creatively for some period of time every day.

• Take up a new hobby or interest ourselves.

PART FOUR

The Right Connections

Alana Perales used to have two good adult friends whom she could count on. One was Yolanda Chavez, her assistant softball coach. Young and attractive, Yolanda worked Alana hard and praised her often, using the word "sweetie" a lot. She liked the same pop music Alana did, and listened sympathetically when Alana talked to her about boy problems after Sunday dinners at Alana's grandparents' house.

Yolanda was killed riding back from a softball game one night during the summer before Alana started sixth grade. The van in which she was riding was hit by another car that ran a stop sign. Alana, following in a car with other members of the team, saw it happen.

In the months that followed, Alana turned to another young woman for support: her father's girlfriend, Lindsay De La Rosa. Alana tended to keep her emotions in check, but with Lindsay she could cry and get a long hug. Lindsay cheered at Alana's games and took Alana and her sister, Angela, to Pueblo, Colorado, over Thanksgiving. She suggested to Alana that they learn to make pottery together.

Lindsay had lived with Alana's father, Harold, for several years when suddenly she decided to move to Pueblo. Within less than two years, Alana had lost the two adults, outside her family, to whom she felt the closest.

Of all the societal changes that have affected adolescents in recent years, the most significant may be the loss of regular, sustained contact with caring adults. This includes contact with parents but is by no means limited to that. Eight of the eighteen kids I originally studied could not name one adult they considered a friend other than a relative. Scientific surveys of much larger populations have pegged the number of such connections even lower.[1]

Most of the kids I observed did not come right out and say they missed adult contact. But their conversations were peppered with references to adults. They talked about growing up in a future that no longer seemed far away, and their questions revealed a hunger to know what that might be like.

Special adults, be they teacher, coach, bus driver, or librarian, give shape and purpose to an adolescent's existence. As adolescents pull away from their parents (and as parents pull away from their kids), these adults can step in to provide the glue that binds together the various pieces of the child's identity puzzle. Kids need these outside adults to help them discover what they're competent in, to make them feel loved and loving, and to reassure them that they are not weird or stupid. The Greek poet Homer recognized this almost three thousand years ago, when he made his hero Odysseus appoint an old friend to guard his son during the Trojan War. That old friend's name was Mentor.

Scientists tell us that kids who enjoy ties to mentors and other adults are more likely to make good grades in school and to enjoy high self-esteem and are less likely to use drugs and alcohol or get into trouble.[2] The kids I studied showed me this: The more alliances they had, the more confident they were in their abilities, the more discriminating they were in their choices of friends, the more sensitive they were to others, and, with a couple of exceptions, the more enthusiastic they were about learning. When schools or other institutions in their communities disappointed or hurt them, adults outside those institutions helped them repair the damage and push forward rather than retreat or drop out.

The Nurture Assumption, published in 1998, stirred up controversy when the author, Judith Rich Harris, claimed that a child's well-being depends almost entirely on peers, not parents. Most of us know, and my experiences support, that it's not an either-peers-or-parents situation. It's not even both-and. Healthy kids are supported by a three-legged stool: peers (I prefer the word "friends"), parents, and other adults.

In chapter ten Michelle Bellamy illustrates what a deliberate connection to someone outside the family can look like in its beginning stages. In chapter eleven, Mario Rawlings's story shows how life-saving formal, long-term connections can be. The section ends with Alana, who drew most of her strength from within her family, particularly from a grandmother whose connections to the community inspired all who knew her.

CHAPTER TEN

Mom's Friend
(Michelle's Story)

It is Christmas night in Tinseltown and Michelle Bellamy is on her way to a party. Not a lavish celebration like some she has attended at the homes of her rich white friends. No, this will be just a little get-together with friends of her mother's, black like she is, in a comfortably middle-class house in West Los Angeles.

She has prepared herself carefully, as always, in the one-bedroom, rent-controlled apartment that she shares with her mom in West Hollywood. She has chosen her nicest pair of denim jeans and a long-sleeved gray shirt that fits snugly over her lithe, just-turned-twelve-year-old body. She has spent at least a half hour searching for her metallic purple nail polish, combing through the piles of magazines, yellowing school essays, and other clutter that accumulates so easily when two people live together in a very small space.

Now, she and her mother, Janice Seton, are walking up the sidewalk toward the home of Henry Turner, a man Janice dated years before Michelle was born. Christmas lights sparkle from every corner of the two-story pink stucco house. Turner is waiting for them, a tall man with the graceful good looks of Harry Belafonte. As he leads them into the foyer Michelle's gaze sweeps the dining room, taking in the table set in red-and-green china and candles floating in crystal bowls. Her eyes then move to *the tall evergreen in the living room swathed in doves and surrounded by gifts. She turns to Janice, both pleased and disturbed.*

"Mom, I hate you!" she whispers. "How come you didn't marry Henry? Why did you choose the frog instead of the prince?" The fact that she wouldn't have been their child escapes her; what she sees is a fabulous house that she wishes could be hers.

Janice is hoping it can become Michelle's, in a way. Thirty years earlier, when she was an art student at a local community college, Janice dated Turner. They kept up their friendship over the years and recently have talked about him assuming an active role in Michelle's life despite his own family obligations. He has a wife and two boys, seven and nine, and they are willing to share him because they understand that Michelle needs a man to replace the father she barely knows.

Janice met Michelle's father, Curtis Bellamy, in her late thirties on a cruise to Mexico. He was the handsome first officer on the S.S. Azure Seas, and they dated for two years whenever he came into port. Then she told him she was pregnant. He sailed out immediately and was in Alaska when Michelle was born.

Janice, forty at that time, was working as an administrative assistant for a computer company. When she gave birth to Michelle, by cesarean section, her doctor ordered a longer bed rest than her company's maternity policy allowed. She chose to stay home—"My baby had no one else"—and she lost her job. She applied for welfare benefits and sought financial support from Curtis, at first on her own and later with the questionable help of Los Angeles County. On this Christmas night, Curtis owes his daughter $14,000 in court-ordered child support.

He held a good job with the Merchant Marines during Michelle's early years. Then when Michelle was about eight, he was laid off, and he has been in and out of work ever since. He claims he can provide no more than an occasional $20 or $25, but Janice thinks that he can give more and believes she is beginning to see in Michelle the result of his neglect. Michelle talks of being unhappy and unnoticed in the sixth grade of the private school she has attended, on scholarship, since kindergarten. She complains that neither her friends nor Janice listen to her. Men are "jerks," especially her dad.

Janice and Michelle have gotten together with Turner—by himself and with his family—several times over the years, and Janice has decided to step up her efforts to connect her daughter and her former boyfriend. As Turner would tell me months later, "Michelle needed someone else in her life besides her mom."

Before the December party, Janice regaled Michelle with tales about Turner—stories about how he wanted to marry her when they were young, how she thought he wasn't ready to settle down, how he flew to Europe at twenty-one and returned regularly to visit his mother and Janice until he fell in love with and married a Dane. During one of her sagas, Janice said to Michelle, "Oh, I've probably already told you this one."

To which her daughter replied, "Yeah, but keep talking. I like hearing it again."

It seemed to Janice that once Michelle entered sixth grade, no matter how much attention and energy Janice lavished on her, it was never enough. She was right. As we have seen with all the kids in this book, a young adolescent needs the nurturing of other adults, much as a young seedling needs water and sun. When she yells at us, hides in her room, or makes home life generally miserable, what she may be saying is, "You can't help me at this moment. Please find me someone who can."

Parents hold the seedling's root structure in place, but other adults, along with same-age friends and acquaintances, push it toward the sun. The goal of these outside connections, like the goal of good parenting, is to endow the child with enough confidence that she can disconnect, gradually, with increasing self-confidence and self-direction. Such adults, often called mentors, benefit the child most if they appear during early adolescence.[1]

When we hear the word "mentor" we may think of a formal association set up by an organization such as Big Brothers, Big Sisters. The reality, however, is more like Michelle's in this chapter or Mario's in the next. Most mentoring relationships—four out of five, according to a recent study by the Commonwealth Fund—develop spontaneously. Parents often bring a child together with the adult, and the mentor and child keep the relationship going.

In African-American communities, such special adults sometimes surface from within a large network of kin, as Eric's half-brother Roger did. Janice, who came from a small family, wasn't able to offer that to her daughter. Nor did she have the financial resources of a middle-class parent, as Chandler's mom did, that would enable her to pay for and provide transportation to after-school activities run by adults. She had secured Michelle a spot in a small, private school where teachers were supposed to take a personal interest in their students, but the school stopped after sixth grade. So she had recently realized that it was time to begin looking elsewhere.

A young man in their church who taught Michelle to play softball and handball was one of her first choices. A woman friend was another. Michelle, displaying the self-absorption typical for this age, thought these adults paid more attention to her mother than to her, and the connections never really took.

The relationship between Turner and Michelle also started tentatively and moved slowly. In order to connect easily to adults she doesn't know well, a young adolescent must first trust and feel fully accepted by the people she does know, particularly her parents and her friends.

Where Did She Belong?

Michelle, as we will see, was strongly attached to her mother but had virtually no relationship with her father. Her connections to friends and acquaintances were fragile as well, for she was different—very different—from most of them.

From the time she was five, she had attended Corinne A. Seeds Elementary School, a lab school at the University of California at Los Angeles. The school took pride in its diverse population—it was coed and half of its five hundred students were non-white—but during the seven years she was there, almost without exception, Michelle was good friends with only the white girls. She occasionally referred to her race in schoolwork, but she showed no interest in pursuing her heritage. "She's not into African stuff," Janice told me.

What she was into were the privileged lives of her friends. "All my friends live in Bel Air, Westwood, and Beverly Hills," she said matter-of-factly on our first visit together in a cafeteria on the UCLA campus. She regaled me that afternoon and on later visits with stories of birthday parties and sleepovers in gated communities where the homes had heated swimming pools and the daughters enjoyed personal beauty consultants, makeovers, and leg waxings. It was difficult to imagine a daily existence more different from the one she lived, where a big deal was to visit a shopping mall and split a $5 lunch with her mother at the food court.

For her eleventh birthday, a couple of her friends threw her a surprise birthday party at Ed Debevics, a 1950s-style diner with turquoise vinyl booths, rock 'n' roll music, and waiters who danced on the tables. She couldn't have been more thrilled. At the same time, she talked about friends as if they were precious jewels that she might lose at any minute.

She hung out with the popular girls when she was five and six, she said, "but then they got together and weren't my friends anymore." A close friend in first and second grades named Mia dropped her for another girl in third and fourth grades. In fifth grade she wasn't especially liked because she didn't dress the way the "in crowd" did. Her best friend that year, Audrey Germaine, turned against her for several months, she told me. "There are lots of mean kids at the school," she complained. "Like in gym class, I say I'm not feeling well and they say, 'Oh, you expect our team to lose just because you don't feel well?' "

She was quite excited, on that first visit, about an upcoming Halloween party at Audrey's house. It was to be her first boy-girl party and she was going as a French maid. She showed me the costume her mother had purchased: a short black dress with a white apron and a white cap.

When I called later to ask about the party, she told me she had been embarrassed because she had been the only guest in costume. She also said that the guests had played kissing games and that she wasn't kissed. "Everybody has someone that likes them except for me," she said with a sigh. "No boy has ever had a crush on me, ever."

During our next interview, she said she was mad at her friends. "Nobody listens to what I have to say. I'll be talking and they'll talk to someone else or walk away. I try to tell them how I feel, but they won't listen to me."

As we saw with Angela Perales, a rift with a friend at this age is of enormous consequence, particularly if one already feels like an outsider. I asked Michelle if schoolteachers or counselors had ever discussed with her and the other students the feeling of isolation that racial and economic differences can stir up. She said no, and the intensity of her answer reminded me of Jessica Johnston's critical observations about Chewning Middle School in Durham.

"People ignore you at this school," Michelle said. "You could walk around naked and they wouldn't notice."

Someone to Notice

Henry Turner would notice Michelle, of that Janice was sure, for he was adept at caring for those around him. He cooked for and entertained many friends. He was crazy about his two sons, taught as a substitute in their school, and was godfather to eleven young people in Denmark. Six of them were planning to visit him during the coming summer. What Michelle admired especially was how he took care of his mother, a sweet woman whom everyone called Mama. "She and I are like white on rice," he told Michelle, a down-home expression that made Michelle giggle. When Turner and his wife, Pia, moved back from Denmark, they settled in Mama's house, and Turner renovated it so that he and Pia could live downstairs. To Michelle, who was so close to her own mother, it seemed like the perfect arrangement.

He possessed traits, in addition to compassion, that seem to appeal consistently to young adolescents. One of those was his success in the adult working world. For fifteen years, Turner had run his own dance and exercise studio in Copenhagen. He taught the basics of jazz, ballet, and aerobic exercise to all ages, from kindergartners to retirees. He sponsored fashion shows and a discotheque on weekends. After he returned to Los Angeles to live, about the time Michelle was born, he continued to teach dance in a private school. He was upbeat, knew how to have fun, and had lots of stories to tell about living in Europe.

Turner, Michelle, and I are having lunch at a boisterous restaurant called The French Marketplace. The menu is the size of a newspaper, large enough for Michelle to hide behind as the waiter hovers at the table, eager for our order. Michelle is having a hard time deciding between the Thai Angel Hair Pasta with Chicken and the Chinese Salad.

"Take your time," Turner tells her as he shoos the waiter away. "There are so many choices, aren't there?"

To choose the wrong thing would be awful, so rare is this opportunity. Michelle finally settles on a third choice, the Shepherd Stew.

"If there's any left over, I can take some home to Mom," she reasons to us. "I know she'll like it."

Michelle listens for a few minutes as Turner begins to tell me about his background, then excuses herself to find a bathroom. She leaves for the bathroom again later, and Turner confides that he is a bit worried about her.

"She does this at our house, too," he says. "She doesn't eat much, then she goes off to the bathroom."

I ask whether he fears she might have an eating disorder. "I don't think so," Turner says. "She and her mother say she eats a lot at home. I don't know. She just seems so into herself."

Michelle returns, and she and Turner begin to talk about school.

"I hear you want to take gymnastics," he says. Sitting at a ninety-degree angle to her, he has turned in his chair to face her and leans forward slightly.

"I want to be more flexible," Michelle responds. "And besides, gymnastics is all girls. The boys at school scare me. They're mean. They yell things like, 'Move it!' Later, maybe I can take dance."

Turner's eyes light up. "Did you know that until I started taking dance, I was extremely shy?" he asks.

"Shy? You?" Michelle can hardly believe it.

"Movement and music made me get in touch with my own body, feel more secure," Turner says. Their talk turns to music, and Michelle says that she would love to see a musical. "I wanted to see 'Phantom of the Opera' but I knew that wouldn't happen."

"You did?" Turner is surprised. "You know if there's something you really want to see, you should tell me. Sometimes I can get free tickets."

When adults think of building relationships with young teens, they tend to think of grand rescue operations in times of crisis—getting tickets to a Knicks game for a kid who is failing in school, for example.

But what matters most to kids is paying attention to them when they're not in trouble, in ordinary ways. Adults can take a tip here from adolescent friendships, which thrive on a sympathetic ear and the sharing of small pleasures. ("How many kinds of nail polish do you have?" "Have you heard the latest Beastie Boys CD?") People are more important than playtime for kids this age; kids are looking for shepherds, not saviors.

Michelle was thrilled to eat lunch at The French Marketplace, a meeting place that caters to an artsy crowd. She was also tantalized by the possibility of seeing a Broadway musical one day, as any child who never got that opportunity would be. But what she talked about most to me later were Turner's questions about her interest in gymnastics and dance, as well as his empathy for her bouts of shyness. Turner knew the secret of connecting to an adolescent; he asked questions in a way that allowed her to set the conversational agenda and then listened carefully to her responses. He signaled that he was interested in Michelle, a big boost to someone who wondered whether there was anything about her to be interested in.

Listening, writes Marc Freedman, author of a book about mentoring programs, "seems to define effective mentors more than any other [characteristic]." He quotes a D.C. physician/mentor named John Hogan: "We [adults] talk so much," Hogan states. "We're telling kids this and that. We forget to listen. We forget to ask, 'What do you think? How do you feel?' It's only after we know how they feel and what they think that we can know what to say."[2]

Robert Blum, a psychologist and expert on adolescent attitudes and behavior, found out how much small things matter when he interviewed kids walking around Minneapolis's Mall of America. What does being connected mean? he asked them. He discovered that "it isn't the trip to Wrigley Field. Being connected is a call after school saying, 'How did the game go? I can't leave work until five but I will be home at six. I just wanted to see how you did.' Being connected is remembering your kid had a test last Thursday in social studies and saying, 'What did you get on that test?' "[3] Blum was talking about parental connections. But his point holds true for any adult who wants to relate to kids.

Repeatedly over the year I observed her, Michelle expressed appreciation for similar ordinary kindnesses. One of her favorite adults at school was a cafeteria aide who would say to her, "Oh, I love that shirt," and celebrate her birthday every year by buying Michelle her favorite soda. The teachers Michelle remembered most fondly not only were "good at teaching" and "helpful when you were bad at something," but people with whom "you could talk about everything." She recalled one fifth-grade math teacher in particular: "He gave us his home telephone number. I still have it." Other adults in Michelle's life—a friend of her mother's who gave Michelle dresses and jewelry, an aunt who took her to

Disneyland—might have been surprised to know that what she really wished for from them was a telephone call just to her, every now and then.

Out of Touch

Her father, Curtis, called her every now and then. But he appeared to be tone deaf to her thoughts and feelings, even on her twelfth birthday.

He had taken her out to dinner, and as the two of them waited for their food to be served, he handed her two gifts. Janice had suggested that he purchase a gift certificate to Contempo, one of Michelle's favorite fashion stores. The first present was flat, and Michelle eagerly unwrapped it, only to discover a package of nuts, grains, and raisins. Trail mix? On her birthday? That was pretty cheap, she thought. She unwrapped the second gift: an autobiography of rhythm-and-blues singer Patti LaBelle. Her heart sank. Patti LaBelle was of her father's generation. Not hers.

Curtis told me later he gave Michelle trail mix because he thought she could snack on it at school. The book about a smart, successful black woman would inspire her, he believed. But Michelle didn't understand his reasoning. She thought he was simply ignoring what she wanted just as he had abandoned her and her mother years earlier. His being out of touch with her desires and her taste bothered her more than the fact that he didn't live with her.

How well a father is tuned in to his child's interests is as important to the child as how often he sees her. Michelle didn't feel odd being raised by her mom alone. Why should she? One out of five kids in this country are in that same situation. As she once said to Janice after reeling off the names of friends whose parents lived apart, "See? We're part of the in-crowd." But when she compared her relationship to her dad to that of her friends with their fathers, it was a different story. Her friend Audrey, for example, bragged about eating at a favorite restaurant with her dad and betting $100 that she would finish her hamburger. She told Michelle that she ate three-fourths of the burger and snared $75.

Michelle loved that story, both for the friendly, teasing bond that Audrey enjoyed with her dad and for the money Audrey's dad had dangled in front of her. Two weeks after her birthday dinner, Curtis telephoned to talk to her, and she was snippy and mean to him. "It felt good," she told me later.

Turner knew from Janice that Michelle felt alternately angry at and sorry for her father. He also realized that the hurt and betrayal she felt hampered his efforts to build a relationship with her. He tried to discuss her situation with Curtis during lunch at The French Marketplace. "Your dad doesn't know what he is missing," he said. Privately, Michelle agreed, but she wasn't ready to talk about something so personal with him.

A few days into the second semester at school, Michelle is standing in line in front of her teacher's desk in the language arts classroom, waiting for an assignment to be critiqued. In this cheerful, inviting room, a giant rug of primary colors is draped across the ceiling, and a dozen wind chimes, made by students, tinkle occasionally.

Michelle's face is far from cheerful, even though a few minutes earlier she was praised for a paragraph she wrote about the European Age of Exploration. She has written more and wants her teacher, Ava De La Sota, to look at it. But other students also have essays to show and are cutting in line. She allows several of them to slide in front of her and eventually gives up trying to advance. She returns to her desk and takes out a doll she has fashioned from pipe cleaners.

During her next class, physical education, she asks to be excused, saying she doesn't feel well. Her PE teacher says okay, and she sits under a large oak tree watching the other kids play soccer. "I used to love to kick the soccer ball," she says. "Now I run away from it."

An old friend, Noelle Okinuk, a dark-skinned native of Papua New Guinea who left the school the year before, shows up for a brief visit and Michelle's spirits pick up. Then the bell rings signaling it's time for math and science, and Michelle takes her place in another classroom, sitting alone at a two-person desk. Her friend Mia used to sit next to her, she explains, but then asked to transfer to another math and science class so she could be with Audrey. This bugs Michelle.

A substitute teacher directs the class to work on a practice sheet of multiplication and division problems. Michelle does the multiplication with ease but struggles with division. Later, the same teacher, now giving instruction in science, tells the class to draw the different parts of a leaf.

Michelle stares down at a blank sheet of paper. "I used to be good at drawing, now I can't draw anything," she complains.

As I first got to know Michelle, I was impressed by how successful she had been in her short life against considerable odds. She loved to read, wrote with flair, made decent grades at a respected private school, frequently got together with friends, enjoyed a close relationship with her mother, and was never in trouble. These were visible and significant signs of promise.

But the longer I knew her, the more I wondered about her psychological resources, namely how confident she felt and how effective she would be at carving out her own life. Gripped in motherlove, she was doing okay, but what would happen in later years? By late adolescence, as a panel of social scientists notes in a recent book about urban families, what best predicts how successful teens eventually are is how well they deal, on their own, with the world outside the family. And psychological supports equip them for that task better than anything else.[4]

In October, Michelle herself told me, "One of my biggest problems is feeling confident." The signs were numerous. She wouldn't raise her hand in class for fear of giving the wrong answer or being laughed at by her classmates. She hated math, which, as psychologist Mary Pipher demonstrates in *Reviving Ophelia*, is a subject that requires confidence and trust in one's judgment because the answers often are not obvious.[5] In January, De La Sota told Janice that Michelle wasn't doing her best, and her math teacher suggested a tutor.

She also hated sports. Athletics and other organized leisure activities are a key way in which young adolescents can build self-esteem, leadership skills, and independence of thought. But Michelle didn't take part in any extracurricular activities either at school or at the city park near her home.

She might have been as harsh on herself if she had lived in the perfect family. Girls her age suffer through occasional slumps in self-esteem, as Pipher and other experts have noted. But Janice worried, and so she had engaged Turner in the task of mentoring her daughter. Privately Turner questioned how effective he could be considering not only Michelle's severed connection to her father but also her bond to her mother, which, in his mind, was too tight.

Sacrificing Everything for Your Child

From the day Michelle was born, she was Janice's job, and in many ways Janice performed her job admirably. She figured out day trips the two could take on very little money, the Santa Monica pier being a favorite. She taught Michelle how to save for things she wanted and how to value the things she had. Perhaps the most important thing she did was go to extraordinary lengths to further Michelle's education. In *Beyond the Classroom*, psychologist Laurence Steinberg says a parent should place a child in a school setting where she is surrounded by confident, smart, ambitious classmates. Janice had done that, at considerable personal cost.

Because they lived on welfare and could not afford a car, Janice accompanied Michelle to school on the bus. This meant leaving home before 7 A.M., walking two long city blocks to the bus stop, taking one bus, then another, getting off the second bus and walking across the sprawling UCLA campus to school. Janice would return home the same way, then retrace her route in the afternoon to pick up Michelle. She spent four hours each day going back and forth, over seven years, even after she developed severe arthritis in her right knee.

She helped Michelle with homework a lot. "We are doing this school project on . . . ," she would say, then catch herself. "I mean, Michelle is doing this project on . . ." As the sixth-grade year wound down, she spent weeks researching new private schools and scholarships for grades seven through twelve, then filling out applications.

She searched periodically for paying jobs for herself but could never find one that gave her the flexibility she felt she needed to raise her daughter. In May 1997, after Los Angeles County cut her welfare benefits, she applied to work at a local hospital and in the Santa Monica school district. She didn't get either job and said Michelle was relieved. Michelle "was a little scared about me working," she said. "She would have to be independent."

Janice had enjoyed an active social life before Michelle was born but that had stopped, she said, because she couldn't afford baby-sitters. When she did go out to dinner with a friend, she almost always took Michelle with her, even as Michelle got older.

Turner would say to Michelle, "I'm so happy your mother has the energy to give you the best." Privately, however, he worried that Janice carried her goodness too far, feeding Michelle's dependence. She required no chores of Michelle and was thrilled when Michelle occasionally cooked dinner. Michelle didn't baby-sit, walk a neighbor's dog, or do any of the little things young teens often do to earn spending money.

She did leave her mom little notes of gratitude and referred to her as "my hero." But she also seemed somewhat weighed down by all that her mother did. "I feel horrible about how much my mother is sacrificing for me," she confided to me.

Although a close parent-child relationship is healthy and desirable, parents need to give their children, as the saying goes, both roots and wings. Turner worried that Michelle's attachment to Janice, essential as it was in earlier years, was beginning to keep her from taking flight. "I know Michelle is your life," he would tell Janice, "but you must be careful you don't steal her life."

Sticking Close to Home

Turner believed that if Michelle were encouraged to go more places on her own and seek out her own contacts, she would become more self-reliant.

"Do you think you're old enough now to ride the city bus by yourself to school?" he asked her at The French Marketplace.

"I could do it," she replied. "And I wish Mom didn't have to."

But Janice felt she did. When Turner suggested to Janice that Michelle ride alone, Janice wouldn't hear of it. "This is California. Strangers can jump out of a car at the bus stop and grab her," she said. "There also are a lot of homeless people around here. We have been verbally attacked by them on the bus."

West Hollywood, a bustling, mixed-income, multiracial community, may or may not have been as dangerous as Janice believed. It probably had a number of what sociologists call "old heads," community figures willing to watch out for kids like Michelle. Many urban neighborhoods do. But that didn't matter to Janice and Michelle. Janice convinced Michelle that West Hollywood, where Michelle had lived her whole life, was a strange and frightful place.

Unlike Eric in the first chapter, Michelle was not allowed to go outside by herself. She never ran to the grocery store for a loaf of bread, discussed platform shoes with clerks in the trendy shops along nearby Santa Monica Boulevard, or strolled through the neighborhood park. Her mother might have let her take walks with friends in the neighborhood, but she had no such friends, one disadvantage of having always attended a school far away.

Once she got into Corinne Seeds, that school became her community. It braced her and her mother emotionally, but, in order to feel truly confident about herself, Michelle needed to feel connected to and safe in her geographic community as well.[6]

An attentive father could have helped Michelle break out of her confined world. Several recent studies indicate that fathers, more than mothers, tend to push adolescents off on their own, encourage them to get out, meet new people, and join organizations.[7] Fathers also tend to encourage mothers to loosen their hold on a child and can provide the moral support that enables mothers to let go confidently.

But because Curtis had so little contact with Michelle, he didn't realize what she was capable of. He supported Janice's philosophy. "If Janice is overprotective, that's better than underprotective," he said.

The one community in which mother and daughter felt safe, other than school, was the shopping mall. I accompanied Michelle and Janice one afternoon to the Beverly Center, a three-hundred-store indoor mall on the border of West Hollywood and Beverly Hills. Michelle visibly perked up once we entered its dazzling caverns. "This is my favorite place," she sighed. "I love it more than life itself."

"Why?" I asked.

"I grew up here," she explained. "I can tell you where every store is."

She wasn't connected to her community, but she was connected to racks of merchandise and nameless clerks.

Eleven people are clustered under the redwood trees at school in early June as Michelle crosses an outside platform to receive her certificate of graduation from sixth grade. They are all relatives or friends of her mother's and include the Turner family. After the ceremony, Janice embraces her daughter, who towers over her in white, four-inch platform shoes.

"Look," she exclaims. "You have more people here than anyone else. Maybe that makes up for all the times you only had me!"

Henry and Pia Turner hug the young graduate, then make a quick get-away, for Henry must finish preparing a luncheon at home in Michelle's honor for her classmates.

When she was younger, Michelle would invite one or two of her class-mates over to spend the night at her apartment. Those visits grew less fre-quent, however, as she got older and became more aware of the contrast between their lifestyle and hers. Turner had planned the graduation lun-cheon as a way for Michelle to give something back to her friends. "You can invite as many friends as you want," he told her.

When Michelle arrives at the Turners' that day, she clasps her hands in awe. Two tables have been pushed together on the deck outdoors. They are draped in white, handmade tablecloths and decorated with assorted flow-ers. Henry Turner has prepared Cornish game hens stuffed with wild rice, spring vegetables, and salad. His fine china and sterling silver are laid out for sixteen. Michelle, Janice, a friend of Janice's, the friend's daughter, and her boyfriend take their seats. Michelle's aunt Ginger and her cousin Tina sit down, as do the four Turners.

Five seats remain empty. Michelle tells Turner that her friends couldn't come, that the school-sponsored graduation party is later that day and her friends have a lot of preparing to do. She doesn't tell him or her mother the real reason. More than a year earlier, she invited two girls over to spend the night and afterward one of them told friends at school that it was the worst time she'd ever had. Michelle later realized that the girl only said that because she was mad at Michelle. But Michelle wasn't about to take another chance.

"I hadn't had that many parties in my life," she told me months after Turner's luncheon. "I was afraid my friends wouldn't have a good time. So I didn't ask them."

Turner believed that one of his roles was to move Michelle out into the world and teach her how she could contribute to it. She needed to learn not only how to receive kindnesses but how to return them, for if her friendships remained one-sided she would ultimately feel demeaned and deflated. As we saw with Jessica Johnston and Jack Richardson, doing useful or thoughtful things for other people can empower shy children in ways that little else can. In order to feel a part of any enterprise—personal, professional, or civic—one must participate in it, not just take from it. This is a tough lesson for some kids to learn, and it was tough for Michelle, who had lived all her life on the generosity of other people.

Waiting for a Fairy Godmother

From the time Michelle was a baby, Janice read fairy tales to her. Their favorite was *Cinderella*. Janice tracked down every version of the story she could find at the public library. Mother and daughter would settle into the deep worn cushions of their couch and read for the hundredth time the story of a beautiful but poor, hardworking maiden blessed by a fairy godmother, discovered by a handsome prince, and whisked away to live happily ever after in the castle of her dreams.

Cinderella resembled Janice's early years: Her mother, on the road acting and modeling, had turned Janice over to a foster family that required Janice to do the household chores. When Janice grew up, however, no fairy godmother came to the rescue. She went to work right out of community college and continued working until Michelle was born. Thereafter, she and her daughter survived on the goodness of mere mortals. As a new mom with little support from her own family, she quickly mastered the art of asking for help from strangers or snapping it up when it was volunteered. She became a master at making connections.

A friend she made one day in the park, when Michelle was a baby, moved to North Carolina and provided her and Michelle with airplane tickets to visit regularly. Another park acquaintance tipped her off to Corinne Seeds. Friends of friends provided Michelle with new clothes and spending money. A woman from the school gave Michelle a violin. Janice always responded with a note or greeting card.

Occasionally a charity would donate a month's supply of bus tokens. A nearby church distributed a turkey on holidays. Cedars of Sinai Hospital provided free medical care. A monthly welfare check, cut from $621 to $525 the year I observed them, covered groceries and rent, barely.

Janice also did what she could to contribute to others. She volunteered occasionally for the American Red Cross and regularly at Michelle's school. When her father fell ill, she tended to him until he died, and she did the same with her mother. She hoped she was teaching

Michelle by example how to approach people as resources—and how to be a resource.

Turner, Scouting Out the Future

In the beginning, Turner's relationship with Michelle seemed informal and easygoing. He and Janice didn't have a plan. They would just talk on the phone from time to time, Janice would drop a hint about something Michelle needed or would like to do, and Turner would take it from there. When Turner found out, months after Michelle's graduation from Corinne Seeds, the true reason that five chairs had sat empty at the graduation luncheon he hosted, he was saddened that Michelle hadn't felt close enough to share her reservations with him.

He realized that if he wanted their relationship to stretch beyond the superficial, he would have to move from the periphery of her life to the center, a relationship that would require a commitment of time, energy, and focused intensity.[8] He would need not only to support her but to expect certain behaviors from her.

As his relationship with Michelle demonstrated, helpful connections with young people sometimes take a great deal of effort to establish and to maintain. Fortunately for Michelle, he had a lot going for him. He shared a past and a present with her mother and thus understood her world more than most outside adults would. He was settled and could continue to see her through high school. He was by no means rich but possessed financial, as well as emotional, resources that her mother did not. He enjoyed a stable marriage and family life that Michelle could observe and perhaps learn from. Most important, he was committed to being there for her.

But he would have to take his cues from her, he realized. If he decided to throw her another party, for example, he would need to ask her whether it was something she would like to do and under what circumstances. He would have to enlist her help rather than do everything for her and make sure she followed through on what she said she would do. New ventures felt risky to her. He could see that now.

He had time to work on their association. The flagging self-esteem that some girls Michelle's age feel usually picks up and stablizes as they reach high school. Periodically, Michelle showed signs of a budding assurance, most notably in her decision to go to Windward School, a prestigious private institution that accepted her for the coming fall on almost a full scholarship. None of her friends had gotten in, so she wouldn't know anybody there, but that didn't deter her. "It's the school I wanted," she said. She talked to Turner about the decision and later said, "You know, I don't spend a lot of time with Henry but it's good to know I can go to him."

CHAPTER ELEVEN

Connections Severed, Connections Made

(Mario's Story)

Starting school in the fall is right up there with cleaning your bedroom as a teenager's idea of a good time. But for Mario Rawlings, a stocky young black man a few days shy of fourteen, the first day of eighth grade is more of a drag than usual. The CIS Academy at Holton, a public school in Durham for at-risk kids who need extra help, will be his third school in three years. He wanted to hang with his friends at last year's school but officials sent him here instead. To make matters worse, his mother has insisted on coming along. He paces far ahead of her in his Tommy Hilfiger jersey and Nautica baggies, hoping no one will notice as the two of them wind their way down freshly waxed corridors and through the door of the main office.

Almost immediately, he is glad she is there.

"I'm here to register my son," Joyce Rawlings tells a pleasant-looking woman behind the counter. This sets off a chain of frenetic activity—papers rifled, phone calls made, consultations with the assistant principal—that ends abruptly.

"Mario doesn't belong at Holton," the assistant principal says. "He is supposed to be at Holloway." That's the alternative school for disruptive and violent students, several blocks away.

"There must be some mistake." Joyce begins to argue, her voice rising. Mario, his face a dark, blank slate, says nothing.

If someone walking by were to sneak a look at him at this moment, the word "sullen" might come to mind. But it would be an inappropriate description of this young man, who as a toddler tumbled from his father's car while his dad was backing out of the driveway and hopped right back in, who volunteered to be a punching bag for his older brother learning to box, who was beaned hard in the eye as a young catcher playing baseball and insisted on staying in the game even as his face swelled. "Self-contained" would be more appropriate. Also suspicious right now, vulnerable to being turned away from school. Again.

Mario has spent much of the last school year at home, suspended. Neal Middle School, which threw him out, gave him neither tutor nor books even though his parents begged for both. The year before that, he was assigned to Bragdon Middle School. Now, as he listens to his mother argue, he realizes he is being sent to yet another school. This time it's one with the worst reputation in the county, a holding tank that even the local juvenile judge has called Durham County's "shame."

His first thought is to call Al Singer, a lawyer and new friend. His second, to go see Mike Benjamin, director of the recreation center around the corner from his house, whom he has known for almost four years.

The story of Mario's eighth-grade year and the adults who figured in it arises from a series of remarkable events that took place eight months before. It was a mess that he desperately wanted to put behind him. Instead, he kept stepping into it.

Early on a school day in January 1996, he had slipped out of his house a few minutes early to meet up with his new pal Jarrod and two other guys on their way to the bus stop in their east Durham neighborhood. Jarrod, a tall, outgoing youth, recently arrived from eastern North Carolina, said that he had a little surprise and headed for a clump of overgrown bushes bordering a dirt road that adjoins Mario's street. Mario and the other boys followed eagerly.

Jarrod pulled a tarnished 32-caliber handgun out of the bushes. These boys were not exactly naive. Plenty went on at Neal Middle School—cigarette smoking out back, marijuana joints in the bathrooms, idle threats with X-Acto knives. But the boys had never touched a real handgun before, and they passed it around like kids trying out a first cigarette. Jarrod pointed the revolver at a couple of the boys in jest.

Then a boy named Preston grabbed it. "Remember when Victor got us with those snowballs?" he asked about a boy not with them. "It's payback time."

The little group headed for the bus stop, where they figured they'd find Victor. Preston held the gun to Victor's neck.

"I'm going to put some cats in you," Preston said. He squeezed the trigger.

Click. The clip was empty. All the boys but Victor had known that it was. Victor was still shaking a few minutes later when the school bus rolled toward them.

Jarrod retrieved his gun from Preston, then tried to hand it off to a boy named Edward.

Edward refused.

"Well, one of y'all hold it," Jarrod said.

Mario admired Jarrod—he talked about his new friend all the time, according to Joyce—and he had learned at home that the quickest way to win approval from someone was to help them out. He took the gun and slipped it into the pocket of his winter jacket, thinking he could give it back to Jarrod when they got to school. "I didn't have no intention of doing anything wrong," he would say later.

But when they got to Neal, Jarrod vanished into the school and Mario decided to stash the gun in his locker. Word that a gun was on campus spread quickly. During Mario's second-period social studies class, a teacher walked in and said he was there to escort Mario to the office of Fred Putney, assistant principal. Victor had told Putney that he had been threatened with a gun. After questioning several witnesses, Putney had pulled in Jarrod and the others and they had fingered Mario.

Surrounded by the principal, Putney, and four sheriff's deputies, Mario said at first that he had thrown away the gun. Then he admitted it was in his locker. Putney and a deputy walked with him to locker number 63, and to Mario's surprise, there was a lock on his locker. He would later swear under oath that he didn't use a lock. After Putney called a janitor to break the lock he found the gun, lying under some books. Putney called Mario's parents at home but couldn't reach them. Once the last bell rang, Putney drove Mario home.

Joyce was there. A security guard, she worked at night so she could be home when Mario, his brother, and his sister got out of school. Putney told her what had happened and that Mario had been suspended for ten days, pending the principal's decision on how much total time he should spend out of school. Putney said that in addition to any discipline the school might mete out, Mario would be charged with a felony in district court. Shortly after Putney left, Mario's dad, Jay, arrived home from his construction job. He heard the story from Joyce, then looked his boy straight in the eye.

"Do you know how much you've hurt me?" he asked. "Why didn't you just drop the gun at the bus stop and walk away?"

"I don't know why," Mario said. He would say that over and over again in the months to come, always convincingly, a sign not that he had no conscience but that he was in search of one, like most kids his age.

That night, Jay whipped him with a belt. He was grounded for six months, until the middle of summer. The only place he could go, Jay and Joyce told him, was the rec center.

"I'll hold your hand, but you will have to face the consequences," Joyce said to him. Neither she nor her son had any idea at the time how severe they would be.

Support Troops

When I drove to the Rawlingses' tidy, brick house for the first time, several days after his mother had tried to place him at CIS, Mario and his dad were waiting out front. Joyce had told me over the telephone that the family would be happy to talk to me. The faces of Mario and Jay told me differently.

"He says he doesn't want to talk about the incident," said Jay, a boyish-looking, slender man not much taller than his son. "I'll go by what he says."

"Is that right?" I asked Mario.

"I don't want no interview," Mario said so low I could barely hear him. "I've been interviewed enough."

"By whom?" I asked.

"The school board," he said.

I suggested a compromise. "Let me talk with your parents for a while. You can be there. Then see how you feel. If you still don't want to be interviewed, I won't go any further. Okay?"

He stared at a patch of parched grass for a minute or two, going deep into that place where children sometimes take refuge. "Okay," he finally agreed.

He warmed up slightly that night and a little more each time I saw him thereafter. But in the months that followed, I thought often of that first snapshot of father and son in front of the little brick house. Mario had done something really stupid, something that his hardworking, decent parents never dreamed he would do. Rather than attack it as his problem, not theirs, and abandon him emotionally, they stood by his side in the battle *and* brought in support troops. They knew they were good parents, but they were not afraid to admit that in a society that is frequently hostile to teens, they needed other, caring people to assist them with the attention, structure, and discipline that their son deserved. The more people who were willing to help them, the better for them and for Mario.[1]

This is not a bad lesson for any of us to remember as our children head into early adolescence. For if they are going to attempt something dangerous, harmful, or against what we think should be their better judgment, ages ten to fifteen are when they're most likely do it.

But First, Strong Parenting

Joyce and Jay had always functioned as a team with their three children. He worked day shifts and she worked nights, which meant he got up in the middle of the night to feed the kids when they were infants. They tag-teamed sporting events so at least one of them would be at every game. Both of them visibly brightened when talking about any of the three.

Joyce telephoned Jay at work right after Putney left on that January day.

"Not Mario!" were Jay's first words when Joyce called him. "He's my right-hand man."

The year before, Jay, the foreman of a drywall company, had taught Mario how to hang a wall. Mario started accompanying him on his weekend side projects, and Jay was so satisfied with Mario's efforts that he paid him the same wage as the grown laborers, $50 to $75 a day.

Therapist/author Michael Gurian says that young adolescent boys are hard-wired to seek out their father's attention, but Mario had followed his dad around from the time he could walk. "It was always 'My daddy this and my daddy that,'" Joyce remembered. "He even told a friend of mine who stopped by to visit to 'Get off my daddy's porch.'"

When Mario was five, Joyce gave birth to his sister, Bethany, who started claiming Jay's attention. "He got real upset by that middle-child stuff," Joyce said.

Both of his siblings proved to be talented individuals. Older brother Jimmy became an All-American baseball player and made junior varsity on a powerhouse high-school football team in the ninth grade. Bethany collected A's in school and medals in softball and cheerleading the way other girls collect dolls. Her red, white, and blue awards stretched all the way across the fireplace mantel directly below a huge, framed baby portrait. To this day Jay calls her "my baby girl."

Mario was an above-average athlete himself, playing shortstop in baseball and point guard in basketball. But he didn't have nearly as many trophies or home run balls on display at home. "He tried to fill [Jimmy's] shoes and he couldn't," Jay said. He had to find other ways to call attention to himself.

At first, he took to playing pranks. He spray-painted his father's truck green, finishing the job with a big green M on the roof. He removed the legs from a pool table. "If something broke, he'd be the one who done it," Jay remembered.

But as he got older, he became everyone's helper. He had a large extended family living in Durham—his grandfather alone had thirteen brothers and sisters—and he was the one the relatives called when they needed their tires rotated or their lawns mowed. One weekend afternoon Joyce looked outside and saw Mario standing over Jay's '73 Ford shortbed truck, polishing its small block engine. She knew Jay hadn't asked him to do it. That was just Mario.

Some people might have called Jay and Joyce authoritarian, so strict were they with their kids. Hanging around outside wasn't allowed, Mario's early morning jaunts to the bus stop the only exception. The kids couldn't go to the mall unless they were accompanied by a parent or adult relative. Everyone had chores: cooking, cleaning, doing their own laundry. No foul language was allowed, and the kids said "yes, ma'am" and "yes, sir" to adults. Jay smoked cigarettes but neither he nor Joyce drank.

The value they stressed the most was education. Joyce had graduated from Durham High School, but Jay had dropped out during his junior year there. They wanted better for their kids: a high-school degree and "some kind of college," in Jay's words. If homework wasn't finished, there was no ball practice. If a teacher called to complain about behavior, Joyce would show up at school the next day. One afternoon at Neal Middle School, Mario got in a shoving match with a student. The next day Joyce accompanied him to all his classes.

The Rawlingses made sure their kids were busy after school and if they weren't, they would be shooed over to the recreational center. Compared to other families they knew, Jay and Joyce thought they had the parenting role down cold. Until Fred Putney showed up at their front door.

Pummeled by the School

Putney's boss, principal Floyd Mitchell, had never met Mario before that fateful January day. Mario had been at Neal less than five months and didn't exactly stand out in the crowd of about eight hundred students. Aside from a couple of lunchtime detentions, he showed none of the behavioral signs that experts in school violence watch for. He wasn't withdrawn, impulsive, or a bully; he didn't complain about being picked on or rejected.[2]

Mitchell would say months later that he didn't consider Mario a risk. Had Mario been caught with a weapon a year earlier, Mitchell probably would have handled the infraction privately. He would have talked to Mario's teachers and parents and to Mario himself. He might have rendered a more judicious verdict than the one he came up with; after all, the evidence confirms that most kids accused of a serious crime never commit another one.[3]

The Rawlingses will never know what Mitchell would have done because a state law adopted in 1995 prevented him from passing judgment. North Carolina legislators, concerned about a fivefold increase in the number of juveniles arrested on weapons charges after 1986, amended statute 115C-391 to require school officials to suspend any child bringing a weapon onto school property for 365 days.[4] The lawmakers allowed school systems to provide an alternative educational setting for such kids but didn't require it.

The day after Mario carried Jarrod's gun to school, Mitchell sent a letter to Mario's parents stating that he had recommended to the interim superintendent that Mario be suspended for a full calendar year, from that January until January 1997. Mario was one of the first Durham students, if not the first, to feel the effect of the new law.

His "co-conspirators" got off more lightly. Jarrod, the gun's owner, was told that he could return to school the next fall, a full semester before Mario. The same applied to Preston, the boy who stuck the gun in Victor's neck. Another boy was told he could return after the initial ten days.

Mitchell, in discussion with the school board attorney, determined that Mario was the most culpable because he brought the gun into school. The other boys "only" played with it on a public street. A school bus stop, the board attorney said, was not considered school property. This difference did not make sense to Mario, his parents, or to Marcia Morey, the assistant county prosecutor in charge of the parallel case in juvenile court. "What happened to the kid who got the gun, to the kids who actually pointed it at someone?" Morey would ask later. "A misdemeanor. Yet some wonderful legislator said [Mario] was a felon. The punishment was far worse than the crime."

Juvenile Judge Elaine O'Neal said that Mario seemed the least culpable and that it was irrational to punish him more than the others. Both she and Marcia Morey disliked the 365-day law because they could foresee the results: suspended youths roaming the streets, too young to hold a job and too old to stay home. When these kids—mostly boys— returned to school they would be a year older than their classmates, putting them at higher than average risk for using drugs, engaging in sex, behaving violently, and dropping out of school.[5] The policy might promote safe schools when the young criminals weren't at school, O'Neal told school officials, but it did not promote safe streets, safe communities, or even safe schools when the kids returned.

A National Trend

Within the last five years, all states have adopted laws similar to North Carolina's 365-day school suspension rule regarding weapons. School administrators have tightened the rules on all kinds of behavior, forcing kids out of school for infractions such as bringing plastic knives from home for lunchtime eating, and writing assigned essays that describe violent scenes too graphically. All students are potentially affected by this new harshness but kids in middle school and junior high particularly so. As we have seen in earlier chapters, these are the years when kids test and break the rules. Yet they are not smart enough to hide what they have done. They don't necessarily do more bad things, they just get caught more often than older kids, delinquency experts say. The result can be seen in the nation's juvenile caseload: Three out of five delinquency cases involve kids younger than fifteen.[6] Minority kids are disproportionately represented. So are adolescent boys.

If young adolescents make one bad mistake in school, as Mario did, they can be removed from their friends at a time in their social development when they most need friends. They can be removed from teachers and counselors just when they're beginning to build ties to adults. They can be punished without due process just as they are beginning to understand and accept adult standards of fairness.

It made no sense to Mario that if he had been found on the street with a loaded gun, standing over a dead body, he would have received a trial. His motives, circumstances, and record would have been weighed. Found in school with an unloaded weapon, he had no such rights.

Being treated unfairly is the number-one reason young adolescents give for feeling disconnected from school.[7] Unjust treatment can also affect the kid's view of social institutions generally. Why should kids subscribe to the community's rules when the most significant piece of that community to them, the school, summarily dismisses them?

Joyce noticed that Mario grew quieter and disappeared into himself often after the suspension. She was furious at a system that seemed bent on destroying her child's spirits and his one road to success. "It wouldn't have affected him so much had he been in high school," she said months later. "But at this age, he knew better, and he had feelings. He still cared about school and about what the people at school thought about him."

"But it says Holton." Al Singer, *a short lawyer with a big presence, is on the phone to the principal at CIS.* "I am reading from this letter signed by [school board chairwoman] Nancy Jirtle. It says Mario will be *allowed to enroll at Holton for the fall semester of the 1996–97 school year."*

After being turned away by CIS authorities, Joyce had called Singer, who ran the Child Advocacy Commission, a nonprofit organization providing legal assistance to families. He had assisted them in their attempts over the last seven months to place Mario back in school, and Mario had come to like him very much, although at first he hadn't been so sure he would.

On the day they first entered Singer's third-floor office on Main Street downtown, Singer, who was on the phone, motioned for them to take a seat in the waiting area. Mario and Jay perched on the edge of a donated lime-green couch. Joyce started reading yellowed newspaper clippings on the bulletin board: "Former Addict Back with Her Children," and "Grandmothers as Primary Caregivers Raising Sons without Fathers."

Singer cut short his phone conversation and ushered the family into his inner office, taking a seat across from them at a desk layered in paper.

Jay, normally reserved, was fuming at the school board for suspending his son. "How can they do this?" he yelled, beating the arm of his chair. Singer explained the statute but kept his eyes on Mario, sizing him up quickly. After ten years of working with the county's most disturbed kids, he could tell that Mario was different. He didn't see the rage in Mario's eyes that he frequently saw in other kids, only confusion and pain. When he finished his explanations to the parents, he turned to Mario and talked straight.

"Stupid," he said to his new young client. "What you did was stupid. You scared a couple of hundred people."

Mario was terrified by this white man with gray hair, goatee, and wire-rimmed glasses. But as he and Singer proceeded later through several hearings together, he realized that Singer was on his side.

The first and, in Mario's memory, the worst hearing was an appeal of Floyd Mitchell's decision to a school system administrator and two assistant middle-school principals. Mario had had to field 143 questions.

"Why didn't you take the gun to Mr. Mitchell or Mr. Putney instead of putting it in your locker?" assistant principal Thomas Gilchrist had asked, according to a transcript of the proceeding.

"I don't know."

"Were you scared to take it to one of them?"

"Yes."

"Well, that's why you didn't do it. You didn't take it because you were scared of what might happen."

Mario had sighed. Gilchrist was putting words in his mouth. He really didn't know, or at least wasn't able to verbalize, why he hadn't turned in the gun. Young adolescent males frequently don't express complex emotional ideas easily. Singer understood this and stepped in to help, acting as a translator as good mentors often do.

He knew, for example, how important it is for young men Mario's age to position themselves favorably in the hierarchy of others their age.

"Were you being macho?" Singer asked.

"Yes."

The panel upheld Mitchell's recommended suspension. Singer then filed an appeal with a three-member panel of school board members, and in March, he, Mario, and Joyce returned to the school board building to argue that appeal. In the two months since the hearing panel, Singer had enlarged his arsenal of arguments and witnesses, and Mario, having learned to trust Singer, was more relaxed. That time he had to answer only thirty-seven questions.

Singer pointed out to the board that Mario benefited from living with both parents at home and that the gun incident was his first offense. He told board members that in a parallel hearing in court, school personnel had testified that Mario was not a risk to other students. A court counselor testified that Judge O'Neal did not consider Mario dangerous. She was going to place him on probation, the counselor said, and require him to do community service and attend a group therapy session with other young offenders once a week.

Singer asked Mario whether he wanted to say anything to the school board.

"I'd like to say that I'm sorry," Mario said, according to the transcript. "I know I did something stupid. But I'd like to get back in school."

"Do you understand what happens by just carrying an empty gun around?" Singer asked him.

"Someone could end up getting hurt and a lot of negative stuff could happen," Mario replied.

Joyce spoke to the board as well. "This law should not apply for just any child," she said. "It should be the background of the child."

She started to cry, then continued in a husky voice: "I want him to stand up for his punishment but don't throw him away just like on the street. 'Cause he'll be a bum on the street. Not that I will let him be. But I have no control when he gets eighteen years old. . . . Until that day comes I'm going to fight for Mario."

One day after the hearing, board chairwoman Jirtle wrote a letter to the Rawlingses giving them a victory of sorts. Mario would have to stay out of school until the fall, when he would be allowed to go to CIS.

It is Jirtle's letter that Singer clutches in his hand this September day as he makes one phone call after another trying to convince the school system that it has to abide by Jirtle's judgment.

Of all the riches denied disadvantaged students, education expert Gene Maeroff writes, the most significant may be the connections that affluent families use to work their way around the obstacles in their children's paths.[8] Affluent families know how the system works, which arguments to make and to whom. They know that if Johnny is suspended from school for three days, there may be a way to get him back in the classroom after only one.

Working-class families such as the Rawlingses do not enjoy these luxuries. That's why someone like Al Singer is so invaluable. "He's handled cases like yours before," Marcia Morey, the prosecutor, told Joyce when Joyce sought Morey's advice concerning the civil case against Mario.

Singer wasn't a miracle worker. He couldn't persuade Neal to provide books and tutoring for Mario while Mario was suspended, even though the school board panel had recommended that Neal do so. But he could make sure Mario didn't hang out on the streets during his suspension. And he could see to it that Mario fulfilled his community service requirement, right under his nose.

The Only Nice White Man

Shortly after the first appeal of Mario's case was denied, Singer offered Mario a job in the Child Advocacy office answering phones and running errands. Mario started taking the city bus to the office and working there from 9 A.M. to 4 P.M., Monday through Friday. He delivered papers to the courthouse, learned to greet office visitors, and answered the phone. "He even learned to say 'advocacy' right," Singer would later tease.

"Mario looked forward to going down there," Jay Rawlings remembered gratefully. "And I was glad he wasn't sitting around the house all day."

It was more than busywork. Singer discussed cases with Mario and took Mario's advice about getting a second telephone line. He laughed when Mario related practical jokes Mario had played on his family. Mario saw himself making a contribution, however small, to Singer's work and well-being. Unlike the relationship between Turner and Michelle, in which Turner gave and Michelle took, Singer and Mario enjoyed an alliance that grew increasingly reciprocal and thus stronger.

When Singer realized that no academic help was forthcoming from Neal, he sought out a tutor with whom Mario worked for a couple of hours each day. He took Mario to night games of the Durham Bulls, the city's triple-A baseball team, and on late afternoons he would cut out of work early and drive Mario and another boy he was mentoring to a basketball court in Few Gardens, one of the city's low-income housing projects. The three of them would play games of Horse and 21, sometimes joined by other kids from the projects. Mario would loosen up and talk about things he'd never bring up at the office. He saw that he wasn't just one of Singer's nine-to-five responsibilities but someone Singer cared about. His defenses melted.

"I gotta stop," Singer would complain about halfway through a game. "My knees, you know."

"Come on, old man, you can do it!" Mario would yell.

Singer was forty-nine. His knees did ache, and his back spasmed occasionally. But he never stopped playing with or working on behalf of his kids. "I'm fed by kids like Mario," he told me.

Singer wanted Mario at CIS, short for Communities in Schools, a network of about two hundred fifty schools, because with classes of ten to twelve students, it was perfect for his client. The week after Mario was turned away, Singer threatened to sue and the school system buckled, slowly. CIS officials agreed to accept Mario but said they had to wait for his records to be transferred from Neal. Administrators at Neal said they could not find the records. Mario started attending Holloway, the school for seriously troubled kids. Four weeks later, his files from Neal were "found," and he headed for his new and very different school.

He continued to see Singer on Wednesdays when he stopped by for group counseling sessions. He attended these sessions faithfully for a year, earning a Walkman radio and a framed certificate for attendance. His mother propped the certificate next to his trophies in the living room.

In December 1996, he arrived home from CIS one afternoon to find a letter waiting for him. He tore the envelope open and read that he had completed the terms of his court-ordered probation. His criminal record had been erased. He smiled a little half-smile to Joyce and said, "I've gotta show this to Dad." Then he picked up the telephone to call Singer.

Singer, he told me months later, is "the only white man who has ever been nice to me. Back when I was in all that trouble, he was my biggest friend." To this day, more than three years after his records were expunged, he calls Singer occasionally, just to talk.

Although Mario tries to forget his unfortunate past, quick scenes prick his memory and his conscience almost every day. Like the afternoon he had to confess the gun incident to his longtime mentor Mike Benjamin.

He had received his mom's permission to walk around the block to the East Durham Recreation Center, a one-story, white, ranch-style building. Benjamin, a commanding black presence over six feet tall, had been recreation director there for a couple of years. He was very popular with the kids, particularly with the young teens, who admired the fact that he had been a successful ballplayer all the way through high school. As an adult he had coached some of the best teams in the county's recreational league. He was also known as a tough disciplinarian; he had once cut his top baseball pitcher for a whole season after the boy refused to stop using foul language on the field.

As Mario ambled slowly toward the center, wondering how in the world he would break the news, he didn't know that Benjamin already knew.

Joyce had dropped in at the center the night before. When, through tears, she told Benjamin what had happened, he couldn't believe he had heard her correctly. Mario wasn't the kind of kid to carry a gun or even to hang around kids who did. Any project Benjamin had, "Mario'd be there to put it up, work it, and take it down," he would say later. When city council members were threatening to cut funds for the city's rec centers, Benjamin had brought Mario to Eastway School to testify against the proposal.

At the time, Mario had told the commissioners, "If it weren't for these clubs, there's no telling what we'd be doing."

Joyce was worried that perhaps Mario wouldn't be able to visit the rec center anymore. Benjamin knew this. He could be tough, but he also believed in giving kids a second chance.

"Every kid is going to do something bad at least once," Benjamin had reassured Joyce. "Between you, his dad, and me, we can deal with this."

He was not quite as conciliatory when Mario walked into the rec center the next day and asked him if they could talk in Benjamin's office. Once inside, Mario told Benjamin the story.

"I really fucked up," Mario concluded. With someone he trusted, he could admit what he really thought.

"Why did you do it?" Benjamin's baritone rang out. "That's not in your act."

Mario was looking at the concrete floor. "I don't know, man."

"You knew it was wrong," Benjamin continued. "You knew kids would tell on you. You had a choice."

"Mike, I'm tired of hearing that."

But he would hear it again and again over the next several months as he followed Benjamin around the center per Benjamin's orders. If Benjamin was at the center, Mario was at the center doing anything his boss asked him to do.

Benjamin yanked him off the basketball team. He wouldn't let Mario go to the bowling alley or skating rink with the rest of the teenagers. Mario complained that Benjamin was being too harsh. But he went along rather than dropping away because he felt he owed it to Benjamin. Benjamin must like him, he thought; two other boys involved in the gun incident had been banned from the rec center altogether.

On the surface, Singer and Benjamin were a study in contrasts. Singer had grown up in a middle-class Jewish family near Philadelphia and graduated from Temple University law school. His passion for kids started with the birth of his first child, a daughter who was severely retarded. Caring for her set him on a collision course with schools and other institutions, and eventually he abandoned the practice of law to run a state agency for the handicapped.

When he took over the Child Advocacy Commission, he inherited kids bruised not by disease but by circumstance. He didn't label them right off with some pathological definition. "Kids are going to make stupid mistakes," he said. "We were teenagers once. Did we forget?"

In Singer's view, his modern rebels were set apart not by their character but by the character of a society that made available so many dangerous ways to rebel. "We should look in the mirror," he said. "How can we tell a kid that guns are wrong when we have so many of them?" Gun control would go a long way toward de-escalating juvenile crime, Singer believed. So would early intervention programs that included identifying a "viable relative" or mentor for a potentially troubled child.

Benjamin helped kids more out of instinct than philosophy. He had been raised by his mother in the Few Gardens projects. He fathered a child when he was thirteen and another when he was fifteen. He married the second child's mother when he was eighteen. He didn't learn to read until he was in the eighth grade and barely made it through high school. He worked with the Durham Housing Authority for a while polishing floors but, at age thirty, was caught with a friend who was selling drugs. He spent eight months in prison for aiding and abetting a crime.

Two events had convinced him to change his life. His brother was shot and killed at Few Gardens because he wouldn't pay up on a $5 bet. Then, when Benjamin got out of prison, a man who ran the Salvation Army Boys & Girls Club, where Benjamin had played basketball, contacted him and asked if he was ready for a change.

He was. He went to work for the Boys & Girls Club and stayed there until the city parks and recreation department approached him about taking over the East Durham program.

The most successful mentoring relationships, some researchers say, are those in which the mentor and the mentored grew up under similar circumstances. More than once Benjamin told Mario and the other kids at the rec center, "There ain't nothin' you can do that I ain't done or seen."

Similar Strategies

Benjamin and Singer used several of the same strategies, enabling them to touch Mario more deeply than he usually allowed. Keeping in frequent contact with him was one of the most important. Mario, like most adolescents, lived in a world of revolving doors. Assigned schools changed, teachers changed, classes and friends changed, neighbors changed. Singer and Benjamin remained. They counseled him, worked alongside him, and played with him for more than two years—a magic number for tying a strong knot, according to a major study.[9]

They also talked straight to him, Singer a little more gently than Benjamin in the beginning. Singer believed that when a boy was angry, it was best not to press him right away on sensitive issues. He didn't mind telling Mario that carrying a gun to school was stupid, but he did not try to tell Mario what he should have done. Benjamin was more direct because he had known Mario longer. Their relationship had moved from one of simple support to one of support and challenge.

Neither Benjamin nor Singer thought of Mario as a delinquent. This was significant: Both men treated Mario as a good kid who had made a bad call, not a bad kid on the road to ruin. A child will test parents and mentors alike—Michael Gurian calls these times "trust moments"—and it is important that we stick with him. This is easier to do when we have worked with the kid, as Singer and Benjamin had, and observed the kind of hard work and good behavior he is capable of.

Benjamin and Singer took responsibility for building their relationships with Mario. They would invite him out, a crucial move since kids this age feel awkward asking an adult to do something with them and so usually don't. If they didn't see him for a couple of days they would find out why. If he didn't return their phone calls (teenagers often don't) they would call him again. They didn't take his lapses of attention personally. And finally, they worked in concert with his parents, which helped assure that the relationships would last as long as Mario wanted them to.

"Mike would talk to Mario like a friend, then he'd tell me some of what he had told Mario," Jay said. "He was not me, but he was about the same type of person as I am, shared the same values." It would have been natural for Jay to feel jealous of Benjamin and Singer, but he never did. "It helped me that Mario got others' opinions," Jay said. "I wasn't the only one telling him certain things."

As fiercely as young adolescents pull away from their parents, most still want to follow their parents' values. Mentors give them an excuse to do that.

Finally, Mario is at the right school—has been, in fact, for five months. It is the day before spring break in late March, and he and I are sitting in the teachers' lounge at CIS.

The school is a mentoring mecca, introducing counselors, health professionals, and tutors, as well as teachers into the lives of students who have dropped out of regular school or are behind in grade. The staff's philosophy seems to be to do whatever it takes to reach their pupils. Some make compromises that they ordinarily might not. Mario's chorus teacher, for example, learns from the class at the beginning of the second semester that singing isn't "cool." So he shows movies that include singing, such as Whoopi Goldberg's Sister Act. He plays songs on the piano and asks students to talk about rap and R&B. By the end of the semester, the class is singing.

In Mario's science class the students learn science vocabulary words by playing Hangman with the teacher on her overhead projector. In academic enrichment, the last period of the day, they get to do their homework or have a class discussion on a topic of their choice. Birdie Midgette, a motherly-looking Caribbean native who teaches the enrichment class as well as language arts, is probably Mario's favorite teacher. Like his other teachers, she has been thoroughly briefed on his past and knows that he has a lot of catching up to do. She assigns him a seat next to her desk and checks on him regularly.

In this nontraditional setting, Mario's spirits and grades picked up at first. "I like my teachers," he told me in late November. "They work with you better and don't just pile work on. You want to come to class." He brought home his first report card the day we spoke and handed it to Joyce right away.

"I like this," she said, pointing to an 87 in algebra. "You need to bring that up," she said about a 73 in language arts. "And look at that! A ninety-three in tech!" After he left the room, she said to me, "Those are the best grades I've ever seen from Mario."

The 93 in his technical skills class, formerly called shop, was the result of a carbon dioxide–powered race car Mario had built. He had carved it out of wood, making it eight inches long, flattening its roof, and painting it green. It had taken first place in a school racing competition among the eighth-, ninth-, and tenth-graders. Mario had set it proudly on the mantel in the living room.

The tech class was over by Christmas, however. As winter rolled into spring, Mario's grades dropped, and his attitude toward school began to sour. Midgette, his language arts teacher, heard him using foul language in the hallway and called his mother. He flunked nine weeks of science — the same class in which he had enjoyed Hangman — and, as a result, Joyce pulled him off a citywide basketball team.

"I don't like any of my teachers," he tells me on this March afternoon. "I just come here, do my work, and go home." He seems more disconnected from his school and teachers than I have ever seen him.

As if to mark what he is going through, his CO_2 car somehow fell off the mantel and broke the week before my visit. When I ask to see it, all that he can show me is its green roof.

Everyone who knew Mario held a different opinion about why his attitude was souring. Singer said his disaffection from school would have happened anyway, the result of age. For reasons educators are only beginning to understand, boys' performance in school, relative to girls', begins to drop late in middle school, by some measures dramatically.[10] Joyce and Jay suspected that he had never gotten over being unfairly treated by the school system. Birdie Midgette said he was torn between seeking the approval of certain popular students and fearing that to get it, he would have to do things he shouldn't.

I thought one problem was that he played no useful role at school. He was a kid who thrived on doing jobs for people, but at school he was supposed to simply sit and absorb information.

Benjamin, who continued to see him at the rec center, had still another theory. He believed that Mario was experiencing a delayed reaction to a murder that had occurred days before he started attending CIS.

Disconnecting, Reconnecting

On a late Thursday afternoon in early October, the telephone had rung at home. Joyce had answered it, screamed loudly, and, without a word to Mario, run out to her car and driven away.

The phone call had come from the police, telling Joyce that her only sister had been found dead, lying next to her dead boyfriend, in his apartment. Police said the boyfriend had shot Joyce's sister, then himself. Two days after the slaying, which brought the city's official murder tally for the year to thirty-six, Durham's police chief, Jackie McNeil, was quoted in *The Herald-Sun* as saying he was unsure what the body count meant to the "vast majority of citizens."

Mario knew what it meant to him. "I was really depressed," he would tell me months later. "My aunt was part of my family. I would think, What if something like that happened to my parents? My brother? My sister?"

At first, however, he held steady, even when, shortly after the murder, his parents decided to take in Joyce's sister's four children, ages four to seventeen. "We don't want them to be separated," Joyce told her own kids. The three girls moved into Bethany's room. The oldest, a boy, moved into the bedroom Mario already shared with Jimmy.

Mario wouldn't tell his parents, but he was mad at their generosity. Sharing his parents' attention with two siblings was bad enough; sharing it with four other kids seemed downright unfair. To make matters worse, his mother said that she likely would be laid off from her job at Liggett & Myers Tobacco Company before Christmas. She was thinking of not looking for another job right away. "The girls need me at home," she said. Who would pay their bills? Mario wondered. Would there be any money for Christmas presents?

Mike Benjamin could tell by the way Mario picked on his cousins at the rec center that he resented them. He pulled Mario aside. The cousins' arrival would not be the big financial drain Mario feared, Benjamin said. They were inheriting some money from their mother's estate. Benjamin tried to play to Mario's sensitive side.

"If that were your mama and daddy who had gotten killed, if you had had to go to someone else's house and your cousin resented you, how would you feel?" he asked. "Your cousins need you now, more than you think they do."

Happy Constants

In May, the teachers at CIS told Joyce they would recommend that Mario repeat eighth grade. As hard as he had tried to catch up, and as much effort as the teachers had put into helping him, he was still performing below grade level. If he continued on to ninth grade, his teachers feared that he would fall further behind, especially if he returned to a large public high school.

Mario was upset because repeating eighth grade would mean he would be almost twenty when he graduated from high school. It seemed that he would never get out of school. But after discussing the matter with him, his parents decided to listen to CIS's recommendations.

The happy constants in his life during this rocky spring and summer were his family and Mike Benjamin. Even the best mentor or parent cannot make school a wonderful experience, but, as we saw with Gay Richardson, Jack's mother, they can work to fill out the other parts of an adolescent's life. Jay assigned Mario to additional construction jobs. The boyfriend of one of Jay's sisters asked him to help with a paper route every weekend.

Benjamin put him in charge of supervising the younger boys at the rec center, and gradually he began to see Mario's spirits pick up. Mario and his seventeen-year-old cousin Derwin started going bowling together. Mario would pull his girl cousins into the kitchen to help him prepare dinner for the family.

Benjamin bragged to Joyce about Mario's attention to the younger boys at the center. "If he sees the bigger guys picking on the little ones, he tells them they better lay off or he'll get on their case," Benjamin said. "I'll look up and see him at the far basketball court teaching the little kids how to play.

"He has told me, 'Mike, I'm gonna be like you. I'm gonna put something back in the community.'" The mentored was becoming a mentor.

As Mario saw it, institutions in Durham had betrayed him, but individuals within his neighborhood had not. Some of them even needed his help. That he could make such distinctions given all that he had gone through—and was willing to follow his civic instincts—testified to the strong moral core that most adolescents possess and to the connections he had made with adults who were in his corner.

CHAPTER TWELVE

The Power of One-Plus
(Alana's Story)

Sixth-grade reading class is about to begin and, with it, a chapter test. But Alana Perales has something even more immediate on her mind. She stands in front of Paula Williams's desk, clutching her hall pass. "Can I go to the bathroom?" she asks. The bell signaling the start of class hasn't rung. She thinks she has a shot at getting permission.

"No," says Williams, firmly. "You have to take the test first." Alana sighs and returns to her desk.

As she scoots through her multiple-choice exam, Williams shows me the chapter on which the class is being tested. It's an excerpt from a novel about a thirteen-year-old girl who emigrates to Canada from Scotland. I ask Williams whether she used the chapter as a jumping-off place to discuss the large migration of Mexicans, such as Alana's great-grandparents, to the United States, and to southwest Kansas in particular.

Sort of, she replies. "There was some discussion about how different immigrants are today, how they live off welfare and don't want to speak English.

"It's bad," she continues. "The kids who don't want to work, who backtalk me, are mostly Mexicans. When we got the first Spanish kids here it was no big deal. But it is a big deal now."

She puts a finger to her lips and motions to a girl who has turned around to stare at us. "*We better stop talking. We're bothering Miss Priss here.*"

During my first conversation with Alana over a pepperoni pizza, she avoided my eyes and barely said more than a few words. I knew from my conversation with her talkative sister, Angela, that her mother, Jessica, had at one time abused alcohol. I knew that her father, Harold, had worked two jobs when she was a baby and that both parents eventually turned over their daughters to Harold's parents. I knew from her uncle Louis that her mom had paid her a visit about four years earlier, and that Alana cried for hours after Jessica left. Given such crushing experiences, I wondered how well she would make it through sixth grade, thought by some experts to be the toughest year of early adolescence for girls.

Indeed, her first reaction to Kepley Middle School was not exactly positive. The rules governing behavior—from when you could visit the bathroom to when you could talk to your friends—drove her crazy, although she followed them obediently. Her classes, she said, consisted mainly of tedious drills and memorization. All but three of her teachers were cranks; one, she confided, had threatened to sue a student after tripping over his backpack on the classroom floor. And almost every day she heard at least one caustic comment from an adult at school about "these Mexicans." She may have been three generations removed from "old Mexico," but the remarks stung.

Yet despite her reservations, Alana tried to be a good student. She was not in-your-face smart, like Angela, but quiet, conscientious, and willing to volunteer for simple chores such as taking attendance. She made A's and B's all year and received top commendations for effort. She also grew increasingly gregarious and self-confident as the year passed.

Like most kids, she had no formal mentor to help her navigate through everyday encounters at home, in the classroom, and with friends. What she did have, however, was a grandmother who loved her ferociously, who was connected to and connected her to an extended family and to dozens of people in the community, who by instruction and example taught her to take on the world thinking of other people as her friends. Alana's experience speaks to the possibilities of kinship care—a family structure that is growing at an unprecedented rate—and to the power that one caretaker can have in the life of one child if that person is assisted by, and trusts, other people. As research psychologist Peter Benson concludes in *All Kids Are Our Kids*, raising healthy, happy, and confident children can begin "with a family, a neighborhood, a congregation . . . Quiet, even solitary beginnings do make a difference."[1]

Inside School

While Alana often said that middle school was boring, she enjoyed learning new facts and skills. One sign of a personally competent child is her ability to separate out and focus on activities that she enjoys within an environment she finds uninviting. Alana was able to do that.[2]

Martha heard about three teachers in particular who helped keep her granddaughter inspired. One was science teacher Ruth Cones, who, as we read in the introduction to part three, rotated students through hands-on experimental labs. Another teacher was Mary Parks, her band instructor. At the beginning of the school year, Alana, who had had no previous musical training, told Parks that she liked the way the flute sounded. She wished she could learn to play "but didn't want to buy a flute," a face-saving way of saying she couldn't afford to. Parks offered to lend her one for the year. After four months, Alana was playing second chair and had her eye on first.

Her favorite teacher, and the darling of many Kepley students I spoke to, was Terry Cantrell. Cantrell, daughter of a much-loved, retired high-school teacher and wife of the community veterinarian, taught math. It was not Alana's best subject—she could not snag an A for the quarter no matter how hard she tried—but it was her favorite class. The class assignment she most enjoyed was planning a trip to anywhere in the world on a budget of $3,000. Alana and her partner chose New Orleans.

"Ms. Cantrell makes learning fun," Alana said, "and she treats everybody the same." The artwork Cantrell chose for her classroom showed the affection she felt for her students. On a big bulletin board she had attached a picture of a cartoonish-looking teacher pointing to a blackboard on which were written, tongue-in-cheek, thirty-three Thou Shalt Nots, including, "No smiling, no wearing weird clothes, no dumb questions . . ." Students who looked at the board knew that she knew the rules they had to follow were excessive. They also knew, however, that they had to control themselves, and another poster told them why. "I care too much about you to allow you to act up in my classroom," it said. "There is no way I will allow you to stop yourself or someone else from learning."

Like Melissa Bartlett in Durham, Cantrell defined her role as helping all students, not just the ones she taught. She often chaperoned student functions that other teachers avoided. At one sixth-grade dance, for example, she was the only teacher there to supervise out of a half-dozen who had been invited.

Alana's uncle Louis Jr., or "Junior" as the family called him, worked as an aide at Kepley and regularly passed on his observations about the school to Martha. He could verify Alana's reactions to school—a sweet affirmation that any adolescent appreciates. His knowledge enabled Martha to listen, with understanding, when Alana talked about her school day.

Martha baked cupcakes and cookies for Alana's school functions, attended her concerts, made sure that Louis, Harold, or Harold's girl-friend watched her games, and looked over her papers and tests. When Alana brought home a grade that wasn't as high as it could have been, her grandmother told her that was all right as long as she raised it. When Alana's work improved, Martha or Louis rewarded her by taking her out for pizza or a hamburger. "I always know what is expected of me," Alana said. "I want to get good grades for them."

"Trouble with the Mexicans"

A recurring topic over Sunday dinner at the Peraleses' was the treatment of Mexican-Americans at school. Seven of every ten students detained at Kepley were Hispanic, according to principal Juan Perez, more than twice the proportion of Hispanics in the 440-pupil school. The number of detentions, which was growing, bothered Louis a great deal. "It's almost like it's done on purpose to weed out students they don't think will stay there anyway," he said.

Many of Kepley's detentions were slapped on students, mostly boys, whose pants dragged the ground, violating the no-sag, no-bag rule. On more than one occasion, Louis raced home at lunch to get one of his own belts and deliver it to a student in need of hitching up his slacks. "To think that the same rules are going to work for everyone, they're just not," he would say.

Martha's daughter Pam called the principal's office to protest the ease with which teachers threw kids into detention. But although the family didn't approve of some of the rules, they told Alana she had to obey them. These discussions forced Alana to think beyond her immediate negative reaction to whether and how one should obey laws with which one disagrees.

In April 1997, an incident at school put the spotlight once again on Mexican-Americans. Four boys, three of them Mexican-Americans, were discovered to have poked seven other students, including one of Alana's close friends, with small medical needles one boy had found in a ditch. County health officials determined that the risk of being infected by hepatitis or AIDS was minimal since the needles were new and unused. But they administered a series of three shots to dozens of students just to be safe. The perpetrators were sent to night school for the rest of the year and forced during the day to work alongside county prisoners wearing bright orange vests. They were also ordered to appear, in their vests, at a school assembly and apologize. "This trouble with the Mexicans seems to never end," Louis said.

"This trouble with the Mexicans" put Alana and Angela in a situation similar to that of Michelle or Jessica, or any minority child in a majority community. Alana and Angela were only half Mexican (their mother was Anglo), and both their father and their father's parents were born in the United States. Yet they were still considered "Mexican" by many of their classmates. If they showed sympathy for other Mexicans during a confrontation at school, they risked alienating their white friends. But if they sided with the Anglos, some of the Mexicans would taunt them.

"Veronica and Patsy and Andrea are my friends," Alana said one day about three Mexican girls. "They're always asking me why I hang out with Beth." Beth was Anglo.

But Alana and Angela were lucky because their relatives knew how to talk to them about surviving social stereotypes. Pam told them there were far fewer Mexicans in the area when she was growing up, and she had been so scared of being picked on that she waited for their father, who was younger than she but bigger and stronger, to accompany her to school each day. Martha told them to ignore the disputes, to focus on the proper behavior she was teaching them, and to try to get along with everybody. "There are always going to be people who don't like Mexicans," she said matter-of-factly.

The girls tried to follow her advice, with differing degrees of success. Angela hung out mostly with white girls and was known to defend herself with her words or her fists on more than one occasion. Alana preferred to sit alone in class to sitting with someone she didn't trust. She had accepted and internalized her grandmother's expectations more successfully than her sister had, and she was learning when to express and when to contain her emotions. She chafed privately at prejudice. "My friend's mom told her not to hang out with me because I'm Mexican," she confided one night. But publicly she tried to stay above the fray.

"I try not to be like the troublemakers," she said. And indeed, she was not. Shortly after the needle episode, the sixth-grade teachers picked two teams of four students to compete in the school-wide Scholastic Bowl. Alana was one of the eight chosen and helped lead her team to a first-place win.

On an Indian summer evening in early September, Alana is sitting with me in the bleachers of the high-school gymnasium. Ostensibly she is there to watch her sister, Angela, play volleyball, but the real reason is to see a couple of classmates who told her they would be at the game.

Angela, number 40 on the Lady Tigers, is all motion, scoring points, high-fiving her teammates, chatting nonstop when on the bench during timeouts. Alana munches on a bag of Doritos, not saying a word, as she waits for friends who never show up.

Eight months later, she has plenty of chums. One of them, Lisa, and she giggle one afternoon about the dumb acrostic puzzles on their place mats at Pizza Hut. They talk about the boy who, at the dance that Cantrell chaperoned, put his hand down a girl's pants on a dare. "It's a complicated story," sighs Lisa, who claims to know the inside scoop on just about everything that happens at Kepley.

Lisa lets me know that the boy she slow-danced with was her old boyfriend, not her current beau. Alana confides that there is now a boy who calls her on the phone. They describe the various cliques at school, then ask if I will take them over to the neighborhood of "one of the snobby girls." We drive by the girl's house, very slowly at their request, in my rented convertible. The top is folded back, of course. They honk the horn and wave. They're not sure the girl is home but they would like to believe she is.

When I first met Alana she seemed to spend most of her free time during the week, when she wasn't doing her homework, watching reruns of *Beverly Hills 90210* on the small television in the bedroom that she shared with her sister. Her family lived in a neat, brown bungalow on the outskirts of Ulysses, and she wasn't allowed to walk alone into town even though it was less than a mile. This made it difficult to get together with kids she hoped would become her friends.

Some of her classmates could be so mean, she sometimes wondered whether it was worth trying to befriend them.

Her uncle Louis came home from work one day and Martha told him that Alana had been crying in her bedroom. Martha wasn't sure why. It turned out that that morning, Alana's gym class had been assigned to swim indoors at the town's recreation center. Alana, self-conscious about her weight and embarrassed to wear a bathing suit, had heard some of her classmates making fun of her.

Taking It Slowly

The Perales family rallied around her concern about her weight, as they did other problems that came to their attention. But they did so carefully and over time. They didn't want to make her so sensitive about her looks that she stopped eating, or binged.

Louis opened the dialogue one night by explaining puberty to her. "Your body is just going haywire right now like any preteenager's body does," he said. He told her that both her father and her sister had been a bit heavy when they were her age but thinned out as they grew older and taller.

He and Martha decided to start taking regular walks with her since she wasn't playing sports at the time. They advised her to stop eating snacks, emphasizing what sweets can do to teeth and complexion as well as body fat. And although Martha loved seeing her granddaughter in tailored clothes, she allowed Alana to wear the baggy T-shirts and jeans that made Alana feel less conspicuous.

Alana did not lose any noticeable weight as the months passed, but her roundness seemed to bother her less and less. She concentrated on improving parts of her appearance that she felt she could control: her smooth complexion, her big blue eyes, and her curly, light-brown hair.

With her family's encouragement—and sometimes, at their insistence—she stayed involved in activities that threw her together with kids her age: the band, an after-school play, volleyball and softball, even the confirmation class at church that she disliked. She became adept at using the telephone with her friends. Gradually, various girls started inviting her to their homes for weekend sleepovers and visiting her on weekday afternoons to watch *Beverly Hills 90210*.

Alana and Angela breeze into a books and music store in nearby Garden City, anxious to browse through the latest compact discs. Angela has no trouble picking out what she wants, the soundtrack from the movie Romeo and Juliet. Alana searches slowly. Finally she picks out a disc by the group Bone Thugs-N-Harmony. Its cover song, she says, is one of her favorites. Called "Crossroads," it's an elegy about death. No, she says, reading my mind. It doesn't make her want to commit suicide.

"Then why do you want to buy it?" I ask.

"Because my friends have it."

She thumbs through Valentines in the greeting-cards section and picks out one to show me. On the front is a baby in a bathtub playing with a rubber duck. Inside, the card says: "Be My Valentine or the Duck Dies." Alana thinks this is funny.

Her real reason for the search becomes clear as she moves to another section of the display. She chooses a floral card with a front inscription that reads: "For your wise advice, I thank you. For the laughter we've shared, I thank you. For the times I have taken comfort in our talks, I thank you."

Inside, in simple bold letters, the card says: "Thanks for being like a Mom to me. Happy Valentine's Day." Martha receives the card and a bear hug two weeks later.

Martha, round like her granddaughter, white-haired and cheerful, was Alana's mother in all but name. Alana said her first word, took her first step, and celebrated her first birthday with her grandparents.

The fact that she spent more time with them in her earliest years than Angela did in her early childhood may help explain why the sisters were so different. Angela, as we saw in chapter six, lived in the crisis-ridden homes of her mom and dad for much of her first five years. Like many first children, she was adored in infancy, abandoned for the second child and, infected by the insecurities of her young parents, driven in later years to win people's approval at considerable cost. "You have to project a certain image," she once told me.

Alana, in contrast, acted like the second child of parents who already knew the ropes. Her uncle drew the contrast in one of our first visits. Angela, he said, "is always asking us questions about her homework." Alana "figures things out for herself." Angela "has so many things that bother her"; Alana "just breezes right through life."

In spite of the confidence in Alana that those observations implied, he and Martha said they worried more about their younger granddaughter. They certainly seemed to pay more attention to her than to Angela, except when Angela broke their rules. One evening in April, Angela had to attend a parent-child banquet at high school by herself because both Martha and Louis were too tired to accompany her. It is doubtful they would have sent Alana off alone like that.

Beyond the Front Stoop

Martha certainly hadn't planned to spend her later years raising two girls. But as she acknowledged, they allowed her to accomplish one of the dreams of her youth. Traveling throughout the Midwest as one of fourteen children in a family of migrant workers, she had wanted nothing more than to someday put down roots in a community. With her own children, she took one step toward that goal by settling on a farm where the family was relatively self-sufficient. In order to care for her grandchildren, though, she had to go further and reach beyond the front stoop.

Hispanics were moving to Kansas at ten times the rate of Caucasians to fill low-skilled jobs in meat processing and petroleum, and as their numbers in Ulysses increased, so did ethnic tensions in the community. Several Mexican families I met there kept to themselves, isolated by language and prejudice, their own as well as their neighbors'.

Martha and her family had lived in similar isolation on the farm but decided to move into town so that Angela and Alana could attend better schools. Martha, working in a nursing home, took a cook's job at the senior citizens center, where she was embraced immediately by the retirees who gathered there every day for a hot lunch. Her reputation as an excellent cook traveled with her to Mary Queen of Peace, the Catholic church she and her family had started attending, and soon she was being asked to volunteer for more church suppers and bake sales than she could keep up with. "I'm one of those crazy people who always says yes when someone calls asking for help," she admitted.

I dropped by the church mid-morning on a day when she was off work and discovered her in charge of making several hundred enchiladas. The enchiladas were to be sold to help pay the costs of cancer treatment for one of the Mexican-American women in town. This woman "didn't want to have anything to do with Anglos and now she's asking for help," Martha said disapprovingly.

As both a paid worker and a volunteer in the community, Martha stayed informed about whose kids were doing what and where they were doing it. She learned of events that her granddaughters might like to take part in and heard about families whom she wanted Alana and Angela to avoid.

In Step with Others

Like Eldon Stanton, the father of Eric in the first chapter, Martha would be the first person to say she could not have raised her granddaughters without the help of a large cast. Ulysses offered no formal support group for surrogate parents such as herself, so she put together her own.

Her husband, Louis Sr., was one member. Having had little schooling, he could not read or write but was accomplished with his hands and worked at a farm equipment shop long past retirement age in order to pay the bills. He would sit in the living room in the evenings when the girls' friends stopped by and say little. But as the friends prepared to leave he would always rise, shake their hands, and say, "You're welcome here anytime."

Martha's daughter, Pam, a legal assistant and married, talked to the girls several times a week either on the phone or in person. Her brother, Louis Jr., had just started community college, planning to become a park ranger, when the girls moved in. "All of a sudden, everything came crashing down," he recalled. "It was to the point where we felt someone's going to have to step in because these girls had been neglected as babies and toddlers. We had a family powwow and realized they've got to come live here.

"Mom was working full-time and Dad was on the farm and I got to thinking this is not going to work. So I thought, I better put my plans on hold and go back and just kind of help out until the situation corrects itself or until their dad comes to get them. But that never happened."

Shortly after the girls' arrival, the family held a conference about what kind of parenting strategy to use.

"We said we could pity them because of their situation and let them have anything and everything that they want," Louis remembered. "Or we could go the other route and require discipline, let them know that there are limits and boundaries and that no means no and yes means maybe, if finances allow it."

Louis moved back home and transferred his passion for animals to kids in need of special help, both his nieces and disabled children. He first worked at the elementary school that Angela, then Alana attended, and when Alana entered Kepley, he followed her there. After school he worked at a center serving school-age children, and he placed a police scanner in the family's living room to alert him to incidents involving "his kids." It was not uncommon for him to rush out at 10 or 11 P.M. to help a kid in trouble.

He said he realized, as Alana and Angela got older, that they deserved the same care and attention he was paying to his pupils. "I knew I needed to give these girls a chance to express themselves, to spend time with them whenever they felt like talking." Martha came to rely on him so much that before she allowed the girls to go anywhere, she told them to check with Junior.

Martha could rattle off dozens of people outside her family who made life with the girls run more smoothly. One was their family physician, who forgave their early doctor bills and never turned them away even when money was tight. Once the family moved into town and the girls were in school, the school bus driver assured Martha that she wouldn't let them off the bus until she saw that an adult was home. An older woman, Inge Mitchell, who lived down the street, kept an eye on the house and the girls.

The school superintendent qualified Alana and Angela for reduced-fee lunches after Martha swallowed her pride one year and asked. Louis Sr.'s boss provided the family with a freezer full of beef each year. "I never have to buy meat, just chicken or fish," Martha said. "He's an angel." In return, she and the girls helped this man with his garden in the summer.

Reciprocity made everything easier, including supervision of the girls when they were away with friends. Martha chatted regularly with the parents of their friends. Realizing that as an older caretaker she had a lot to learn about a younger generation, she listened to the observations of the parents she trusted. "We kind of take care of each other's kids," she said.

She found that she was growing in her understanding of how to raise adolescents and was much more relaxed with her grandchildren than she had been with her children. She didn't fuss if their bedroom got messy. She hugged them and paid them compliments—two things she had never done with her own children, she said. But what made the most difference as they got older, she believed, was her decision, which came relatively late in Angela's adolescence, to communicate openly. After several escapades by Angela, Martha realized that in order to convince the girls to talk to her so that they might solve their problems together, she had to be willing to hear whatever they said no matter how much it hurt. She also had to share her own feelings, a skill that did not come easily.[3]

By the end of Alana's sixth-grade year, Martha was beginning to learn, in her words, "to sit down and listen to the girls and let them say whatever was on their mind. We'd talk and cry and talk and cry again."

Louis Jr. occasionally wondered whether he had done the right thing by changing his life course to help raise the girls. But Martha never expressed any reservations. She was, as so many grandparents are, fiercely loyal to her granddaughters and increasingly aware, as they got older, of the ways in which they had enriched her life. Raising them had enabled her to talk more openly to her own children, she said, and to show more affection toward them. She was so busy with Alana and Angela "that I didn't have time to think about my aches and pains. It has been a good experience, you bet."

The girls were lucky to have such an optimist taking care of them, according to psychologist Martin E. P. Seligman. "When you teach your child optimism, you are teaching him to know himself, to be curious about his theory of himself and of the world," he writes in *The Optimistic Child.* "You are teaching him to take an active stance in his world and to shape his own life, rather than be a passive recipient of what happens his way."[4]

On my last visit with Alana that year, she rattled off the ways in which she thought she had changed.

"I draw well. I'm good in all my subjects. I'm now the number-one flute player."

"Anything else?" I asked.

"I'm more mature. Not so childish."

Really? I reminded her of the recent school dance, when she and a group of friends jerked their bodies, wobbled their knees, and clawed the air in what they called "the chicken dance." The six of them had looked pretty silly to me.

She met my gaze. "Well, you know what that shows, don't you?"

No, what?

"I'm part of it. I'm not watching from the sidelines anymore."

AS PARENTS WE CAN

• Make sure our child enjoys a good relationship with at least one adult to whom she is not related. The degree of intimacy and amount of time needed will vary.

• Give him a chance to connect on his own first; listen for names of adults he talks about frequently and let those adults know how important they are.

• Assure any significant adult that kids don't expect grand gestures. They want to be listened to and noticed for the little things: what they're wearing, who their favorite rock group is.

• Allow the attachment to grow on its own. Listen carefully if the adult offers advice, a compliment, or a less-than-flattering observation.

• Help her think of ways to show appreciation for her adult friend; discuss possible projects they could do together.

• Connect him to an adult who understands the legal system if he gets in trouble. This person should be his advocate and guide as well as ours.

• Seek connections ourselves, particularly to other adults who can share information or skills that will make us better parents.

School Year 1999–2000

Eric Stanton

At seventeen, Eric described himself as "an entrepreneur" who had "no time for girls."

The first part of his senior year started, strangely enough, like his ninth-grade year, tending to a parent who was temporarily bedridden from an operation. This time it was his mother, Denice Stanton. For more than three months, he did her banking and shopping and changed the bandages on her foot.

At school he maintained an A/B average and played drums in the marching band. Music consumed more and more of his life. He started a rock and jazz band with a friend. He played drums in church on Sundays. He found himself a weekend job as a restaurant host and used some of his earnings to purchase a small sound system, a microphone, and lights. He then set up a small deejay business.

It had always been his parents' dream that he would go to a four-year college. But given his burgeoning enterprises, as well as his proficiency in music, neither Eldon nor Denice Stanton was surprised when Eric told them that he wanted to attend Los Angeles Community College immediately after high school, while searching for a university program in sound engineering.

"I told him he's at least got to have a plan," Eldon said.

Chandler Brennan

Chandler barely made it into her senior year at Northern High School. Lacking the credits to graduate in May because she had failed so many courses, she said she intended to complete her high-school education in the fall at a local technical school. After that, she was considering nursing school or cosmetology.

She was dating a young man who had dropped out of high school and lived at home. Her mother, Tracy, couldn't talk her into ending the relationship. Daughter and mother had become somewhat closer since the first year I met them; over Christmas 1999, they enjoyed working together as Santa's helpers at a local shopping mall.

When Chandler looked back on her tumultuous ninth-grade year, she believed her parents had done the right thing in sending her to John Umstead Hospital. "I hate it that I went," she said, "but I don't know where I'd be now if I hadn't gone."

Her mood had stabilized as her parents' relationship ended. Her father, Daniel, left Tracy in March 1998, and they were divorced a year later. Chandler and her younger sister, Ashley, stayed with Tracy in their house.

After fractious legal proceedings with Daniel that continued into the year 2000, Tracy was left with the house, which was still mortgaged to the bank, and some furniture. She took on a day job as a secretary and started waitressing at night. As angry as she felt, she enjoyed her work and the opportunity to meet new people. She told Chandler and Ashley, "Make your career first and your own money. Then find yourself a husband."

Shannon Steele

Shannon, who was starting seventh grade when I met her, took charge of her life in tenth grade as her parents, Brenda and Gary, backed off. She decided not to play sports at school but to manage several boys' teams instead. She was hired as a referee at the town's recreation center and joined a leadership/service organization whose members elected her vice president. She began bringing home A's and B's from school instead of C's and D's.

The one area in which she didn't exercise enough control was her diet. No matter how often her parents reminded her about the health risk she ran eating sweets, they would find candy wrappers and cookies in her car and backpack. They decided to stop nagging her, that she was old enough to assume responsibility for her health. In three years, they reminded themselves, she would be away at college. She talked about attending the University of Kansas to study sports medicine.

"We have seen a real turnaround this year," Brenda said. But she and Gary were holding their breath, for ninth grade was barely over and it had been a year from hell.

That year Shannon fought constantly with them over the rules of the house.

The climax took place one week in December. Brenda and Gary had made her quit basketball several weeks earlier because of her grades, and when they gave her permission to return, the coach refused to take her back. Toward the end of that week, Brenda and Gary told her that she couldn't stay with her boyfriend and his family the coming weekend while they were out of town.

On Friday, while home for lunch, she injected herself with a large amount of insulin in an effort to scare her parents. She almost died as a result.

After her recovery, the Steeles as a family started seeing a social worker. Shannon went by herself as well, and learned several techniques for managing her anger.

During one of their battles, Brenda wrote me by e-mail: "I'm not sure what but we're going to have to put Shannon somewhere for a while." A few lines later, echoing Tracy Brennan, Chandler's mother, three and a half years earlier, she asked, "Where did the daughter I know go?"

Unlike Tracy and Daniel, Brenda and Gary did not send their daughter away. They discussed their own behavior and resolved to consistently reinforce family rules together. A physician who examined Shannon at the hospital decided to change her insulin, and her blood sugar stabilized. By late spring of ninth grade, she was beginning to settle down, the result, Brenda now thinks, of all the things they did plus simple maturation.

As her sophomore year began, Shannon bought a cross-stitched wall hanging for her mom that read: "If I didn't have you for a mother, I'd choose you for a friend."

Libby Sigel

Libby's tenth-grade year, like Shannon's, was much smoother than eighth and ninth. "I don't fight with my parents as much, partly because I'm not around as much and partly because there's nothing to fight about," she said.

In eighth grade, she continued to do things with friends she knew she wasn't supposed to, all the while analyzing why. She hosted a party at her house in late fall, for example, and a hundred kids showed up. Her mother, Rebekah, caught some of them smoking and told Libby everyone had to go home. "It was a bad party," Libby said later.

Rebekah occasionally searched Libby's room for signs of drugs; once that year she found marijuana in her daughter's wallet. Also that year, Libby tried to lock her mother out of her room, but Rebekah brought in a locksmith to change all the locks in the house so that none of her children could lock anyone out.

The relationship between Libby and her mother began to improve in the summer after eighth grade, when Libby and her younger brother traveled to India by themselves. "I was born in Bombay; I always wanted to see it," Libby said. Moved by the poverty she witnessed there, she started working at a homeless shelter when she returned. In tenth grade, she took calls for a crisis hotline and counseled students at her high school. She talked about one day becoming a psychologist.

Inspired by her English teacher, she wrote poetry and songs. She took up the guitar and played keyboard in a coffeehouse. With less time to socialize than she had had in middle school, she became more selective in whom she chose to hang out with. They were the friends "who matter most," she said, and included several kids she had known in middle school.

One of those friends, a recovering drug user, had run away from home a couple of times. Libby told her mom that she was troubled by the fact that the girl's mom "has no control over her daughter."

"You know all those times you were controlling and checking up on me?" she asked Rebekah one morning. "Well, it's because of you that I would never run away or do the stuff she has done. Even if you weren't around I wouldn't do it."

Chip Thomson

The year 2000 found Chip in a group home in Durham and attending Jordan High School. He should have been a senior but instead was a junior, barely. He had spent the previous two years living in two residential drug treatment programs and had fallen behind in his high-school credits as a result.

The second program, during the school year 1998–99, was at John Umstead Hospital, the same institution where Chandler had lived two years earlier. Chip made progress there: He enjoyed his classes, particularly woodworking, and his therapist.

Marianne and Brian drove for an hour to Umstead every Tuesday night that year to take part in family counseling. They also visited on weekends. They included Chip in family trips to Ireland and the beach. "He can be a lot of fun, real nice to be around," Marianne said.

They came to believe that he was better off living away from home. So when his year at Umstead ended and hospital authorities recommended he be placed in a group home, a step-down unit, they consented. In November 1999, a worker at the group home found marijuana in Chip's bedroom. Chip was charged with possession. At about the same time, school authorities caught him writing his name on a bathroom wall. He was charged with defacing public property.

After his court appearance on both charges, his mother told me, "He still needs lots of supervision. It's one step forward, three-quarters of a step back every week." Chip would turn eighteen in July, she noted, and that would alter the family's legal and financial obligations to him in ways that she and Brian had not yet fully explored. "Whether he will ever be able to come home, I don't know. We need a chance to regain our sanity and give Justin a normal life." The Thomsons had placed Justin, Chip's brother, in a private school after what they considered Chip's disastrous experience with public schools, and were pleased with his performance there.

The same night I talked to Marianne, Chip described with enthusiasm how much he liked being back at Jordan, how he had met new friends there and worked on the technical crew for a play production. He was attending Narcotics Anonymous regularly, he said.

He played down the marijuana arrest. "I don't have any real desire to do drugs anymore," he said. "Things are going good with my parents. I'll be coming home in a couple of months."

Angela Perales

Angela's accomplishments at school her senior year would have filled several paragraphs in a *Who's Who* reference book. She was a member of the National Honor Society, a starting player on both varsity volleyball and softball teams, a nurse in the school musical "South Pacific," and a contender in regional chorus competitions. She waitressed about twenty hours a week, squirreling away money for Kansas State University, where she had been accepted for admission in the fall of 2000 with a partial scholarship. She seemed well on her way to becoming the first person in her family to go to a four-year college.

Her personal life, however, was not as satisfying. Her great-grandmother, a tiny woman she affectionately called "Lil' Grandma," died, and Angela missed visiting her on weekends in the nursing home. Her dad moved to Wichita and then to Denver before returning to Ulysses without a job. Her mother remarried and gave birth to another baby girl. And in the summer before twelfth grade, she started dating a young man whom her grandmother, Martha Perales, called a bum.

He was seven years older than her, only sporadically employed, and had seen the inside of a police station more than once. Martha and other relatives told Angela to stay away from him. Angela snuck out with him anyway but didn't feel good about it.

"I don't want to have to go behind my family's back," she said. "I don't like making them mad. But James makes me feel good."

Martha blamed the relationship on the young man, mostly, but also bemoaned the fact that several of Angela's girlfriends were hanging out with older guys. These friends had replaced Stacy and Kimberly in Angela's daily affections.

By early winter, Angela had stopped seeing James but was continuing to battle family rules. One evening, Martha and Louis, Angela's uncle, decided to open a free-ranging discussion with her while Harold, her father, was present. "You have to make us understand why you are so unhappy," Martha said. Angela spilled out questions that had bothered her for years. Why was her father never around? Why did he seem to prefer the affections of different women to the love of his daughters? Why had her mother really left?

Both Angela and Martha said later that that long and tough evening marked a turning point in their relationship. She started coming home when expected or calling when she was going to be late.

"I think we're going to make it," Martha said late in the year.

Rodney Kincaid

Ninth grade at a new school heralded a promising beginning for Rodney. He brought home B's and C's instead of C's and D's. His teachers told his mom, Veronica, that he was "willing to learn." And of particular joy to him, he made the golf team in the spring.

His mother attributed this progress to the fact that the family had, finally, moved out of Los Angeles to a suburb called Torrance. The majority of students at Norbonne High School were white, and she thought that made a difference. "The teachers expect more," she said. Rodney agreed. "It's definitely tops on the scale," he said. He volunteered another reason he was performing better: "I moved away from my old friends." He felt more comfortable asking and answering questions in his new classes, he said.

The migration to Torrance was not by choice. Rodney's dad, Big Rodney, had fallen behind paying the mortgage on their house in South-Central LA, and the bank had foreclosed on their mortgage. Veronica, furious with her husband for losing her childhood home, asked for a separation. Big Rodney moved into a house with a friend, and she found a two-bedroom rental apartment in Torrance. "Rodney didn't understand what had happened, and to tell you the truth, neither did I," Veronica said later. "But I tried to keep things on a positive note."

Rodney had been inching ahead in his studies ever since his calamitous sixth-grade year. In seventh and eighth grades, authorities at Audubon Middle School placed him in the school's Sports Academy, a full day and afterschool program of academics, tutoring, and sports with a reputation for successful interventions. He struck up a close friendship with his English teacher, whom he still talked about a year later. He also grew about six inches and no longer felt puny alongside his classmates.

On weekends he stayed with his dad at his dad's friend's house, enjoying a computer that the friend allowed him to use. He looked forward to formal instruction at school in computer programming and computer repair. "I might want to go into computer technology someday," he said.

Jessica Johnston

Jessica started ninth grade at the Christian school her mother had suggested three years earlier. The route there was far from straight, however.

The beginning of seventh grade found her back at Chewning Middle School. That fall, her mother, Teresa McNamara, filed for divorce from her husband Glenn. Teresa then started dating other men, and, at the same time, an older sister moved into their house with a boyfriend. Jessica was twelve by then, the age her mother had said she could start visiting her father. She announced that she was going to live with him.

"You've got an attitude," Teresa told her the night she packed her bags.

"Did you ever think it might be y'all?" Jessica responded.

In Jessica's eyes, Ray Johnston symbolized stability. He lived in the house in which she was born and worked for the same trucking firm he started with in the late 1970s. After he and Teresa divorced, he had married a woman he met at work; together, they had a son and appeared to be content.

Shortly after she moved into his house, Jessica started attending the school run by her church, Fellowship Baptist. She finished her seventh-grade year there. But she missed her old friends at Chewning and returned to Chewning for eighth grade.

Chewning's test scores continued to lag behind most of the other schools in Durham County, and Jessica found the school environment even more hostile to learning than two years earlier. She took up smoking with her school friends and drank beer a couple of times with the son of a man her mother married. She missed seeing her brother Joseph and her stepbrothers Justin and Joel. Late in her eighth-grade year she started going back to Fellowship Baptist Church on Sundays and resumed the church's home visits that she had so enjoyed in sixth grade. She took part in all the youth activities, inspired by the youth pastor and his wife. She began to feel that her life was back on the right track.

"I realized that if I didn't have my mom or my sisters to look to as examples, I had people at church who loved me and took care of me," she said.

In ninth grade, she left the public school system for the school that Fellowship ran. She excelled in her courses there just as she had at Chewning. For the almost four years I knew her, she never lost sight of the fact that she needed to do well in school and college in order to lead a more successful life than so many people she knew.

"I want to be able to support myself, and not be dependent on any man," she said. "I'm trying to learn from my family's mistakes."

Jack Richardson

By the time he entered tenth grade at Ulysses High School, Jack's life had settled into a quiet, steady hum. Horticulture had taken the place of ceramics as his favorite class; basketball had replaced football as the school sport he preferred, partly because at six feet four inches, he was tapped to be starting forward. He was an A/B student but continued to prefer outdoor activities to his studies.

He learned to hunt pheasant, but roping was still his number-one hobby. Together with a friend he won several local roping competitions and qualified to enter a national rodeo contest in Colorado. During spring breaks and summers he worked ten- and twelve-hour days for several farmers and ranchers, including Jess Hammer. The farmers took to his friendly, unassuming personality and so did their wives. One farmer's wife "called me her other son," Jack said proudly.

One reason he worked so hard was to pay for the upkeep on an old Chevrolet truck that his dad, Phillip, bought for him. Phillip had been hired for the federal meat inspector's job he had sought during Jack's seventh-grade year, and this had stabilized the Richardsons' income.

The only blip in their increasingly steady life was the behavior of Jack's younger brother, Zeb. Zeb would slip out of the house at night and not tell his parents where he was going. He was caught shoplifting a package of cigarettes and was placed on probation. His grades at school seesawed. Gay and Phillip took him to see a counselor and toughened up the house rules.

"Jack is comfortable with who he is," Gay said. "Zeb isn't, yet."

Michelle Bellamy

Michelle visited her adult friend Henry Turner less frequently as she got older, until by ninth grade she scarcely saw him at all. "That's because he's working a lot," she told me. Indeed, Turner had assumed a full-time job as an English teacher in a Los Angeles middle school that held classes year-round. He confided to Michelle's mom, Janice Seton, that he was worn out most days.

He made an effort to reach out to both Michelle and her mom. When an affordable two-bedroom apartment became available across the street from his home, he urged Janice to snatch it up. She declined because she believed the neighborhood was less safe than the one in which she and Michelle were living. He also continued to invite Janice and Michelle to his house from time to time, but frequently Janice went alone because Michelle preferred to spend time with friends.

These were acquaintances from Windward School, the exclusive private school she had entered, on scholarship, in seventh grade, and their favorite activity was shopping. The mall at Century City replaced the Beverly Hills Center as the cool place to hang out. After window-shopping there and eating dinner, she would return home and tell her mom, "I feel like a real teenager!"

She spent a couple of hours each day on homework. The time consumed by French, math, and other subjects, coupled with her mother's lack of a car, kept her out of any extracurricular activities. She still wouldn't consider taking city buses by herself, and her mother remained staunchly opposed to the idea as well.

Their financial status was no better than when I first met them. Michelle's father, Curtis Bellamy, owed $22,000 in child support by the middle of Michelle's ninth-grade year.

Janice launched what she called a "Help Janice campaign," with goals of losing weight and finding a job. She took two free computer courses, then attended a job skills class that helped her prepare a résumé. She volunteered at Windward, just as she had at Michelle's elementary school.

Michelle said she was considering working someday in fashion or interior design, but of two things she was certain: "College is a must . . . and I want to always be with my mom."

Mario Rawlings

Through his sophomore year, Mario stayed out of serious trouble and made passable grades. He rarely saw his old adult friends Al Singer and Mike Benjamin, but he thought about them frequently and fondly.

He had repeated eighth grade at Holton against his wishes. But by ninth grade he had decided on his own that he should finish high school there instead of transferring to the regular high school. He enjoyed that year: One of his teachers took a special interest in him, and his achievement improved dramatically; he started dating a girl whom his parents liked; and his older brother, Jimmy, was suspended from high school for being seen with a gun on campus. Having been the focus of his parents' worry in years past, Mario was relieved to see that attention shift away from him, even as he felt sorry for his brother.

The incident that caught up his brother bore an eerie resemblance to what had happened to Mario. Jimmy had slipped into a friend's car at the friend's request, intending to drive it off the high-school property. He spied a shotgun in the front seat and moved it to the backseat; another student saw him do this and reported it to school authorities.

Once again, Joyce and Jay Rawlings had to appear at a hearing to plead that their son be allowed back into school. Once again, they consulted Singer. They succeeded in getting Jimmy's suspension reduced to two months; Jimmy later dropped out of high school and took a job in construction, telling his parents that he would work on his high-school equivalency degree.

At seventeen and still in the tenth grade, Mario was a prime candidate to abandon school like his brother. He had stopped playing sports except for an occasional basketball game with friends. He no longer visited the recreation center, saying "I guess I grew out of it." On weekends he hung around the house or worked on construction sites.

But having fought so hard to get back into school, he swore he was going to finish it. And what did he plan to do after that?

"I don't even know," he said.

Alana Perales

The self-assuredness that Alana began to display near the end of sixth grade blossomed as she got older. "I'm not shy anymore," she said in the winter of ninth grade at Ulysses High School. "When new people come to school, I'll go up and talk to them. I try to do a lot more things."

She was earning A's in all her classes at the time of our conversation, even though the work was more difficult and the classes were longer. She attributed this in part to better teachers and to a relaxed atmosphere at school. "They treat us more like grown-ups," she said. "We can chew gum. We can go home for lunch."

The high school offered a larger and more varied collection of books in its library than middle school had, and she discovered that she loved to read, mysteries and crime stories especially. Art class gave her a chance to explore sketching in black and white. Her favorite pursuit, however, remained playing the flute. Still using the flute on loan from her sixth-grade teacher, she assumed first chair in the band, even though she was only a freshman, and was asked to play in the pit band for the annual school play. She received a guitar for Christmas and started teaching herself to play it; she said she would like to learn to play the violin. Going to college was "definitely" in her plans, she said, financed partly, she hoped, by a band scholarship.

She grew taller, as her uncle had predicted she would, and assumed a solid shape of which she was proud. "People look at me like I'm big but I think I'm strong," she said. "Everyone picks me for their team in PE." Her strength made her a better volleyball and softball player, she noted.

She saw her father occasionally when he came to visit her grandmother. But she didn't visit him at his house because, she said, "I'm tired of meeting all his girlfriends." Her relationship with her grandmother and uncle remained strong, although she felt jealous when her sister, Angela, acted out and attracted their attention.

She felt close to her sister when Angela confided in her but got angry when Angela asked her to cover for her. She believed that her grandmother and uncle kept a tighter rein on her because of their experience with Angela, and she thought that was unfair. Her uncle Louis started working at the high school the same year she arrived there, saying he wanted to continue to assist the students he had helped in middle school. "He says he's not following me but I know he is," she said. "They think I'm going to turn out like my sister. I'm nothing like she is."

Some Concluding Thoughts

If you were sitting in my living room and we were sharing a pot of coffee, here is what I would tell you I have learned about raising young adolescents:

Early adolescence is partly about loss. Our kids lose their innocence, their unquestioning faith in adults, and their certainty about themselves and their place in a world they no longer know. It is about loss for us, as well. We lose their adoration, their physical need for us, and our sense of control.

It doesn't happen overnight. Adolescence creeps up on us. It seeks out the shadows. Then it slams a door in our face or flees up the stairs in tears and we awaken to the fact that in a few years (four? five? six? The exact number doesn't matter) our children will be gone. When they return home, they won't be the same. The grief we experience at that moment, repeated in each clash over the next few years, feels like someone has reached inside our chests and yanked out a fistful of heart. The confusion the kids feel, as they anticipate that leaving, makes them wonder if they have a heart.

But adolescence is also about gains—big gains. In giving up their old roles, our kids take on new ones, and we have front-row seats. At one time on stage ourselves, we find ourselves more and more in the audience watching as they leap, then lunge; as they don leotards, then armor. Sometimes we are so wrapped up in anticipating the next act that we forget to enjoy the one on stage; we focus too much on the not yet, ignoring the pleasures of the already.

Each act is not as dire as popular books or well-meaning relatives would have us think. The majority of adolescents do not turn into some unrecognizable Jekyll and Hyde monster. They just become more of who they are. If we liked them most of the time when they were three, four, and five, chances are we'll like them when they're thirteen, fourteen, and fifteen—most of the time.

Perhaps best of all, with guidance from us and other adults, as well as a measure of good luck in the companions they choose, our kids will one day become our friends, unlike any we will ever have. And in the process of helping them reach that point, we will have been stretched in ways we could never have anticipated and learned things about ourselves and the world we otherwise would never have known.

There are steps we can take, indeed must take, if we want to increase the odds that our sons and daughters will become the kind of adults we would like to share with the world. The families in this book, as well as scientists I have come to respect, have taught me most of these things. I have also learned a great deal from the experience my husband and I have had raising our son, Jeff, as well as from my stepdaughters, now grown, and from other members of my family and my friends. I am privileged to have a large circle: In writing, as in raising kids, it is easier to row with a boat full of sailors than with a lone oarsman.

Let Go, but Stay in Touch

The first thing to know when raising young adolescents is that we must relinquish the very idea of control. Events will yank it out of our hands anyway. This does not mean that we relinquish our influence over our children. It means that we replace control with communication. Our children must learn to take control of their own lives, and how well we communicate with them will help determine the success with which they are able to do that.

An admission here: I told myself when I started this project that I would never use the C word. Everyone uses it when talking about teenagers, and almost nobody explains what it means. Then I met Rebekah Sigel, Libby's mother. I watched her ask Libby questions when Libby got in trouble, not accusatory questions ("Why in the world did you do that?") but questions worded to make Libby think ("What does it mean to do that kind of thing with your friends?"). I also met Denice Stanton, who regularly traded questions with her son, Eric, while they were watching the evening news, reading the Bible together, or enjoying a dinner out. These parents and others taught me that communication starts by asking good questions and listening carefully to the answers before jumping in with our own thoughts. This can require a lot of willpower, but only then will we know what to pay attention to and what to do.

I also learned that communication means how (and whether) we communicate about our kids and on their behalf to our spouses, relatives, teachers, coaches, neighbors, the people we worship with and buy groceries from, our kids' friends and their parents—in other words, all the people who make up our children's world. The first definition of "communicate" in *Webster's New Collegiate Dictionary* is "to share." I like that way of putting it. As our kids enter adolescence we begin to share them with a wider audience. They forget to tell us, or don't want to tell us, lots of things, but if we're plugged into this larger community we learn many of those things anyway. The most successful parents I met were those who talked regularly with each other and everyone else about their children. They may have stood on the edges of their children's lives, but they knew what was at the center.

There is still more to communication. By the time our kids are nine or ten, they are sophisticated enough to match our actions against our words. Actions win out almost every time. We best communicate our values and morals, our likes and dislikes, through our behavior. How will our children learn skills that take years to acquire, such as maintaining friendships or working toward long-term goals, if not by watching us?

As I observed and listened to each child in this book, I considered three primary questions: Was the child learning how to treat others with respect? Was he or she given meaningful responsibilities? Did he or she enjoy helpful, trusting relationships with adults?

As the stories show, communicating these three ideas successfully is a two-way street. If we want our teenagers to treat us with respect, we have to demonstrate respect for them in the smallest gestures. If we want them to shoulder more responsibility, we must act responsibly. If we want them to enjoy healthy relationships with people of all ages, we have to resist the temptation to focus solely on our immediate families. We must reach out to other adults and other kids.

Treat Them with Respect

One major way we show respect is by viewing our children's behavior through a positive lens whenever possible, focusing on healthy aspects of their personality. This can be difficult to do in a society that would rather slam-dunk teenagers than high-five them.

Many of the things they do that drive us crazy—arguing, tying up the phone or the computer, standing in front of a mirror for what seems like hours—are things they are supposed to do, from a developmental point of view. Once we understand that, we can agree on some limits while enjoying the marvelous ways in which their bodies and minds are growing. We can explore the process of growing up with them rather than looking constantly for results. When they come home from school, we can inquire first about the most interesting thing they learned that day instead of immediately asking what grade they got on their math test.

When they bring up the things that matter most—a soured relationship, a battle with someone over something they believe—we can let them know we think that they are capable of handling the situation. If we ask them to try to figure things out for themselves, assuring them that we are there if they cannot, they will.

Give Them Responsibility

Successful parents help their kids find jobs at home or outside the home that challenge them to think and act like adults. Performing adult tasks and being recognized for a job well done feels like a million dollars. When Mario Rawlings hung drywall with his father, Jay, he no longer thought of himself as a lawbreaker. He was a mason. And when Jay called Mario "my right-hand man," Mario, near the bottom of the heap at school, felt on top of his world.

At home, we need to ask ourselves not only whether our kids can wash the dishes but what other, more significant responsibilities they can assume. Build a bookcase? Shop for groceries? Balance a checkbook? One reason so many kids this age become whizzes at the computer is that they know their parents are not. They love being the in-house expert.

When making big decisions that affect the family we must draw our kids into the process, as Denice Stanton did when she was trying to decide whether to quit her second job and instead turned the job over to her son. Sometimes we'll be met with "I don't care what you do," though they'll be flattered that we asked. But at other times, they will enjoy adding their two cents' worth.

Parents are often reluctant to allow kids to take outside jobs, either volunteer or for pay, for fear that their studies will suffer. That's probably true for young people whose day planners resemble a CEO's. But as we help our children choose their activities, we need to keep in mind that collaborating on a job with a responsible adult may do more for a kid's self-esteem, study habits, and manners than playing a mediocre game of soccer. Jobs give kids lots of practice at making decisions in structured environments.

Volunteer work is better for most kids this age than a paying job and often appeals to their newfound idealism. Working no more than six to eight hours a week for money, however, is not a bad option for some kids if it is tied to learning about saving money, donating money, or paying their own way at the movies.

Share Them with Other Adults

By early adolescence, our children need the regular company of adults other than us. Other men and women see traits in our kids that we see only dimly. They and our kids can talk unencumbered by the worn baggage that accompanies most family discussions. Significantly, our kids believe them.

When my son, Jeff, was eleven, a Babe Ruth baseball coach took him aside and told him that he had the arm of a pitcher. My husband had been catching balls for him in our backyard for years, but Jeff had always been reluctant to step up to the mound in a real game.

After those few words from Paul Ahrens, an amazing metamorphosis took place. Jeff began thinking of himself as a pitcher. He started pitching for Paul and has never stopped pitching. It is his favorite position in his favorite sport.

Encouraging other adults to assume roles in our adolescents' lives is good for us, too. Like the nanny who joins a household to take care of a baby, these adults offer us respite as well as a sounding board.

Plug Them In

Some kids this age will adopt adult friends on their own, but most need help. There are numerous places to search: youth organizations, sports teams, houses of worship, our own neighborhoods. This is one area in which parents must exercise their influence: They need to insist that their child be consistently involved in at least one outside activity. Psychologists and educators now consider such pursuits so important that they no longer call them extracurricular activities. They use the word "cocurricular."

In general, parents should let kids choose how they want to spend their time, but sometimes they have to weigh in. When Jeff started high school, he wanted to drop orchestra after playing string bass for three years. He said he wanted to take up chorus instead because he had heard it was more fun. Carl and I told him he should give the new orchestra a try for one year, and if he wanted to switch in his sophomore year, he could. After proclaiming repeatedly that it should be his decision, he agreed. Less than a month into ninth grade, he was so satisfied with the quality and camaraderie of the orchestra that he started plotting his schedule to figure out how he could stick with orchestra over the next three years.

The activities that the kids of my book enjoyed the most were those in which they helped make key decisions and in which they could take leadership roles. Several found such opportunities in their church. Angela Perales sang parts of the liturgy regularly at Mass. Eric Stanton read the Bible from the lectern of his Baptist church. Jessica Johnston helped organize and carry out mission visits to low-income neighborhoods. These children seemed to enjoy church more than others who simply sat in the pews during worship.

Introduce Them to the Spiritual

Few kids this age are enthusiastic about formal religious instruction unless they are blessed with a particularly talented instructor. But it is important that they be exposed to the idea of a spiritual life, as a possible resource for the future. They are also well served by learning the principles of the Jewish, Christian, and Muslim faiths so they can better understand American history, world history, and current events. And in some congregations, they may be lucky enough to find a youth group in which they are encouraged to ask questions that they are just beginning to articulate about morality and the meaning of their lives.

I witnessed an example of this in Ulysses, in a warehouse being used temporarily by a new evangelical Christian church called Faith Fellowship. A half dozen young people had gathered there on a Sunday evening. "Who influences you the most?" asked the youth director, a trim, dark-haired man who didn't look much older than his charges. "Who helps you decide where you take a stand . . . what you believe . . . how you see yourself . . . ?" Behind him, a giant posterboard proclaimed in orange and pink a line from the first chapter of Timothy in the New Testament: "Don't Let Anyone Look Down On You Because You Are Young." In smaller letters it continued: "But set an example for the believers, in speech, in life, in love and in purity."

These words are good advice for adults as well as young people. Those youth most active in religious and other organizations had parents who were also involved, sometimes in the same organization as their kids (almost always a good idea), sometimes in others.

Don't Stop Playing with Them

Playfulness is as important to our relationship with our adolescents as it was when they were younger. It may even be more important, since our time with them otherwise is frequently spent reminding them to study for their French test or complaining that they tie up the computer.

But play is no longer as simple as building a block tower and may require more negotiation. Adolescents' tastes change and so does their willingness to be seen doing anything with their parents. We have to be creative. Going to a movie on a weekday rather than a weekend or taking

a quick trip out of town to a chess tournament or a ball game are possibilities. Even painting the house together can be fun if the young painter
is allowed some freedom on how he does the job.

Some fun times should be just one-on-one. Denice and Eldon Stanton told Eric that no matter how much it hurt him that they lived apart,
when he was with either of them he benefited from that person's full
attention. They were amazed by what they could find out when they
were relaxing alone with him.

Sip from Their Cup

On their adventures with Eric, Denice and Eldon paid attention to the
things he wanted to talk about and do. We need to take an interest in the
popular culture of our kids, no matter how foolish or even disturbing
some parts of it may appear to us. How can we expect to understand what
our kids are talking about if we limit ourselves to the perspectives of
adults?

Some parents are lucky enough to have kids who carry the world right
through the door, while other parents must do a little sleuthing. We can
consult other teenagers we know. We can listen to the music our kids enjoy
(at least occasionally). We can watch one or two of their favorite TV shows
with them on a regular basis. Participating every now and then in their
activities or interests—not too often, since we don't want to steal their
lives—gives us something to talk about when we're taking them to the
dentist. If we dismiss the things in their lives that seem small to us, they will
be slow to talk to us about the big things—schoolwork, curfews, friends.

We may even get hooked. I'm now a big fan of "The X-Files." I read
Michael Crichton and listen to Big Bad Voodoo Daddy. My son's
technicolor/Dolby stereo world has brightened up my black-and-white
existence considerably.

Accept Them

When a wobbly fourteen-month-old takes a tumble, we don't say, "Boy
what a klutz. She'll never learn to walk." We say, "Oops! Try again."
That's exactly the attitude we need to adopt with our young teens. We
must not be fooled by their often sophisticated appearance; they will

make mistakes, sometimes the same mistake several times. They are growing more erratically than they will at any other stage in their lives. Some don't evolve into the consistent maturity we associate with adulthood until their late twenties, and a few never do. As Chip's mother said, "The story isn't over yet." But if we continue to accept them as wonderful works in progress, they will have a better shot at becoming the kind of people we want them to be.

Of course, there is one big difference between the mistakes of a fourteen-month-old and those of a fourteen-year-old: The actions of the latter can have severe consequences for the child himself and for others. I believe kids know this. What they sometimes don't know is what, in our minds, are the big blunders. We've all heard the admonition "Pick your battles." Kids need to know in advance, as much as possible, what those battles will be. I'll indulge Jeff in having a messy room most of the time. But I will be deeply disappointed if he lies to me. And he knows that if he does, some of his most precious privileges will be taken away.

Own Up to Your Mistakes

If we expect our kids to take responsibility for their mistakes, we must be willing to admit ours. Parents who are always blaming other people raise kids who do the same, and everybody is unhappy. Parents who have come to terms with their mistakes, even things they did years ago, are more likely to raise kids who are also at peace with themselves. Young adolescents can handle almost any truth if we let them know we think they can.

These lessons were brought home to me most vividly by Marcy and Tim Hoover, a farm family I met in Ulysses. One afternoon several months after I visited them, Marcy received an unexpected phone call. "This is your daughter Andrea," said the caller, whom Marcy had given up for adoption nineteen years earlier—when she was nineteen and in love with a young man she was dating.

Marcy and Tim agreed to allow Andrea to meet the family. But first they would have to tell their four children, two of them adolescents, about the daughter Marcy had given up. Marcy was most worried about the way her teenage son would respond.

"But, Mom, these aren't the values you've been raising us with!" he said.

"I know that, and I also know we make mistakes," Marcy told him. "As you can see, mistakes sometimes have big consequences."

Marcy, who worked at the local high school, and Tim, who raised milo and wheat, were two of the most calmly self-assured parents I have ever met. They had not had easy lives growing up. Both had had alcoholic parents. Neither had particularly wanted to farm but, in their words, "kind of fell into it." The type of farming they pursued, dryland as opposed to irrigated, was a humble and unsettled existence in what used to be called the Dust Bowl. They were always praying for rain. But they accepted the decisions they had made and found many things to enjoy in their rural community, including their kids, who, not surprisingly, were pretty content themselves.

Turn Your Face to the Sun

The farmer and those who depend on the farmer's harvest are "next-year people," Marcy's father, John Summers, told me one weekday afternoon. "It takes a big dose of faith, deep, spiritual faith, to depend upon the elements." His granddaughter Meredith, Marcy's daughter, walked to his house from Kepley Middle School that day as she did most afternoons. As she listened to us talk, I thought how lucky she was to be growing up around two generations of men and women who believed that no matter what the financial or family circumstances of the moment, tomorrow would be better.

Kids are naturally optimistic. Their world, however, is full of cynics: Even parents can be as negative as Homer Simpson as we get older. We start our conversations with "What's wrong with . . ." and "What's missing from . . ." Our kids are not the only ones who scowl.

Kids can withstand the assaults of a cynical culture if we hold on to our hope about the course of our lives and theirs. If we cannot, we shouldn't be surprised when they bring home a C or a D in English and say, "That teacher's so lame. I'll never make a better grade."

Give Them Constancy

The disruptions in kids' lives these days are numerous and constant, more so than ever before. As I researched this book, I would regularly hang up the telephone and say to my husband, "You're not going to believe what happened to . . ." And this was with families chosen initially for their ordinariness.

The universe can shift virtually overnight for all kinds of reasons. Parents may separate, divorce, or remarry (such family dissension frequently occurs when at least one child is in early adolescence). Mom or Dad or both may change jobs or take on second jobs. Several kids in this book spent no more than one year in any given school during grades five through nine.

These changes occur just at the time of the most noticeable change of all, their bodies. Thus, routines and rituals can be important, and we need to give our kids as many as we possibly can: breakfast or dinner together, phone calls at the same time every day or every week, holidays celebrated in the same manner, vacations to the same beach. And we certainly shouldn't add to the chaos, as more than one parent in this book did, by promising to do something with them and then not doing it.

Manage Your Fears

We can teach our children inner security if we do not let fear limit our world or theirs.

Many of us remember a time when communities were safer, when neighbors kept an eye on kids even when they weren't asked to do so. We remember a time when a mom could let a kid out the back door after school and say only, "Be home in time for dinner." We remember a time when we didn't see every shooting, every riot, every robbery in our living room every evening.

That was the world for the fortunate among us. But this is our kids' world, the only one they know. As therapist Jim Hancock writes in *Raising Adults:* "Trying to protect kids from exposure to the world they live in is like trying to put a wetsuit on a porpoise. It's too late; they live in the water. What we can do is create the kind of consequential environments that will help kids keep swimming and breathing."[1]

Despite our hesitations—sometimes well founded, sometimes not— we must encourage kids to make their own way, to explore block by block each leafy curb and concrete alley, to be able to put names to each of their neighbors. Too many kids I talked to did not have intimate knowledge of the places in which they were growing up or see that they had a stake in where they lived. If they didn't feel a connection to their local geography, could they find one in the larger universe they would soon inherit?

Some of the parents I met tended to keep their kids too close for too long and continually talked about how dangerous the world was. This is unfortunate. How kids perceive the world and their ability to live in it is more important to their ultimate health and happiness than how safe or dangerous the streets really are. As Eldon Stanton demonstrated and Janice Seton didn't, kids are not meant to live in caves. Parents must launch them toward the mountaintop even as they warn them away from the cliffs.

Of course, kids vary in their maturity, and parents must set limits on this exploration accordingly. What was permissible when we were their age may not be today. When our kids cannot understand our cautiousness, we must explain it to them as matter-of-factly as we can, emphasizing what they are already capable of doing.

Sometimes we should consider allowing them to exceed the limits, giving them slightly more responsibility than the experts might suggest they are ready for. Eric Stanton did more than most kids his age when he sold his mother's wares by himself at the age of twelve on Venice Beach; Libby was braver than many thirteen-year-olds when she took her younger brother to India.

Occasionally, some kids are going to make an intentional break for the cliff, and they should be disciplined accordingly. But we need to remember that they are not testing us as much as they are testing themselves. Recalling some of the tests we set for ourselves when we were their age will help us keep their behavior in perspective.

Other kids want to huddle in the cave forever. These reticents can learn to be more adventurous by watching us try a new activity that involves risk. Kids who do not learn to go boldly into the world take the biggest risk of all, that of turning into fearful, nervous adults who are less safe than their plucky peers.

Nurture Friendships

Good friends help kids know when to plunge ahead and when to hold back. Before I started this book I did not appreciate how critical friends are to the well-being of young teenagers, how important it is that kids feel they are what psychiatrist David Hamburg calls members of a valued group. The saddest, most troubled kids I met were those who felt isolated from or, worse, rejected by the kids in their most significant social universe, the school. I also did not understand what allies good friends can be to a parent.

Good friends bring out in kids the values we are trying to instill, such as generosity and empathy. One way we can tell whether someone is a good friend to our child is what kind of person our kid is when the two are together.

Years before a child enters adolescence, the observant parent or teacher can predict how easy or difficult it will be for him to make friends during the teen years. Introversion and extroversion tend to be genetic traits. The techniques we use to encourage a child's social skills before middle school or junior high will vary according to who our child is. But our goal is the same: helping the child learn such skills early with children both he, and we, like.

This may mean asking that he be placed in a class with or without a specific child. It may mean enrolling him in a particular school or in activities in which he is likely to make friends whose characters we admire. It always means opening our home to his friends and talking to them as much as he will allow. It always means encouraging him to explain to us his perspective about things and insist that he listen to ours—conversational skills he can use with his friends. And it also always means paying attention to problems he has with classmates—not overreacting but also not just assuming that kids will be kids, and that they will work it out. Kids can have a day or two to think about a given problem and try to solve it themselves. But if they can't and it's still bothering them, it's time to intervene. They need opportunities and guidance.

It can be difficult to know much about our kids' companions or the parents of those companions as our children move into schools that are out of our neighborhood. And kids' inclination at this age to switch from group to group doesn't make the task any easier.

The best way to stay on top of their new acquaintances is to volunteer some time each week in their school. Teachers, guidance counselors, even other parent volunteers love to talk, and gossip at this age is protective. Also, in every group of kids, one parent usually knows what's going on. This parent probably has a chatty kid or a house where kids congregate. She or he is someone worth knowing.

Encourage Learning by Doing

Afraid of this social side of young adolescents, too many educators try to corral "raging hormones" in middle school by enforcing dozens of rules and sticking to a "sage on the stage" teaching style that ignores the way kids this age learn best. Judging by the glazed eyes and doodling that I saw in many classrooms, we are losing more kids to worksheets than to weapons.

We have an "if it was good enough for me . . ." attitude about instruction at this age that is baffling and destructive. Often it was good enough for us because few of us knew any better. We don't have that excuse anymore. Study after study has shown that preteens and young teens retain more information when they've used most of their senses learning it. The best teachers and principals understand this and deserve our encouragement at every opportunity.

The only things keeping some kids interested in school, besides the opportunity to see friends, are their elective classes. Art, music, and diversified technology (what we knew as home economics and shop) allow kids the opportunities for creativity and movement that their core courses do not. We must pay attention not only to the quality of math and English instruction but also to these electives. And we must resist efforts under way in some school systems to eliminate them or to offer them only after school.

Stay Engaged

In order to determine the quality of the education our kids are receiving, we first must learn the names of their teachers and their subjects. It amazed me how many parents didn't know these facts. What do we convey to our children about our interest in their learning if we don't take the time to memorize, at most, six or seven names? Eldon Stanton had trouble remembering which of Eric's teachers taught which subject, so he typed the information into his computer and reviewed it regularly.

We can gradually relinquish other jobs related to school that we used to do: going over homework or running to the teacher at the first hint of a problem without first encouraging our kid to try to solve it himself. These are critical years for impressing upon kids that education is their responsibility. And for honing their thinking skills in ways that many teachers no longer find the time to do, by asking questions such as "How do you know that?" or "What if you did that problem this way?"

Count Them In

Our society increasingly sees teenagers as problems, not resources, and it is hard not to get caught up in the faultfinding. We make casual, negative quips such as "So-and-so is acting just like an adolescent." When a group of teenagers, particularly teenage boys, approach us, we cross the street, avoiding eye contact. When teenagers are in a room with us, we talk over them as if they were senile old relatives dozing off in the corner.

We throw kids out of school for stupid infractions and send them in record numbers to adult prison, where they are housed in abusive conditions. Our fear of kids has trumped our good sense; "zero tolerance" has taken the place of justice. What's the difference between zero tolerance and intolerance? None, as far as kids are concerned.

In a 1997 national survey by Public Agenda, a nonprofit policy organization, almost three out of five Americans said today's kids will either make the world a worse place when they grow up or make no difference at all. I know that adults have ragged on the young from the days of Aristotle and probably before. But the broad cynicism expressed in that poll is frightening.

I am particularly concerned about the preteens and younger teens caught up in this wave of negativism. As we have seen, young adolescents are sponges, able to comprehend fully for the first time what people think of them. It is not until later in adolescence that they are able to separate what kind of person they believe themselves to be from what others say they are. Our expressions have the potential to provoke the very kind of behavior we expect; in fact, some might say they already have.

If Americans continue to think of kids as problems they will be less likely, not more likely, to invest money in the resources that kids and their families need. This is particularly true in communities with growing numbers of ethnic or racial minorities.

Consider what is happening in Ulysses. Ulysses is, in many ways, a great place to raise kids. And it may have had very sound reasons for each individual action it took that affected its teenagers: closing the teen center, failing to fund a new recreation center, turning down kids' requests to hold dances at the senior citizen center, redesigning parks so kids could no longer use skateboards and Rollerblades, restricting what kids wore to school and, increasingly, their freedom of movement at school and on the streets. But taken together, these events, all of which occurred within two years, delivered a major blow. As Angela Perales interpreted it: "They just don't want us around anymore." What is needed in Ulysses, as elsewhere, are parents and youths who understand the impact of such actions on kids and are willing to speak up in the media, at council meetings, and at school-board sessions.

I believe that many parents would like to change their negative attitudes about teenagers but are not sure how to start. When my son was in middle school, the PTA sent out to hundreds of parents a questionnaire asking which subjects they would like to see addressed at evening seminars. Ten possibilities were listed, including drugs, violence, sex, gender issues, and one called "The Positive Traits of Young Adolescents."

More than one wag returned the form with that topic circled and a query scribbled next to it: "You mean there are some?" But the subject drew more requests by far than any other.

Relax a Little

People frequently ask me whether writing this book has changed my relationship with my own young adolescent. To get the real answer to that I suggest that they ask Jeff. But I believe it has.

I am more relaxed around him than I used to be. When he behaves in a way that bothers me, I recognize it as normal behavior (usually) and don't take it personally (usually). The advice I read somewhere when he was a toddler still applies: Think of the behavior as the stage acting out, not the kid. Sometimes, as I listen to him argue with me or his dad in a particularly persuasive manner, I even cheer him on silently as he exercises his mind.

Because I'm more at ease I'm able to pick up on the funny, insightful, and just plain interesting things he says and does every day. We laugh a lot, sometimes tussle with each other (kids this age are very physical), and poke fun at each other and at my husband, Carl, in a good-natured way. But I use humor carefully, and I try never to make fun of him or criticize him in front of other people. I have seen too many kids cringe when a parent did that.

When he's feeling blue for no reason he can think of, I am able to reassure him that that's normal for his age. Of course I am relieved when he bounces back in a few hours or by the following day because I also know that if he didn't, his depression might point to something more serious.

I try not to be as protective as I once was, but I sometimes fail. One weekend morning he asked if he could bike alone about a mile through our wooded, middle-class neighborhood to meet some friends at his middle school. I said yes, but only if he called me once he got there. He agreed, but gave me a funny look, as well he should have. He was thirteen. Since then, as he has proved himself capable in several unusual situations, I've loosened my grip. His increasing maturity, like the maturation I witnessed among most of the kids in this book, is reassuring.

He does not talk a lot with me or with his dad about what is going on in his life, but I learn tidbits from others to whom he does talk. And I never doubt that I am important to him. Granted, he no longer comes running to the door, dragging his favorite teddy bear, when I return from a trip. But the phone calls at work and our late-night conversations let me know where I stand. I also know because of the kids I interviewed. Dozens of times they brought up the subject of parents when we weren't talking about parents at all.

When I began this book, I wanted to minimize the significance of parents and emphasize the importance of other adults. The kids themselves kept leading me back to their families. I listened to a boy virtually abandoned by his mother make excuses for two years about why she couldn't see him. I listened to a girl rant about her mother for more than an hour and then watched her run to her mom for a big hug as soon as we returned home. I watched a proud boy cry at something his father said about him, then sit at his dad's feet to have his head rubbed. We must remember this: Despite appearances to the contrary, our adolescents' love for us is bone-deep.

So is their need for us to return that love. I have become better at using my time so that I am there for Jeff when he requires it *and* when I do. The most successful parents I met during my research made tangible sacrifices for their kids; the most involved parents had the most fun. These parents taught me that closeness is earned.

Pay Attention to, and Enjoy, the Details

Being home, in and of itself, or driving Jeff to every sports event, every movie, and every party, will not necessarily connect us. In order to connect with him I must pay attention to the small details of his life as well as to the large dramas. This requires focused attention more than time. I have to know enough about his schoolwork, for example, to be able to call him from work and ask how his biology project on duckweed is progressing and whether his partner found the obscure journal article he was searching for. As one friend says, "We can demonstrate in a thousand ways that we're right there."

Someday, of course, I will not be "right there." I catch hints from time to time that if I were hit by a meteor tomorrow, he would still grow into a competent and caring man. That's one of the best feelings a parent can have.

The balance of power between us is shifting. I seek his advice more frequently. I am sometimes consoled by him and often inspired by him. The early adolescent years are not only our last best shot at guiding our children, they're our last best shot at being guided by our children before we lose them to the world. Because of Jeff I am stronger, wiser, and braver than I would otherwise be.

The best example I can think of occurred two summers ago in a boat on the North Carolina sound. Our family has vacationed on the northern Outer Banks for ten years. For six of those years, Jeff and Carl have gone parasailing.

Parasailing, for the uninitiated, means sitting in a cloth swing with a huge, colorful parachute attached to your back. You perch on the back of a motorized boat, hooked to a cable that is attached to the boat. The boat shoots forward in the water, gradually increasing in speed, and you rise steadily into the air behind the boat, borne aloft by the parachute. You can soar as high as fourteen hundred feet above the water.

The first two years Carl and Jeff took flight I was so terrified of this sport that I stayed behind on the shore, sure that I was going to lose my husband and child to the Currituck Sound. The next couple of years I accompanied them on the boat. Jeff started pressuring me to go up myself. You'd enjoy it, he told me.

No way, I said the first, second, and third time he brought it up. But in the summer of 1998, I changed my mind. Maybe it was a coincidence, but I was in the middle of writing the chapter on Jack Richardson, whose forty-year-old mother had decided to learn to rope steers on horseback along with thirteen-year-old Jack.

As our captain steered us out into the sound and I watched Jeff volunteer to go first, I remembered a quote from the writer Annie Dillard: "You can't test courage cautiously." And so on that sunny July afternoon I allowed a blond, bronzed, twenty-something first mate to hook me up to a parachute that resembled a small house. Off I went, and as I rose to one hundred feet, then five hundred feet, and finally one thousand feet I could see my speck of a son snapping photographs.

I once had asked a teenage girl who parasails what she does if she gets scared. "I sing," she told me. So I sang loudly the first song that came to mind, "Amazing Grace."

Less than ten minutes later I was pulled back in and Jeff was waiting for me in the stern. He gave me a thumbs-up.

My friends and relatives find it hard to believe this story. But Jeff still has the pictures.

NOTES

Part One

Introduction
1. Peter C. Scales, *Boxed In and Bored* (Chapel Hill, NC: The University of North Carolina, Center for Early Adolescence, 1996), 20.

Chapter One (Eric's Story)
1. Frank F. Furstenberg, Jr., et al., *Managing to Make It: Urban Families and Adolescent Success* (Chicago: The University of Chicago Press, 1999), 219.
2. Bruce E. Compas et al., "Adolescent Development: Pathways and Processes of Risk and Resilience," *Annual Review* (1995): 270.
3. Daniel Keating, "Adolescent Thinking," in S. Shirley Feldman and Glen Elliott, eds., *At The Threshold: The Developing Adolescent* (Cambridge: Harvard University Press, 1990), 64.
4. Huda Akil, co-director, Mental Health and Research Institute, University of Michigan, interview with author, 1997.
5. Jacquelynne Eccles, professor of psychology, University of Michigan, interview with author, 1997.
6. Mihaly Csikszentmihalyi et al., *Talented Teenagers: The Roots of Success and Failure* (Cambridge: Cambridge University Press, 1994), 14.
7. Ibid., 149.

8. Carnegie Corporation of New York, *A Matter of Time: Risk and Opportunity in the Nonschool Hours* (Woodlawn, MD.: Wolk Press, Inc., 1992), 32; Furstenberg et al., *Managing to Make It*, 71.
9. Furstenberg et al., *Managing to Make It*, 46.
10. "Boys with Absentee Dads Twice as Likely to Be Jailed," *The Washington Post*, Aug. 21, 1998.
11. William Damon, *Greater Expectations: Overcoming the Culture of Indulgence in America's Homes and Schools* (New York: The Free Press, 1995), 235.
12. Furstenberg et al., *Managing to Make It*, 71.

Chapter Two (Chandler's Story)
1. Wade F. Horn and Carol Keough, *New Teen Book* (Des Moines: Meredith Press, 1999), 10.
2. Inge Seiffge-Krenke, *Stress, Coping, and Relationships in Adolescence* (Mahwah, NJ: Lawrence Erlbaum, 1995), 148–49.
3. Horn and Keough, *New Teen Book*, 55.
4. North Carolina Governor's Commission on Juvenile Crime and Justice, 1997 report.
5. Edward L. Deci and Richard M. Ryan, *Intrinsic Motivation and Self-Determination in Human Behavior* (New York: Plenum Press, 1985), 159.
6. Laurence Steinberg with Wendy Steinberg, *Crossing Paths: How Your Child's Adolescence Can Be an Opportunity for Your Own Personal Growth* (New York: Simon & Schuster, 1994), 254.
7. Ibid., 142.
8. Michael Resnick et al., "Protecting Adolescents from Harm: Findings from the National Longitudinal Study on Adolescent Health," *Journal of the American Medical Association* (Sept. 10, 1997): 831.
9. Chris Hayward, associate professor of psychiatry, Stanford University, at workshop entitled "New Research on the Biology of Puberty and Adolescent Development," sponsored by the Forum on Adolescence, National Research Council, March 1998.
10. "News and Trends," *The Youth Connection*, Institute for Youth Development, (Sept. 1998): 8.
11. Laurence Steinberg, "Autonomy, Conflict, and Harmony in the Family Relationship," in Feldman and Elliott, eds., *At the Threshold*, 266.
12. Kenneth G. Rice et al., "Coping with Challenge in Adolescence: A Conceptual Model and Psycho-Educational Intervention," *Journal of Adolescence* 16 (1993): 241; Compas, "Adolescent Development," 284.
13. Winifred Gallagher, *The Power of Place* (New York: Poseidon Press, 1993), 137–38.
14. Lynn Ponton, *The Romance of Risk: Why Teenagers Do the Things They Do* (New York: Basic Books, 1997), 6–7.

15. Peter C. Scales, *A Portrait of Young Adolescents in the 1990s* (Chapel Hill: The University of North Carolina, Center for Early Adolescence, 1991), 11.

16. Stanton E. Samenow, *Before It's Too Late: Why Some Kids Get into Trouble and What Parents Can Do About It* (New York: Times Books, 1989), 46; "Inside the Teen Brain," *U.S. News & World Report*, Aug. 9, 1999.

17. Scales, *Boxed In*, p. 23; Marilyn Jacobs Quadrel et al., "Adolescent Invulnerability," *American Psychologist* (Feb. 1993): 111.

18. Stuart T. Hauser and Mary Kay Bowlds, "Stress, Coping and Adaptation," in Feldman and Elliott, eds., *At the Threshold*, 395–96.

19. Adrian Angold, psychiatrist, Duke University Medical Center, interview with author, 1997.

20. Furstenberg et al., *Managing to Make It*, 81.

21. Peter C. Scales and Nancy Leffert, *Developmental Assets: A Synthesis of the Scientific Research on Adolescent Development* (Minneapolis: Search Institute, 1999), 31.

22. Scales and Leffert, *Developmental Assets*, 132.

23. Robert Wm. Blum and Peggy Mann Rinehart, *Reducing the Risk: Connections That Make a Difference in the Lives of Youth* (Analysis of data from the National Longitudinal Study on Adolescent Health) (Minneapolis: University of Minnesota, 1997), 21–24.

24. Scales and Leffert, *Developmental Assets*, 32–33.

25. Horn and Keough, *New Teen Book*, 68.

Chapter Three (Shannon's Story)

1. Scales, *Portrait*, 12–13.

2. Daniel Offer et al., *Patterns of Adolescent Self-Image* (San Francisco: Jossey-Bass, Inc., 1984), 5.

3. Forum on Adolescence workshop on puberty, March 1998.

4. Richard Lansdown and Marjorie Walker, *Your Child's Development from Birth Through Adolescence* (New York: Alfred A. Knopf, 1991), 341.

5. Winifred Gallagher, *I.D.: How Heredity and Experience Make You Who You Are* (New York: Random House, 1996), 137.

6. The Search Institute, *Developmental Assets: A Profile of Your Youth*, June 1997.

7. Robert Wm. Blum and Peggy Mann Rinehart, *Reducing the Risk*, 20.

8. Bonnie Barber, psychologist, speaking at the Society for Research in Child Development meeting, April 1997.

9. William S. Rholes et al., "A Developmental Study of Learned Helplessness," *Developmental Psychology* 16, 6 (1980): 616–24.

10. Elena O. Nightingale, adjunct professor of pediatrics, Georgetown University Medical School, and co-editor, *Promoting the Health of Adolescents* (New York: Oxford University Press, 1993), interview with author, 1999.

11. Ibid.
12. Rosenberg self-esteem scale, found in Morris Rosenberg, *Society and the Adolescent Self-Image* (Princeton: Princeton University Press, 1965).

Part Two

Introduction

1. Mihaly Csikszentmihalyi et al., "The Ecology of Adolescent Activity and Experience," *Journal of Youth and Adolescence* (1977): 281–94, as reported in Seiffge-Krenke, *Stress*, 227; Ritch C. Savin-Williams and Thomas J. Berndt, "Friendship and Peer Relations," in Feldman and Elliott, eds., *At the Threshold*, 278.

Chapter Four (Libby's Story)

1. Peter Bearman et al., *Peer Potential: Making the Most of How Teens Influence Each Other*, a report from the National Campaign to Prevent Teen Pregnancy, 1999, 23.
2. Laurence Steinberg, *Beyond the Classroom: Why School Reform Has Failed and What Parents Need to Do* (New York: Simon & Schuster, 1996), 147–48.
3. Bearman et al., *Peer Potential*, 15.
4. *U.S. News & World Report*, Aug. 9, 1999.
5. Bearman et al., *Peer Potential*, 43.
6. Laurence Steinberg, *You & Your Adolescent: A Parent's Guide for Ages 10–20* (New York: Harper & Row, 1990), 182; B. Bradford Brown, "Peer Groups and Peer Cultures," in Feldman and Elliott, eds., *At the Threshold*, 191.
7. Brown, in Feldman and Elliott, eds., *At the Threshold*, 192.
8. Horn and Keough, *New Teen Book*, 46.
9. Steinberg, *Beyond the Classroom*, 17.
10. Michelle Englund et al., "Development of Adolescent Social Competence," presented at the Society for Research in Child Development meeting, April 1997.
11. Bearman et al., *Peer Potential*, 16.

Chapter Five (Chip's Story)

1. M. L. Clark and Monnie L. Bittle, "Friendship Expectations and the Evaluation of Present Friendships in Middle Childhood and Early Adolescence," *Child Study Journal* (1992): 117; Michael Gurian, *A Fine Young Man* (New York: Tarcher, 1998), 53.
2. Scales and Leffert, *Developmental Assets*, 63; Horn and Keough, *New Teen Book*, 147.

3. Bearman et al., *Peer Potential*, 35.
4. Stanley I. Greenspan, *Playground Politics* (New York: Perseus Press, 1994), 94–96.
5. "Adoption: Numbers and Trends," National Adoption Information Clearinghouse, March 1999.
6. *U.S. News & World Report*, Aug. 9, 1999.
7. Ibid.
8. "Snapshot of Durham Middle Schools," *The [Raleigh] News and Observer*, July 6, 1997.
9. "The Health of Adolescent Boys," a survey conducted by Louis Harris and Associates, Inc., for The Commonwealth Fund, June 1998, 5.
10. Horn and Keough, *New Teen Book*, 92.
11. Fact sheet from the Center for Substance Abuse Research, University of Maryland, June 29, 1998, and information supplied by the National Center on Addiction and Substance Abuse at Columbia University.
12. Gail Caissy, *Early Adolescence: Understanding the 10 to 15 Year Old* (New York: Plenum Press, 1994), 79–80.

Chapter Six (Angela's Story)
1. AARP Grandparent Information Center; U.S. Census Bureau.
2. Scales, *Portrait*, 16; Horn and Keough, *New Teen Book*, 39.
3. Feldman and Elliott, eds., *At the Threshold*, 297.
4. Ibid.
5. John Cotterell, *Social Networks and Social Influences in Adolescence* (New York: Routledge, 1996), 185.
6. Bearman et al., *Peer Potential*, 18–19.
7. M. Lee Van Horn et al., "Dating as a Social Activity: The Importance of Peers," and Melanie J. Zimmer-Gembeck, "The Emergence of Heterosexual Relationships in the Lives of Female Adolescents and Their Reorganization of Peer Relationships," papers presented at the Society for Research in Child Development conference, 1997; interview with Zimmer-Gembeck.
8. Sarah Brown, director, the National Campaign to Prevent Teen Pregnancy, interview with author, 1999.
9. Bearman et al., *Peer Potential*, 17.
10. Cotterell, *Social Networks*, 116.
11. Interview with Sarah Brown, director, the National Campaign to Prevent Teen Pregnancy, 1999.
12. Ponton, *The Romance of Risk*, 89.
13. Savin-Williams and Berndt, in Feldman and Elliott, eds., *At the Threshold*, 280; Bearman et al., *Peer Potential*, 30.
14. Cotterell, *Social Networks*, 60, 71.

Part Three

Chapter Seven (Rodney's Story)

1. Huda Akil, co-director, Mental Health and Research Institute, University of Michigan, interview with author, 1997; "*Great Transitions: Preparing Adolescents for a New Century,*" Concluding Report of the Carnegie Council on Adolescent Development, 1995, 29–30.
2. "This We Believe: Developmentally Responsive Middle Level Schools," position paper of the National Middle School Association, 1995, 15.
3. Gene I. Maeroff, "Altered Destinies," *Phi Delta Kappan* (Feb. 1998): 425–32.
4. Scales, *Boxed In*, 12.
5. "This We Believe," 15.
6. Furstenberg et al., *Managing to Make It*, 81.
7. Ronald Kotulak, *Inside the Brain: Revolutionary Discoveries of How the Brain Works* (Kansas City, MO: Andrews and McMeel, 1997), 183.
8. Furstenberg et al., *Managing to Make It*, 44.
9. Anne C. Lewis, "Yo! Pay Attention to Me!", *Phi Delta Kappan* (Nov. 1997): 179.
10. As cited in Dr. Steven Schinke, "Educational Enhancement Program: Final Research Report" (New York: Columbia University School of Social Work, August 1997).
11. Joseph S. Renzulli, "Developing the Gifts of All Students," *Phi Delta Kappan* (Oct. 1998): 105–11.

Chapter Eight (Jessica's Story)

1. Scales and Leffert, *Developmental Assets*, 150.
2. Thomas Lickona, *Raising Good Children from Birth Through the Teen Years* (New York: Bantam Books, 1994), 12.
3. Scales and Leffert, *Developmental Assets*, 150–53.
4. Michelle Foster, "Intergroup Relations in Culturally Diverse Classrooms and Communities," at Workshop on Research to Improve Intergroup Relations Among Youth, Forum on Adolescence, National Research Council, Nov. 1998.
5. Janet Schofield, "Improving Intergroup Relations Among Students," in J. A. Banks and C. A. McGee Banks, *Handbook of Research on Multicultural Education* (New York: Macmillan, 1995), 642.
6. "U.S. Struggles to Solve Its Math Problem," *The Washington Post*, Jan. 23, 1997.
7. James W. Stigler and James Hiebert, "Understanding and Improving Classroom Mathematics Instruction," *Phi Delta Kappan* (Sept. 1997): 14–21.
8. Alfie Kohn, "How Not to Teach Values: A Critical Look at Character Education," *Phi Delta Kappan* (Feb. 1997): 434.
9. Lickona, *Raising Good Children*, 154–55.

10. Edward L. Deci and Richard M. Ryan, "The Support of Autonomy and the Control of Behavior," *Journal of Personality and Social Psychology* 53 (1987): 1027.

Chapter Nine (Jack's Story)
1. Kotulak, *Inside the Brain*, 185.
2. For example, Michael Schulman, *The Passionate Mind: Bringing Up an Intelligent and Creative Child* (New York: The Free Press, 1991).
3. Kathleen Burge, "Prodigies," *Attache* (April 1998): 80–87.
4. Richard deCharms, "The Origins of Competence and Achievement Motivation in Personal Causation," *Achievement Motivation: Recent Trends in Theory and Research* (New York: Plenum Press, 1980), 22–33. See also Deci and Ryan, "The Support of Autonomy."
5. Nel Noddings, "Thinking About Standards," *Phi Delta Kappan* (Nov. 1997): 189.
6. Interview with author, April 1996.
7. Jacquelynne Eccles et al., "Grade-Related Changes in the School Environment: Effects on Achievement Motivation," *Advances in Motivation and Achievement* (Greenwich, CN: JAI Press, Inc., 1984), 283–331.
8. Michael Gurian, *A Fine Young Man* (New York: Jeremy P. Tarcher, 1998), 38–39.
9. *Great Transitions*, 105; Scales, *Boxed In*, 39.
10. Gregory Pettit, "After-School Experience and Social Adjustment in Early Adolescence," paper presented at meeting of the Society for Research in Child Development, April 1997.
11. John Taylor Gatto, "Why Schools Don't Teach," *Hope* (Sept./Oct. 1996): 18–24.
12. Robin L. Jarrett, "Successful Parenting in High-Risk Neighborhoods," in *The Future of Children: When School Is Out*, a report by the David and Lucile Packard Foundation, Fall 1999, 45–49.
13. Chris Stevenson, *Teaching Ten to Fourteen Year Olds* (New York: Addison-Wesley Longman, 1998), 113.
14. Ibid., 138.

Part Four

Introduction
1. Scales and Leffert, *Developmental Assets*, 38.
2. Ibid., 27; "Mentoring Makes a Difference: Findings from The Commonwealth Fund 1998 Survey of Adults Mentoring Young People," July 1998.

Chapter Ten (Michelle's Story)

1. Richard Weissbourd, *The Vulnerable Child: What Really Hurts America's Children and What We Can Do About It* (Reading, MA: Addison-Wesley, 1996), 230.
2. Marc Freedman, *The Kindness of Strangers: Adult Mentors, Urban Youth and the New Voluntarism* (San Francisco: Jossey-Bass, 1993), 101.
3. Robert Blum, "The Connections That Help Kids," *The Youth Connection* (Institute for Youth Development), July 1998, 2–3.
4. Furstenburg et al., *Managing to Make It*, 50, 199.
5. Mary Pipher, *Reviving Ophelia: Saving the Selves of Adolescent Girls* (New York: Ballantine, 1994), 63.
6. Scales and Leffert, *Developmental Assets*, 51.
7. Wade F. Horn, president, National Fatherhood Initiative, interview with author, 1998.
8. Freedman, *Kindness*, 66–67.

Chapter Eleven (Mario's Story)

1. Gurian, *A Fine Young Man*, 65.
2. "Early Warning/Timely Response: A Guide to Safe Schools," U.S. Department of Education, Aug. 1998, 8–9.
3. Delbert Elliott at Workshop on Safety and Security of Adolescents, Forum on Adolescence, National Research Council, Sept. 18, 1997.
4. Figures on increase from 1997 report by North Carolina Governor's Commission on Juvenile Crime and Justice.
5. Resnick et al., "Protecting Adolescents," 831.
6. Juvenile Court Statistics, 1986–1995, Office of Juvenile Justice and Delinquency Prevention.
7. Blum and Rinehart, *Reducing the Risk*, 21–22.
8. Maeroff, "Altered Destinies," 426.
9. Commonwealth mentoring study.
10. Gurian, *A Fine Young Man*, 179.

Chapter Twelve (Alana's Story)

1. Peter L. Benson, *All Kids Are Our Kids: What Communities Must Do to Raise Caring and Responsible Children and Adolescents* (San Francisco: Jossey-Bass, 1997), 231.
2. Thomas P. Gullotta et al., *Developing Social Competency in Adolescence* (Newbury Park, CA: Sage, 1990), 100.
3. These skills are described in Gullotta et al., eds., *Developing Social Competency*, 127.
4. E. P. Seligman as quoted in Nancy Leffert et al., *Starting Out Right: Developmental Assets for Children* (Minneapolis: Search Institute, 1997), 83.

Conclusion
1. Jim Hancock, *Raising Adults: Getting Kids Ready for the Real World* (Colorado Springs: Pinon Press, 1999), 86.

BIBLIOGRAPHY: GENERAL RESOURCES ON ADOLESCENCE

This is a sampling of some general resources related to adolescence that may be useful, including publications, websites, and listserv discussion groups listed in alphabetical order. It is by no means an exhaustive list. A caveat regarding the chatrooms, message boards, and listserves (where you can post questions related to teens and parenting and engage in discussions with other parents): Some lists have a lot of traffic and will fill up a mailbox quickly. Check out a list's archives before subscribing to see if it is what you are looking for.

Books and Magazines

Ames, Louise Bates, Frances L. Ilg, and Sidney M. Baker. *Your Ten- to Fourteen-Year-Old.* New York: Dell Publishing, 1989.

Dillard, Annie. *An American Childhood.* New York: Harper & Row, 1998.

Elkind, David. *Ties That Stress: The New Family Imbalance.* Cambridge, MA: Harvard University Press, 1995.

Fenwick, Elizabeth, and Tony Smith. *Adolescence: The Survival Guide for Parents and Teenagers.* New York: DK Publishing, Inc., 1996.

Freeman, Carol Goldberg. *Living with a Work in Progress: A Parents' Guide to Surviving Adolescence.* Columbus, OH: National Middle School Association, 1996.

Giannetti, Charlene C., and Margaret Sagarese. *The Roller-Coaster Years: Raising Your Child Through the Maddening Yet Magical Middle School Years.* New York: Broadway Books, 1997.

Greydanus, Donald E. *Caring for Your Adolescent: Ages 12 to 21: The Complete*

Authoritative Guide. The American Academy of Pediatrics, New York: Bantam Books, 1991.

Hamburg, David, M.D. *Today's Children: Creating a Future for a Generation in Crisis.* New York: Times Books, 1994.

Hersch, Patricia. *A Tribe Apart: A Journey Into the Heart of American Adolescence.* New York: Ballantine Publishing Group, 1999.

Holmes, George R. *Helping Teenagers into Adulthood: A Guide to the Next Generation.* Westport, CT: Praeger, 1995.

Kimball, Gayle. *The Teen Trip: The Complete Resource Guide.* Chico, CA: Equality Press, 1997.

Lickona, Thomas. *Raising Good Children from Birth Through the Teenage Years.* New York: Bantam Books, 1994.

Lipsitz, Joan. *Growing Up Forgotten: A Review of Research and Programs Concerning Early Adolescence.* New Brunswick, NJ: Transaction Books, 1980.

Mednick, Fred. *Rebel Without a Car: Surviving and Appreciating Your Child's Teen Years.* Minneapolis, MN: Fairview Press, 1996.

Myers, Bob. *Raising Responsible Teenagers.* London, Eng.: Jessica Kingsley Publishers, 1996.

Palladino, Grace. *Teenagers: An American History.* New York: Basic Books, 1997.

Phelan, Thomas W. *Surviving Your Adolescents: How to Manage and Let Go of Your 13–18 Year Olds, 2nd edition.* Glen Ellyn, IL: Child Management Inc., 1998.

Riera, Michael. *Uncommon Sense for Parents with Teenagers.* Berkeley, CA: Celestial Arts, 1995.

Rosenzweig, Susan. *Families with Young Adolescents: A Resource List, revised edition.* Chapel Hill: Center for Early Adolescence, University of North Carolina, 1987.

Schlegel, Alice, and Herbert Barry III. *Adolescence: An Anthropological Inquiry.* New York: The Free Press, 1991.

Steinberg, Laurence D., and Ann Levine. *You and Your Adolescent: A Parent's Guide for Ages 10 to 20, revised edition.* New York: HarperCollins Publishers, Inc., 1997.

Takanishi, Ruby, and David A. Hamburg, editors. *Preparing Adolescents for the Twenty-First Century.* Cambridge, Eng.: Cambridge University Press, 1997.

Weissbourd, Richard. *The Vulnerable Child: What Really Hurts America's Children and What We Can Do About It.* Reading, MA: Addison-Wesley Longman, Inc., 1997.

Youngs, Bettie B. *Safeguarding Your Teenager from the Dragons of Life: A Parent's Guide to the Adolescent Years.* Deerfield Beach, FL: Health Communications, Inc., 1993.

Websites and Listservs

Adolescence Directory On-Line (ADOL), http://education.indiana.edu/cas/adol/adol.html or 812-856-8113

An online directory that provides links to web resources and articles focusing on the social and emotional growth of adolescents.

Carnegie Corporation of New York, http://www.carnegie.org/ or 212-371-3200

From 1986 to 1995, the Carnegie Council on Adolescent Development issued many reports that focused attention on the problems and opportunities of adolescence. Its website lists all the publications and how to acquire them.

Connect for Kids: Guidance for Grown-ups, http://www.connectforkids.org/ or 202-638-5770

Sponsored by the Benton Foundation, this website includes articles, ideas for action, and resources.

ERIC (Educational Resources Information Center) Clearinghouse on Elementary and Early Childhood Education at the University of Illinois at Urbana-Champaign, http://ericeece.org/ or 800-583-4135

Provides information through the website and toll-free number on the development, education, and care of children from birth through early adolescence. Questions may be e-mailed to: askeric@ericir.syr.edu. An answer should arrive within two business days, which includes relevant abstracts or articles, bibliography citations, a listing of internet sites, and additional sources.

Family Education Network (FEN), http://familyeducation.com/

Geared for parents and educators, this website provides articles, advice, discussions, and activity suggestions. Website partners include the National PTA, National Education Association, and The American School Counselor Association.

National Parent Information Network, http://npin.org/ or 800-583-4135

Provides parenting-related materials.

The National Parenting Center, http://www.tnpc.com/

Parenting source providing advice, articles, and discussions.

PARENTING-L. An e-mail discussion group for parents on parenting-related issues and concerns. To subscribe, send an e-mail message to: listserv @postoffice.csu.uiuc.edu with : subscribe PARENTING-L {Firstname} {Lastname} in the body of the message. An archive of past messages is on the web at: http:// www.askeric.org/Virtual/Listserv__Archives/Parenting-L. html. PARENTING-L is run by the ERIC Clearinghouse on Elementary and Early Childhood Education (ERIC/EECE).

The Search Institute, http://www.search-institute.org or 800-888-7828

Provides research and resources on youth development and how the organizations that serve them can be more effective.

YouthInfo, http://youth.os.dhhs.gov/

Provides statistics on adolescents, links to reports and publications of interest. Developed by the U.S. Department of Health and Human Resources.

Part One: Knowing Who They Are

Chapters 1–3

Here is a sampling of resources. Please also refer to the other resource lists for additional sources on the issues discussed in this section.

Books

Bluestein, Jane. *Parents, Teens and Boundaries: How to Draw the Line.* Deerfield Beach, FL: Health Communications, Inc., 1993.

Committee on the Health and Safety Implications of Child and Youth Labor of the National Research Council and Institute of Medicine. *Protecting Youth at Work: Health, Safety, and Development of Working Children and Adolescents in the United States.* Washington, DC: National Academy Press, 1998. (On the web at: http://www.nap.edu/catalog/6019.html.)

Csikszentmihalyi, Mihaly, Samuel Whalen, and Kevin Rathunde. *Talented Teenagers: The Roots of Success and Failure.* New York: Cambridge University Press, 1993.

Dryfoos, Joy G. *Adolescents at Risk: Prevalence and Prevention.* New York: Oxford University Press, 1990.

———. *Safe Passage: Making It Through Adolescence in a Risky Society.* New York: Oxford University Press, 1998.

Eagle, Carol J., and Carol Colman. *All That She Can Be: Helping Your Daughter Maintain Her Self-Esteem.* New York: Fireside Press, 1994.

Feldman, S. Shirley, and Glen R. Elliot. *At the Threshold: The Developing Adolescent.* Cambridge, MA: Harvard University Press, 1993.

Gurian, Michael. *A Fine Young Man: What Parents, Mentors, and Educators Can Do to Shape Adolescent Boys into Exceptional Men.* New York: Jeremy P. Tarcher/The Putnam Publishing Group, 1999.

Horn, Wade F., and Carol Keough. *Better Homes and Gardens New Teen Book: An A-to-Z Guide for Parents of 9- to 16-Year-Olds.* Des Moines, IA: Meredith Books, 1999.

Jessor, Richard, ed. *New Perspectives on Adolescent Risk Behavior.* Cambridge: Cambridge University Press, 1998.

Marone, Nicky. *How to Father a Successful Daughter: Reassuring Advice for Fathers to Help Their Daughters Become Happy, Confident Women.* New York: Ballantine Publishing Group, 1998.

Millstein, Susan G., Anne C. Petersen, and Elena O. Nightingale. *Promoting the Health of Adolescents: New Directions for the Twenty-first Century.* New York: Oxford University Press, 1994.

Nelsen, Jane, and Lynn Lott. *Positive Discipline for Teenagers: Resolving Conflict with Your Teenage Son or Daughter* (Developing Capable People Series). Rocklin, CA: Prima Publishing, 1994.

Pipher, Mary Bray. *Reviving Ophelia: Saving the Selves of Adolescent Girls.* New York: Ballantine Books, 1994.

Pollack, William. *Real Boys: Rescuing Our Sons from the Myths of Boyhood.* New York: Henry Holt & Company, 1999.

Ponton, Lynn E. *The Romance of Risk: Why Teenagers Do the Things They Do.* New York: Basic Books, 1998.

Pruitt, David B., ed. *Your Adolescent. What Every Parent Needs to Know: What's Normal, What's Not, and When to Seek Help. Emotional, Behavioral, and Cognitive Development from Early Adolescence Through the Teen Years.* New York: HarperCollins, 1999.

Scales, Peter C. *A Portrait of Young Adolescents in the 1990s: Implications for Promoting Healthy Growth and Development.* Minneapolis: Search Institute, 1991.

Shulman, Samuel, and Inge Seiffge-Krenke. *Fathers and Adolescents: Developmental and Clinical Perspectives.* New York: Routledge, 1997.

Simmons, Roberta G., and Dale A. Blyth. *Moving into Adolescence: The Impact of Pubertal Change and School Context.* New York: Aldine De Gruyter, 1987.

Slap, Gail B., and Martha M. Jablow. *Teenage Health Care: The First Comprehensive Family Guide for the Preteen to Young Adult Years.* New York: Pocket Books, 1994.

Stark, Patty. *Sex Is More Than a Plumbing Lesson: A Parent's Guide to Sexuality Education for Infants Through the Teen Years.* Dallas: Preston Hollow Enterprises, 1990.

Steinberg, Laurence, and Ellen Greenberger. *When Teenagers Work: The Psychological and Social Costs of Adolescent Employment.* New York: Basic Books, 1988.

Steinberg, Laurence, and Wendy Steinberg. *Crossing Paths: How Your Child's Adolescence Can Be an Opportunity for Your Own Personal Growth.* New York: Simon & Schuster, 1994.

Zimmerman, Jean, and Gil Reavill. *Raising Our Athletic Daughters: How Sports Can Build Self-Esteem and Save Girls' Lives.* New York: Doubleday, 1998.

Websites

Adolescence: Change and Continuity, http://www.personal.psu.edu/nxd10/adolesce.htm
This website, produced by students at Pennsylvania State University, introduces some of the developmental changes between puberty and the end of college. Website includes autobiographies of several adolescents focusing on identity development.

Advocates for Youth: Helping Young People Make Safe and Responsible Decisions About Sex! http://www.advocatesforyouth.org, or (202) 347-5700
Works to prevent pregnancy, sexually transmitted diseases, and HIV in teens. Website includes fact sheets, an area for teens only, as well as a link to Youth Resource for gay, lesbian, bisexual, and transgender youth.

American Academy of Child & Adolescent Psychiatry, http://www.aacap.org, or (202) 966-7300, extension 124 (Information Line)
Focuses on the developmental, behavioral, and mental disorders affecting children and adolescents. Fact sheets are available on the website under "Facts for Families."

The American Academy of Pediatrics, http://www.aap.org
Provides information on the physical, social, and mental health of infants, children, adolescents, and young adults. Click on You and Your Family. Using the Search function on the website is an easy way to find information on adolescence. If you click on Advanced Search, you can type in multiple terms (i.e., adolescent sexuality).

The Board on Children, Youth, and Families, under the National Research Council and the Institute of Medicine of the National Academy of Sciences, http://nationalacademies.org/cbsse/bocyf, or (202) 334-3965
The Board's Forum on Adolescence looks at the role of parents in promoting adolescent development, health, and well-being; sleep needs and difficulties of adolescents; and promoting child and adolescent development during the after-school hours. On the website under Reports you can access full-text publications, including: *Risks and Opportunities: Synthesis of Studies on Adolescence* (1999); *Adolescent Development and the Biology of Puberty* (1999); *Adolescent Decisionmaking* (1999); *Research to Promote Intergroup Relations* (1999).

Focus Adolescent Services: Resources, Support, and Information to Help Troubled Teens and Families, http://www.focusas.com, or (877) 362-8727
Provides resources and links to articles on a range of topics, including fire-setting, eating disorders, depression, attention disorders, sexual behavior, directories of support organizations and services by state, and more.

Institute for Youth Development, http://www.youthdevelopment.org/, or (703) 471-8750
Organization devoted to promoting risk avoidance for youth in five interrelated areas: alcohol, drugs, sex, tobacco, and violence. Website includes access to publications, helpful suggestions, and links to other resources.

National Campaign to Prevent Teen Pregnancy, http://www.teenpregnancy.org
Website includes tips for parents; tips from teens; facts and statistics; a parents' resource guide for talking with teens about love, sex, and relationships; as well as links to additional sources.

National Center for Fathering, http://www.fathers.com, or 1-800-593-3237
Research and education organization providing practical resources that dads can use in relating to their kids.

Planned Parenthood Federation of America, Inc., http://www.plannedparenthood.org, or 1-800-829-7732
Planned Parenthood is dedicated to providing access to sexual and reproductive health care and information. Click on Sexual Health on the website to find Teen Issues. In the Bookstore, click on Family Communication. Planned Parenthood also has a website specifically geared toward teens at: http://www.teenwire.com.

Sexuality Information and Education Council of the United States (SIECUS), http://www.siecus.org
Promotes comprehensive education about sexuality. On the website, For Parents provides in-depth tips and instruction for talking to your kids, publications, fact sheets, and more.

Talking with Kids about Tough Issues, http://www.talkingwithkids.org, or 1-800-244-5344
National campaign sponsored by Children Now (http://www.childrennow.org) and the Kaiser Family Foundation (http://www.kff.org) providing parents with information on how and when to talk with their kids about tough issues, including sex, HIV/AIDS, violence, drugs, and alcohol.

Women's Sports Foundation, http://www.womenssportsfoundation.org, or 1-800-227-3988
Works to increase opportunities for girls and women in sports and fitness. Provides research on the psychological, social, and physiological effects of sports and fitness on girls and women.

Youth Service America, http://www.servenet.org/ysa
Provides volunteer opportunities for all ages.

YouthTree USA, http://www.youthtree.com
Internet directory of national and local youth and family programs, services, hotlines, and resources.

Part Two: The Company They Keep

Chapters 4–6

Please refer to the resource lists in other chapters for additional sources on the topics discussed in this section.

Books

Benson, Peter L., Eugene C. Roehlkepartain, and Anu Sharma. *Growing Up Adopted: A Portrait of Adolescents and Their Families.* Minneapolis: Search Institute, 1994.

Cotterell, John. *Social Networks and Social Influences in Adolescence.* London, England: Routledge, 1996.

de Toledo, Sylvie, and Deborah Edler Brown. *Grandparents As Parents: A Survival Guide for Raising a Second Family.* New York: Guilford Press, 1995.

Gallagher, Winifred. *I.D.: How Heredity and Experience Make You Who You Are.* New York: Random House, 1996.

——. *The Power of Place: How Our Surroundings Shape Our Thoughts, Emotions and Actions.* New York: Poseidon Press, 1993.

Garbarino, James. *Raising Children in a Socially Toxic Environment.* San Francisco: Jossey-Bass Publishers, 1999.

Greenberg, Gregory, and Wade F. Horn. *Attention Deficit Hyperactivity Disorder: Questions and Answers for Parents.* Champaign, IL: Research Press, 1990.

Greenspan, Stanley I., with Jacqueline Salmon. *Playground Politics: Understanding the Emotional Life of Your School-Age Child.* Cambridge, MA: Perseus Books, 1994.

Gullotta, Thomas P. *Developing Social Competency in Adolescence.* Newbury Park, CA: Sage Publications, 1990.

Hauser, Stuart T., with Sally I. Powers and Gil G. Noam. *Adolescents and Their Families: Paths of Ego Development.* New York: The Free Press, 1991.

Kindlon, Dan, and Michael Thompson. *Raising Cain: Protecting the Emotional Life of Boys.* New York: Ballantine Books, 1999.

Koch, Joanne Barbara, and Linda Nancy Freeman. *Good Parents for Hard Times: Raising Responsible Kids in the Age of Drug Use & Sexual Promiscuity.* New York: Simon & Schuster Trade, 1992.

Koetzsch, Ronald E. *The Parents' Guide to Alternatives in Education: The First In-Depth Guide to the Full Range of Choices in Alternative Schooling, with*

All the Information You Need to Decide What Kind of Education Is Right for Your Child. Boston: Shambhala Publications, Inc., 1997.

Laursen, Brett, ed. *Close Friendships in Adolescence.* San Francisco: Jossey-Bass Inc., 1993.

Newberger, Eli H. *The Men They Will Become: The Nature and Nurture of Male Character.* Cambridge, MA: Perseus Books, 1999.

Samenow, Stanton E. *Before It's Too Late: Why Some Kids Get Into Trouble—and What Parents Can Do About It.* New York: Times Books, 1999.

Schaefer, Charles E., and Theresa Foy DiGeronimo. *How to Talk to Teens About Really Important Things: Specific Questions and Answers and Useful Things to Say.* San Francisco: Jossey-Bass Inc., 1999.

Seiffge-Krenke, Inge. *Stress, Coping and Relationships in Adolescence.* Mahway, NJ: Lawrence Erlbaum Associates, 1995.

Smilansky, Moshe. *Friendship in Adolescence & Young Adulthood.* Gaithersburg, MD: Psychosocial and Educational Publications, 1991.

Wiener, Valerie. *Gang Free: Friendship Choices for Today's Youth.* Minneapolis: Fairview Press, 1995.

Youniss, James, and Jacqueline Smollar. *Adolescent Relations with Mothers, Fathers and Friends.* Chicago: The University of Chicago Press, 1987.

Zeigler Dendy, Chris A. *Teenagers with ADD: A Parents' Guide.* Bethesda, MD: Woodbine House, 1995.

Websites

The American Council for Drug Education, http://www.ACDE.org/, or 1-800-488-3784

Substance abuse prevention and education agency that provides parents with tips for talking with their children about drugs and signs and symptoms of drug use on its website.

Campaign for Our Children, http://www.cfoc.org/

Works to reduce the incidence of teenage pregnancies. Website provides Parent Resources, Ask the Experts, Sexual Responsibility, and statistics, fact sheets, and links to more resources.

Children and Adults with Attention-Deficit/Hyperactivity Disorder (CHADD), http://www.chadd.org/, or 1-800-233-4050

National support, education, and advocacy organization. Website provides answers to frequently asked questions, fact sheets, *Attention!* Magazine online, chapter locator, links.

Grandparent Information Center, http://www.aarp.org/getans/consumer/grandparents.html, or (202) 434-2296

Established by AARP, this clearinghouse provides information about services and programs to help improve the lives of grandparent-headed households. Publications, newsletter, referrals available.

National Adoption Information Clearinghouse, http://www.calib.com/naic, or 1-888-251-0075
This is a service of the Children's Bureau of the U.S. Department of Health and Human Services' Administration for Children and Families. Publications and resources available.

National Clearinghouse for Alcohol and Drug Information, http://www. health.org/, or 1-800-729-6686, or 1-877-767-8432 for Spanish-speakers
A service of the U.S. Department of Health and Human Services' Substance Abuse and Mental Health Services Administration providing alcohol and substance abuse prevention, intervention, and treatment information. Provides referrals, publications, information specialists.

National Council on Alcoholism and Drug Dependence, Inc., http://www. ncadd.org/, or 1-800-622-2255
Works to prevent and treat alcoholism and other drug addictions through education and advocacy. Website includes information, publications, and links to resources and referrals to local services.

The National Information Center for Children and Youth with Disabilities, http://www.nichcy.org/, or 1-800-695-0285
Information source for disability-related topics regarding children and youth, birth through twenty-one, operated by the Academy for Educational Development and the Office of Special Education Programs of the U.S. Department of Education. Provides fact sheets, parent guides, referrals, links.

Parent's Handbook: How to Talk to Your Children About Developing Healthy Relationships, http://www.lizclaiborne.com/lizinc/lizworks/women/ parents. asp, or 800-449-7867
Produced by Liz Claiborne, Inc., in conjunction with the Parenting Institute of New York University, provides tips for communicating with children about how to develop healthy peer and dating relationships.

Partnership for a Drug-Free America, http://www.drugfreeamerica.org/, or (212) 922-1560
Works to educate the public primarily through an ad campaign. Website offers help and resources for parents.

The Ups & Downs of Adolescence: A Newsletter About and for Young People, Parents and All Concerned Adults, http://www.ianr.unl.edu/ianr/ fcs/upsdowns/
National monthly newsletter written by staff and faculty at Land Grant Universities across the country, and hosted on the Internet by the University of Nebraska, Lincoln. Past issues through 1995 are available at: http://ianr-www.unl.edu/ianr/fcs/upsdowns/pastups.htm.

Part Three: Learning In and Out of School
Chapters 7—9

Please refer to the other resource lists for additional sources on the issues discussed in this section.

Books

Benson, Peter L. *All Kids Are Our Kids: What Communities Must Do to Raise Caring and Responsible Children and Adolescents.* San Francisco: Jossey-Bass Inc., 1997.

Borba, Michele. *Parents Do Make a Difference: How to Raise Kids with Solid Character, Strong Minds, and Caring Hearts.* San Francisco: Jossey-Bass Inc., 1999.

Comer, James P. *Waiting for a Miracle: Why Schools Can't Solve Our Problems—and How We Can.* New York: Dutton, 1997.

Damon, William. *Greater Expectations: Overcoming the Culture of Indulgence in America's Homes and Schools.* New York: The Free Press, 1996.

———. *The Youth Charter: How Communities Can Work Together to Raise Standards for All Our Children.* New York: The Free Press, 1997.

George, Paul S., and William M. Alexander. *The Exemplary Middle School,* 2nd edition. New York: Harcourt Brace Jovanovich, 1993.

Greenspan, Stanley I., with Beryl Lieff Benderly. *The Growth of the Mind and the Endangered Origins of Intelligence.* Cambridge, MA: Perseus Books, 1998.

Kidder, Tracy. *Among Schoolchildren.* New York: Avon Books, 1990.

Lipsitz, Joan. *Successful Schools for Young Adolescents.* New Brunswick, NJ: Transaction Books, Rutgers University, 1984.

Louv, Richard. *The Web of Life: Weaving the Values That Sustain Us.* Berkeley: Conari Press, 1998.

Nabhan, Gary Paul, and Stephen Trimble. *The Geography of Childhood: Why Children Need Wild Places.* Boston: Beacon Press, 1994.

Offer, Daniel, Eric Ostrov, and Kenneth I. Howard. *Patterns of Adolescent Self-Image.* San Francisco: Jossey-Bass Inc., 1984.

Ryan, Kevin, and Karen E. Bohlin. *Building Character in Schools: Practical Ways to Bring Moral Instruction to Life.* San Francisco: Jossey-Bass Inc., 1998.

Scales, Peter C. *Boxed In and Bored: How Middle Schools Continue to Fail Young Adolescents—and What Good Middle Schools Do Right.* Minneapolis: Search Institute, 1996.

Schofield, Janet Ward. *Black and White in School: Trust, Tension or Tolerance?* New York: Teachers College Press, 1989.

Steinberg, Laurence, B. Bradford Brown, and Sanford M. Dornbusch. *Beyond* the Classroom: Why School Reform Has Failed and What Parents Need to Do. New York: Simon & Schuster Trade, 1997.

Stevenson, Chris. *Teaching Ten to Fourteen Year Olds.* New York: Addison-Wesley Longman, Inc., 1997.

Tracy, Louise Felton. *Grounded for Life?! Stop Blowing Your Fuse and Start Communicating with Your Teenager.* Seattle: Parenting Press, Inc., 1994.

Turning Points: Preparing American Youth for the 21st Century. Report of the Task Force on Education of Young Adolescents. New York: Carnegie Council on Adolescent Development, 1989.

Websites

Boys & Girls Clubs of America, http://www.bgca.org/, or 1-800-854-2582

Neighborhood-based youth organization providing activities and a safe place after school and on weekends with full-time, trained youth development professionals. Website includes information on how to find local clubs.

Center for Adolescent Studies, http://www.education.indiana.edu/cas/, or (812) 856-8113

Located at the School of Education, Indiana University, Bloomington. Works to advance the understanding of the psychological, biological, and social features of normal adolescence. Teacher Talk offers online practical advice, strategies, and lesson plans for secondary teachers who want to enhance the social and emotional growth of their students. Teacher Talk Forum provides links to learning resources and lesson plans for secondary students, their parents, and educators.

Center of Education for the Young Adolescent, University of Wisconsin-Platteville, http://www.uwplatt.edu/~ceya/, or 1-800-208-7041

Works to improve the education and lives of adolescents. Offers a resource center with a library on adolescence. Issues include: how the standards movement affects young adolescents; violence, safety, and raising adolescents to be responsible; curriculum; adolescent relationships and developmental stages; communication; adolescent brain research. Also publishes brochures.

Families and Education, http://www.rmcres.com/famed/

This site, run by RMC Research, works to help parents and educators understand how schools and other educational programs work; how children learn, and how parents and families can best contribute to the learning process. Brochures available.

Federal Resources for Educational Excellence, http://www.ed.gov/free/

Website makes hundreds of federally supported resources for teaching and learning easier to find. Subjects range from an architectural tour of the National Gallery of Art's East Building to a mutual fund cost calculator from the Securities and Exchange Commission.

Harvard Education Letter, http://www.edletter.org/, or 1-800-513-0763
A bimonthly newsletter from the Harvard Graduate School of Education geared toward parents and teachers. Examines the research about pressing school issues such as retention.

Indiana Prevention Resource Center, Indiana University, http://www.drugs. indiana.edu/
A special issue of their newsletter focuses on the after-school hours of middle-school youth, *Three Critical Hours—Three Critical Years: Toward Precision Targeting in Prevention.*

MIDDLE-L is an e-mail discussion group for those interested in middle-school education. To subscribe, send an e-mail message to: listserv@postoffice.csu. uiuc.edu, with/:/ ~ subscribe MIDDLE-L {Firstname} {Lastname} in the body of the message (eg.: Subscribe MIDDLE-L Jane Doe).
An archive of past messages is on the web at: http://www.askeric.org/ Virtual/Listserv_Archives/MIDDLE-L.html. MIDDLE-L is run by the ERIC Clearinghouse on Elementary and Early Childhood Education (ERIC/EECE).

National Dropout Prevention Center/Network, http://www.dropoutprevention.org
Nationwide membership organization of educators and professionals located at Clemson University that works to reduce America's dropout rates. Website provides statistics, feature articles from around the nation, resources on dropout prevention and service learning.

National Education Association, http://www.nea.org
Teacher's union that works to advance and improve public education and teacher quality. Website has sections geared toward parents and teachers.

National 4-H Council, http://www.fourhcouncil.edu, or 1-888-779-6884
Nonprofit educational organization that provides experiential programs and activities for young people across the country. Publications cover youth development, youth-adult partnerships, leadership development, cultural diversity, conflict resolution, environmental education, workforce preparation, and more.

National Middle School Association, http://www.nmsa.org/, or 1-800-528-6672
Resource Center includes book recommendations (including for parents), research summaries, and more. Publications include: A Parent's Guide to Young Adolescents on the web at: http://www.courttv.com/choices/ guide/index.html and A Teacher's Guide to Working with Young Adolescents at: http:// www.courttv.com/choices/teachers/. Also offers a fax-on-demand information line, 1-888-329-6672, to receive NMSA documents by fax.

National Parent Teacher Association (PTA), http://www.pta.org, or 1-800-307-4782

Child-advocacy membership organization. Website provides parenting information resources, including helping your kids to succeed in middle and high school, and building successful partnerships with teachers and school administrators. Also publishes *Our Children* magazine.

Parent Soup, http://www.parentsoup.com/community/teens.html
Gives parents of teens a place to talk with other parents. Provides chat rooms, message boards (a place to post a question and check back later to see if anyone's posted a response), a daily parent tip, and expert advice.

Phi Delta Kappa International, http://www.pdkintl.org/, or (812) 339 1156
International organization that promotes quality public education. Offers a special report on middle grades (on the web at: http://www.pdkintl.org/kappan/kmidad.htm).

U.S. Department of Education, http://www.ed.gov/, or 1-800-USA-LEARN (872-53276)
Website includes programs and services, publications and products, picks of the month. Check out their Think College Early website at: http://www.ed.gov/thinkcollege/early/.

Part Four: The Right Connections
Chapters 10–12

Please refer to the other resource lists for additional sources on the issues discussed in this section.

Books

Apter, Terri. *Altered Loves: Mothers and Daughters During Adolescence*. New York: St. Martin's Press, 1991.

Baker, Colin. *A Parents' and Teachers' Guide to Bilingualism (Bilingual Education and Bilingualism, No. 5)*. Bristol, PA: Multilingual Matters, 1995.

Bassoff, Evelyn S. *Between Mothers and Sons: The Making of Vital and Loving Men*. New York: Dutton, 1995.

Benson, Peter L., Judy Galbraith, and Pamela Espeland. *What Teens Need to Succeed: Proven, Practical Ways to Shape Your Own Future*. Minneapolis: Free Spirit Publishing, Inc., 1997.

Berrol, Selma Cantor. *Growing Up American: Immigrant Children in America, Then and Now*. New York: Macmillan Library Reference, 1995.

Blum, Robert William, and Peggy Mann Rinehart. *Reducing the Risk: Connections that Make a Difference in the Lives of Youth*. Minneapolis: Division of General Pediatrics and Adolescent Health, University of Minnesota, 1997. (On the web at: http://www.peds.umn.edu/centers/ihd/AddHealth.pdf%20 copy.)

Esman, Aaron H. *Adolescence and Culture*. New York: Columbia University Press, 1990.

Faber, Adele, and Elaine Mazlish. *How to Talk So Kids Will Listen & How to Listen So Kids Will Talk*. New York: Avon Books, 1999.

Ford, Judy. *Wonderful Ways to Love a Teen: . . . Even When It Seems Impossible*. Berkeley: Conari Press, 1996.

Garbarino, James. *Lost Boys: Why Our Sons Turn Violent and How We Can Save Them*. New York: The Free Press, 1999.

Igoa, Cristina. *The Inner World of the Immigrant Child*. New York: Lawrence Erlbaum Associates, Inc., 1995.

James, Donna Walker, ed. *MORE Things That DO Make a Difference for Youth: A Compendium of Evaluations of Youth Programs and Practices*. Washington, DC: American Youth Policy Forum, 1999.

Lucas, Tamara. *Into, Through, and Beyond Secondary School: Critical Transitions for Immigrant Youths*. McHenry, IL: Delta Systems/Center for Applied Linguistics, 1997.

Mace-Matluck, Betty J., Rosalind Alexander-Kasparik, and Robin M. Queen. *Through the Golden Door: Educational Approaches for Immigrant Adolescents with Limited Schooling*. McHenry, IL: Delta Systems/Center for Applied Linguistics, 1998.

Olsen, Laurie. *Embracing Diversity: Teachers' Voices from California Classrooms*. Oakland: California Tomorrow, 1990.

——. *Made in America: Immigrant Students in Our Public Schools*. New York: New Press, 1997.

Olsen, Laurie, and Ann Jaramillo. *Turning the Tides of Exclusion: A Guide for Educators and Advocates for Immigrant Students*. Oakland: California Tomorrow, 1999.

Olsen, Laurie, Ann Jaramillo, Zaida McCall-Perez, and Judy White. *Igniting Change for Immigrant Students: Portraits of Three High Schools*. Oakland: California Tomorrow, 1999.

Peshkin, Alan. *The Color of Strangers, the Color of Friends: The Play of Ethnicity in School and Community*. Chicago: University of Chicago Press, 1991.

Websites

100 Black Men of America, Inc., http://www.100blackmen.org/, or (404) 688-5100

National alliance of leading African-American men of business, industry, public affairs, and government. Focuses on youth mentoring, anti-violence, education, and economic development programs. Website includes links to local chapters.

ASPIRA Association, Inc., http://www.aspira.org/, or (202) 835-3600

National nonprofit organization devoted to the education and leadership development of Latino youth. Website provides information on finding scholarships, links to homework support, resources for parents, publications, and more.

Big Brothers Big Sisters of America, http://www.bbbsa.org, or (215) 567-7000
Volunteer youth mentoring organization that matches children in need with caring adult mentors. Some affiliates also offer opportunities for high-school students to mentor grade-school students. Website includes links to local Big Brother Big Sister agencies.

The Center for the Study and Prevention of Violence, http://www. colorado.edu/cspv, or (303) 492-8465, or (303) 492-1032
The Center, based at the University of Colorado at Boulder, works to understand and prevent violence, particularly adolescent violence. Offers publications, information about programs that work in preventing violence, and places to go for more information.

ERIC Clearinghouse on Urban Education, http://eric-web.tc.columbia.edu/, or 1-800-601-4868
A service of the U.S. Department of Education based at the Institute for Urban and Minority Education at Columbia University's Teachers College. Website offers articles, annotated bibliographies, and reviews and summaries of publications and provides links to immigration issues.

National Criminal Justice Reference Service, http://www.ncjrs.org/, or 1-800-851-3420
Resource for information on criminal and juvenile justice. Publications include: *Mentoring—A Proven Delinquency Prevention Strategy.*

The National Mentoring Partnership, http://www.mentoring.org/, or (202) 729-4345
National organization promoting mentoring and its benefits. Website provides suggestions for finding a mentor, as well as research on the benefits of mentoring to youth. Resources include opportunities by area, a guide on how to be a successful mentor, and information on starting and running mentoring programs.

—Compiled by Stacey Relkin Winkler

INDEX

ACKNOWLEDGMENTS

Writing, although largely a solitary pursuit, has its roots in the communities in which we grow up. One of those communities for me has been *The Washington Post* newsroom. I am grateful to Len Downie, executive editor, for encouraging *Post* writers to take on new challenges; to Style department heads David Von Drehle and Gene Robinson and assistant Style editor Deborah Heard for allowing me to pursue my dream; to my base family in Style Plus for their encouragement; and especially to my editor Peggy Hackman, whose eye for stories that affect ordinary people's lives is unmatched. Thanks also to Alison Howard and Lexie Verdon for critiquing this book and to the dozens of writers and editors at the *Post* who amaze and motivate me every day with their perceptive reporting and graceful writing.

The inspiration for this book came from David Hamburg and a community of scientists and communicators he assembled while he served as president of Carnegie Corporation of New York. David and his wife, Betty Hamburg, have done more to support the study of adolescence, particularly early adolescence, than any other people I know. I feel blessed to know them. Carnegie provided me with wonderful friends and guides including Ruby Takanishi and Avery Russell. My heartfelt thanks to both of them.

For two years, I had the privilege of being a visiting scholar at the Board on Children, Youth, and Families, a research team within the National Academy of Sciences. My thanks to Karen Hein, Barbara Torrey, and Faith Mitchell; to Deborah Phillips, Rosemary Chalk, Michele Kipke, and Anne Bridgman; and to the rest of a hardworking staff. I am also indebted to sociologist Donald Hernandez, on temporary assignment to the board, for his assistance from beginning to end, and to the board's advisor and resident wise woman, Elena Nightingale, for her insightful questions and steady presence.

Several other social scientists reviewed my work and kept me on track: Keith Brodie, president emeritus at Duke University; William Damon, director of the Stanford Center for Adolescence; and Jacquelynne Eccles, professor of psychology at the University of Michigan. Peter Benson and Peter Scales, president and senior fellow, respectively, at the Search Institute in Minneapolis gave me much-needed advice, as did Sarah Brown, director of the National Campaign to Prevent Teen Pregnancy. Research assistants Julie Ash, Steven Kelts, and Jason Wagner helped me wade through hundreds of books, journal articles, and newspaper clippings.

The staff at the Casey Journalism Center for Children and Families deserves acknowledgment, in particular Cathy Trost and Stacey Relkin Winkler. Among other wonderful friends, I would like to thank crime writer Patricia Cornwell for her deep insights, unflagging encouragement, and ability to make me laugh. The steady support of Lorin Buck, Demetra Nightingale, Nancy Harlan, Tony and Emily Mauro, and Kathy Cullinan also carried me through these last four years.

The teachers and counselors at my son's middle school, many of the parents there, and principal Margaret McCourt-Dirner lived this book with me. The congregation of Holy Trinity Lutheran Church in Falls Church kept me grounded from conception through birth. Particular thanks go to the church's Friday Night Group, whose attention to my son and to other young church members showed me what caring relationships between adults and adolescents can look like.

Several individuals at the three sites I visited went out of their way to assist me and make me feel welcome. In Los Angeles, I owe a lot to Lou Dantzler, founder of the Challengers Boys & Club, and to his dedicated staff. In Durham, North Carolina, Marcia Morey, former assistant prosecutor and now a judge, put me in touch with families I otherwise would not have met and provided insight into that city's schools and juvenile justice systems. Judy Alig, tireless champion for kids in Ulysses, Kansas, earned my respect over and over. And Lynda Fort, owner of Fort's Cedar View in Ulysses, furnished me with not only a comfortable place to stay and the best coffee I've ever had but also with a better understanding of that remarkable part of the country known as the High Plains.

This book would not have been possible without the generosity of five foundations: Carnegie, W. K. Kellogg, Robert Wood Johnson, W. T. Grant, and the Foundation for Child Development. I am also indebted to the English-Speaking Union for working on my behalf.

The world's best agent, Esther Newberg, found just the right home for this book at Riverhead Books and just the right editor, Cindy Spiegel. Both in-house publicist Ken Siman and the staff at Pro-Media, an outside firm, have been terrific.

My parents, my sisters, and my sisters' families have been unfailingly supportive, as have my son, Jeff, my stepdaughters, Ashli and Amber, and my husband, Carl. Carl, a writing professor, likes to say that if you work hard at your craft, the magic will come. I thank him for teaching me that that is true about marriage as well as literature.

I have saved the real heroes for last: the young people, parents, and other adults whose stories fill this book. I remain touched by their candor and humbled by their courage. I have become a better parent because of what they taught me.